The Usability Engineering Lifecycle

A PRACTITIONER'S HANDBOOK FOR USER INTERFACE DESIGN

DEBORAH J. MAYHEW

MORGAN KAUFMANN PUBLISHERS, INC.
San Francisco, California

Senior Editor: Diane Cerra
Director of Production & Manufacturing: Yonie Overton
Production Editor: Sarah Burgundy
Cover Design: Wall-to-Wall Studios/Pittsburgh, PA
Cover Image: ©Henryk Kaiser/The Stock Solution
Text Design: Mark Ong, Side by Side Studios
Editorial Illustration: Carrie English, canary studios
Technical Illustration: Cherie Plumlee
Compositor: Seventeenth Street Studios
Copyeditor: Judith Brown
Proofreader: Jennifer McClain
Indexer: Ty Koontz
Printer: Courier Corporation

Designations used by companies to distinguish their products are often claimed as trademarks or registered trademarks. In all instances where Morgan Kaufmann Publishers, Inc. is aware of a claim, the product names appear in initial capital or all capital letters. Readers, however, should contact the appropriate companies for more complete information regarding trademarks and registration.

Morgan Kaufmann Publishers, Inc.
Editorial and Sales Office
340 Pine Street, Sixth Floor
San Francisco, CA 94104-3205
USA
Telephone   415/392-2665
Facsimile   415/982-2665
Email   mkp@mkp.com
WWW   http://www.mkp.com
Order toll free   800/745-7323

Library of Congress Cataloging-in-Publication Data

Mayhew, Deborah J.
    The usability engineering lifecycle : a practitioner's handbook for user interface design / Deborah J. Mayhew.
        p. cm. — (The Morgan Kaufmann series in interactive technologies)
    Includes bibliographical references.
    ISBN 1-55860-561-4
    1. User interfaces (Computer systems)   2. Computer software—Development.   I. Title. II. Series
    QA76.9.U83M395 1999
    005.4'28—dc21   99-19111
                                                                              CIP

Dedicated to
Katie Ann with love

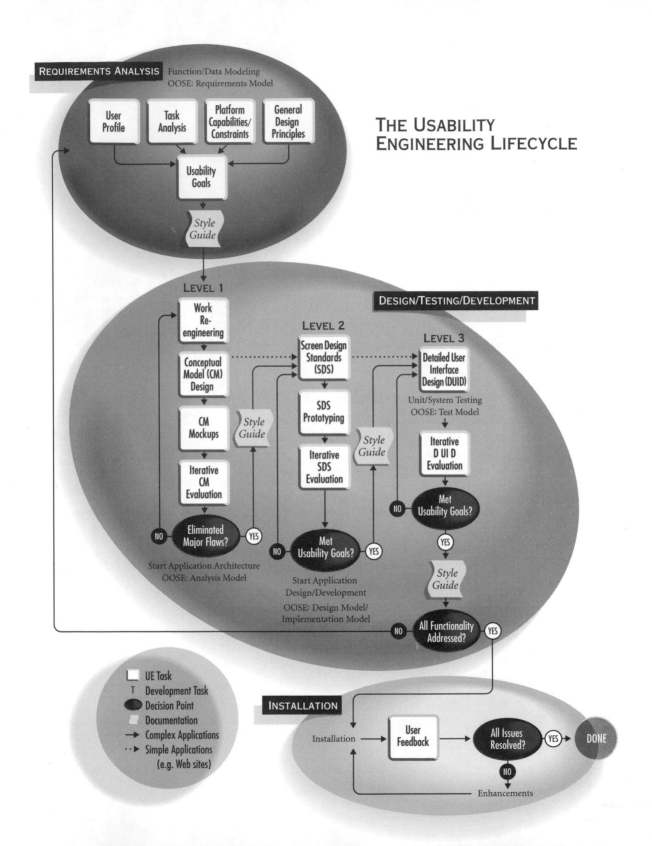

THE USABILITY ENGINEERING LIFECYCLE

Contents

vii

Preface

One client, an insurance company, first approached me after a $3 million development project simply failed. Their users flatly refused to use the application, saying it was too difficult to learn and unusable. Another client, this one a product vendor, contacted me because they had stiff competition in the marketplace, and a market survey had indicated that ease of learning and efficiency of use were crucial criteria in their potential customers' buy decisions.

Yet another client had an internal business goal of increasing their volume of transactions by 10 percent without increasing staff. They correctly reasoned that more efficient work tools (in this case computer-based information systems) could help accomplish this goal.

Most recently, I was called in by a large contractor company who had recently completed building and installing a large information system for a government agency. The vast majority of users the system was intended to support found it too difficult to learn and use and ended up delegating its use to a small number of dedicated users. Thus, instead of facilitating the existing jobs in the organization, the new system necessitated the creation of a new job. The client company insisted that the vendor provide them with a new, more *usable* system.

Clients often report to me astounding expenditures on user training and customer support for their software applications, very low levels of productivity, and very high turnover rates, all often directly attributable to unusable software. I read of one software vendor who actually lost money on a product because the customer support required per customer was more costly than the profit margin on the product (Nielsen 1993, 84).

The costs of less-than-user-friendly software can be astonishingly high—the combined result of unnecessarily high training and customer support costs, unnecessarily low productivity, and lost market share. These days, buyers and users of software applications expect a high level of usability. Unfortunately, your average software engineer has no idea how to deliver it, and your average software development methodology simply does not address it.

Currently, well-established techniques for achieving software usability are available, and the bottom-line benefits of incorporating these techniques into standard product development methodologies invariably outweigh the costs (Bias and Mayhew 1994). The potential benefits of product usability can impact the bottom line of vendors, contractors, and internal product developers. Achieving it requires two basic things:

◆ General user interface design principles and guidelines
◆ A structured engineering approach to user interface design

In my first book (Mayhew 1992), I brought together all the then currently available software user interface design principles and guidelines in one convenient source. In this book, I offer a detailed, structured approach to product user interface design in the form of a Usability Engineering Lifecycle. Since 1984, I have been developing, updating, refining, documenting, teaching, and promoting a comprehensive, detailed Usability Engineering Lifecycle set in the context of a typical software development lifecycle.

I did not invent the concept of a Usability Engineering Lifecycle. Nor did I invent any of the Usability Engineering tasks included in the lifecycle or any of the various techniques that can be applied to accomplish these tasks. However, the Usability Engineering Lifecycle as described in this book differs from those described by other authors in several important ways:

◆ It is more comprehensive and specific in its inclusion of Usability Engineering tasks in the overall lifecycle.
◆ It is more detailed in specifying how to integrate usability tasks into an already existing software development lifecycle.
◆ It is more detailed in its specification of how to carry out tasks and techniques in the lifecycle.
◆ In particular, it provides more structure and detail for the actual process of user interface design.

Other excellent books cover individual Usability Engineering tasks or techniques in the lifecycle quite extensively (see, e.g., Beyer and Holtzblatt 1998; Wixon and Ramey 1996; Hackos and Redish 1998, on task analysis; and Nielsen and Mack 1994; Dumas and Redish 1993, on evaluation). This book is unique, however, in its comprehensiveness. It covers the entire Usability Engineering Lifecycle, with all its tasks and representative techniques, embedded within an existing software development lifecycle; and in particular, it shows how *all* the Usability Engineering tasks in the lifecycle support and drive each other.

The Usability Engineering Lifecycle consists of a set of Usability Engineering tasks applied in a particular order at specified points in an overall product development lifecycle. The lifecycle as I practice it is based on my work in the field of Usability Engineering, which dates from 1981, and most particularly from my consulting practice, which dates from 1986. I have had many opportunities to practice and hone the lifecycle approach, as well as the techniques I employ for the different tasks, in many different organizations and on many different types of development projects.

Although my consulting practice has focused primarily on the design of mainstream software user interfaces, and most of my clients have been developing applications under the Microsoft Windows operating system on PCs, I have also consulted on the user interface design to more specialized software products based on very different hardware and software platforms. Examples of such products include factory equipment, medical technology, scientific data gathering instruments, and Web sites. I have found that the overall approach of the Usability Engineering Lifecycle is equally applicable to the successful design and development of usable products of these kinds, even when much of the design involves more traditional "knobs and dials" hardware interface design. Designers of such products need only use their imagination a bit to apply the Usability Engineering Lifecycle to their unique products and development methodology. Thus you should bear in mind that while the discussions, examples, and sample work products and templates in this book are often based on typical office software applications, the underlying lifecycle and its tasks, techniques, and principles will apply equally well to the design and development of other types of software, such as Web sites and applications and, in fact, any kind of interactive product. To reinforce this very general applicability of the Usability Engineering Lifecycle, where appropriate throughout the book, I have used the term "product"—rather than "application," "software," or "system"—to refer to the interactive products you might be designing.

In addition, the Usability Engineering Lifecycle can be adapted to support internal development projects, commercial development projects, and contract development projects. I have applied it in all these contexts. And it can be adapted to projects varying in size, complexity, time frame, and budget. I have used it across such varying contexts as well. Note, however, that the lifecycle as it is described in this book is oriented towards development projects that have already been defined, planned, and scoped (as opposed to projects intended to completely reengineer a business and identify opportunities for new products, as is the focus in Beyer and Holtzblatt 1998). It is also oriented towards development projects creating fairly new products, as opposed to reworkings of existing projects. With a little imagination, however, you can draw upon the tasks and techniques of the lifecycle as it is described in this book to support these kinds of projects as well. For example, if you do have the opportunity or need to do major business reengineering before the development of specific automated tools, and you have used Beyer and Holtzblatt's Contextual Design technique to do this, you will know that their technique leaves off just where actual user interface design begins in the Usability Engineering Lifecycle. So, you could pick up where they left off by using the tasks and techniques described in Chapters 8–17 of this book.

This book is meant for practitioners. It is not a theoretical book, but a practical book that attempts to teach concrete, immediately usable skills to practitioners in product development organizations. Each task in the lifecycle is treated in a single chapter that includes step-by-step procedures for carrying out that lifecycle task. The book also includes examples of work products from Usability Engineering tasks from my own practice and "war stories" related to carrying out these tasks in the real world—also from my own experience. If you are also interested in further study, many references to available literature in the field are cited. Product managers, product developers, User Interface Designers, and Usability Engineers will all find this book useful. It will also serve well as a textbook for a course on Usability Engineering.

The costs of unusable software are high. With the help of this book, you can put the maturing discipline of Usability Engineering to work in your product development organization to eliminate those costs.

About This Book

Chapter 1 provides an introduction and background to the topic of Usability Engineering and a high-level overview of the Usability Engineering Lifecycle. Chapters 2 through 17 provide complete descriptions of each of the lifecycle tasks illustrated in the chart at the beginning of every chapter. There is a common structure to all of these chapters, as follows:

◆ **Lifecycle Illustration:** At the beginning of each chapter, the lifecycle illustration is displayed, with a magnifying glass indicator showing the location of the task treated in that chapter in the overall lifecycle. This will bring you back to the "big picture" and the context within which each lifecycle task is set.

◆ **Table of Contents:** A table of contents is given for the chapter, to facilitate lookup later when you are using the book as a quick reference and reminder.

◆ **Purpose:** The purpose and goals of each task are offered within the context of the overall lifecycle and general usability goals. This provides the motivation for the task.

◆ **Description:** A high-level description of the task is offered. Here, you get an overview that provides context for two later sections, Sample Technique—A Step-by-Step Procedure and Alternative Techniques—A Review.

◆ **Scheduling and Integration with Other Tasks:** The lifecycle chart suggests the order in which tasks should be carried out. Interdependencies between the task under discussion and other lifecycle tasks (as well as other general development tasks) are noted here, further clarifying the order in which tasks should be carried out and how they interact with other tasks. Where tasks can overlap or be conducted in parallel, this is noted.

◆ **Roles and Resources:** This section describes how different roles with different skill sets can work together to accomplish the task. Three main usability roles are assumed: the Usability Engineer, the User Interface Designer, and the User Interface Developer. These roles are briefly defined in Chapter 1 and discussed in detail in Chapter 21.

◆ **Sample Technique—A Step-by-Step Procedure:** The high-level task description offered in the Description section is expanded upon by offering a detailed step-by-step procedure for carrying out one alternative technique for the task. My choice of which technique to describe here in detail is based on two factors: I chose the more rigorous techniques, because "quick and dirty" techniques or shortcuts tend to be based on these more formal techniques. And I chose techniques with which I have extensive experience, as I am better able to describe these in detail and to offer sample work products.

◆ **Level of Effort:** In this section, a sample level of effort (i.e., person hours by staff type) required for the sample technique is offered to help readers inexperienced with these tasks and techniques to make initial estimates for planning purposes. Many factors will influence level of effort, including product complexity, techniques chosen, and available resources. The samples offered in this section are meant only to give very rough ideas of effort estimates. You might adapt and use these sample estimates in your initial planning efforts, but then you will need to adjust them based on your own experience.

◆ **Alternative Techniques—A Review:** Here I briefly describe and comment on alternatives to the technique described in the previous two sections. I also offer references, so that you can pursue these alternative techniques further through other literature if you wish.

◆ **Shortcuts:** In each chapter, the sample technique for carrying out a task as described in the Sample Technique—A Step-by-Step Procedure section is a fairly rigorous one. As such, it is highly recommended because it offers the biggest potential payoff in terms of accurate and thorough results. But it is also often the most labor intensive and costly. Often these techniques are simply not practical, or at least it is not practical to carry out every task in the lifecycle with the most rigorous and expensive technique. In the Shortcuts section, alternative "quick and dirty" techniques for each task are offered.

◆ **Web Notes:** In general, the Usability Engineering Lifecycle can be effectively applied to Web development projects as well as to more traditional software and other kinds of product development projects. But Web development is unique in some ways. Here I offer ways in which techniques can be adapted to support the development of Web sites and applications.

◆ **Sample Work Products and Templates:** In this section, I offer examples of real (although adapted and disguised) work products from my own extensive experience in conducting these tasks during my consulting projects. I also sometimes offer blank forms or "templates" to support the accomplishment of the task. These examples and structured formats make the task descriptions in the Description and Sample Technique—A Step-by-Step Procedure sections less abstract, and they provide tools for you to use as you try to learn and use these Usability Engineering techniques.

You should note that the sample work products across tasks are not all from one coherent project. I decided not to fabricate one simple coherent set of work products based on a hypothetical project, but rather to include actual work products from real projects, even though they came from different projects. It is my hope that the realism and richness of real work products will be more valuable as tools to practitioners than a fabricated and simplified set of work products would be.

Chapters 18–21 cover topics not strictly part of the lifecycle, but closely related to it. These include how to promote and implement the Usability Engineering Lifecycle in development organizations (Chapter 18), how to plan Usability Engineering efforts (Chapter 19), how to cost-justify Usability Engineering efforts (Chapter 20), and how to organize resources for Usability Engineering (Chapter 21). The organization of these chapters is similar (but not identical) to the structure of Chapters 2–17 as described above.

References to the literature are provided at the end of the book. For each chapter, both those referred to in the text of the chapter and others that represent useful readings relevant to the task under discussion are listed.

I recommend initially reading the entire book sequentially. Then, as you begin to apply the Usability Engineering Lifecycle approach in your development projects, you can first review Chapters 18–21 to help you plan and sell your Usability Engineering proposals to management. Finally, as it comes time to apply each task, you can refer to the Sample Technique—A Step-by-Step Procedure, Alternative Techniques—A Review, Shortcuts, Web Notes, and Sample Work Products and Templates sections of the pertinent chapter to help you carry out that task.

ABOUT THE AUTHOR

I am the owner and principal of Deborah J. Mayhew & Associates, a consulting firm based in Massachusetts, USA. I offer courses and consulting on all aspects of Usability Engineering and user interface design. You can contact me at

Dr. Deborah J. Mayhew & Associates
88 Panhandle Road
POB 248
West Tisbury, MA 02575

Phone: 508-693-7149
Fax: 508-693-9726
email: drdeb@vineyard.net
URL: http://vineyard.net/biz/drdeb/index.html

THE USABILITY ENGINEERING LIFECYCLE WEB SITE

The Deborah J. Mayhew & Associates Web site includes a link to a forum on the Usability Engineering Lifecycle as described in this book. I encourage you to send email to this site with your comments, questions, and experiences using this book and its contents. I will periodically post answers to questions and summaries of comments and experiences. Through this Web site, we as a community can learn from each other and contribute to the evolution of the Usability Engineering Lifecycle and its tasks and techniques so it will best meet our collective needs.

ACKNOWLEDGMENTS

Much of the content of this book is based in one way or another on the excellent works and publications of my many Usability Engineering colleagues over the past two decades. My thanks to them for their contributions to our field.

I would also like to thank my many consulting clients over the last thirteen years for the opportunity to work with them and try out and hone the various tasks and techniques that make up the Usability Engineering Lifecycle, as well as for the opportunity to introduce the lifecycle itself into their development organizations. I always learn as much from my experiences with my clients as they learn from me.

In particular, I would like to thank Brenda Kerton, a project manager at London Life Insurance Company in London, Ontario. Brenda brought me in to assist in her efforts to introduce the Usability Engineering Lifecycle to her development organization, and a number of the work products and examples in this book are adapted from her project (see Chapters 3, 7, and 13).

In addition, while I am not free to name them, I would like to thank the project leader and his team from a project I worked on with a metropolitan police department. Again, many of the examples and work products in this book are adapted from that project. You know who you are—thanks for the terrific opportunity to put a lot of the ideas in this book into practice.

I would also like to thank my colleagues Ron Perkins, of Design Perspectives, and Jack Mayhew, of The Computer Lab, for working with me on the police project. They were a pleasure to work with, and I learned a lot from them too.

Thanks especially to my anonymous reviewers, who provided a great deal of sound advice on how to improve early drafts of this book.

Finally, my thanks to Diane Cerra, my managing editor, Sarah Burgundy, my production editor, and Judith Brown, my copyeditor at Morgan Kaufmann Publishers, for the best experience I've had working with a publisher.

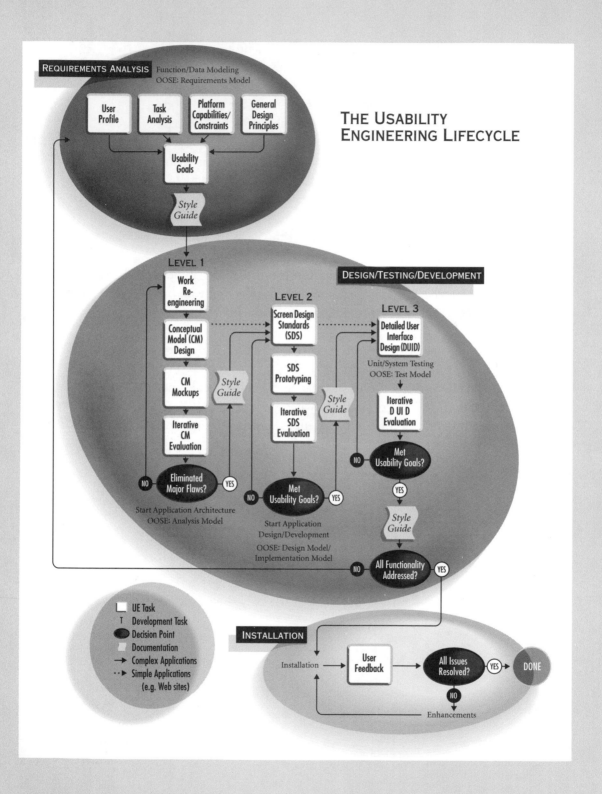

THE USABILITY
ENGINEERING LIFECYCLE

1

Introduction

BACKGROUND

This book is about achieving usability in product user interface design through a process called Usability Engineering. The **user interface** to an interactive product such as software can be defined as the languages through which the user and the product communicate with one another. In the case of software applications, this usually means the way displays and feedback are designed (the application-to-user language) and the way users indicate to the application what they want to do next through interactions with display elements via input devices such as a mouse or keyboard (the user-to-application language). As far as users are concerned, the user interface *is* the product. Just about their entire experience with the product is their experience with its user interface.

Usability is a measurable characteristic of a product user interface that is present to a greater or lesser degree. One broad dimension of usability is how *easy to learn* the user interface is for novice and casual users. Another is how *easy to use* (efficient, flexible, powerful) the user interface is for frequent and proficient users, after they have mastered the initial learning of the interface.

To achieve usability, the design of the user interface to any interactive product, including software, needs to take into account and be tailored around a number of factors, including:

◆ Cognitive, perceptual, and motor capabilities and constraints of people in general

◆ Special and unique characteristics of the intended user population in particular

The user interface consists of the languages through which the user and product communicate

1

- Unique characteristics of the users' physical and social work environment
- Unique characteristics and requirements of the users' tasks, which are being supported by the product
- Unique capabilities and constraints of the chosen software and/or hardware and platform for the product

In the words of Karat and Dayton (1995), "A usable software system is one that supports the effective and efficient completion of tasks in a given work context."

The bottom-line benefits of more usable, or user-friendly, products to business users include

- Increased productivity
- Decreased user training time and cost
- Decreased user errors
- Increased accuracy of data input and data interpretation
- Decreased need for ongoing technical support

The bottom-line benefits of usability to development organizations (including internal development organizations, vendors of commercial products, and contract development organizations) include

- Greater profits due to more competitive products/services
- Decreased overall development and maintenance costs
- Decreased customer support costs
- More follow-on business due to satisfied customers

(See Chapter 20 for a complete cost-benefit analysis of Usability Engineering.)

Usability Engineering provides structured methods for optimizing user interface design during product development

Usability Engineering is a discipline that provides structured methods for achieving usability in user interface design during product development. It is a discipline with roots in several other basic disciplines, including cognitive psychology, experimental psychology, ethnography, and software engineering.

Cognitive psychology is the study of human perception (vision, hearing, etc.) and cognition (human memory, learning, problem solving, decision making, reasoning, language, etc.). From cognitive psychology, Usability Engineering draws knowledge about these aspects of human information processing and applies it to the design of the user interfaces to interactive products in such a way as to exploit the strengths and support the weaknesses of human information processing. Basing user interface design on what we know about human cognition helps us to design interfaces that will be easier to learn, easier to use, and otherwise tailored to optimally support the specific target users doing the specific work tasks a product is intended to support.

Experimental psychology uses empirical methods to measure and study human behavior. Usability Engineering draws upon these methods to measure user performance and satisfaction with product user interfaces.

Ethnography, a science used by social and cultural anthropologists to investigate, study, analyze, interpret, and describe unfamiliar cultures, lends itself to studying users and determining user and usability requirements for product design.

Software engineering is an approach to software development that involves defining application requirements, setting goals, and designing and testing in iterative cycles until goals are met. While there are many different methods of software engineering, they all have this basic approach in common. Usability Engineering adapts these general components of software engineering to provide an engineering-like process for the design and development of usable product user interfaces.

According to Karat and Dayton (1995), "In most cases of the design and development of commercial software, usability is not dealt with at the same level as other aspects of software engineering (e.g., clear usability objectives are not set, resources for appropriate activities are not given priority by project management)." However, any development organization that produces interactive products (software or other kinds), and has an interest in and motivation to produce *usable* interactive products, needs at least two things:

◆ Knowledge and application of known user interface design principles and guidelines
◆ Knowledge and application of structured methods for achieving usability

For some types of interactive products, such as generic business software, there are well-established design principles and guidelines available that are based on objective research and reported in the literature. Development organizations need staff who are fluent in these design guidelines to participate in design efforts, so this general accumulated knowledge will find its way into their products. Development organizations also need structured methods for achieving usability in their products. Just having a design guru on board does not guarantee that design principles and guidelines will find their way into products. Design is complex, and there is no cookbook approach that can rely on general principles and guidelines alone.

Optimal design cannot be achieved with generic principles alone—every product and its users are unique. Conversely, applying structured methods without also following well-established design guidelines may fail

Either of these two things alone is necessary but not sufficient. Optimal design cannot be accomplished by the application of generic guidelines alone, because every product and its intended set of users are unique. Design guidelines must be tailored for and validated against the unique product requirements, and this is what the structured methods accomplish. Conversely, applying structured methods without also drawing upon well-established design principles and guidelines is inefficient at best and may simply fail at worst. Without the benefit of the initial guidance of sound design principles during first passes at design, a particular project with its limited resources may never stumble upon a design approach that works.

Methodological approaches to Usability Engineering have been evolving since the 1970s. An early reference to a Usability Engineering methodology was offered by Gould and Lewis (1985). They described a very general approach to Usability Engineering involving three global strategies:

- Early focus on users and tasks
- Empirical measurement
- Iterative design

Although Gould and Lewis did not specify exactly how these global usability strategies could be integrated into an overall software development lifecycle, or what techniques to apply, their ideas were quite revolutionary at the time. They offered a case study in which they applied their approach, but it involved a small project team, heavily populated with usability experts, and a fairly simple product. They also cited all the many obstacles present in larger, more complex development projects and project team organizations, which make incorporating their usability approach difficult.

Since Gould and Lewis's classic article, others have offered general frameworks for Usability Engineering (Mantei and Teorey 1988; Nielsen 1992; Shneiderman 1992; Wixon and Wilson 1997). Button and Dourish (1996) point out that, historically, the field has been evolving through three distinct approaches to introducing Usability Engineering into product development organizations:

1. Adding cognitive scientists to design teams to provide input on design
2. Inserting Usability Engineering methods and techniques with specific, written work products into the existing development process
3. Redesigning the whole development process around Usability Engineering expertise, methods, and techniques

The Usability Engineering Lifecycle described in this book represents the spirit of Button and Dourish's third approach above. Although it is described mostly in the context of developing typical office software applications, it is equally applicable to projects developing more specialized and unique software-based products based on very different hardware and software platforms, such as factory equipment, medical technology, scientific data-gathering instruments, Web sites and applications, and, in fact, any kind of interactive product.

The lifecycle can be adapted to support internal development projects, commercial development projects, and contract development projects. It can also be adapted to projects varying in size, complexity, time frame and budget. As described in this book, the lifecycle is oriented towards development projects that have already been defined, planned, and scoped, as opposed, for example, to projects intended to completely reengineer a business and identify opportunities for new products, as is the focus in Beyer and Holtzblatt (1998). The orientation is also towards projects creating fairly new products, as opposed to reworkings of existing projects. With a little imagination, however, you can draw upon the tasks and techniques of the lifecycle as it is described in this book to support these other kinds of projects as well.

Although the lifecycle is described mostly in the context of developing typical office software applications, it is equally applicable to projects developing any kind of interactive product

The lifecycle can be adapted to support internal, commercial, and contract development projects of any size, complexity, time frame, and budget

THE USABILITY ENGINEERING LIFECYCLE—AN OVERVIEW

The Usability Engineering Lifecycle consists of several types of tasks, as follows:

- Structured usability requirements analysis tasks
- An explicit usability goal setting task, driven directly from requirements analysis data

◆ Tasks supporting a structured, top-down approach to user interface design driven directly from usability goals and other requirements data

◆ Objective usability evaluation tasks for iterating design towards usability goals

Chapters 2 through 17 describe each Usability Engineering task within the lifecycle in detail and discuss how the tasks are interrelated and all work together to achieve the goal of usability. In this chapter, we'll look at the overall lifecycle. The chart at the beginning of this chapter is a graphical representation of all three lifecycle phases: Requirements Analysis, Design/Testing/Development, and Installation. Usability Engineering tasks within each phase are presented in boxes, and arrows show the basic order in which tasks should be carried out. Much of the sequencing of tasks is iterative, and the places where iterations would most typically occur are illustrated by arrows returning to earlier points in the lifecycle.

The plain text provides the context of an overall software engineering lifecycle, in which the Usability Engineering Lifecycle must be embedded and integrated. Two general types of software engineering methodologies are included. The first line of text at any point represents a task in a typical modern rapid prototyping development methodology, while the second line of text at any point indicates a task in a particular, and currently popular, methodology: Object-Oriented Software Engineering, or OOSE (see Jacobson et al. 1992, for a complete book on this methodology, and a later section of this chapter for an overview).

The following sections briefly describe each usability task. The highly iterative nature of the Usability Engineering Lifecycle, illustrated in the chart, becomes even clearer in these task descriptions.

The User Profile will drive tailored design decisions and identify major user categories for study in the Contextual Task Analysis task

PHASE ONE: REQUIREMENTS ANALYSIS

User Profile: A description of the specific user characteristics relevant to user interface design (e.g., computer literacy, expected frequency of use, level of job experience) is obtained for the intended user population. This will drive tailored user interface design decisions and also identify major user categories for study in the Contextual Task Analysis task.

Contextual Task Analysis: A study of users' current tasks, work-flow patterns, and conceptual frameworks is made, resulting in a description of current tasks and work flow and an understanding and specification of underlying user goals. These will be used to set usability goals and drive Work Reengineering and user interface design.

Usability Goal Setting: Specific *qualitative* goals, reflecting usability requirements extracted from the User Profile and Contextual Task Analysis, and *quantitative* goals, defining minimal acceptable user performance and satisfaction criteria based on a subset of high-priority qualitative goals, are developed. These usability goals focus later design efforts and form the basis for later iterative usability evaluation.

Platform Capabilities and Constraints: The user interface capabilities and constraints (e.g., windowing, direct manipulation, color) inherent in the technology platform chosen for the product (e.g., Apple Macintosh, Microsoft Windows, product-unique platforms) are determined and documented. These will define the scope of possibilities for user interface design.

These first four Requirements Analysis tasks are documented in a work product called the product Style Guide.

The Requirements Analysis tasks are documented in the product Style Guide

General Design Principles: Relevant general user interface design principles and guidelines available in the Usability Engineering literature are gathered and reviewed. They will be applied during the design process to come, along with all other project-specific information gathered in the first four tasks.

PHASE TWO: DESIGN/TESTING/DEVELOPMENT

This phase of the lifecycle is divided into three levels. Design level 1 contains four tasks dealing with high-level design issues.

Work Reengineering: Based on all Requirements Analysis data and the usability goals extracted from it, user tasks are redesigned at the level of organization and work flow to streamline work and exploit the capabilities of automation. No user interface design is involved in this task, just abstract organization of functionality and work-flow design.

Conceptual Model Design: Based on all previous tasks, initial high-level design alternatives are generated. At this level, navigational pathways and major displays are identified, and rules for the consistent presentation of work products, processes, and actions are established. Screen design detail is not addressed until design level 2.

Conceptual Model Mock-ups: Paper-and-pencil or prototype mock-ups of high-level design ideas generated in the previous task are prepared, representing ideas about high-level functional organization and Conceptual Model Design. Detailed screen design and complete functional design are not in focus here.

Iterative Conceptual Model Evaluation: The mock-ups are evaluated and modified through iterative evaluation techniques such as formal usability testing, in which representative end users attempt to perform representative tasks with minimal training and intervention, imagining that the mock-ups are a real product user interface. This and the previous two tasks are conducted in iterative cycles until all major usability bugs are identified and engineered out of the level 1 (Conceptual Model) design. Once a Conceptual Model is relatively stable, system architecture design can commence.

Design level 2, also with four tasks, is concerned with setting standards.

Screen Design Standards will ensure coherence and consistency across the user interface

Screen Design Standards: A set of product-specific standards and conventions for all aspects of detailed screen design is developed, based on any mandated industry and/or corporate standards (e.g., Microsoft Windows, Apple Macintosh), the data generated in the Requirements Analysis phase, and the product-specific Conceptual Model Design arrived at during level 1. Screen Design Standards will ensure coherence and consistency—the foundations of usability—across the user interface.

Screen Design Standards Prototyping: The Screen Design Standards (as well as the Conceptual Model Design) are applied to the design of the detailed user interface for selected subsets of product functionality. This design is implemented as a running prototype.

Iterative Screen Design Standards Evaluation: An evaluation technique such as formal usability testing is carried out on the Screen Design Standards prototype, and then redesign/reevaluate iterations are performed to refine and validate a robust set of Screen Design Standards. Iterations are continued until all major usability bugs are eliminated and usability goals seem within reach.

Style Guide Development: At the end of the design/evaluate iterations in design levels 1 and 2, you have a validated and stabilized Conceptual Model Design and a validated and stabilized set of standards and conventions for all aspects of detailed Screen Design. These are captured in the document called the product Style Guide, which already documents the results of Requirements Analysis tasks. During Detailed User Interface Design, you will follow the Conceptual Model Design and Screen Design Standards in the product Style Guide to ensure quality, coherence, and consistency—the foundations of usability.

In level 3, the design is completed, based on the results of the first two levels.

Detailed User Interface Design: Detailed design of the complete product user interface is carried out based on the refined and validated Conceptual Model and Screen Design Standards documented in the product Style Guide. This design then drives product development.

Iterative Detailed User Interface Design Evaluation: A technique such as formal usability testing is continued during product development to expand evaluation to previously unassessed subsets of functionality and categories of users, and also to continue to refine the user interface and validate it against usability goals.

PHASE THREE: INSTALLATION

User Feedback: After the product has been installed and in production for some time, feedback is gathered for use in enhancement design, design of new releases, and/or design of new but related products.

Table 1.1 lists all the tasks in the Usability Engineering Lifecycle and summarizes key points that are elaborated upon in subsequent chapters.

GENERAL PHILOSOPHY BEHIND THE USABILITY ENGINEERING LIFECYCLE

As you review the tasks in the Usability Engineering Lifecycle, there are some tips you will want to keep in mind that apply to the lifecycle as a whole.

User interface design is key. I present Usability Engineering tasks in the foreground, with less emphasis on overall software engineering tasks, to

Table 1.1 Task summary chart

Task	Purpose	Description	Techniques	Work Products	Integration
User Profiles	Establish user characteristics around which the UI design must be tailored.	Develop a description of the intended user population in terms of characteristics relevant to UI design.	Questionnaire distributed to users. Interviews with people knowledgeable about users.	Questionnaire/ interview form Data summary Analysis and conclusions.	Drives virtually all other tasks except Platform Capabilities/ Constraints.
Contextual Task Analysis	Obtain a user-centered model of work as it is currently performed and extract from this the usability requirements for the product.	Conduct a study of users in their actual work environment performing their real work.	Contextual observations/ interviews. Affinity diagrams. Formal work models. Brainstorming with task scenarios. Trajectory mapping. Multi-dimensional scaling. Interviews with people knowledgeable about user work tasks and environment.	Work environment analysis Task scenarios Task analysis document Current user work models.	Users to study are identified in User Profile. Drives virtually all other tasks except Platform Capabilities/ Constraints.

continued

Task	Purpose	Description	Techniques	Work Products	Integration
Usability Goal Setting	Establish specific qualitative and quantitative usability goals that will drive UI design.	Extract qualitative usability goals from previous tasks and also from general business goals to drive UI design, and quantify a subset of high-priority goals to be used in usability testing as acceptance criteria.	Extract goals from User Profile and Contextual Task Analysis. Extract goals from general business goals. Establish benchmark data.	Documented qualitative usability goals. Documented quantitative usability goals.	Derived directly from the User Profile and Contextual Task Analysis tasks. Drives virtually all other tasks except Platform Capabilities/ Constraints.
Platform Capabilities/ Constraints	Establish the capabilities and constraints of the technology platform, which will limit UI design alternatives.	Study the user interface capabilities and constraints of the chosen technology platform for the product.	Review platform documentation. Interview platform experts.	Documented platform capabilities and constraints.	Can be performed anytime during Requirements Analysis. Drives all design tasks in later phases.
General Design Principles	Identify all general principles and guidelines from the Usability Engineering literature that may be relevant to the product under development.	Consult the available literature and experts to identify relevant general design principles.	Review any relevant platform, corporate, and product family Style Guides. Perform a literature review. Consult with usability experts. Consider automated development tools with guidelines built in.	(none)	Can be performed any time during Requirements Analysis. Integrated with all Requirements Analysis data to drive all design tasks in later phases.

continued

Table 1.1 Task summary chart

Task	Purpose	Description	Techniques	Work Products	Integration
Work Reengineering	Reengineer the current user work model for the purposes of realizing the potential of automation and more effectively supporting business goals, yet minimizing retraining and maximizing productivity.	Reengineer the current user model and document it in a model describing how product functionality will be organized and structured. Validate the reengineered work model with users.	The current user work model is changed only as necessary to exploit the capabilities of automation and better meet business goals. The reengineered work model can be validated with the card sorting technique or with Task Scenario walkthroughs.	Reengineered work model.	Driven directly from work model derived during Contextual Task Analysis. Considers output from User Profile and Usability Goal Setting tasks. Feeds directly into Conceptual Model Design and other design tasks.
Conceptual Model Design	Establish and define a coherent and rule-based, high-level UI design framework that will set the stage for design at lower levels. Support users' natural expectation of a unifying model across the UI.	Conduct the first pass at actual UI design. Design a set of high level presentation and interaction rules, and identify major displays and navigational pathways between them.	Adapt from platform Style Guide (e.g., MS Windows, Apple Macintosh). Generate presentation rules that map to the reengineered work model.	Conceptual Model Design.	Driven directly from the reengineered work model. Considers output from all Requirements Analysis tasks. Feeds directly into Conceptual Model Mock-ups, Iterative Conceptual Model Evaluation, and later design tasks.

continued

Task	Purpose	Description	Techniques	Work Products	Integration
Conceptual Model Mock-ups	Support evaluation, refinement, and validation of the Conceptual Model Design.	Incorporate the design rules that define the Conceptual Model Design in a mock-up of a subset of total product functionality.	Paper-and-pencil mock-ups. Running prototypes.	Paper-and-pencil mock-ups or running prototypes representing the Conceptual Model Design.	Based directly on the Conceptual Model Design. Used to evaluate, refine, and validate the Conceptual Model Design in the Iterative Conceptual Model Evaluation task.
Iterative Conceptual Model Evaluation	Evaluate, refine, and validate the Conceptual Model Design.	Apply one of a variety of objective techniques to iteratively evaluate, refine, and validate the Conceptual Model Design.	Formal usability testing. Usability inspection methods.	Evaluation plan. Evaluation materials. Evaluation data. Data analysis. Conclusions and recommendations for design changes.	Performed on Conceptual Model Mock-ups. Results fed back into Conceptual Model Design.

continued

Table 1.1 Task summary chart

Task	Purpose	Description	Techniques	Work Products	Integration
Screen Design Standards	Establish and define a set of design standards that, along with the Conceptual Model Design, will set the stage for Detailed UI Design. Support users' natural expectation of consistency across displays.	Conduct the second level of UI design. Design a set of Screen Design Standards that will ensure consistency in UI design across the displays and interactions in the product UI.	Adapt from platform Style Guide (e.g., MS Windows, Apple Macintosh). Generate standards to meet the unique usability requirements of the product.	Screen Design Standards.	Some standards may be adapted from a platform, corporate, or product family Style Guide. Designed in the context of all Requirements Analysis data and the Conceptual Model Design. Feeds directly into the Screen Design Standards Prototyping task. Ultimately directly drives the Detailed UI Design.
Screen Design Standards Prototyping	Support the evaluation, refinement, and validation of the Screen Design Standards.	Incorporate the Screen Design Standards in a prototype of a subset of total product functionality.	Running prototypes.	Running prototypes representing the Screen Design Standards.	Based directly on the Screen Design Standards. Used to evaluate, refine, and validate the Screen Design Standards in the Iterative Screen Design Standards Evaluation task.

continued

Task	Purpose	Description	Techniques	Work Products	Integration
Iterative Screen Design Standards Evaluation	Evaluate, refine, and validate the Screen Design Standards.	Apply one of a variety of objective evaluation techniques to iteratively evaluate, refine, and validate the Screen Design Standards.	Formal usability testing. Usability inspection methods.	Evaluation plan. Evaluation materials. Evaluation data. Data analysis. Conclusions and recommendations for design changes.	Performed on Screen Design Standards prototypes. Results fed back into Screen Design Standards.
Style Guide Development	Document the Conceptual Model Design, the Screen Design Standards, and the output from all Requirements Analysis tasks. Enhance communication regarding UI design across the project team.	Document the Conceptual Model Design, Screen Design Standards, and the output from all Requirements Analysis tasks as they are completed in one, evolving document, the product Style Guide.	A single, prestructured document can be developed as the product proceeds through the lifecycle.	A Style Guide document containing the final validated Conceptual Model Design and Screen Design Standards, as well as the main results of all Requirements Analysis tasks.	The repository of all Usability Engineering Lifecycle task outputs except the Detailed User Interface Design and User Feedback tasks.
Detailed User Interface Design	Design the complete, detailed product UI.	Conduct the third level of UI design. Design and document the entire product UI in detail as a UI specification.	The product Style Guide standards are applied to design the UI to all product functionality.	Detailed UI Design specification.	Driven by data and design standards in the Style Guide. Feeds directly into development and the Iterative Detailed User Interface Design Evaluation task.

continued

Table 1.1 Task summary chart

Task	Purpose	Description	Techniques	Work Products	Integration
Iterative Detailed User Interface Design Evaluation	Evaluate, refine, and validate key subsets of the Detailed UI Design. Expand the scope of all previous UI evaluation tasks.	Apply one of a variety of objective evaluation techniques to iteratively evaluate, refine and validate the Detailed UI Design as it is developed.	Formal usability testing. Usability inspection methods.	Evaluation plan. Evaluation materials. Evaluation data. Data analysis. Conclusions and recommendations for design changes.	Performed on the product as it is developed. Results fed back into Detailed UI Design.
User Feedback	Obtain usability data after a product has been installed and used. Inform the UI design for later releases of a product and related products.	Apply one of a variety of objective evaluation techniques to obtain feedback from actual experienced users of an installed product.	Formal usability testing. Questionnaires. Interviews. Focus groups. Usage studies.	Usability feedback.	Performed after a product is in production. Results fed back into the UI design for later releases of the product or related products.

communicate my belief that user requirements and user interface design should drive the overall development process, rather than be driven by it or be incidental to it. After all, the whole point of interactive products is to serve the users, and as far as users are concerned, the user interface *is* the product.

User requirements and user interface design should drive the development process

Integration of Usability Engineering with software engineering must be tailored. The chart at the beginning of this chapter illustrates how Usability Engineering tasks *parallel* or *overlap* traditional development tasks and are tightly intertwined with them. As is communicated by the somewhat loose placement of traditional development tasks relative to Usability Engineering tasks, the exact overlapping of the two types of tasks is not completely clear. The most appropriate relationship between them is probably not absolute, but is most likely dependent on various project-specific factors and on the particular software development methodology with which the lifecycle is integrated.

The exact overlapping of Usability Engineering and software engineering tasks is not completely clear. The most appropriate relationship between them depends on various project-specific factors

For example, traditional systems analysis and Contextual Task Analysis are highly related tasks, but they are not the same thing and require very different kinds of expertise. Exactly how to integrate them to avoid duplication of effort and yet produce the intended and necessary outputs of both is a topic for future work. In the meantime, I simply adapt how I integrate Usability Engineering tasks with an overall product development methodology on a project-by-project basis. You must do the same. The section Customizing the Usability Engineering Lifecycle later in this chapter offers some insights.

Requirements Analysis pays off. Note the fairly extensive effort in Requirements Analysis represented in the chart. Like Karat and Dayton (1995), I strongly believe that " . . . *careful* (and usually collaborative) design and *informal* evaluation, rather than *casual* design and *formal* evaluation, are where the leverage is for producing good interfaces in the real world of industrial software development" (italics mine). In my experience, a good job at requirements analysis brings you closer to the mark in your first pass at design, thus increasing the likelihood of—and reducing the number of iterations of design and evaluation required for—meeting usability goals.

A top-down, struc-
tured approach to
design deals with
high-level issues
first, then detailed
standards, then
complete design

Design can be approached in a top-down, structured process. Note that the Design/Testing/Development phase is divided into three levels. The idea here is that you can (and usually should) take a top-down approach to user interface design. This means dealing with high-level design issues first (i.e., Conceptual Model Design), followed by detailed *standards* (i.e., Screen Design Standards), and then complete design (i.e., Detailed User Interface Design). At each level you conduct iterations of design and testing to finalize that level of design decisions before moving on to lower-level design issues. In the words of Wixon and Wilson (1997):

> Iterative design allows development teams to break large product designs into manageable stages and eliminate major problems early in design and lesser problems as development proceeds. One practical and political advantage of iterative design is that it allows the team to see successive improvements early.

Design, testing, and development should be iterative. Rather than having design, testing, and development be three distinct, linear phases in the lifecycle—as was the case in traditional "waterfall" software engineering methodologies—they are done iteratively, in bundles of functionality, and in different levels of design detail, all intertwined in one overall phase. This is a hallmark of modern software engineering methodologies, especially OOSE, and is equally appropriate in the Usability Engineering Lifecycle, which must be embedded in these methodologies.

The whole lifecycle can be layered across subsets of functionality. Note the layered approach to functionality in the lifecycle, in which the entire Design/Testing/Development phase is conducted on one subset of functionality at a time and then repeated for subsequent subsets, or layers, of functionality (see the "More Functionality?" decision point at the end of the Design/Testing/Development phase in the lifecycle chart). This is in contrast again to the more monolithic, classical "waterfall" development methodologies, which completed each lifecycle phase for *all* functionality before moving on to the next phase in a rigid, linear order. This early approach produced many problems and inefficiencies.

Modern methodologies, and OOSE in particular, advise taking a layered approach. In this way, the team can get valuable feedback and learn valuable lessons from each layer's iteration before expanding their efforts to additional functionality. This philosophy seems particularly fitting in the Usability Engineering Lifecycle.

There are a variety of techniques for carrying out each lifecycle task. The Usability Engineering Lifecycle identifies a set of Usability Engineering tasks that should be carried out in a particular order and integrated in particular ways with the existing systems development lifecycle. For any particular lifecycle task, the practitioner has a set of techniques to choose from to accomplish the basic goals of that task. In the following chapters, which cover the lifecycle tasks one at a time in detail, I describe certain techniques that I have found to be useful in my practice. Note, however, that there are usually a variety of techniques available for carrying out any particular task. My intent is to describe at least one technique in enough detail so that you can carry it out based on your reading of the chapter, and this precludes a detailed and exhaustive review of all available techniques for every task. Instead, I have provided brief descriptions of, and references to, literature on alternative techniques for each task.

Alternative techniques make the lifecycle flexible and adaptable. The distinction between tasks and techniques is an important one that makes the Usability Engineering Lifecycle flexible and adaptive across all kinds of development projects, small to large, simple to complex, regardless of platform and underlying development methodology.

A Usability Engineering *task* can be defined as an activity that produces a concrete work product that is a requisite for subsequent Usability Engineering tasks. Each task has some conceptual goal that defines it. For example, the goal of the User Profile task is to gain a clear understanding of those characteristics of the intended user population that will have a direct bearing on which design alternatives will be most usable to them.

A *technique*, on the other hand, is a particular process or method for carrying out a task and for achieving a task goal. As I've already stated, usually there are a number of alternative techniques available for any given task. For example, for the User Profile task, alternative techniques include distributing user questionnaires and conducting user or user manager interviews. Generally, techniques vary in such things as how costly and time consuming they are to execute, the quality and accuracy

A layered approach allows the team to get valuable feedback from each iteration before attempting additional functionality

In order to achieve optimal usability, all lifecycle tasks should be carried out for every development project

of the work products they generate, how difficult they are for nonspecialists to learn and use, and the sophistication of the technology required to carry them out.

Always adapt your approach by selecting techniques based on project constraints

The key to the general applicability and flexibility of the Usability Engineering Lifecycle lies in the choice of which *techniques* to apply to each task, *not* in the choice of which *tasks* to carry out. I strongly believe that *all* the tasks identified in the lifecycle should be carried out for every development project involving an interactive product in order to achieve optimal usability. However, I always adapt my approach to any given project by a careful selection of techniques based on project constraints. When project constraints simply will not support the resources required for more rigorous techniques for all tasks, I often select "quick and dirty," or shortcut, techniques.

For example, a project I am often hired to perform is an expert assessment, sometimes called a Heuristic Evaluation (see Chapter 10), of the user interface of a product prototype. Typically, I take about forty hours to complete such a project—not much time to carry out all the lifecycle tasks. What I do in this case, however, is to conduct a minimal—you might even say "miniature"—requirements analysis. I collect my user profile, task analysis, platform capabilities and constraints, and usability goals in a matter of hours, simply by interviewing the most qualified people available. Obviously, the data I collect in this manner is not as accurate or complete as it would be if I used more rigorous data collection techniques like those described in the later chapters of this book. However, I always present my final analysis by stating that my conclusions are only as good as the information I was given to base them on.

Based on that context information, I perform my assessment, which is simply a shortcut technique for user interface evaluation (the design has already been done!). I do one iteration, no more—again, a shortcut. I assess all aspects of interface design, from conceptual model to screen design standards to detailed design, in one round, and offer redesign suggestions at all three levels. Again, a shortcut. I may even perform a form of user feedback if there are users available who have some experience with the prototype.

In the end, at least in one form or another, and to varying degrees of accuracy and completeness, I have carried out all the tasks in the lifecycle. My selection of techniques is the only thing that distinguishes such a short, simple project from ones on which I spend a year or more of effort. From the simplest to the most complex and comprehensive of my consulting projects, I employ *all* the tasks in the lifecycle.

You can do the same thing in adapting the Usability Engineering Lifecycle to your projects. Use the more rigorous and accurate techniques described or referenced in this book when you can. But don't hesitate to use the shortcut techniques also described for any given task when necessary. They are always better than skipping a task altogether.

Often usability practitioners are called in late in the development cycle and expected to make a contribution. For example, you might be called in to perform a usability test without the opportunity to do a User Profile or Contextual Task Analysis. In these cases, again, you should carry out at least shortcut versions of earlier tasks in the lifecycle to provide context for the later tasks you are invited to perform, because without that context, the value of the later task is severely limited. You don't have to be invited in at the inception of a project to use the Usability Engineering Lifecycle; you just need to understand how to perform the shortcut versions of each task.

Optimal implementation of the lifecycle requires full participation of cross-functional teams. Most Usability Engineering Lifecycle tasks are best carried out not in isolation by usability experts, but by a whole cross-functional project team in which usability experts represent one of many important skill sets and perspectives (see Wixon and Ramey 1996, 60, 63; Rowley 1996, 125–127, 135–138; Juhl 1996, 216; Dray and Mrazek 1996, 147; Coble et al. 1996, 246; Holtzblatt and Beyer 1996, 305–307; Chin, Rosson, and Carroll 1997).

In traditional approaches, different kinds of specialists (e.g., marketing personnel, analysts, system architects, usability experts, programmers) perform different steps in the software engineering process, and communication between steps/specialists is accomplished through documents. It takes time to write, read, and understand documents, and usually many holes in understanding remain, with no easy process for obtaining answers or clarification. In addition, the knowledge and perspectives of some specialists do not impact the work of other specialists who work in earlier phases of the process, so that a certain amount of revisiting earlier work is almost always necessary to address all issues. Finally, specialists working later in the lifecycle have little "buy-in," or commitment to the work of specialists working earlier in the lifecycle,

Most lifecycle tasks are best carried out by a cross-functional project team in which usability experts represent one of many skill sets and perspectives

because they weren't there and don't understand the processes or rationale behind the earlier decisions.

The idea of a *cross-functional team* is that all team members perform all steps together in the overall process, each bringing his or her particular perspective and skill set to all major project decisions. In this way, communication is facilitated, and a deeper shared understanding of issues across team members results. In addition, all participating specialists get their issues addressed, as each step is performed to minimize rework downstream in the process. Finally, team members who ultimately will make design decisions not only understand requirements issues but have bought into the goal of addressing them explicitly in the design (see, e.g., Page 1996, 209).

It can be extremely effective to have users participate in many lifecycle tasks as active participants

A usability expert may be the only one on a project team currently skilled at the techniques described in this book, but I strongly recommend that *all* project team members carry out lifecycle tasks jointly, so that they develop a shared understanding of the requirements and design issues. In addition, it can be extremely effective to have users participate in many Usability Engineering lifecycle tasks, not just as objects of study or sources of information, but as active participants.

For example, Chin, Rosson, and Carroll (1997) describe an approach in which users participate in all analysis and design activities as fully empowered, and even dominant, team members. Their approach, which they call Participatory Analysis, involves a structured technique for analyzing the kind of "Task Scenarios" obtained through the contextual observations/interviews of a Contextual Task Analysis (see Chapter 3). In this technique, prominent features of the current work process or system are identified from concrete Task Scenarios, or examples of real work, and analyzed for their pros and cons. All analysis and documentation is done in language and terms completely and concretely tied to real work and thus familiar to users. No analysis techniques and terms from traditional software engineering (e.g., data modeling) are employed. This has the effect of not only drawing in, motivating, and empowering the users on the team, but also clearly establishing them as the most important experts on the team. Contrast this with the way users are often involved in requirements analyses and design—by inviting them to attend meetings run by technologists, on methods and terminology familiar only to technologists. Chin and colleagues demonstrate through a study of the use of their approach that when users are provided with a structured approach that relates directly to their area of expertise—their work—they can be effective participants in analysis and design. At the same time, someone needs to assume overall responsibility for directing and managing specific Usability Engineering Lifecycle tasks, and the logical person to do this is one of the usability experts assigned to a project.

ISSUES RELATED TO THE LIFECYCLE TASKS

In addition to the lifecycle tasks, four other Usability Engineering issues arise during product development. The last four chapters in this book address these issues:

Promoting and implementing the lifecycle. Development organizations not currently practicing Usability Engineering techniques need to be sold on their value and need to make process changes in order to incorporate Usability Engineering into their overall development methodology.

Usability project planning. Level of effort, start and end dates, and assigned staff must be estimated and planned for each of the Usability Engineering tasks in the lifecycle and then integrated with the overall project plan.

Cost-justification. A traditional cost-benefit analysis can be adapted and applied to the Usability Project Plan, both to refine it and to gain approval for funding.

Organizational roles and structures. There are different roles that usability specialists with different skill sets can play on projects, and different ways to place usability staff within organizational reporting structures. Designing organizational roles and structures for Usability Engineering can have a profound impact on the successful application of Usability Engineering techniques to product development.

Designing organizational roles and structures can profoundly impact the successful application of Usability Engineering techniques to product development

In this book, I refer to three main usability roles: Usability Engineer, User Interface Designer, and User Interface Developer. These roles are briefly defined here and discussed in detail in Chapter 21.

The **Usability Engineer** is assumed to be generally skilled in carrying out all the tasks and many of the available techniques in the lifecycle. This role would require education and experience in at least some of the disciplines from which Usability Engineering draws its knowledge and methods. Usability Engineers are skilled in performing, for example, User Profiles, Contextual Task Analyses, and usability testing.

The **User Interface Designer** requires good design skills but does not require education and experience in other Usability Engineering techniques. User Interface Designers perform the actual design tasks within the Usability Engineering Lifecycle.

The **User Interface Developer** is responsible for the architecture and actual building of user interface code and must have the prerequisite skills to do so, along with sensitivity to usability issues and receptivity to Usability Engineering tasks and techniques.

CUSTOMIZING THE USABILITY ENGINEERING LIFECYCLE

All lifecycle tasks will always apply, but they can be expanded or contracted depending on the requirements, characteristics, and resources of a particular project

Every development organization has its own unique overall product development methodology to which the integration of the Usability Engineering Lifecycle tasks must be tailored. All the lifecycle tasks will apply, but where, when, and how they are integrated with other development tasks can be customized to minimally alter the existing methodology, yet best support the goal of usability. The tasks can be expanded or contracted depending on the requirements, characteristics, and resources of particular development projects.

For complex products with a high need for usability, a high probability of a major payoff for usability efforts, and a high level of available resources, the full-blown lifecycle with rigorous techniques for each task, as described in Chapters 2–17, is appropriate. This means, for example:

◆ Applying rigorous techniques for the User Profile and Contextual Task Analysis tasks

◆ Conducting all three design levels in the Design/Testing/Development phase, including iterative evaluation in each

◆ Taking full product functionality through the whole lifecycle in three or more layers

By contrast, for relatively simple projects with minimal resources available, such as simple Web sites and applications, we could contract the lifecycle as follows:

◆ "Quick and dirty" versions of the User Profile and Contextual Task Analysis tasks could be applied.

◆ Designers could rely more heavily on general design principles and guidelines available in the literature.

◆ The three design levels could be collapsed into a single iterative design process (but note that it is still essential to carefully consider and consciously design at all three levels).

◆ Documenting design standards in a product Style Guide could be skipped.

For projects falling between these two extremes, all manner of variations are possible. For example:

◆ In the Design/Testing/Development phase, design level 1 could be carried out as specified, but design levels 2 and 3 could be collapsed into a single iterative process covering standards and detailed design simultaneously.

◆ Total functionality could be taken through the lifecycle in two or three layers, rather than one or many.

◆ "Quick and dirty" techniques for most lifecycle tasks can substitute for the more rigorous techniques discussed in the following chapters (see the "Shortcuts" section of each chapter).

Another factor in tailoring the lifecycle within particular product development organizations has to do with the available Usability Engineering skills in that organization. For example, when software developers are experienced in Usability Engineering techniques and, in particular, in designing from a product Style Guide, then Detailed User Interface Design can be left up to them, with usability specialists providing support and review. When this is not the case, it may be more efficient and effective to have usability specialists do Detailed User Interface Design and document it as specifications, and to let developers work from these specifications.

In general, some techniques depend on specialized Usability Engineering skills more than others, and some are easier to pick up with no past education or experience. Development organizations can start introducing those Usability Engineering techniques that they have the skill sets to carry out, and work slowly towards more rigorous techniques as they

Some techniques depend on specialized Usability Engineering skills more than others, and some are easier to pick up with no past education or experience

train or hire people to provide the requisite skills. For example, it's easier to teach and learn basic design principles and how to do simple usability testing than it is to teach and learn how to conduct the more rigorous User Profiles and Contextual Task Analysis techniques effectively.

Sometimes the nature of the work being automated will require that the lifecycle and its tasks be adapted in particular ways. For example, Brown and Motte (1998) have found that many traditional techniques for lifecycle tasks are very hard to implement when designing products for use in a medical trauma environment. They note, for example, that a Contextual Task Analysis can be difficult to carry out, as work in a trauma center is unscheduled, often frenzied and chaotic, cannot be interrupted for introspection and questions, often takes place in a small room already crowded with people and equipment, and usually cannot be videotaped due to confidentiality and liability issues. Similarly, formal usability testing in this work environment is impossible for obvious reasons, while simulating the work environment in a lab is next to impossible.

Nevertheless, Brown and Motte emphasize that there are no viable substitutes for the *tasks* of Contextual Task Analysis and Iterative Evaluation, and they recommend, based on experience, adapting *techniques* to the constraints of this unique environment. For example, they recommend conducting structured interviews with clinical experts prior to field observations, and having a clinical expert accompany usability experts and designers during field observations, to help interpret what is happening. In addition, they suggest having clinical experts prioritize and add to the list of requirements generated by field studies to further refine requirements. They also suggest having a team consisting of a clinical expert and a usability expert perform Heuristic Evaluations (see Chapter 10) as an alternative evaluation technique for early design ideas. In these ways, Brown and Motte tailor the techniques used to carry out the tasks of the lifecycle without significantly altering the choice or sequence of tasks.

The best way to tailor the lifecycle to your project is to prepare alternative usability project plans and then subject them to cost-benefit analyses

The best way to decide exactly how to tailor the Usability Engineering Lifecycle to your project is to follow the instructions in Chapters 19 and 20 on preparing alternative usability project plans and then subject them to cost-benefit analyses. The best way to tailor the overall Usability Engineering Lifecycle and *institutionalize* it within the overall development methodology of an organization is to create and fund an explicit project to do just this. To help accomplish this goal, hire a usability specialist (either in-house or as a consultant) with the appropriate skill set and level of experience to work with the development organization and the keepers and educators of the development methodology. Chapter 18 offers some advice on introducing and integrating the Usability Engineering Lifecycle into a development organization and its existing methodology.

THE USABILITY ENGINEERING LIFECYCLE AND OOSE

The philosophy and approach of Object-Oriented Software Engineering (OOSE), a current and popular software development methodology, is very compatible with the Usability Engineering Lifecycle. I include references to this methodology in the Usability Engineering Lifecycle charts presented at the beginning of each chapter. Here, I pause to give readers unfamiliar or only a little familiar with OOSE a brief overview, including a definition of key terms and concepts. I refer you to the book by Jacobson and his colleagues (1992) for more detail on OOSE concepts. Terms defined here are used throughout this book to help you tie Usability Engineering techniques into the OOSE approach to software engineering.

The philosophy and approach of OOSE is very compatible with the Usability Engineering Lifecycle

OOSE divides development into three high-level phases: Analysis, Construction, and Testing. During the **Analysis phase**, two models are constructed. First, a **Requirements Model** is formulated. This consists of two major pieces, Actors and Use Cases. **Actors** are categories of users, or roles users can play. Examples of Actors might be, for a medical application: physician, surgeon, technician, nurse, and receptionist. For a police department application, they might be police officer, station commander, clerk, and property clerk.

Individual **Users** are considered to be *instances* of Actors. A distinction is drawn between **Direct Users**, who interact directly with an application, and **Indirect Users**, who do not interact directly with, but are affected by, an application. For example, in a medical clinic workstation, the physicians, nurses, and system administrators are Direct Users; and patients and other physicians who receive records and reports from the physicians who use the workstation would be Indirect Users.

Primary Actors are the key user types for a system, and **Secondary Actors,** while they are Direct Users of the system, are not considered to be the main users. For example, in a medical clinic workstation, the physician would be considered the Primary Actor, and a system administrator and nurses or assistants might be considered Secondary Actors.

A Use Case is a generalization that tries to capture the nature of a whole category of related activities

Use Cases are coherent, relatively independent, meaningful tasks that Actors carry out in their current work. More than one Actor may participate in a particular Use Case. Examples of Use Cases for a clinical workstation in a medical environment might be to review patient records, read/interpret radiology images, and schedule patients. The Use Case describes exactly how the general task is carried out and also captures any significant variations in the task. It documents the task as a sequence of steps, as a procedure. A Use Case is a generalization that tries to capture the nature of a whole category of related activities. The actual work that users perform at given points in time are *instances* of Use Cases. A key characteristic of Use Cases is that they reflect work as it is currently done and are written in everyday language. Thus, they reflect the user's perspective and are easily validated by the user because they are easy to understand.

Use Cases are generally self-contained, while in real life, users often perform multiple parallel tasks, or one task may temporarily interrupt another. To capture this, OOSE offers the concept of an Extension to a Use Case. An **Extension** specifies how one Use Case description may be inserted into another. Both Use Cases can occur independently, and the Extension captures special cases in which they intertwine. For example, there may be a Use Case describing routine reading/interpreting of radiology images and an Extension describing a related task or Use Case that is triggered only when the image reveals certain characteristics.

The second type of model constructed in the Analysis phase, which is based on the Requirements Model, is the Analysis Model. The **Analysis Model** begins to structure the requirements documented in the Use Cases from a systems point of view. Here you move from a description of how work is performed today (Use Cases) to how it will be performed with the automated system. The Analysis Model is *object-oriented* in that it structures the functional requirements as a set of objects interacting with one another.

An **object** consists of both information and behavior. It is defined by a number of behaviors or operations and a state that remembers the effect of these operations. Objects can be related to one another in several ways. One key concept is that of **inheritance**—objects can be defined by inheriting information and behaviors from other objects and then adding unique behaviors and information.

Three kinds of objects are defined in the Analysis Model. **Interface Objects** specify functionality that is directly dependent on the application environment—that is, the parts of the application that interact with the outside world, including other applications and users. All aspects of the application user interface are thus encapsulated in Interface Objects. **Entity Objects** model information the application will handle over long periods of time, even after individual Use Cases have been executed. **Control Objects** basically specify functionality that does not naturally fall into Interface Objects or Entity Objects. They often act as the "glue" that relates other types of objects in the course of a Use Case.

Objects can be common across multiple Use Cases. They are in fact extracted quite naturally directly from the Use Cases identified in the Requirements Model. They tend to reflect real-life objects that have meaning for users. Examples of objects might be medical records, radiology images, and schedules.

In the **Construction phase** of OOSE, two models are generated: the Design Model and the Implementation Model. Finally, in the **Testing phase**, a Test Model is constructed. In the words of Jacobson and his colleagues (1992, 157), "The requirements model will be *structured* by the analysis model, *realized* by the **design model**, *implemented* by the **implementation model** and *tested* by the **testing model**" (bold and italics mine). (These models are indicated in the Usability Engineering Lifecycle charts at the beginning of each chapter.) The details and constraints of the actual hardware and software environment and tools do not come into play until the development of the Design Model in the Construction phase. In the Analysis phase, everything is still quite abstract and independent of implementation details.

One final key concept in OOSE is the idea of a highly iterative approach to developing these models. Functional requirements are not exhaustively defined before any design begins, and design is not exhaustively specified before construction begins. Instead, small subsets, or layers, of functionality are taken through several models, validated in various ways, and then expanded to include additional functionality. This is consistent with the basic philosophy of Usability Engineering, which also

Objects can be defined by inheriting information and behaviors from other objects and then adding unique behaviors and information

takes a highly iterative approach to user interface design; I have built this concept into the Usability Engineering Lifecycle charts presented at the beginning of each chapter.

Referring to this chapter's chart, you can now study how the Usability Engineering Lifecycle can be integrated into the OOSE approach to software development. For example, the User Profile and Contextual Task Analysis tasks should parallel the development of the Requirements Model in the Analysis phase of OOSE. The Work Reengineering task corresponds roughly to the construction of the Analysis Model in the Analysis phase of OOSE. Actual user interface design, which begins in the Conceptual Model Design task, will enhance the Design Model in the Construction phase of OOSE. Thus, Usability Engineering tasks that are independent of hardware/software platform and tool choices occur along with the OOSE activities that are also independent of implementation choices.

OOSE has a user-centered philosophy, but it doesn't address many fundamental Usability Engineering goals and techniques

OOSE, as described by Jacobson and his colleagues (1992), has a user-centered philosophy. However, even in OOSE, many fundamental Usability Engineering goals are still not addressed, and many fundamental Usability Engineering techniques are still not applied. For example, OOSE does not explicitly refer to a "Work Environment Analysis." This important part of a Contextual Task Analysis points to aspects of the users' actual work environment that should drive user interface design decisions (see Chapter 3). And OOSE does not emphasize "contextual" observations of work, or even the need to tap into current user task organization and task sequence models in the design of the user interface.

The Usability Engineering techniques offered in this book can be thought of as extensions to OOSE that will greatly enhance the ultimate usability of object-oriented software systems

The tasks and techniques of the Usability Engineering Lifecycle described in this book can greatly enhance OOSE's user-centered philosophy by supplementing the techniques of OOSE. Usability Engineering and OOSE are not competing approaches, but rather are potentially complementary approaches to software development. OOSE without Usability Engineering techniques, while espousing a user-centered philosophy, will not necessarily result in optimally usable software systems. In the parlance of OOSE, we might think of the Usability Engineering techniques offered in this book as potential *extensions* to OOSE that will greatly enhance the ultimate usability of object-oriented software systems.

Recent work in the field of Usability Engineering has attempted specifically to integrate Usability Engineering techniques with object-oriented design and development. An interesting paper by Rosson and

Carroll (1995) reports on an experimental software design and development tool that supports tight integration of one aspect of Contextual Task Analysis—Task Scenario development—with what I am calling Work Reengineering, and user interface design and software development. In their words:

> Our work on the Scenario Browser embodies a new perspective on the gap between task specification and implementation. Rather than rely only on the empirical feedback available through a rapid prototyping process, we propose that tasks [here they mean a combination of what I am calling Work Reengineering and the three levels of user interface design] and implementation be developed jointly, within an analytic framework that supports recognition and management of their interdependencies. Specifically, we have created a design tool that might integrate use-oriented reasoning with reasoning about software abstractions, using scenarios as the unit or context of analysis and design. In this we are integrating two converging areas of research, that on scenario-based design of human-computer interaction, and that on the use of scenarios in object-oriented analysis and design. . . .
>
> . . . Our work investigates the proposition that scenarios of the *same sort* we have been collecting and constructing to guide envisionment of the "external" system, the system as directly experienced by the user, can provide a use-oriented context for object-oriented analysis and design. (Italics mine)

The tool described in their paper seems to support a tight integration of the requirements analysis and design tasks I have separately described as Contextual Task Analysis, Work Reengineering, Conceptual Model Design, Screen Design Standards, and Detailed User Interface Design, with the software engineering tasks of analysis, design, and implementation in the specific context of object-oriented development. Their tool, as they point out, is still in the experimental stages, and it is unclear how well it would support complex development projects (the project they describe in their paper is fairly simple). However, the idea of developing such tools seems promising, and we can hope that more resources will be allocated to the development of such tools in the future.

In the meantime, the *spirit* of their tool, which involves close collaboration at all times between users, usability practitioners, and developers is a fundamental cornerstone of good Usability Engineering. In Chapters 7 and 8, I return to this idea and to the ideas from Rosson and Carroll's paper.

Requirements Analysis

I

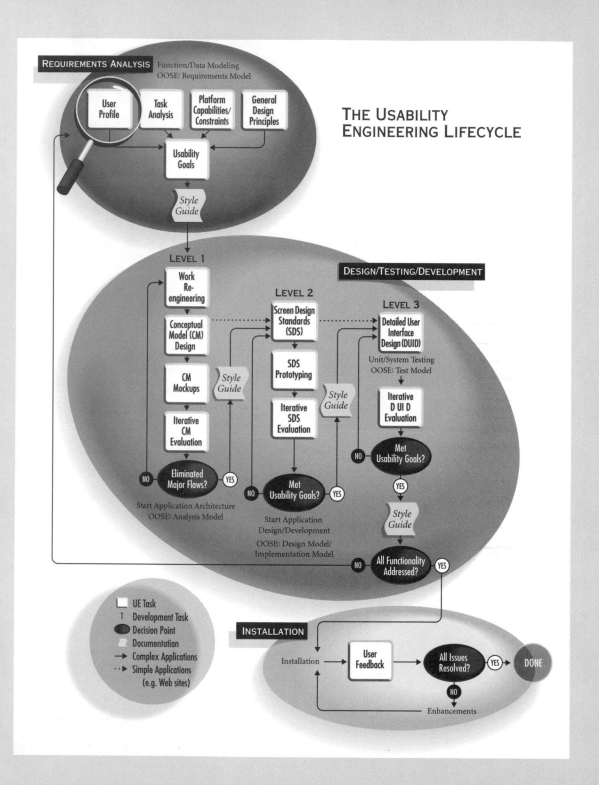

THE USABILITY
ENGINEERING LIFECYCLE

2

User Profiles

PURPOSE

There is no single best user interface style or approach for any and all types of users. Specific interface design alternatives that optimize the performance of some types of users may actually degrade the performance of other types of users. For example, an infrequent, casual user needs an easy-to-learn and easy-to-remember interface, but a high-frequency, expert user needs an efficient, powerful, and flexible interface. These are not necessarily the same thing. Similarly, a highly skilled typist might perform better with a keyboard-oriented interface, while a low-skill typist might do better with a GUI.

Unless User Interface Designers (see Chapters 1 and 21 for definitions of all Usability Engineering roles) know the specific characteristics of a population of users (e.g., expected frequency of use, level of typing skill), they cannot make optimal user interface design decisions for them. The purpose of a User Profile is thus to establish the general requirements of a category of users in terms of overall interface style and approach.

If you want an immediate and concrete sense of what a User Interface Designer needs to know about the users and why, skip to the Sample Work Products and Templates section later in the chapter, read it, and then return here.

DESCRIPTION

For the User Profile task, you must first determine who will use the planned product. How you do this depends on what type of development

Unless User Interface Designers know the characteristics of users, they cannot make optimal design decisions for them

35

organization you are working in, and the procedure is described in the later section Sample Technique—A Step-by-Step Procedure. After you determine who your users are, you obtain a description of the whole user population in terms of characteristics relevant to user interface design. These characteristics include

- Psychological characteristics (e.g., attitude, motivation)
- Knowledge and experience (e.g., typing skill, task experience)
- Job and task characteristics (e.g., frequency of use, task structure)
- Physical characteristics (e.g., color blindness)

You can determine user characteristics by gathering data through interviews and/or a User Profile questionnaire (see the Sample Work Products and Templates section later in the chapter). In the case of vendor organizations, certain User Profile data can also be obtained indirectly from marketing personnel. In the case of internal development organizations and contract developers, some User Profile data can be obtained indirectly from human resources personnel.

From the summarized data, you draw high-level conclusions regarding interface design requirements and document these in a narrative format (see the Sample Work Products and Templates section).

A separate User Profile should be summarized for each significant category of users (e.g., doctors, technicians, nurses, receptionists) within a market segment or business unit. You should perform the data collection and analysis part of this task only once for each significant user category. Then for each new product intended for that user category, simply refer to the relevant User Profile conclusions and design implications.

When products are radical innovations, it may be impossible to do a User Profile

If you work for a vendor company, as opposed to an internal development company or contract development organization, you might think that it will be difficult to identify actual users and get questionnaire responses from them. If your product is new, rather than a new release of a current product, maybe you are not even sure who your users will be. In such cases, when products are radical innovations, it may indeed be difficult to identify and get access to representative potential users, and doing a User Profile might be next to impossible. You may have to wait until your initial product is out and perform a User Profile before designing your second release or related products.

But often, even in a vendor situation, users are well known and accessible. You will find that marketing and sales organizations have good contacts in customer organizations, and in fact themselves have a lot of useful knowledge about users that you can tap into just by asking the right questions. Often customers are invested in your future products and will give you access to users. If not, or if your product is intended for the general public, you can provide incentives (e.g., payment, discounts, or entries in a raffle) for potential users to participate in a questionnaire study. In my experience, in the vast majority of situations, it is possible to get User Profile data in some form.

It is important to revalidate User Profiles every few years, especially if user populations are changing due to turnover or new hiring practices. For example, one of my clients knew that a large percentage of users in a particular category would retire over the next several years. They also knew that management planned to hire replacements who were younger and better educated. Thus, there was a planned change in the User Profile for that user category, and we incorporated this expected User Profile into our designs.

Revalidate User Profiles every few years, especially if turnover or new hiring practices change user populations

SCHEDULING AND INTEGRATION WITH OTHER TASKS

Certain interdependencies exist between Usability Engineering Lifecycle tasks themselves and between Usability Engineering Lifecycle tasks and standard software development lifecycle tasks. Tasks must be scheduled so that the output from each task can provide essential input to other tasks. In each chapter on a specific task, this section describes the relationship of the task to the whole process.

The User Profile task fits into the overall Usability Engineering Lifecycle in the following ways:

◆ The User Profile task is the first task in the Usability Engineering Lifecycle.

◆ This task feeds directly into the Contextual Task Analysis task by identifying categories of users whose tasks and work environment must be studied in that later task.

◆ This task feeds directly into the Usability Goal Setting task because usability goals are in part driven directly by user characteristics (e.g., a low frequency of use indicates a need for ease of learning and remembering). Thus, different usability goals will be extracted from the profiles of different categories of users.

◆ Ultimately, the User Profile task will have a direct impact on all design tasks, which focus on realizing usability goals, which in turn are based in part on User Profiles.

◆ This task will also drive the selection of usability evaluation issues and test users.

◆ Output from this task will be documented in the product Style Guide.

The User Profile task fits into the underlying software development methodology in the following ways:

◆ This task can *parallel, overlap,* or *follow* development of the Requirements Model in the Analysis phase in OOSE (or function and data modeling in the requirements phase of a traditional rapid prototyping methodology). It could either define Actors for the Requirements Model or take the definition of user categories from the Requirements Model as its starting point.

◆ This task (along with all other Usability Engineering Lifecycle Requirements Analysis tasks) should precede development of the Analysis Model in the Analysis phase of OOSE (or the application architecture design in a traditional rapid prototyping methodology).

ROLES AND RESOURCES

For each task, certain Usability Engineering roles, such as the Usability Engineer and the User Interface Designer, should participate. These and other Usability Engineering roles are defined briefly in Chapter 1 and in detail in Chapter 21. This section describes how the roles work together to accomplish each task.

If the questionnaire technique is used in the User Profile task (see the next section), the usability roles might participate as follows:

Task leader: A Usability Engineer should direct this task, bringing to bear his or her skills in questionnaire design and data analysis. The Usability Engineer should also at least direct, review, and provide significant input to the conclusions drawn from the questionnaire data.

Other resources: Project team members and/or the User Interface Designer can carry out most of the main steps of this task. Users would participate in the design of the questions, in the pilot questionnaire, and as the ultimate respondents of the final questionnaire.

If the interview technique is used (see Alternative Techniques—A Review), the usability roles might participate as follows:

Task leader: The User Interface Designer could take main responsibility for the task.

Other resources: A Usability Engineer will be useful in helping to decide which user characteristics to profile and also in drawing conclusions. Other project team members can carry out the steps. User representatives would serve as interviewees.

Sample Technique— A Step-by-Step Procedure

There are two main ways to obtain a User Profile, depending on available time and other resources: questionnaires distributed to actual users or interviews with people knowledgeable about the whole population of users. The technique that produces the most accurate and reliable results is to gather data directly from intended users through a questionnaire. This can be time consuming and requires a skill set that includes questionnaire design and data analysis. However, once a User Profile is obtained through this method, it can be reused across applications for the user population profiled, and thus the cost of obtaining it can be "amortized" across projects, reducing the actual cost per development project.

The following steps describe how to obtain a User Profile in the most reliable and accurate way—using a questionnaire. I also refer you to the Sample Work Products and Templates section of Chapter 17 for an example of a report from a questionnaire study that also provides insights into the use of questionnaires as a general information-gathering technique.

❶ **Determine user categories.** First you must determine who the intended users for a product are. Often they fall into already defined categories (e.g., doctor, nurse, technician, receptionist). How you determine users and user categories depends in part on what kind of development organization you work in.

If you work for an internal development organization or a contract development organization, the business unit for which a product is being developed will in most cases already have a definition of users, usually by job category. Defining the users is also usually part of the standard systems development methodology in an internal development organization, and as a usability specialist, you need only ask to get a list of user categories.

If you work for a vendor company, neatly identifying and defining future users can be a bit trickier. But your marketing organization (or whatever organization is responsible for planning and defining new products) has probably formulated a definition of potential customers for a planned product. Again, you need only ask the right people to get a simple identification of intended user categories.

❷ **Determine relevant user characteristics.** Start with the questionnaire template provided (see the Sample Work Products and Templates section) or with other questionnaires developed in-house, and hold meetings with the appropriate project team members, the User Interface Designer, the Usability Engineer, and some representative and knowledgeable users to gather input on user characteristics that should be polled in the User Profile.

❸ **Develop a draft questionnaire.** Revise and expand the questionnaire template to tailor it to specific organization or project needs. Add and delete questions as appropriate. Write an introduction explaining the purpose and benefits of the questionnaire, again following the format of the questionnaire template in the Sample Work Products and Templates section.

❹ **Get management feedback on the draft.** You will need management's input and approval on your draft questionnaire.

❺ **Revise the questionnaire.** At this stage, revise the questionnaire to incorporate management feedback.

❻ **Conduct a pilot questionnaire with interviews.** Interview a small sample of potential questionnaire respondents by going through each question with them and checking for clarity of wording, completeness, mutual exclusivity of multiple-choice answers (see the Sample Work Products and Templates section), and appropriateness of questions. Two to three interviewees per major user category will suffice.

❼ **Revise the questionnaire.** Now revise the questionnaire to incorporate interview feedback.

❽ **Select a user sample.** In general, the response rate to mailed questionnaires is about 10 percent. However, in my experience, response rates from invested internal computer users, when questionnaires are properly motivated, has been much higher. In a vendor company with internal users, I got a return rate of 33 percent out of 180 questionnaires distributed, while in an insurance company, I got back 75 percent of 400 distributed. In a police department, on the other hand, with the signature of a high-ranking officer on the cover letter, I got 100 percent—800 out of 800 returned! As a rule of thumb, until your own in-house experience proves otherwise, assume a response rate of no more than 30 percent from internal users and no more than 10 percent from external users.

Unless the total population is very large (over about 3,000), aim for a final sample of 10 percent of the total population. With internal users, this means sending out questionnaires to a minimum of roughly 33 percent, expecting to get 30 percent of these back (with external users you might have to send out 100 percent to get 10 percent back). When user populations exceed about 3,000, as is often the case in a vendor situation, it becomes impractical to distribute and analyze questionnaires from even as little as 10 percent of the total population. In these cases, aim for a final sample of at least 100 or so users *from each significant user category.*

Representative sampling is very important. Make sure to send questionnaires to equal numbers of each known, significant user category (e.g., physicians, nurses, technicians, receptionists). If the first distribution does not produce roughly equal returns from each category, send a second distribution to underrepresented categories. Also sample representatively within each major user category. For example, in an insurance company, perhaps major user categories include clerical staff, managers, and claims adjusters, but there are two distinct types of claims adjusters and two distinct types of managers, and all user types reside in different geographical locations, some of which are currently more automated than others. In this case, include equal numbers of the five categories of users in the initial distribution, and try to include equal numbers from the various locations and various levels of automation within those categories.

❾ **Distribute the questionnaires.** You can use interoffice mail, regular mail, or email (but don't use email if it is likely to cause a bias in response; i.e., only some users routinely use email, and thus only they will get it and respond). Make returns as easy as possible. For example, if using regular mail, include a preaddressed, stamped envelope for returns. Give a clear return deadline, but also encourage users who miss the deadline to return the questionnaire whenever they can.

⑩ **Design data entry/analysis.** Using a spreadsheet, statistics package, tailored data entry and analysis program, or just paper, pencil, and calculator, design a data entry format and analysis technique, assuming an ultimate data summary format similar to the template in the Sample Work Products and Templates section (two data entry and analysis templates are shown). Also plan to collate and summarize any free-form comments.

⑪ **Enter data.** As questionnaires are received, enter data as planned.

⑫ **Summarize data.** When all questionnaires are returned, or upon the deadline date (perhaps allowing a grace period of several days), analyze data as planned and produce a data summary similar in format to the template included in the Sample Work Products and Templates section.

⑬ **Interpret data.** Here it is particularly useful to have a Usability Engineer take the lead (see Chapters 1 and 21 for definitions of all Usability Engineering roles). Write a short (several pages) summary providing a synopsis of the key characteristics of each user category and drawing specific implications for user interface design. Do not make any assumptions about the relative importance of different categories of users at this point. Summarize the general needs of each different user category and variations within the category.

For example, if managers were found to be primarily low-frequency, computer-illiterate, and computer-phobic users, while clerical users were found to be mostly high-frequency, computer-literate users with positive attitudes towards technological tools, the general needs of the former could be summarized as *ease of learning* and remembering, and the general needs of the latter as *ease of use*, flexibility, and power. Then examples of how to achieve these general goals could be offered. For more information on how User Profile data should drive design decisions, see Mayhew (1992, ch. 2).

The Sample Work Products and Templates section offers a sample of User Profile conclusions and design implications. Which user category to favor in the overall interface (if any) will be decided on during Usability Goal Setting, a later task.

⑭ **Present results.** Distribute the narrative conclusions and design implications, with the data summary form as an appendix, to all interested parties, including at least the User Interface Designer and other project team members. The results should also be folded into the product Style Guide (see Chapter 14). If appropriate, summarize these work products in an oral presentation as well.

LEVEL OF EFFORT

Table 2.1 gives a sample level of effort for the questionnaire technique. Level of effort will vary significantly, depending on how many questionnaires are distributed and how many are received and must be analyzed. After experience conducting this task in your own development environment, you can revise these estimates to better reflect your own experience.

Table 2.1
Level of effort—User Profiles

Usability/Development Time		User Time	
Step	Hrs	Step	Hrs
Needs finding	24	Needs finding	24
Draft questionnaire	12		
Management feedback	2	Management feedback	2
Revise questionnaire	6		
Pilot questionnaire	8	Pilot questionnaire	8
Revise questionnaire	6		
Select user sample	4		
Distribute questionnaire	6	Respond to questionnaire	50
Data analysis	24		
Data interpretation/presentation	24		
Document User Profiles	24		
Total	140	Total	84

ALTERNATIVE TECHNIQUES— A REVIEW

As an alternative to the questionnaire, you can simply design the User Profile data summary template (see the Sample Work Products and Templates section) and use it to collect data in interviews with selected user representatives. User representatives might be managers or user category leaders or even marketing staff in a vendor situation—anyone expected to be familiar with a broad range of users from the intended population. You ask them to describe the overall user population according to the characteristics covered on the data summary template.

This technique is much quicker and thus cheaper than the questionnaire technique, but the reliability of the data will depend on how accurately the people interviewed know the user population. Often, no one really has an accurate picture of the whole user population.

If you use the interview technique, start with step 12 from the Sample Technique—A Step-by-Step Procedure outlined earlier, developing the data summary template (see the Sample Work Products and Templates section) with input from project team members, management, and user representatives regarding what the relevant user characteristics might be. Then use the template to interview selected user representatives and get their best guess as to how users are distributed across the categories in each user characteristic (e.g., what percentage of users are low-, medium-, and high-skilled typists).

The level of effort for the interview technique can be extrapolated from the level of effort for a questionnaire, given in the preceding section. Needs finding still must be done, as well as data analysis and data interpretation/presentation. Intervening steps, however, are skipped, and interviews are substituted. This might take about three hours per user type.

SHORTCUTS

Obtaining the best guess of people likely to know the users well is acceptable when you can't gain data from real users

The interview technique is a shortcut to the questionnaire technique for gathering User Profile data. Although nothing compares with actually gathering data from a representative sample of the users themselves, the best guess of people most likely to know the users well is an acceptable alternative. Also bear in mind that once a User Profile is conducted for a given user population, this profile can be reused on any project developing a product for the same user population. Thus, once it's done, the "shortcut" on subsequent projects is simply to reuse the User Profile from the previous project.

A good example of this kind of reuse is given in Comstock and Duane (1996). They describe a project in which they reused User Profile (and Task Analysis) data from previous projects aimed at the same user categories to formulate and establish usability goals and design approaches on a new project. You should note, however, that it is probably advisable to redo User Profiles about every two years, as user populations do change in important ways over time.

Getting an Accurate User Profile

For two of my clients, I first interviewed project team members (developers) to get a general sense of the user population before I designed a User Profile questionnaire. In one case, the project team was convinced the users would have a generally low level of familiarity with the Microsoft Windows platform they planned for their product, and they were thus prepared to depart significantly from the Windows standards in their product user interface. When the User Profile questionnaire revealed a generally high level of Windows experience, I strongly advised them to adopt the Windows standards as closely as possible. Team members were still interested in creating their own unique user interface, but early testing of several alternative designs that varied in how faithfully they followed Windows standards clearly showed that the more consistent the design was with Windows standards, the more easily users learned to use it.

On the other project, the development team felt quite confident that users would generally have high levels of computer literacy. An extensive User Profile questionnaire of over 800 users, however, revealed that a very small percentage of potential users had any experience with computer software at all, let alone the Windows standards. In this case, based on this User Profile data, we designed (and validated through testing) a very simplified user interface that departed significantly from the Windows standards.

In both cases, you can see two things: project team members often have serious misconceptions about important characteristics of the users, and these misconceptions can lead them to design very inappropriate user interfaces for those users. Thus, while I use shortcuts to the questionnaire technique when I have no choice, I am careful to choose interviewees who are likely to have a more accurate picture of users than developers usually do, and I am careful to explain to my client that my design recommendations will only be as good as the user data on which I am basing them.

Web Notes

The problems of doing a User Profile for a Web site or application are very like doing one for a vendor company: the users are not so accessible or even known. However, a User Profile is still doable. You can get help from marketing personnel to identify and get access to potential users. You can do a "quick and dirty" User Profile based on interviewing marketing personnel or others who may have contact with potential users (see the earlier section Alternative Techniques—A Review). And, after the Web site or application is implemented, you can at least solicit User Profile information through the site itself. You can then use this information to update and improve the new versions of the Web site and to build new related Web sites and applications. You might create a link that takes users to a User Profile questionnaire, and provide some incentive (discounts, raffle entries, etc.) for them to fill it out and send it back.

Sample Work Products and Templates

The following sample work products and templates for the User Profile task are offered here:

- User Profile Questionnaire Template
- User Profile Data Entry and Analysis Templates
- User Profile Data Summary Template with Sample Data
- Sample User Profile Conclusions and Design Implications

User Profile Questionnaire Template

The following template can be used as a starting point for any User Profile questionnaire. Some notes on how the template is laid out will help when creating your own User Profile questionnaire from this template. First, in the questionnaire itself, the titles in parentheses should be removed (they are there to cue you regarding how these questions relate to the Data Summary Template shown later).

Some questions should be kept together and in the order they appear in the template, such as questions 1–4, which establish membership in predefined user categories, and questions 17–23, which refer to one another and therefore should be kept together and in order. Other questions should be randomly distributed across the questionnaire to reduce response bias; for example, questions 5–9 poll attitudes and motivation, and questions 10–16 address knowledge and experience.

Many of these sample questions must be tailored to fit what is already known about the intended respondents. For example, question 1 should list the known job types within the target user population, and question 2 should be much more specific, listing actual locations of offices if possible.

A short cover letter should be provided with the questionnaire, pointing out the purpose and benefits of User Profiles. It is helpful to have the cover letter signed by a well-known and highly placed person, to help motivate respondents to participate (obviously, permission must be obtained from such a person before using his or her name). An example cover letter is offered here, but you should tailor it to the particular circumstances.

The template uses two formatting techniques that I highly recommend. First, bold is used to highlight key aspects of questions and answers. This enhances clarity and readability. Second, considerable white space is used, especially where respondents are expected to write in answers. Although this makes the questionnaire appear longer and thus may put some users off, the increased readability and ease of response outweigh any drawbacks. If length is an issue, you can produce a double-sided questionnaire and give users an estimate of the time it will take to complete it, pointing out that it is mostly multiple choice.

When adding questions that poll attitudes or opinions, order choices in an ascending or descending order (e.g., "like," "neutral," "dislike"), but vary the order from question to question, so that some have the positive choice first and others have the negative choice first. This helps to avoid introducing a response bias due to implicitly leading the user in one direction or the other. However, in self-assessment questions, such as typing skill, educational level, or computer literacy, order from lowest to highest skill level to avoid encouraging users to overinflate their assessments.

In general, always design questions to be neutral, so as not to inadvertently lead users in their answers and introduce a response bias into the data. Finally, make sure your multiple-choice answers are *mutually exclusive*. For example, don't have "1–3" as one choice and "3–6" as another: which would you choose if your answer was 3? And make them *exhaustive* (don't make your last category "10–15" if somebody's answer might be 16 or greater).

Many of the sample questions must be tailored to fit what is already known about the intended respondents

Provide a short cover letter with the questionnaire that is signed by a well-known and highly placed person and that points out the purpose and benefits of User Profiles

XYZ Insurance Application—
User Profile Questionnaire

Dear XYZ Insurance Application User:

This questionnaire has been prepared by the XYZ Insurance Application project team to help us learn more about you, the potential end users of our system. **The information you and other future users of the XYZ Insurance System provide through this questionnaire will help us to design and develop a higher-quality application** that will be better tailored to your needs and thus easier to learn and easier to use.

The questionnaire is anonymous, and we will be summarizing all responses to describe whole categories of users, rather than referring back to any single questionnaire. The more candid and accurate you are in your responses, the more useful the information gathered through this questionnaire will be in helping us to meet your needs.

It should only take you about 15–20 minutes to fill out this questionnaire. It may look long, but most questions are simple multiple choice. Your input will have the most impact if you return your completed questionnaire in the enclosed stamped, addressed envelope by **Friday, October 22, 1999.** However, we will find your input useful no matter when it gets to us, so even if you miss this important deadline, please return it whenever you can. To ensure your anonymity, do not put a return address on the envelope. Your participation is greatly appreciated.

Best regards,

_____

Mr. Important
XYZ Insurance Company

XYZ Insurance Application—
User Profile Questionnaire

(User Category Identifiers)

1. Check the **job title** that best describes your current job:
   - _____ **Clerical**
   - _____ **Internal Claim Rep**
   - _____ **External Claim Rep**
   - _____ **Supervisor**
   - _____ **Manager**
   - _____ **Other** (please describe) _____

2. In which **geographic area** is your main office located?
   - _____ **Northeast**
   - _____ **Southeast**
   - _____ **Midwest**
   - _____ **Southwest**
   - _____ **Northwest**
   - _____ **California**

3. Please estimate **how many** people in your job title are working in your geographic area: _____
   (If you have no idea, write "N/A.")

4. Describe the current **level of automation of your job title** in your office by checking one choice below:
   - _____ **None** (No users in my job title have or use a computer workstation.)
   - _____ **Low** (All users in my job title who use the computer share a workstation with other users.)
   - _____ **Medium** (Some users in my job title who use the computer share a workstation with other users, but some have their own workstations.)
   - _____ **High** (All users in my job title have their own workstations.)

"XYZ Insurance Application—User Profile Questionnaire," cont. next page

"XYZ Insurance Application—User Profile Questionnaire," cont.

(Attitude and Motivation)

5. In general, **how do you feel** about working with computers?
   - _____ I **don't like** working with computers.
   - _____ I have **no strong like or dislike** for working with computers.
   - _____ I **like** working with computers.
   - _____ **Other** (please explain) _____

6. How have computers **affected your job**?
   - _____ Computers have made my job **easier.**
   - _____ Computers have **not affected** my job in any particular way.
   - _____ Computers have made my job **more difficult.**
   - _____ **Other** (please explain) _____

7. Is the amount of **time it takes to learn** new software applications usually **worth it**?
   - _____ **Yes**, it pays off because computer systems usually help me do my job better or faster.
   - _____ **Sometimes** it pays off, and sometimes it doesn't.
   - _____ **No**, computer systems are usually not useful enough to justify the training time.
   - _____ **Other** (please explain) _____

8. Do you **enjoy learning** how to use new software applications?
   - _____ **Yes**, it's usually challenging and interesting.
   - _____ **Sometimes**, depending on the application.
   - _____ **No**, it's usually tedious and frustrating.
   - _____ **Other** (please explain) _____

9. In general, are you **interested in computers**?
   - _____ I am **not interested** in computers and would avoid using them if I could.
   - _____ I am interested in computers but **only as a means** to help me do my job better and faster.
   - _____ I am **interested** in computers in general, and I enjoy using them.
   - _____ **Other** (please explain) _____

(Knowledge and Experience)

10. What is your level of **typing skill**?
    _____ **"Hunt and peck"** typist (less than 15 words per minute)
    _____ **Moderately skilled** touch typist (between 15 and 50 words per minute)
    _____ **Highly skilled** touch typist (greater than 50 words per minute)

11. What is your **highest academic degree**?
    _____ **no** degrees
    _____ **High school** degree
    _____ **Trade** or vocational school degree (beyond the high school level)
    _____ **College** degree (for example, B.A., B.S., Associate College degree)
    _____ **Graduate** degree (for example, M.A., M.S., Ph.D., Ed.D., M.D., R.N.)
    _____ **Other** (please explain) _____

12. How would you describe your **experience level** in your current **job title**?
    _____ **Novice** (less than 1 year)
    _____ **Experienced** (1–3 years)
    _____ **Expert** (more than 3 years)
    _____ **Other** (please describe) _____

13. What is your native language?
    _____ **English** (go to question 16)
    _____ **Spanish**
    _____ **Other** (please name) _____

"XYZ Insurance Application—User Profile Questionnaire," cont. next page

"XYZ Insurance Application—User Profile Questionnaire," cont.

14. If your native language is **not English**, how well do you **speak English** (leave blank if English is your native language)?
    _____ **Poorly** (I have trouble communicating with English speakers.)
    _____ **Adequately** (I speak well enough to get around.)
    _____ **Fluently** (I speak almost as well as a native speaker.)
    _____ **Other** (please describe) _____

15. If your native language is **not English**, how well do you **read English** (leave blank if English is your native language)?
    _____ **Poorly** (I have trouble reading documents in English.)
    _____ **Adequately** (I read well enough to get around.)
    _____ **Fluently** (I read almost as well as a native speaker.)
    _____ **Other** (please describe) _____

16. How would you describe your general level of **computer experience**?
    _____ **None** (I have never used any software applications.)
    _____ **Low** (I have used only one or two software applications.)
    _____ **Moderately low** (I have learned and used between three and ten different software applications.)
    _____ **Moderately high** (I have learned and used more than ten different software applications but have no programming skills.)
    _____ **High** (I have used many different software applications and have some programming skills.)
    _____ **Other** (please describe) _____

(Job and Task Characteristics)

17. Please name all the **software applications you currently use** in your job, and indicate how long you have been using them. Under **"Business Applications"** (1–5), list any specialized applications built by or through MIS at XYZ Insurance Co. to service your business. Only list systems you personally use. Under **"Office Applications"** (A–E), list any general-purpose commercial packages such as word processors, spreadsheets, and so on that you use.

Years/Months

APPLICATION **EXPERIENCE**

Business Applications:

1. _____ _____

2. _____ _____

3. _____ _____

4. _____ _____

5. _____ _____

Office Applications:

A. _____ _____

B. _____ _____

C. _____ _____

D. _____ _____

E. _____ _____

"XYZ Insurance Application—User Profile Questionnaire," cont. next page

"XYZ Insurance Application—User Profile Questionnaire," cont.

18. On the average in your geographic area, **how long** do people **stay in your job title** before leaving the company, being promoted to other titles, or leaving the job for any other reason?
    _____ **I don't know**
    _____ **Less than six months**
    _____ **Six months to a year**
    _____ **Over a year, up to three years**
    _____ **Over three years**

19. Approximately what percentage of your total work time do you spend doing your work in the following different **locations** (your answers should add up to 100 percent)?
    _____ **Your field office**
    _____ **Your home**
    _____ **A hotel room**
    _____ **A claimant's location**
    _____ **Another field office**
    _____ **Other** (please name) _____

(Physical Characteristics)

20. Are you:
    _____ **Male**
    _____ **Female**

21. Are you:
    _____ **Right-handed**
    _____ **Left-handed**
    _____ **Ambidextrous** (equally coordinated with both hands)

22. Are you **color blind** in any way?
    _____ **No**
    _____ **Yes** (please describe) _____

23. **How old** are you?
    - _____ **18–25**
    - _____ **26–40**
    - _____ **41–55**
    - _____ **over 55**

24. Do you wear **glasses or contact lenses**?
    - _____ **No**
    - _____ **Yes** (Please describe your vision problem and correction method, for example, nearsighted, farsighted; bifocals, contact lenses.) _____

25. Do you have any **physical handicaps** other than vision deficiencies that computer technology would need to accommodate or support (for example, hard of hearing, arthritis in hands, wheelchair)?
    - _____ **No**
    - _____ **Yes** (Please describe) _____

USER PROFILE DATA ENTRY AND ANALYSIS TEMPLATES

Separate data entry and analysis should be done for each major user category, if relevant. For example, the data from all clerical staff should be entered and analyzed separately from the data for the internal claims reps, external claims reps, supervisors, and managers. Similarly, data from all physicians should be entered and analyzed separately from the data for technicians, nurses, and receptionists. An analysis of the whole population can always be synthesized from the separate analyses, but you will want to draw conclusions and implications for each user category separately as well.

Here I offer two User Profile data entry and analysis templates, one assuming a spreadsheet program, and the other assuming just paper, pencil, and calculator. The sample spreadsheet below shows the data from two questions and three users. Raw data is entered from each respondent's questionnaire, putting a 1 in any cell that represents an answer chosen for that question by that user, and leaving blank or entering 0 in cells representing all other answers to that question. Then, sums and percentages across users for each question are calculated by entering simple formulas in the cells of the Sums and % rows.

As you can see in the spreadsheet at the bottom of this page, after the raw data was entered, the spreadsheet calculated that 67 percent of users answered "Yes" to question 8 about whether they enjoy learning new computer systems, and 33 percent answered "Sometimes." In response to question 9 about how interested in computers they are, 67 percent answered "Only as a means to get my work done," and 33 percent answered "I am interested in computers." In most cases percentages across answers within a single question should add up to 100 percent (unless there is missing data, i.e., some respondents failed to answer some questions).

If data entry and analysis cannot be automated, you can still make up a simple data entry sheet onto which raw data can be collated and analyzed. A sample of such a format, using the same two questions and three respondents appears on page 57. As you go through each questionnaire, you would enter a tick mark in the Tally column for the answer the respondent chose for each question (here you can see that two users chose "Yes" to question 8, and one user chose "Sometimes," etc.). Then compute the percentage by dividing each sum by the total number of respondents. Again, in most cases percentages across answers within a single question should add up to 100 percent unless there is missing data.

XYZ Insurance Application—User Profile Data

Respondents	Q 8 Yes	Enjoy Learning Computers		Q 9	Interested in Computers	
		Sometimes	No	Not interested	Only as a means	Am interested
1	1					1
2		1			1	
3	1				1	
Sums	2	1	0	0	2	1
%	0.67	0.33	0.00	0.00	0.67	0.33

XYZ Insurance Application—User Profile Data

Question	Answer	Tally	Sum	%
Q 8: Enjoy learning computers?	Yes	//	2	.67
	Sometimes	/	/	.33
	No		∅	.00
Q 9: Interested in computers?	Not interested		∅	.00
	Only as a means	//	2	.67
	Am interested	/	1	.33

USER PROFILE DATA SUMMARY TEMPLATE WITH SAMPLE DATA

Following is a template for summarizing the data from the data entry and analysis templates in a more readable way. The header section identifies the set of users whose data is summarized on this form, and a separate summary should be developed for each major user category, if relevant.

Each question from the original questionnaire is recorded on the form, using question numbers and abbreviated phrases for both questions and answers (only the first several questions from the questionnaire are represented here to give the idea of the format). The questions are grouped in related categories, rather than in the exact order in which they appear on the questionnaire (where order was intentionally randomized). The percentage of respondents who answered in each multiple-choice category is recorded for each question. For example, in question 5, an attitude question, the data might indicate that 13 percent "don't like," 48 percent are "neutral," and 39 percent "like" computers. In most cases percentages should add up to 100 percent (unless there is missing data, i.e., some respondents failed to answer some questions).

XYZ Insurance Application—
User Profile Data Summary

Overall Business Organization: <u>Individual Insurance</u>

User Category:
Job title:	Supervisors
Geographic area(s):	All
Total respondents:	43
% of total at geographic area:	33%
Level of automation:	High

Attitude and Motivation:

5. Feel about computers
- <u>.13</u> don't like
- <u>.48</u> neutral
- <u>.39</u> like

6. Affected your job
- <u>.16</u> more difficult
- <u>.56</u> neutral
- <u>.28</u> easier

7. Learning pays off
- <u>.24</u> no
- <u>.39</u> neutral
- <u>.37</u> yes

8. Enjoy learning apps
- <u>.74</u> no
- <u>.14</u> sometimes
- <u>.12</u> yes

9. Interested in computers
- <u>.10</u> not interested
- <u>.78</u> only as a means
- <u>.12</u> interested

Knowledge and Experience:

10. Typing skill
- <u>.91</u> < 15 wpm
- <u>.06</u> 15–50 wpm
- <u>.03</u> > 50 wpm

11. Highest degree
- <u>.00</u> no
- <u>.05</u> high school
- <u>.00</u> trade
- <u>.76</u> college
- <u>.19</u> graduate

12. Job experience
- <u>.05</u> < 1 year
- <u>.07</u> 1–3 years
- <u>.88</u> > 3 years
- <u>.00</u> other

SAMPLE USER PROFILE CONCLUSIONS AND DESIGN IMPLICATIONS

The sample offered here is based on a User Profile of seven categories of plant floor workers in a manufacturing company, which is in turn based on a questionnaire and data analyses and summaries similar to those offered in the preceding templates. The categories of users in the complete User Profile included production workers, managers, supervisors, quality assurance specialists, clerical workers, skilled tradespeople, and engineers. This sample contains the analysis and conclusions in the User Profile for two user categories: production workers and engineers. Pay particular attention to the differences in user characteristics between the two categories and the corresponding difference in user interface requirements. Also included is a summary table linking key, general usability goals to user categories according to user characteristics revealed in the User Profiles. This table gives an example of how to link information gained during the User Profiles task with goals set during the Usability Goal Setting task.

ABC Factory Applications—User Profile Conclusions

Production Workers

General Description

Production workers are hourly workers, including machine operators, assemblers, and hourly personnel other than skilled trades. They include people performing job functions as an integral part of the production process, such as an assembler on a final assembly line. Other production workers work as machine operators, responsible for the operation of one or more pieces of production equipment.

There are a total of 7,834 production workers, representing 62 percent of the total plant floor workforce, working in four different plants all in the same city.

"ABC Factory Applications—User Profile Conclusions," cont. next page

"ABC Factory Applications—User Profile Conclusions," cont.

User Characteristics

Among production workers, general *attitude* and *motivation* towards computers are fairly high, but not as high as most other user categories (e.g., clerical and QA). However, nearly 73 percent of these users do not perceive computers to be important to their jobs.

Educational level is generally high school degree or less—lower than any other user category. By inference, reading skill would probably average around the eighth-grade level.

Job experience levels are quite high, comparable to other user categories. *Turnover* is low, and generally lower than other categories.

Computer experience, by contrast, is quite low, and considerably lower than other user categories. *Frequency of computer use* is quite low, and significantly lower than other user categories, and use is most often *discretionary.*

These users get very little, and brief, *training* support for new systems—less than any other user category.

A majority have no *typing skills,* and only a small fraction are experienced typists, significantly less than in other user categories.

A majority of these users are *male*—a mix not terribly discrepant from other user categories. By inference, a little over 7 percent (599) have some form of *color vision deficiency.* A substantial majority (69 percent) wear *corrective lenses,* comparable to other user categories. Virtually 100 percent wear protective eyeglasses on the job.

This user category is currently about 67 percent over forty in *age,* comparable to other categories except engineers, who are generally younger.

Usability Requirements

Production workers have a high need for *ease of learning*, especially in the general *computer* (as opposed to job and task) aspects of usage, due to their lower educational levels, low computer experience, low frequency of use, discretionary use, minimal training support, and their perception that computers are currently not particularly important to their jobs.

However, they are very experienced on the *job*, their attitude and motivation regarding computer usage are high, and their turnover rate is low. This suggests that *power without complexity* (i.e., *simplicity*) is also important. That is, the power ought to be immediately perceivable, not hidden by a complex and difficult-to-learn user interface.

Very low typing skills suggest an interface with absolutely *minimal typing requirements.*

Low reading skill and the prevalence of corrective lenses suggest that *icons and visual displays* (rather than verbal ones) will be useful. Any text that is displayed should be written at about the fifth-grade reading level. The prevalence of corrective lenses and the general older age of these users also suggest that *text and symbols should be adequately large*.

The fact that most production workers are male suggests that the *use of color* must take into consideration a significant (8 percent) incidence of color blindness.

"ABC Factory Applications—User Profile Conclusions," cont. next page

"ABC Factory Applications—User Profile Conclusions," cont.

Engineers

General Description

Engineers are trained, salaried employees who design, purchase, install, and support production processes and equipment. They include process engineers, plant engineers, controls engineers, and other professions that support plant processes and operations.

There are a total of 972 engineers, representing 9 percent of the total workforce, working in four different plants all in the same city.

User Characteristics

Among engineers, *attitude* and *motivation* towards computers are generally high, higher than among production workers, comparable to skilled tradespeople and managers, but not as high as among clerical and QA users. Of these users, 82 percent perceive computers to be important to their jobs.

Educational level is very high, with 96 percent possessing at least one college degree. This is significantly higher than any other category. By inference, reading skill would conservatively average between tenth- and twelfth-grade level.

Job and *task experience levels* are moderate to high, with 54 percent possessing eleven years or more experience, although this percentage is significantly less than any other user category. A significant portion of the total category (35 percent) possess three years or less experience in their current job. As compared with other categories, engineers have the highest *turnover* rate, with 21 percent turnover per year.

Computer experience is moderate to high, generally a bit higher than most of the other nonhourly categories, and considerably higher than the hourly categories. *Frequency of computer use* is moderate, higher than production workers and skilled tradespeople but lower than other categories. This category is second only to supervisors in the percentage of members using four or more different computer applications (66 percent). Use is most often *discretionary*.

Engineers have moderate levels of *training* support for new systems available to them, less than some categories but more than others. Training is typically eight hours or less in duration.

A majority are experienced *typists,* second only to the clerical user category.

A majority of these users are *male*—a mix not terribly discrepant from other user categories. By inference, a little over 7 percent (65) have some form of *color vision deficiency.* A substantial majority wear *corrective lenses* (77 percent), comparable to other user categories.

Only about 38 percent of engineers are currently over forty in *age,* and engineers are thus significantly younger than any other category.

Usability Requirements

Engineers are very experienced on the *job*, and their frequency of use is relatively high, their educational levels are high, their computer experience is moderate to high, their training support is moderate, and their perception is that computers are important to their jobs. This suggests that *ease of use* and *power* are important.

High levels of typing skills suggest that *typing requirements* will not be a problem.

High educational and reading skill levels suggest that icons and visual displays are not as important as to other user categories. The prevalence of corrective lenses suggests that *text and symbols should be adequately large.*

The fact that most engineers are male suggests that the use of color must take into consideration a significant (7 percent) incidence of *color blindness.*

"ABC Factory Applications—User Profile Conclusions," cont. next page

"ABC Factory Applications—User Profile Conclusions," cont.

Usability Requirements Summary

The following table summarizes the important usability requirements according to user category.

Key: blank = not important, x = important, xx = very important

	Ease of Learning	Ease of Use	Simplicity	Visuals/ Icons	Minimal Typing	Color Vision Deficit	Other Vision Deficit
Production	xx	x	x	x	xx	x	x
Engineering		x				x	x
Clerical		xx					x
QA	x		x		x	x	x
Supervisor	x		x	x	x	x	x
Skilled	xx	x	x	x	xx	x	x
Manager		x	x		x	x	x

Usability requirements named in the table are defined below.

Ease of learning: How easily and quickly can users learn to use new computer systems, with or without training? This is important for infrequent users and/or users who may not have access to formal training. It is also important for users with negative attitudes and low motivation regarding computers and their jobs, and/or with low computer literacy.

Ease of use/power: How quickly, easily, and efficiently can users accomplish tasks once they have been learned, and what range of tasks can be easily accomplished? This is important for users with high experience levels, high frequency of use, positive attitudes, high motivational levels, and a need for efficiency and speed.

Simplicity: Is there a need for a low level of complexity in order to accomplish tasks? This includes *conceptual* complexity (minimizing new concepts required to perform additional tasks) and the complexity of actually *performing* human-computer interactions (minimizing the actions required to communicate with the system).

Use visuals/icons: Should information be presented as icons and in other visual, graphical formats, as opposed to text and numbers? This includes the use of visual cues such as color, reverse video, bold, and so on. Many users will benefit from the use of graphics and visuals, but particularly users with low ability in reading or other language skills.

Minimize typing: How significant are typing skills and familiarity with keyboards? "Point and select" is an alternative interaction style to "remember and type."

Color vision deficit: How common is color blindness? Special care must be taken in using colors in the interface if a significant number of users have some form of color blindness. In particular, pure, saturated reds and greens should be avoided or used only with some other redundant cue.

Other vision deficit: How common are other vision problems? The interface must be usable by users with imperfect eyesight if significant numbers of such users are part of the target population. This means text must not be too small, and graphics and selections must be large and detailed enough so that users can discriminate among them.

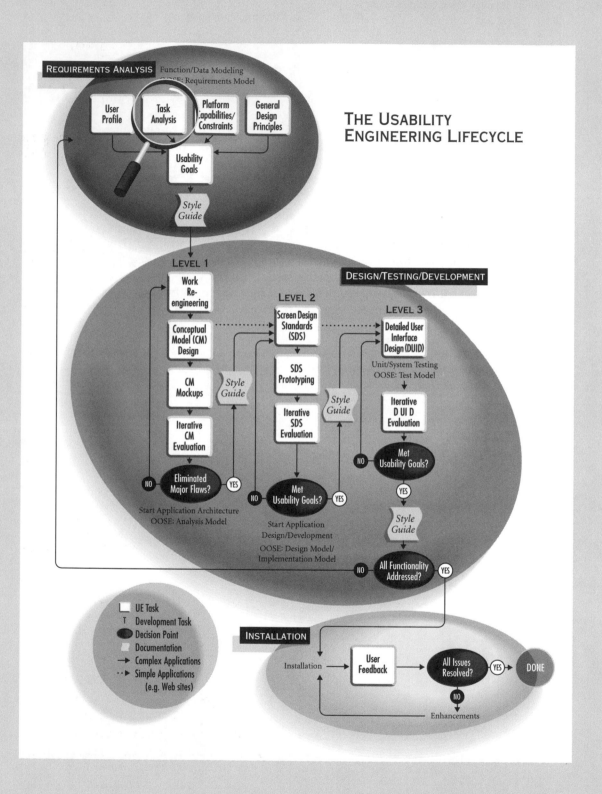

Contextual Task Analysis

PURPOSE

As in the rest of the Usability Engineering Lifecycle tasks described in this book, the focus of Contextual Task Analysis is on projects in which a specific product has already been identified, defined, and scoped. Other task analysis techniques focus on major business reengineering efforts that include identifying opportunities for new products or on identifying basic features that should be included in new products. See, for example, the excellent book by Beyer and Holtzblatt (1998) and the valuable reference book edited by Wixon and Ramey (1996). If you do have the opportunity or need to do major business reengineering before the development of specific automated products, and you have used Beyer and Holtzblatt's Contextual Design technique to do this, I might point out that their technique leaves off just where actual user interface design begins in the Usability Engineering Lifecycle. So, you could pick up where they left off by using the tasks and techniques described in Chapters 8–17 of this book.

Contextual Task Analysis as it is described here is most appropriate when you already have a set of functions and features identified and scoped out for automation; you primarily need to understand the identified current work in order to optimally support it with a new product such as a software application. On such a project, major business reengineering efforts such as those described by Beyer and Holtzblatt would simply be out of scope.

Here, the purpose of this task is to obtain a user-centered model of work as it is currently performed. That is, you want to understand how

The focus of Contextual Task Analysis here is on projects in which a specific product has already been identified, defined, and scoped

67

users currently think about, talk about, and do their work in their actual work environment. Ultimately, the reason for this is that when you design the new product and its user interface, you want to find an optimal compromise or trade-off between three goals:

- Realizing the power and efficiency that automation makes possible
- Reengineering work processes to more effectively support identified business goals
- Minimizing retraining by having the new product tap as much as possible into users' existing task knowledge, and maximizing efficiency and effectiveness by accommodating human cognitive constraints and capabilities within the context of their actual tasks

Traditional software development methods focus mostly on the first goal. As a result, some of the second goal and most of the third are lost, because designers and developers never really understand the users' work and their current work models. A great deal of work "reengineering" occurs in application design, and only some of it serves the first two goals above. Much of it is unnecessary and results in training and usage burdens on the user. You cannot factor in the third goal—minimizing the training overhead and maximizing efficiency and effectiveness—unless you first have a clear picture of users' current work models: how they do their work in the realities of their everyday work environment, and how they think and talk about it.

To obtain a current user work model, you must perform a Contextual Task Analysis, which differs from a traditional systems analysis as described in Table 3.1.

The purpose of this task is to define usability requirements and to point towards ways of meeting those requirements

Traditional systems analysis usually results in the inclusion of all required data and low-level functions, and structures them in a robust implementation architecture. Without a truly user-centered approach, however, it often fails to organize and present that data and functionality in a manner that supports and optimizes the work performance of real users in their real work environment. This missing piece is the whole point of a Contextual Task Analysis. Thus, the purpose of this task is to supplement more traditional types of systems analyses in order to define usability requirements and point towards ways of meeting those requirements. Then, in later tasks, these requirements can be applied directly to making user interface design decisions.

Table 3.1 Traditional systems analysis vs. Contextual Task Analysis

	Traditional Systems Analysis	**Contextual Task Analysis**
Goal	Input to the design of: software processes and data structures	Input to the design of: the user interface
Output	Function models and data models	Work Environment Analysis, Task Analysis, Task Scenarios, and Current User Task Organization Model
Impacts	Implementation architecture	Reengineered task organization and task sequence models, Conceptual Model Design, Screen Design Standards, and Detailed User Interface Design
Focus	Technical information processing limitations, data characteristics, and implementation architecture considerations	Human information processing limitations, current work, and current user work models
Objects of Analysis	Data and functions	Users, users' work environment, and users' work goals

Contextual Task Analysis techniques tie in rather neatly with Object-Oriented Systems Engineering (OOSE—see Jacobson et al. 1992). Chapter 1 provided a brief introduction to OOSE concepts and terms that are relevant to this task. In this chapter, these concepts and terms are referred to, and the tie-ins are noted.

DESCRIPTION

In Contextual Task Analysis you perform the following basic steps:

- Gather background information about the work being automated.
- Collect and analyze data from observations of and interviews with users as they do real work in their actual work environment.
- Construct and validate a model of the users' current task organization.

A central step in Contextual Task Analysis is the second step above, referred to in this book as contextual observations/interviews. The idea is that you must observe and interview users in their real-life work context

Observe and interview users doing their actual work to understand and discover their work models. Only then can you present a user interface that supports their work models and tasks

to understand their work and discover their work models. Only then can you structure and present functionality in an application user interface in a way that taps into users' current work models and optimally supports their tasks.

An abstract modeling of users' tasks, which is the focus of more traditional types of systems analysis, does not typically take into consideration key aspects of actual work flow, the users, and their work environment. Another way of putting this is that traditional systems analysis models work in the abstract. They don't consider the basic capabilities and constraints of human information processing, the particular characteristics of the intended user population, the unique characteristics of the work environment, and how users themselves model, carry out, and talk about their tasks.

Actors and Use Cases in OOSE are abstract concepts capturing generalities across individual users doing similar tasks. They do not necessarily capture things like common user errors, breakdowns in the task process, bottlenecks, work-arounds devised by users, ways the task overtaxes human capabilities, and so on. In a Contextual Task Analysis, you observe instances of Actors (real people) and instances of Use Cases (real work, called Task Scenarios). From these direct observations, you will gain insight into both the optimal structuring of the work from the point of view of automation and the key aspects of the user's work environment and models that will have direct implications for designing a usable user interface.

Based on an analysis of your direct observations, construct a model that represents the users' point of view: how they think about, talk about, and do their work

Based on an analysis of your direct observations, you then construct a model that represents the work from the users' point of view: how they currently think about, talk about, and do their work. This model is not directly designed into the application or its interface. It feeds into only one of the goals referred to earlier—that of tapping into existing user knowledge, habits, and capabilities—and it is juggled with the other two goals of supporting general business goals and exploiting the power of automation. This juggling happens in a later task, called Work Reengineering, described in Chapter 7.

A detailed technique for carrying out a Contextual Task Analysis is given in the Sample Technique—A Step-by-Step Procedure section later in the chapter. This technique is adapted from the field of ethnography, a science used by social and cultural anthropologists to investigate, study, analyze, interpret, and describe unfamiliar cultures (see, e.g., Button and Dourish 1996). Several key principles come from this field and can be applied directly to the problem of understanding the "culture" of a user group, their work environment, and work for the purpose of designing a new interactive product (see Ford and Wood 1996):

◆ Much behavior in the target culture is tacit and cannot be extracted by direct questioning; therefore, extended direct observation of the target culture is necessary.

◆ Investigators cannot have a highly structured approach to their study because they have no a priori knowledge or understanding of what is important in the target culture. Only a semistructured approach is possible because unlike other types of research, the investigation does not start with any hypotheses.

◆ It is important to observe how artifacts in the culture are used to accomplish real goals, rather than to impose some classification scheme on them based on the investigator's use of the same artifacts.

◆ Similarly, it is important not to distort the meaning of the target culture's language through a mechanical translation into the investigator's language, but rather to observe and understand how terms are actually used.

◆ In order to study the target culture, the investigator must learn to speak the language of that culture, rather than expect the culture to learn his or her language.

◆ It is important to have no implicit assumptions that might bias interpretation and to test explicit assumptions in a rigorous way.

Note that these principles fly directly in the face of most traditional approaches to systems analysis.

In ethnographic terms, if you wish to truly understand the culture of Borneo so that you can improve the lives of the natives in some way, you must go to Borneo, learn the language spoken there, and live in several villages, trying to partake in their everyday life and adopt their perspectives and philosophies. You cannot assume that natives of Borneo think and work like you do. And you cannot simply find a second-generation immigrant from Borneo, sit him down, and ask him a lot of questions about life in Borneo.

Similarly, if you wish to truly understand the work of a set of users so you can provide them with a useful tool (such as a software application) you must go to their workplace, learn the user jargon, and observe and talk with a representative set of users of all key types. You cannot

To truly understand the work of a set of users, go to their workplace, learn the user jargon, and observe and talk with a representative set of users of all key types

You cannot assume that users will think or work like you, and you cannot simply assimilate a former user into your project team

We can borrow and adapt methods from ethnography, but ultimately we will be altering the behavior we study in a Contextual Task Analysis

assume that users will think like you or work like you. And you cannot simply assimilate a former user into your project team (and into the development culture) and use him or her as a source of information about actual users. Work modeling techniques like "Use Cases" (see Jacobson et al. 1992) and prototypes (which users can readily understand) help communicate and validate your understanding of users' work. You need to avoid constructs like those used in data modeling, which force the users to learn a whole new language to communicate about their work with designers.

Note that the field of ethnography seeks only to define and describe actual behavior. We can borrow and adapt methods from the field of ethnography, but bear in mind that ultimately, through technology, we will be altering the very behavior we study in a Contextual Task Analysis (for more discussion on this point, see Button and Dourish 1996). How you get from an understanding of current work practice to the design of future work practice is addressed in Chapter 7 and the design chapters, Chapters 8, 11, and 15 (see also Chin, Rosson, and Carroll 1997).

Contextual Task Analysis techniques are relatively new and therefore not yet commonplace in product development organizations even when usability experts are present. However, variations of the technique described in the section Sample Technique—A Step-by-Step Procedure have been successfully used in a number of organizations, including Microsoft, U.S. West, Digital Equipment, IBM, Varian, Hewlett-Packard, ATL (a medical equipment vendor), Claris, WordPerfect, Lotus, BJC Health System (a health-care organization made up of fifteen hospitals), the University of Washington Medical Center (see Wixon and Ramey 1996, for many case studies), The National Science Foundation (Chin, Rosson, and Carroll 1997), the International Monetary Fund (Harper and Sellen 1995), and Tektronix (Lewis et al. 1996).

Several authors have reported that information gathered through Contextual Task Analysis techniques sometimes radically altered the direction the organization had been taking on a project (see Bauersfield and Halgren 1996, 192; Wixon et al. 1996, 71–85; Ramey et al. 1996, 8–13; Muller and Carr 1996, 29; Lewis et al. 1996, 67–8; and Page 1996, 205–208). Others (see Wixon and Ramey 1996) have reported successfully using Contextual Task Analysis techniques to

◆ Generate ideas for new products
◆ Identify key features to include in products

◆ Design the user interface for products that have already been identified and scoped

◆ Improve the usability of products already in production

In this chapter I focus on using these techniques to design the user interface for products that have already been identified and scoped.

SCHEDULING AND INTEGRATION WITH OTHER TASKS

The Contextual Task Analysis task fits into the overall Usability Engineering Lifecycle in the following ways:

◆ The User Profile task feeds directly into Contextual Task Analysis by identifying categories of users (Actors) whose tasks must be studied.

◆ Contextual Task Analysis feeds directly into the Usability Goal Setting task by helping to identify different primary goals for different task types (Use Cases) and by identifying bottlenecks and weaknesses in current work processes that can be improved through good user interface design.

◆ Contextual Task Analysis feeds directly into the Work Reengineering task. Current user work models are "reengineered" only as much as necessary to exploit the power of automation and contribute to explicit business goals. Current user knowledge and experience are exploited as much as possible to facilitate usability.

◆ Contextual Task Analysis will be documented in the product Style Guide.

◆ Ultimately, this task will have a direct impact on all design tasks, the selection of usability testing and evaluation issues, and the design of usability testing materials.

The Contextual Task Analysis task fits into the underlying software development methodology in the following ways:

◆ This task can *parallel, overlap,* or *follow* development of the Requirements Model in the Analysis phase of OOSE (or function and data modeling in the requirements phase of a traditional rapid prototyping methodology). It could either identify Use Cases for the Requirements Model or take the definition of Use Cases from the Requirements Model as its starting point for constructing Task Scenarios.

◆ This task (along with all other Usability Engineering Lifecycle Requirements Analysis tasks) should precede development of the Analysis Model in the Analysis phase of OOSE (or the application architecture design in a traditional rapid prototyping methodology).

ROLES AND RESOURCES

The usability roles might participate in the Contextual Task Analysis task as follows:

Task leader: A Usability Engineer should direct this task, bringing to bear specialized skills in Contextual Task Analysis.

Other resources: The User Interface Designer and all project team members should participate in all aspects of this task. The work of contextual observations/interviews can be split among project team members. All other work, as described in the next section, can be delegated to team members under the direction of the Usability Engineer. Users participate by being the subjects of contextual observations/interviews and the Task Sorting exercise. They can also be active participants in the analysis process (see, e.g. Chin, Rosson, and Carroll 1997).

SAMPLE TECHNIQUE— A STEP-BY-STEP PROCEDURE

Currently in the field of Usability Engineering, there is no well-established, universally applied, practical, and highly structured technique for performing a Contextual Task Analysis that will drive the user interface design for a product that has already been identified and scoped. It is more art than science at this point, with each usability practitioner using his or her own informal approach. However, some structured techniques are beginning to emerge, and several authors are reporting their experience with them (see, e.g., Beyer and Holtzblatt 1998; Hackos and Redish 1998). Some techniques that have worked well in my extensive experience are structured and documented in the eleven steps described here. They can be roughly grouped and summarized as follows:

◆ Gather background information about the work being automated (steps 1–4).

◆ Collect and analyze data from contextual observations/interviews of real users doing real work in their actual work environment (steps 5–8).

◆ Construct a users' task organization model of the current work (steps 9–11).

The steps are depicted in the process model in Figure 3.1. In this model, steps are enclosed in boxes, and the output of steps is indicated in free text around the arrow leaving a step. Although steps 5–8 are described separately and linearly, in fact, I usually conduct them in an iterative fashion. The discussion in step 5 explains how all of these steps are interrelated.

As indicated in the process model, in some cases, the output of a step is a specific type of document. Examples of these documents are offered in the Sample Work Products and Templates section later in the chapter.

These steps are written from the point of view of a Usability Engineer who is introducing Usability Engineering techniques into a development process and culture that has not previously applied these techniques. The following steps outline how the Usability Engineer in this situation can best introduce the techniques and integrate them with other development activities that are standard practice.

GATHER BACKGROUND INFORMATION ABOUT THE WORK BEING AUTOMATED

❶ **Review requirements specifications (if available).** Sometimes usability experts are not brought in until a traditional systems analysis (or an object-oriented analysis) has been carried out and a requirements specification for the intended system has been completed (i.e., a traditional functional spec or, in OOSE, a Requirements Model). If this is the case, reading the requirements specification is a good starting point to get an overview of the user tasks that will be automated. If it is too early in the project and a requirements specification has not been completed, simply proceed to step 2 below.

Your goal here is to understand the boundaries around the work to be automated and to get a high-level picture of how the project team is planning to approach the automation of that work. This will provide context for step 5.

❷ **Meet with project team members.** Conduct interviews with project team members (e.g., managers, analysts, architects, developers) to get a high-level picture of the

Figure 3.1 Contextual Task Analysis—A process model

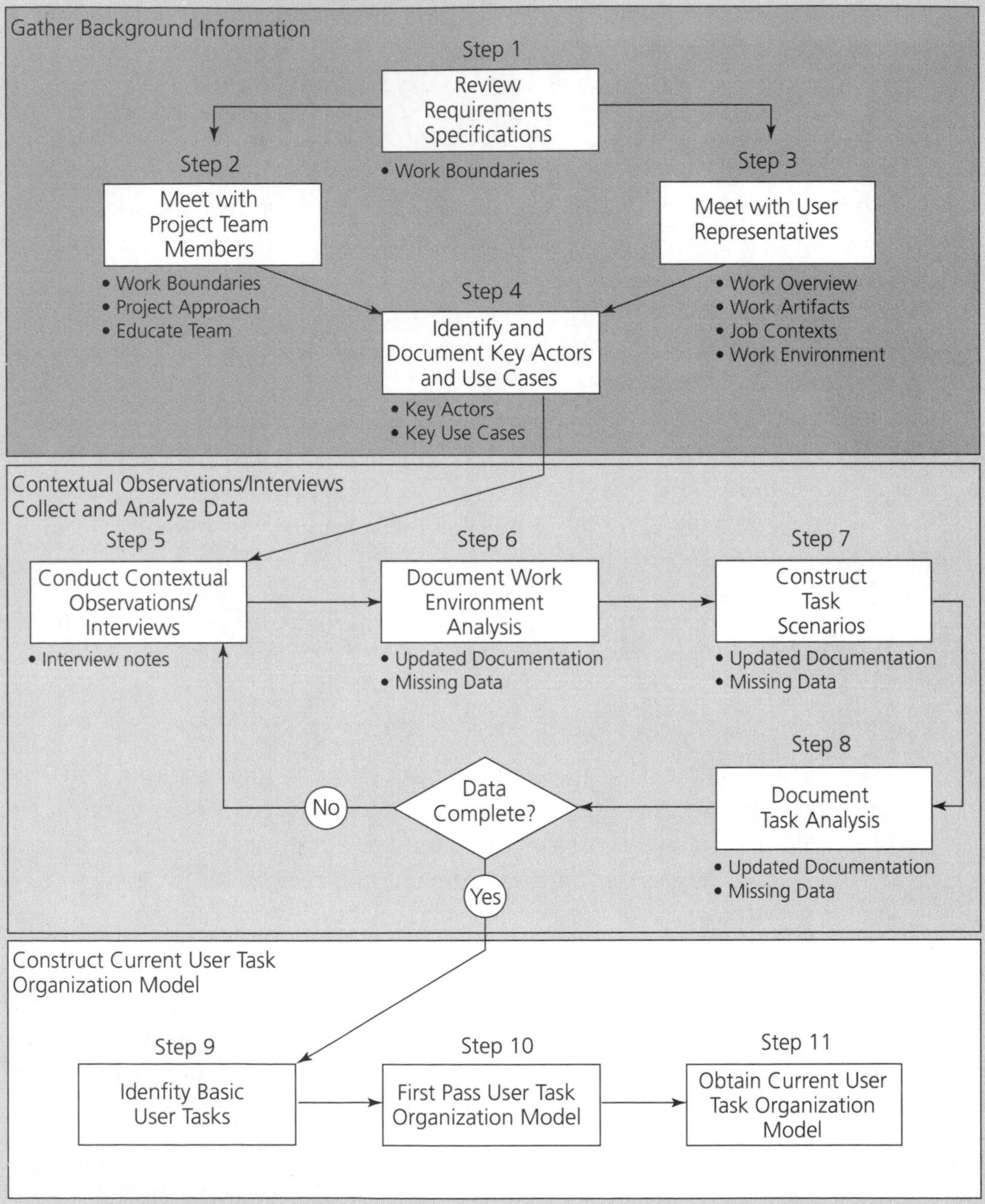

Gather Background Information

Step 1
Review Requirements Specifications
• Work Boundaries

Step 2
Meet with Project Team Members
• Work Boundaries
• Project Approach
• Educate Team

Step 3
Meet with User Representatives
• Work Overview
• Work Artifacts
• Job Contexts
• Work Environment

Step 4
Identify and Document Key Actors and Use Cases
• Key Actors
• Key Use Cases

Contextual Observations/Interviews
Collect and Analyze Data

Step 5
Conduct Contextual Observations/ Interviews
• Interview notes

Step 6
Document Work Environment Analysis
• Updated Documentation
• Missing Data

Step 7
Construct Task Scenarios
• Updated Documentation
• Missing Data

Step 8
Document Task Analysis
• Updated Documentation
• Missing Data

Data Complete?
No
Yes

Construct Current User Task Organization Model

Step 9
Idenfity Basic User Tasks

Step 10
First Pass User Task Organization Model

Step 11
Obtain Current User Task Organization Model

jobs/tasks being automated. Their perspective (and the requirements specification reviewed in step 1) will have a technical slant to it, and may reflect a systems-centered approach, but nevertheless is a good starting point to understand what the application needs to offer. At the same time, describe the approach laid out in the steps below to educate the team on the new techniques, win their confidence, and assure their cooperation.

Your goal here again is to understand the boundaries around the work to be automated and to get a high-level picture of how the project team is planning to approach the automation of that work. This will provide context for step 5. Another important goal here is to educate and get buy-in from project team members to assure their participation in all steps of the Contextual Task Analysis technique outlined below.

❸ Meet with user representatives. Conduct interviews with user representatives (e.g., user managers, user group leaders, subject matter experts or "SMEs")—called Indirect Users in OOSE parlance—to get a high-level picture of the jobs/tasks being automated. In some cases Indirect Users might even be outside the user organization. For example, actual customers would be considered Indirect Users of a customer support system used by customer support representatives. Similarly, travel agency customers would be Indirect Users of a travel agent's on-line reservation system. Even though they are not Direct Users or end users, Indirect Users' perspectives can be key in addressing the business goals of an on-line customer support or travel agent system.

By combining the big picture from a more user-oriented perspective with information gained from the User Profiles, you will sharpen your focus for your contextual observations/interviews (see step 5) with end users (Direct Users).

Spend some time with user representatives getting a list of (and copies of, if possible) the main *artifacts,* or *objects,* involved in the tasks being studied (see Wood 1996). Artifacts or objects might include paper forms, documents, and other types of work products, and tools such as software, special types of containers, and so on. Then look at how these artifacts or objects are used in the work tasks. Together, these objects give you a high-level overview of the "what" and "how" of the work tasks. This will provide important orientation and context for your contextual observations/interviews (see step 5).

Your goal here is to start to focus on *key* tasks (Use Cases), user types (Actors), and the artifacts or objects associated with them, and become alert to any special concerns and issues that the user organization might have. Also, you can learn something about the physical and sociocultural work environment, which might not have become apparent from previous steps and which you can pursue further in your contextual observations/interviews (see step 5). In addition, you should focus on getting information about the whole job context of the users for whom the planned product will be just one tool supporting certain tasks. Without this, there is little hope of designing a tool that will fit with all the other tools, processes, and environment that represent the world in which the user lives and works (see Holtzblatt and Beyer 1996, 305; Beyer and Holtzblatt 1998). For one organization's approach to gathering this type of information, see Butler and Tahir (1996).

I want to emphasize that this step is not a substitute for contextual observations/ interviews (see step 5), where you observe and interview real end users (Direct Users) in their actual work environment. The perspectives of SMEs and other regular partners from the user organization are helpful and important, but they are often very different from the perspectives of end users (see, e.g., Brown 1996, 161, for a contrast between a medical equipment vendor's regular "luminary" physician partners and actual end users of their products).

❹ **Identify and document key Actors and Use Cases.** Based on the User Profiles, the previous three steps, and on any OOSE requirements analysis that has been done, identify from the complete set of Actors (major user categories) and Use Cases (major types of user tasks) a subset of Actors and Use Cases on which to focus the Contextual Task Analysis.

A complex product may have a large number of Use Cases and Actors. It is often not practical or effective to study them all exhaustively at this point in the Usability Engineering Lifecycle; instead, select a small number of key Actors (Primary rather than Secondary Actors) and key Use Cases (e.g., those performed by Primary Actors and accounting for the majority of critical transactions) that do a good job of representing the whole scope of the product. The idea is that if you base a *user interface architecture* (i.e., reengineered work, Conceptual Model Design, and Screen Design Standards) on an analysis of and design for these key Actors and Use Cases, that architecture will probably extend well to the whole product. This is more efficient and probably more effective than an exhaustive analysis of Actors and Use Cases, and it is also consistent with the layered design philosophy that is the foundation of OOSE (see Jacobson et al. 1992, 16, 24).

COLLECT AND ANALYZE DATA FROM CONTEXTUAL OBSERVATIONS/INTERVIEWS

⑤ **Conduct contextual observations/interviews.** Because this step is so complex, it is further broken down into subsections. We begin with an overview.

Overview. Contextual observations/interviews are absolutely central to a Contextual Task Analysis. Here, you go out and observe and talk with actual intended end users (Direct Users) in their real work environment while they do real work (i.e., perform instances of Use Cases). Focus on those user tasks (Use Cases) that are relevant to the automation project, but also attend to the context of the user's overall job, which may be wider than the tasks being automated. Your main goals are to

- Identify the main work artifacts or objects.
- Collect Task Scenarios, or instances of Use Cases.
- Gain insight into the actual user and business goals underlying Use Cases.
- Gain insight into users' work models.
- Learn the users' language (their terminology and jargon).
- Gather statistics about Use Cases, for example, relative frequency, range and average time to complete, number and types of errors.
- Gain insight into problems, bottlenecks, errors, and other opportunities for improvement in the current work process (whether manual or automated).
- Gather data about the work environment.

Users' knowledge about their work is often tacit or no longer conscious (see Wood 1996, 38), so simply interviewing them outside their work context is not a reliable source of accurate information. By observing in the work context, you can see what the user actually does and then probe for details and underlying goals (see Butler and Tahir 1996, 260). Users are better able to reflect on and explain their own actions while they are performing them, as their own actions stimulate memory retrieval.

Also note that work practices documented in "policies and procedures" manuals often inaccurately reflect *actual* work practices, as users always modify these procedures in practice, finding work-arounds and adapting them to the real world (see Holtzblatt and Beyer 1996, 308). Users interviewed out of context will usually not report these work-arounds, either because they do them almost unconsciously or because they are reluctant to report how they deviate from official procedures in their everyday work. Yet product designers often use these formal, "official" procedures as the main (or even the only) source of information about work practices.

A simple example of what can be missed by not doing contextual observations/interviews is found in Coble et al. (1996, 231). This report describes the use of contextual observations/interviews to study the functional requirements of physicians for a clinical workstation:

> Before the . . . session started, a physician explained the purpose and details of each section in his office chart . . . Later, when he was doing actual work in context, the person performing the . . . session noticed that the note he was looking at was written with red ink. She probed and the physician said it told him the previous encounter with this

---

WAR STORY

AN ARRESTING CONTEXTUAL TASK ANALYSIS

As an example of what can be missed by not doing a Contextual Task Analysis, I was performing such an analysis in a metropolitan police department. Police officers used a system of standardized paper forms to inventory confiscated property. I observed infrequent users of the forms struggling with them (there were many complex forms and many unwritten rules about how to fill them out), and I later observed how frequent users handled them. The frequent users tended to ignore the forms initially and take free-form notes describing the property they had to document in a format very different from that required on the forms. They then transcribed their own notes onto the forms as required. It was clear from this observation (and from follow-up interviews

with the frequent users) that the forms were not designed in a way that supported the users' task, and a lot of what I learned about how frequent users worked around the forms went into designing better on-line forms. A traditional systems analysis would typically not involve studying users actually using paper forms in their actual work, but would have instead taken the paper forms themselves as a description of the work to be automated. Problems with the forms would have been missed entirely and perpetuated in the on-line version of the task.

There are always a great many things that users simply will not think to report during an off-site interview or "focus group." They only emerge during contextual observations/interviews of people doing real work in their workplace. Such things can have major implications for product user interface design.

patient was a hospital visit. That fact told him he needed to review the hospital discharge summary and hospital laboratory results before entering the patient's exam room. *The physician was surprised that he had not mentioned that need before.* It was so ingrained in how he worked that he did not even process that highly relevant detail consciously anymore. (Italics mine)

Having identified a small subset of key Use Cases and Actors, you now observe and interview three to six users of each key user type or role, for several hours each, making sure that you observe instances of all key user tasks across all users. Different project team members can perform the contextual observations/interviews with different users and then consolidate their findings (see steps 6–10 below).

As a final note, if your product development project is intended to automate work that is not currently being done, it is still possible to use Contextual Task Analysis techniques to gather useful information that can help drive design.

In most cases, even when a particular job is not currently being performed, something highly related to that job *is* being done, and this can be the focus of a Contextual Task Analysis. If nothing at all related to the work your product is automating is currently being done, there is a good chance you are building a product that nobody needs! Good products are always driven by real user needs. Keep in mind also that once an initial release of a product is in production, you could perform another Contextual Task Analysis to discover how it is being used and where it breaks down, and use these insights to drive the design of later releases.

The next subsections of step 5 are meant to help you structure your contextual observations/interviews. Later steps tell how to analyze, document, and apply your findings. None of the steps as described here are as structured and clear-cut as I would like them to be. Contextual Task Analysis techniques are still evolving in the Usability Engineering field. Likewise, ethnographic research methods, which contextual observations/interviews are based on, are inherently only semistructured. But in my experience, even when designers and developers carry out contextual observations/interviews without a structured approach for collecting, analyzing, documenting, and applying this information, they gain amazing insights that help them design an application and user interface that best support real users doing real work in their real environment. So, after reading the rest of this step, even if you do not feel entirely clear about what information you should gather and how to go about getting it and applying it, *just do it!*

W A R   S T O R Y

DISCOVERING HOW USERS DO WORK BEFORE THEY DO IT

One of my clients was building a software application to help their users track work resources, such as supplies and equipment, not only to keep track of these resources and find them when needed, but also to justify budget plans for future years based on resource usage in the current year. As it happened, the user organization did not previously track work resources, and so a new job was being introduced at the same time as the software tool to facilitate the job. The client initially thought that since users were not currently doing the job (*tracking* the resources), there was nothing to do a Contextual Task Analysis on. However, as I explained to them, users were currently *using* the work resources; and so we could observe the way they found and used these resources, as well as how they named them, talked about them, and thought about them. These observations would undoubtedly give us important insights into how to present users with a way to record and track the resources in a software user interface.

I cannot overemphasize that there is nothing more valuable, important, and likely to yield key insights than spending some time actually living in the shoes of your users (see also Page 1996, 208). Once you start to do this, you may recognize additional structured approaches that work well in your organization.

Iterating through steps 5–8. Steps 5–8 should usually be performed in an iterative manner (see Figure 3.1). These steps are

Step 5: Conduct contextual observations/interviews

Step 6: Document the work environment analysis

Step 7: Construct Task Scenarios

Step 8: Document the task analysis

Some authors (Holtzblatt and Beyer 1996; Beyer and Holtzblatt 1998) advocate constructing detailed formal work models representing the types of information described in steps 6–8 *after each individual contextual observation/interview,* and then consolidating the individual models to capture commonalities after all observations/interviews are complete. In the context of developing a product already identified and scoped (as opposed to a major business reengineering effort), I find stopping to analyze and formally model every contextual observation/interview individually too time consuming, unnecessarily thorough, and inefficient. I also find the formal models do not do a very good job of communicating important data. They are hard to interpret, and much of the richness of the data is lost.

On the other hand, it is a mistake to conduct too many contextual observations/ interviews without stopping to digest and analyze what you have learned (see, e.g., Brown 1996, 174). You will lose the information that your notes might prompt you to remember if the experience is fresh in your mind, and you will simply find the interpretation, analysis, and documentation tasks overwhelming. Instead, I prefer to proceed through steps 5–8 by conducting observations/interviews in small batches, with interim analysis and documentation sessions between batches, and I prefer to document the data in written documents rather than as formal models. Usually, I conduct between three and six contextual observations/interviews for a given user type (Actor) over several days, then stop to analyze, organize, and document what I have learned in the format of the documents described in steps 6–8. Then I see where the holes are in my data and conduct the next batch of contextual observations/ interviews, trying to focus on those holes. After each batch of contextual observations/interviews, I update my documents. In relatively simple projects with only one main type of user (Actor), sometimes only one or perhaps at most two iterations of steps 5–8 are necessary, with a total of three to six contextual observations/interviews. In more complex projects with many user types, more iterations are necessary, with a total of fifteen or more contextual observations/ interviews.

Finally, Page (1996, 211) offers some good advice regarding the whole process described in steps 1–11. He points out that you should not be a perfectionist about technique, or focus too much on the process itself. It is the results—that is, the ultimate impact on design—that are important. He also suggests that any organization trying out these techniques should schedule time periodically to reflect on the process and share their "learnings" with the rest of the organization.

Training observers/interviewers. Both developers and users tend to misunderstand the purpose and appropriate technique of contextual observations/interviews. As you want to have a cross-functional team perform these analyses (see Chapter 1), I highly recommend that all participating team members receive some training in ethnographic and Contextual Task Analysis techniques before taking part in contextual observations/interviews. I have personally seen whole sessions derailed by developers who had not been sufficiently briefed about how to conduct contextual observations/interviews, and many authors in Wixon and Ramey (1996) report similar experiences. Everyone present, including the users, must understand the goals and techniques of the contextual observations/interviews and allow the most skillful interviewer present to direct and control the session.

Selecting users. Select between three and five users of each key user type (Actor). Initially, choose users known to represent "best practices," that is, users known to be task experts who do their tasks both accurately and efficiently. Users who have performed tasks frequently and for some time usually have worked out optimal ways of doing the tasks, have insights into the bottlenecks and weak points in the current system (whether manual or automated), and have devised effective and successful workarounds. In addition, they are better able to describe what they do in terms of underlying principles and abstractions (Wood 1996, 45). Later, it will be important to round out your contextual observations/ interviews to include less experienced, less frequent users, to see what their special problems and needs are; but it helps first to have, as context, a picture of the experts' approaches to tasks.

WAR STORY

WAITING FOR TASKS TO HAPPEN

On one project, I was doing a Contextual Task Analysis of property processing tasks in a large city police department. Most property is taken in as part of an arrest, and obviously arrests are not scheduled in advance. When an arrest with property is being processed, there is a great deal of time pressure to get things done and done correctly, and also a lot of distractions. Given this work environment, the best I could do was to hang around in police stations for whole days at a time, hoping I would get lucky and be there when certain tasks occurred. When things were slow, I would corner potential users and try spontaneously to interview them. Although this was inefficient and difficult to control, it worked, and I got the bulk of the information I needed. For another example of a challenging scheduling situation in a medical environment, see Brown (1996,166).

Scheduling contextual observations/interviews. Scheduling contextual observations/interviews is simple and straightforward in some situations and very difficult in others. When users do fairly independent tasks, and their work is scheduled or self-paced, it is relatively easy to arrange to be there during a certain type of task. In other cases, it's a real challenge to be there when tasks of interest are being done and have the chance to ask enough questions so you understand what is going on.

Starting contextual observations/interviews. Begin each contextual observation/interview by explaining why you are there and what you hope to gain. This is not only common courtesy but also can be crucial to the success of the observation/interview (see, e.g., Coble et al. 1996, 234; Brown 1996, 160). Give a brief description of

◆ Who you are (organizationally).
◆ The overall project these contextual observations/interviews will support.
◆ Your specific goals in this contextual observation/interview (e.g., to learn generally about the user's job; to observe specific tasks being performed; to get a general description of a certain type of task; to gain insight into current bottlenecks and problems; to learn about user jargon and mental models). These may vary across contextual observations/interviews, with early ones being very unstructured and later ones having a specific focus.
◆ What you expect of the user (e.g., just do your job and tell me about it; answer a set of specific questions; give me a grand tour of your work). Again, these will vary across contextual observations/interviews.
◆ How long the contextual observation/interview will last.
◆ How the user's input will help improve the products under development.

If you are conducting an international study using these techniques and you have brought an interpreter along, be sure the interpreter also has a clear understanding of your goals and plans so she or he will not "filter" out important data in translations of users' responses (see, e.g., Brown 1996, 165; Dray and Mrazek 1996, 148–149).

It's easy to be misperceived as Big Brother doing an inspection; this perception discourages users from being candid about their problems and the unofficial and informal work practices they have developed. So, it is especially important to break the ice and build rapport with users before beginning the contextual observation/interview.

One set of analysts (see Dray and Mrazek 1996, 150), who were interviewing people in their homes, found that bringing dinner and having some informal time before beginning work influenced the success of the contextual observations/interviews. Even when users understand that talking with you is part of their job, it is important to take the time to establish trust so that users are comfortable reporting accurately and candidly about their work.

Conducting observations/interviews. Probably the optimal number of interviewers per user is two. One interviewer can direct the contextual observation/interview and the other can take notes, or one can direct and take notes, and the other can operate a video camera (see the later section Data Capture Techniques). Any more than two observers/interviewers can have an inhibiting effect on users and also make it hard for one interviewer's train of thought and questioning to be coherently followed. (For other similar simple tips and rules of thumb about performing contextual observations/interviews, see Beyer and Holtzblatt 1996, 44–50.)

A good model to keep in mind, at least for the initial contextual observations/ interviews, is *apprenticeship*. Remember that the user is the Master, or expert, and you are the Apprentice, or novice. As noted by Holtzblatt and Beyer (1996, 308–309), this model has the following implications:

◆ The contextual observation/interview cannot be highly structured beforehand because the Apprentice does not yet know enough about the job to know what is important to look for and ask about.
◆ A one-on-one contextual observation/interview is best (although observers and note takers can also be present) because each Apprentice needs to be able to learn in his or her own way and pace (see also Coble et al. 1996, 235).
◆ The Master is in control of the observation/interview but allows the Apprentice to probe to clarify his or her understanding.

In later contextual observations/interviews, you (the Apprentice) can introduce more structure and take more control, because you now have some basic under-standing and are just trying to fill in gaps in your knowledge base.

As you conduct contextual observations/interviews, while bearing in mind the apprenticeship model suggested above, keep the contextual observation/interview focused so as not to waste either your or the user's time. Users have no idea what — of all the information they could volunteer—is and is not important or useful to you.

You must walk the fine line between focusing on the right kind of information and not losing opportunities to learn something unexpected. Remember that task analysis is like ethnography—until you get to know the culture somewhat, you don't really know what to look for and what will be important. On the other hand, you are not conducting an academic study, and you do not have unlimited time. So you must help the user to understand what sorts of things you are after. A great deal of tact is required when interrupting a user and redirecting the discussion. Don't be afraid to do so, as usually users will welcome the direction, but do so without being judgmental or critical (see Butler and Tahir 1996, 263).

When designers and developers do their first contextual observations/interviews, a common pitfall is to slip out of *information-gathering* mode and into *design* mode or user *education* mode (see Butler and Tahir 1996, 258; Coble et al. 1996, 235). Refrain from brainstorming technical solutions as the user describes his or her current process and its problems, and refrain from taking the time to educate the user in any depth about technological plans and projects (any more than a brief orientation to justify your contextual observation/interview). Remember, you are not designing yet, and you are not there to provide the user with information (see Butler and Tahir 1996, 262). You are there to gather information from the user. The user should always be doing most of the talking, taking direction from you only to change the area of focus.

Even when you are doing your best to focus on the right things, users will often derail you in similar ways. Sometimes they hope or expect that the session will provide training or solutions to their problems. Sometimes, rather than talk about their work as they do it today, they want to dictate technological solutions (see, e.g., Brown 1996, 160). Sometimes users bring along their co-workers, expecting a focus group format (see Page 1996, 200). You must work hard to keep things on track, and it is important to manage users' expectations about the purpose and format of the session both beforehand, when you schedule the interview, and at the beginning of the session. If problems still occur, gently remind the user of the purpose and necessary format of the session; and if possible, you can offer to get their personal agenda addressed at some other time in some other way (see, e.g., Butler and Tahir 1996, 258).

As you learn from your first contextual observations/interviews, work hard to adopt the users' language and jargon as quickly as possible, and use it in stating your questions (Wood 1996, 42). Do not translate users' language into technical, data modeling, or OOSE language and try to force the user to speak this language. If you do this, you will lose important information as the user tries to help you understand the work by reformulating it instead of sharing with you what their actual work model is. For a good description of the format of a contextual observation/interview in a medical environment, see Coble et al. 1996, 233–235).

Types of data to capture. As context, be sure to first ask each user some basic questions about his or her background, such as

- How long have you worked at this location?
- How long have you worked in your current job/role?
- What relevant background/education do you have (e.g., academic background, additional course work, computer literacy, job-specific training)?

The best set of additional background questions can be identified from the User Profile, which has identified key user types (Actors). You will want to note not only what overall type each user observed/interviewed is, but also a couple of other characteristics known to vary widely for that user type. For example, some key questions to ask of physicians in the study by Coble et al. (1996, 237–238) included type of practice, subspecialty, location of practice, and typical number of patients in hospital at one time.

During the contextual observations/interviews, focus on obtaining Task Scenarios (see step 7 later in the chapter). A Task Scenario is an *instance* of a Use Case—a step-by-step description of an actual, detailed procedure that a user followed to accomplish some task. It captures the *sequence* of steps required to get a task done. For example, say the general Use Case is for a travel agent to make a set of reservations for a customer's trip. A real instance or Task Scenario might involve making airline, rental car, and hotel reservations for the Smith family (two adults, one child, and one infant) to go to Disneyland on July 23rd for a week, and trying to accommodate specific requests for such things as preferred airline and preferred hotel. The Task Scenario would identify the exact sequence of steps an agent followed to complete this specific task.

In addition to gathering Task Scenarios, ask users the following kinds of questions as you observe them at work:

- When . . . ? (to understand what triggers tasks)
- Where . . . ? (to determine the location of tasks in the workplace)
- How . . . ? (to understand steps in carrying out tasks)

- What . . . ? (to understand the objects or artifacts associated with tasks)
- Why . . . ? (to get at underlying goals)
- How often . . . ? (to identify frequent and infrequent activities)
- How long . . . ? (to get benchmark data on time to complete tasks)
- What do you call that? (to discover user jargon and terminology)
- What *errors* typically occur?
- How do you discover and correct these errors?
- What are the main *bottlenecks* in this task?
- What are the main *problems* you encounter when doing this task?
- What *work-arounds* have you found to get around the problems and bottlenecks?
- Are there any *exceptions* to normal procedures?
- What things would you most like changed?
- Do you have any specific ideas for improvement?

Data capture techniques. The main data capture technique in contextual observations/interviews is free-form note taking, but this can be supplemented by formatted data collection sheets (see this chapter's Sample Work Products and Templates section), copies of artifacts and work products, video- and audiotapes, and still photos.

Sometimes, in high-pressure, time-critical, or very difficult jobs (e.g., air traffic control, customer service, surgery, sales), it is not possible to interview users while they are doing their work. In such cases it is still very important to *observe* them in the context of their actual work, but you can also interview them outside of doing their tasks, based on notes taken during the observation. If possible, do this in their work environment, where they will be reminded of important aspects of their work and can show you work artifacts. If even this is not practical (e.g., when the task is doctors performing surgery, and the operating room is always in use), a good alternative is to videotape users as they work, and then review the videotape with them later and ask questions then (see, e.g., Ramey, Rowberg, and Robinson 1996).

Even when there are no obstacles to observing and interviewing users, you may want to use videotaping. It can be especially helpful when multiple observers/interviewers cannot get together in person to consolidate their findings. It can also be an effective way to train others to conduct contextual observations/interviews. A proficient observer/interviewer can videotape some of her or his work and then show it to others as an example of how to conduct a contextual observation/interview. Videotaping can also be particularly useful in observer/interviewers' early experience. Their note taking may not be very effective early on, and the videotapes (or even audio-tapes—see Coble et al. 1996, 234) will preserve valuable data. With more experience, observers/interviewers learn to take better notes and rely on recordings of sessions less.

I do not recommend using videotaping routinely to free yourself from taking notes during the contextual observations/interviews. Videotaping more than doubles the time to conduct an observation/interview—two to three hours to conduct it, then two to five hours to view the tape and take notes. Project teams have reported cases in which they videotaped every contextual observation/interview and then never had the time to review many of the tapes (see Rowley 1996, 141; Bauersfield and Halgren 1996, 188, 193). Unless you budget the time in advance, do not count on videotapes as your primary data collection technique. Take lots of detailed notes.

When you want to videotape, but it is unacceptable to users (sometimes it will be), audiotaping may be acceptable and will still provide a useful record from which to reconstruct data after a contextual observation/interview (see, e.g., Coble et al. 1996, 234). Also, still photos can be an effective way to capture details of the work environment. And it is often appropriate to ask users for copies of work artifacts, such as forms, documents, or database reports (see Dray and Mrazek 1996, 150–152).

When using videotape as a data collection technique, bear in mind the following guidelines from Mackay (1995) for ethical use of video. In general, consider the right to privacy of users, and keep their best interests in mind when making and using videotapes.

Before videotaping:

◆ Get informed consent.
◆ Make sure users always know when the camera is on.
◆ Explain the purpose of videotaping.
◆ Explain who will have access to the video.
◆ Explain possible settings for showing the video.
◆ Explain possible consequences of showing the video.
◆ Describe potential ways the video might be disguised.

After videotaping:

◆ Treat videotapes as confidential.
◆ Allow users to view videos and reconsider their permission.

◆ If the use of the videotape changes, seek permission again.

Editing videotapes:

◆ Avoid misrepresenting overall findings by biased use of video clips.
◆ Reveal any special effects.

Presenting videotapes:

◆ Protect the users' privacy.
◆ Do not present video clips that make users look foolish unless their identity is disguised.
◆ Do not rely on the power of a video to make a weak point.
◆ Summarize data fairly—do not misrepresent isolated incidences through video clips.

Distributing videotapes:

◆ Do not use videos for purposes for which they were not intended.

Document the tasks you observe in each contextual observation/interview in some common format (see the Sample Work Products and Templates section for an example). These tasks will form the foundation for construction of Task Scenarios in step 7. Also take lots of notes on whatever you observe about the physical work environment, the sociocultural environment, and the context of the task within the user's overall job (see step 6), whether tied directly to a particular task or not. These notes will feed into the development of the Work Environment Analysis document (see step 6) and the Task Analysis document (see step 8).

Generally I find that, in my earliest iterations and with very complex work situations, it is hard to know in advance the best way to capture the data, and so I just take freeform notes. In contextual observations/interviews of simpler work, and in later iterations when I have already learned something about the work and am ready to get more focused, using a tailored format something like the one offered in the Sample Work Products and Templates section is very useful.

Ending the observations/interviews. Be sure to express your appreciation for the user's time at the end of the contextual observation/interview. In some cases, users are paid for their time, and in others they are volunteers or are directed by their management to cooperate. In any case, be sure to thank them. If they are not compensated, it can be a nice touch to send thank-you notes or give them tokens such as project mugs or T-shirts. Remember that you will probably want to do future contextual observations/interviews in the user organization, and users will talk among themselves about their experiences. Set the stage for future user receptivity to participating in Contextual Task Analyses (see, e.g., Coble et al. 1996, 234–235) by making it a positive experience and expressing your appreciation.

Greasing the wheels. To ease this whole process and help users take it in stride, it can be useful to set up a "Product Development Partnership" (Rowley 1996, 138). To do this, you recruit users on a volunteer basis before any particular project is begun and keep track of them in a database so that they are easily accessible and already understand the agenda when they are asked to participate in a contextual observation/interview. There are often organizational barriers to direct contact between developers and users, and these barriers must be broken down if true user-centered design is to be accomplished. In my experience, most users are delighted and more than willing to contribute to the design of the tools they will have to use. Sending out a general notice describing the kind of Usability Engineering work that is planned and asking for volunteers to occasionally put in time as a design partner will usually attract a large and enthusiastic response. Then, when they are contacted for scheduling contextual observations/interviews to support a particular project, users already have a general idea of what to expect, and they have already made a commitment to participate.

Wilson and colleagues (1997) point out some additional ways to facilitate user involvement in product design and development in general:

- ◆ **Motivate all stakeholders.** Users *and* user managers must be educated on and convinced of the benefit of their participation.
- ◆ **Ensure active management buy-in.** Simple agreement from user management to have users participate is not enough. Managers need to communicate to users that they can take time off from their daily work to participate in project activities when they are asked to do so.
- ◆ **Educate users about the whole design process.** Users who understand the whole user-centered design approach at a high level will be more effective participants in the process.
- ◆ **Facilitate later involvement through earlier involvement.** Users who participate early on in the project are more effective participants at later stages than

users who start later and don't understand the process or the current state of the project.

Public relations. A side effect of conducting contextual observations/interviews as part of product development is that it can be excellent PR. I have had many users express delight and appreciation for involving them in the design of their tools, and I generally find users eager to have input. Other authors report this as well (see Wixon and Ramey 1996). By and large users seem flabbergasted that anyone from their development organization is truly interested in the details of their work and is going to the trouble to learn from them. This is a sad comment on the history of relations between user and development organizations. Through Usability Engineering techniques, you have an opportunity not only to build better products, but also to build more cooperative, respectful, and productive relationships between users and developers.

It is very important, however, to manage users' expectations. Sometimes users expect to see an impact from their input immediately and directly (see, e.g., Brown 1996, 173), and they become frustrated and disillusioned when they do not. They need to understand the nature of the whole development process and how their input will feed into it.

6 Document the work environment analysis. This step and steps 7 and 8 are a joint effort by all observers/interviewers and other team members (including users—see Chin, Rosson, and Carroll 1997) involved in design. At this point in the overall process, it is a good idea to establish a design room (Holtzblatt and Beyer 1996, 322–323). It should be a room the team can use for the duration of the project, where team meetings can be conducted and information and design can be recorded and left in the working state.

As discussed in step 5, it is highly recommended that this step, along with steps 7 and 8, be performed iteratively. That is, an initial round of contextual observations/interviews should be performed and then immediately documented as described in steps 6, 7, and 8. Then, more contextual observations/interviews should be carried out, and after each round, the documents described in these three steps can be refined and updated. This approach avoids having to deal with an overwhelming amount of data at one time (see Rowley 1992, 135–136, 141; Coble et al. 1996, 232–233; Dray and Mrazek 1996, 152–153). It also allows observers/interviewers to digest, capture, and analyze information between rounds of contextual observations/interviews. It is easy to get burned out by all the new information and simply be unable to process more new information effectively. Finally, with this approach, early contextual observations/interviews can be more open-ended, so as not to miss important issues, needs, and aspects of work; and later contextual observations/interviews can focus on clarifying vague data and filling in gaps that may not be apparent during one long course of observations/interviews.

In step 6, based on extracting work environment details from the most recent round of contextual observations/interviews, write (or update) a general description of the work environment, drawing specific implications for user interface design (see the Sample Work Products and Templates section for an example). Include descriptions of the following:

◆ The physical work environment (e.g., open/closed work areas, lighting, heat, noise level, distractions and interruptions)
◆ The sociocultural work environment (e.g., morale, motivation, interuser support and teamwork, past experience with and attitudes towards automation)
◆ The job contexts (e.g., frequency and importance of tasks within overall job, physical and sociocultural aspects of work environment unique to job)

Tools must be designed for the context in which they will be used, and this step ensures the context is fully understood. Imagine you are designing a screwdriver, and all you know is the size of the screw head. So, you design something like a traditional screwdriver, with the correct sized blade. But suppose it then turns out that the user needs to apply the screw from the inside of a narrow pipe in order to assemble some piece of equipment. Clearly, a traditional screwdriver will be useless in this context.

Similarly, suppose you know you want to design a software application for a set of users, but you have never gone to their actual work environment. So you assume a traditional officelike environment, and design assuming a traditional workstation. But suppose it turns out that in the actual work environment, users are constantly moving all around the environment to get different parts of an overall job done. Software for a traditional workstation simply will not work. You might need to design for a smaller and more portable device that can be carried around with the user, like the units carried by UPS delivery staff.

In one more example, suppose you have never visited the users' workplace, and you assume they all work in closed offices. So you design a system with voice input and output. But it turns out that users work in one big open area with desks located right next to one another. The noise from all those people and workstations will render the system useless since most voice recognition systems simply don't work with acceptable accuracy in a noisy environment. The point is, there are many aspects of the actual work environment that will determine how well a tool will work, and so the environment itself must be studied and the tool tailored to it. That is the purpose of a work environment analysis.

One way to extract work environment data from the contextual observation/ interview notes is by having the different observers/interviewers codevelop the document (as described in step 8). Another way is through a technique known as constructing an "affinity diagram" (see Holtzblatt and Beyer 1996, 318–319, and the Alternative Techniques—A Review section later in the chapter). These two techniques can also be used for developing the Task Analysis document in step 8.

❼ Construct Task Scenarios. Based on a consolidation of all contextual observations/ interviews, write (or update) two to five key, representative, high-frequency Task Scenarios, or *instances* of key Use Cases, representing real-life work tasks, for *each* major user type or Actor (see the Sample Work Products and Templates section for examples). These can be composites, constructed by merging parts of different observed scenarios in realistic ways. You need not exhaustively represent every major variation of a Use Case or cover every Use Case for each Actor; just select a small number that seem representative. The whole team of observers/interviewers—along with some key users (see Chin, Rosson, and Carroll 1997)—should develop these Task Scenarios together, from their combined experiences and notes.

Write the Task Scenarios abstractly (but in user terms), with little or no reference to existing or future computer systems, as a list of steps. They will help capture important aspects of work flow (sequencing of steps within tasks) and will provide a representative focus and realistic context for design and testing later (see, e.g., Rosson and Carroll 1995). It can also be useful to have some videos of actual observed scenarios to take into the next step, as well as documented scenarios (see Chin, Rosson, and Carroll 1997).

❽ Document the Task Analysis. Write (or update) a document containing Task Scenarios and other descriptions of insights gained from the contextual observations/ interviews. Sections of this document might include

◆ Purpose and Structure of this Document
◆ Identification of Tasks and Users (this would refer to all, but also point to the

subset of key Use Cases and Actors that will be the initial focus of the design process)

◆ Task Scenarios (these provide realistic instances of Use Cases)
◆ Analysis of Current Tasks, for example:
  • Range of Task Complexity
  • Volume of Transactions across the Organization
  • Range of Frequency of Transactions by User Category
  • Level of Training
  • Error Rates
  • Level of Redundant Data Entry
  • Breakdowns in the Process
  • Bottlenecks in the Process
  • Degree of User Mobility during Tasks
  • Degree of Interrupts during Tasks

An example of content in such a document is given in the Sample Work Products and Templates section. Another good example of the type of content that might be found in this document for a medical system is given in Ramey, Rowberg, and Robinson (1996, 8–13).

When there are only a small number of observers/interviewers on a project, this document (and the one developed in step 6) can be codeveloped. One observer/interviewer goes through all of her or his notes from one batch of contextual observations/interviews and writes a first draft of the document, organized in a way that makes sense to the observer. Then other observers/interviewers, one at a time, add to that document from their batch of contextual observations/interviews, inserting their notes into the defined structure and modifying the structure if necessary. I have successfully and efficiently used this simple approach on projects with two observers/interviewers.

CONSTRUCT THE CURRENT USER TASK ORGANIZATION MODEL

Task Scenarios describe the sequence of steps users currently use to complete individual tasks. Across the final three steps in the sample technique, you will determine how users think of the relationship between tasks (the Current User Task Organization Model). Task Scenarios and the Current User Task Organization Model then lay the foundation for a later task in the Usability Engineering Lifecycle: Work Reengineering. Here, you will identify all basic user tasks that will be automated in the new product and model the way users currently think about them and organize them. These are the steps:

◆ Identify the basic user tasks.
◆ Take a first pass at a Current User Task Organization Model of those tasks.
◆ Obtain a Current User Task Organization Model of those tasks directly from users.

Often, your model will take the form of a task hierarchy. However, a hierarchical structure is not the only way to represent a Current User Task Organization Model. It may simply not be appropriate for some types of work. But studies of expert knowledge suggest that such knowledge is generally organized hierarchically (Wood 1996, 37), and it is a structure that has proven appropriate over and over in my experience. I suggest starting with a hierarchical task structure and turning to something else only if it does not seem to capture the nature of the users' task organization models (see the section Alternative Techniques—A Review).

Bear in mind that here you are trying to determine the organization *across* tasks —the way users currently think about tasks and do them in their daily work—rather than the flow or sequence of steps *within* tasks. You have already obtained insights into within-task flow from the Task Scenarios you constructed from your contextual observations/interviews. Your Use Cases and Task Scenarios have given you a good start at identifying all basic user tasks, and you might have already gained some insights into a Current User Task Organization Model, but the steps in this section provide a specific technique for extracting a model directly from users.

❾ **Identify basic user tasks.** In a meeting attended by all observers/interviewers and other project team members involved in design (see Holtzblatt and Beyer 1996, 310–311, 319–320), the group goes through all documented contextual observation/interview notes and Task Scenarios, with each team member serving as the expert on his or her own notes. Together the group constructs a single list of all the discrete work tasks that make up the users' overall jobs (see the Sample Work Products and Templates section for examples). These may correspond to Use Cases, or they may represent the building blocks of Use Cases. For example, basic user tasks in the job of tracking property in a metropolitan police department might include

◆ Enter incoming property from a new incident in property log.
◆ Document property from a new incident on proper forms.
◆ Get station commander's approval on property documentation.

- Turn over property to the property clerk.
- Prepare property transfer forms.
- Transfer property to a warehouse.
- Transfer property to a lab.
- Deposit cash in a bank.
- Return property to an owner.
- Update property log after property transfers.
- Destroy property.
- Auction property.
- Determine present location of property.

Similarly, basic user tasks in a customer support job at an insurance company might include

- Look up policy information.
- Change policy beneficiary.
- Change customer address.
- Take out a loan on a policy.
- Order office supplies.
- Provide customer information to sales rep.

If users do not participate directly in step 9, they should at least validate the final list of basic user tasks you generate.

⑩ Take a first pass at Current User Task Organization Model. I have found this technique to be useful for modeling users' task organizations (see Alternative Techniques—A Review for other techniques). Based on your contextual observations/interviews, organize the basic user tasks you identified in the previous step into a hierarchy reflecting a model of current user task organization, grouping things that seem to belong together both logically and in terms of work flow (see the Sample Work Products and Templates section for an example). In the next step, you will get input on this model directly from users; the purpose of this step is to set up some context in which the user input can be interpreted.

This is *not* an attempt to reengineer the work in the automated product. That comes in a later lifecycle task, Work Reengineering. It also says nothing about how functionality will be presented in the user interface to the system; you are not doing user interface design yet. Independent of any automation at all, this first pass is a reflection of your understanding of how users currently think about and do their work.

⓫ **Obtain a Current User Task Organization Model.** Now you want to empirically obtain a model that represents the way users organize the activities and artifacts of their work. One way to do this is to conduct a *task sorting exercise* with users to see how they organize low-level tasks into a hierarchy (you will most likely find important deviations from the first pass you generated in step 10).

To conduct a task sorting exercise, write each basic user task on an index card (in user terminology and using explanatory text if necessary). Recruit three to five users for each key user type (Actor) and schedule them for one to two hours each. For *each* user:

◆ Show them the housekeeping analogy (see the template for the task sorting exercise in the Sample Work Products and Templates section) as a way of explaining this exercise. (Read it over yourself now, to better understand the purpose of and how to conduct this exercise.)

◆ Ask them to group the basic user tasks in a way that makes the most sense, given how they think about and do their actual work. Encourage them to divorce themselves from artifacts of their current tools and focus on what is inherent and would be most natural, given their work.

◆ Ask them to take their groups and form subgroups if they haven't already done so and if this makes sense to them.

◆ Ask them to give labels to all groups and subgroups.

◆ Document the hierarchy from each user (see the Sample Work Products and Templates section for an example).

After getting input from a sample of users, compare the hierarchies and try to construct one hierarchy that captures all commonalities. Document it in the same format as the example in the Sample Work Products and Templates section. The final consolidated Current User Task Organization Model can be documented in the Task Analysis document that also contains the Task Scenarios.

Work Reengineering, a later task in the Usability Engineering Lifecycle described in Chapter 7, will be to take this Current User Task Organization Model as a base and "reengineer" it to be the task organization model upon which the application and its user interface will be based.

LEVEL OF EFFORT

Table 3.2 gives a sample level of effort for the Contextual Task Analysis task. The work effort will vary widely depending on the complexity of the application and the techniques chosen and applied. It will also depend in large part on how familiar the analysts are with the work domain, and how complex the work domain is.

This sample represents a simple to moderately complex application with two observers/interviewers, in which they apply the technique described in the Sample Technique—A Step-by-Step Procedure section. Very complex projects with many more observers/interviewers and different techniques could take considerably more staff time, although not necessarily more elapsed time, because much of the work can be done by different teams of observers/interviewers at the same time. Analysts who have used various techniques on a variety of projects report an elapsed time of anywhere between two weeks and six months to complete the Contextual Task Analysis task (see Wixon and Ramey 1996).

Table 3.2
Level of effort—Contextual Task Analysis

Usability Time (two staff sharing all tasks)		User Time	
Step	Hrs	Step	Hrs
Review requirements spec	24		
Interview project team	16		
Interview user reps	16	Interview user reps	8
Identify key Actors/Use Cases	8		
In-context observations	80	In-context observations	40
Work Environment Analysis	24		
Task Scenarios	16		
Task Analysis document	24		
Low-level tasks	16		
First pass task model	8		
Obtain user task model	32	Obtain user task model	18
Document task model	8		
Total	272	Total	66

ALTERNATIVE TECHNIQUES— A REVIEW

Two recent books (see Beyer and Holtzblatt 1998 and Wixon and Ramey 1996) do an excellent job of documenting alternative techniques for Contextual Task Analysis. I refer you to these books for details; here, I offer quick summaries of alternative techniques for some of the steps in the Contextual Task Analysis described in the Sample Technique—A Step-by-Step Procedure section.

Another way to approach the analysis aspect of documenting the results of contextual observations/interviews (see step 8 in the sample technique) that might work better when there is a larger number of observers/interviewers is known as constructing an "affinity diagram" (see Holtzblatt and Beyer 1996, 318–319; Beyer and Holtzblatt 1998, 154–163). In this approach, each observer/interviewer re-records each individual observation or piece of data from his or her own set of notes onto a separate self-sticking note. Examples of the level of detail recorded might be

Another approach to analyzing and documenting the results of the observations/ interviews is constructing an affinity diagram

This user only does this task about four times a year.

This user commented that there is never any time to train.

Prisoners rarely get copies of property forms as they should because the paperwork is so tedious it is rarely done before they are released.

Very high noise level in this police station: babies crying, prisoners shouting, many police officers present and talking.

This user says he often waits in line two to three hours to get his task done.

This police station is one big open room divided into different areas where different tasks are performed.

Then all observers/interviewers meet and as a group put their respective notes up on a big blank wall one at a time, clustering notes together that seem to be related. As more and more notes go up, the emerging structure of clusters is rearranged in ways the group agrees upon. In this way, a final structure of distinct groups of issues and observations evolves. Then the team members label clusters and group them into higher-level categories (note that some clusters will relate specifically to the work environment and will be recorded in the Work Environment Analysis document from step 6 in the sample technique). Thus, all the rich data gathered across a large number of contextual observations/ interviews by a large number of individuals can be exhaustively documented and shared as well as organized and reduced to their commonalities. Team members can then brainstorm about the general implications that these issues and observations raise for usability requirements.

An affinity diagram can help identify gaps in the data and thus focus additional contextual observations/ interviews

When an affinity diagram is developed partway through the iteration of steps 5–8 in the sample technique discussed earlier, it can also serve to identify gaps and areas that lack clarity in the data, thus helping to focus subsequent contextual observations/interviews (see, e.g., Coble et al. 1996, 239–240). Based on the structure of issues and observations in the final affinity diagram, and the related implications that emerge from this process, one team member can then write the Task Analysis and Work Environment Analysis documents. (For another example, see Coble et al. 1996, 244.)

Still another useful approach to analyzing and documenting the output of the contextual observations/interviews is described in Chin, Rosson, and Carroll (1997). Here a multidisciplinary team of users, technologists, and usability engineers base their analysis on the Task Scenarios gathered during the contextual observations/interviews. They identify features of the current scenarios and analyze these features in terms of their pros and cons.

A number of different ways for modeling users' work are described in other literature. Use Cases describe " . . . a specific way of using the system by performing some part of the functionality. Each use case constitutes a complete course of events initiated by an actor and it specifies the interaction that takes place between an actor and the system" (Jacobson et al. 1992, 159). Holtzblatt and Beyer (1996, 312–318, 319–320) and Beyer and Holtzblatt (1998, ch. 6) offer five others. These include Flow Models, which model how different roles interact and communicate to get work done; Sequence Models, which model the sequence of steps people take to accomplish some work task; Artifact Models, which model things people create, use, and modify in the course of their work; Cultural Models, which model the culture in which work takes place; and Physical Models, which model the physical environment in which work takes place.

Other techniques for eliciting task organization models from users can be used when tasks are not necessarily expected to fall into a hierarchical structure. Lokuge, Gilbert, and Richards (1996) describe two methods and provide references for them. In one—the Multi-Dimensional Scaling method (MDS)—users are asked to rate all possible pairs of items (e.g., basic user tasks) on a scale of relative similarity on a single specified dimension, such as functional relatedness or likelihood to be used in sequence. Then the MDS analysis algorithm is applied to the data, generating clusters of items that represent groupings meaningful to users along the single specified dimension.

In the other technique, called Trajectory Mapping (TM), users are asked to imagine a conceptual feature or property that links each pair of items and then order all remaining items along that dimension. The data is then subjected to the TM analysis algorithm, which generates clusters of items related along multiple dimensions of salience *to the user*, rather than along a single dimension predefined by the experimenter.

Through techniques such as these, you can extract from users how they actually think about and organize information and activities in their own work models, given their current work process and tools, even if a hierarchical structure is not appropriate and the task sorting technique will not work.

If you are enhancing or maintaining an existing product or developing products highly related to a current product, as opposed to developing brand-new products, then in place of or in addition to the contextual observations/interviews technique described earlier, you could apply other techniques aimed at soliciting feedback from users about current products. These techniques include questionnaires, usage studies, interviews, and focus groups, and they are described in detail in Chapter 17. Usage and assessments of current products by users can provide insights that will be directly applicable in the development of new releases and related products.

Other techniques for eliciting task organization models from users can be used when tasks are not necessarily expected to fall into a hierarchical structure

SHORTCUTS

If you can afford the effort but must limit the elapsed time for a Contextual Task Analysis, keep in mind that you can reduce the elapsed time by having the whole team divide responsibility for contextual observations/interviews and conduct them simultaneously.

When you enter a project late, or resources are not available for a thorough Contextual Task Analysis as described in this chapter, or the project is small in scope and relatively simple, you can at least perform a scaled-back version of this task by conducting a small number of contextual observations/interviews in one round (rather than a truly representative set in iterative batches) and skipping all documentation tasks.

If even this is impractical, you can at least find one or two representative users (or knowledgeable project team members) and interview them together to get Task Scenarios, Current User Task Organization Models, and an understanding of the users' work environment. This is no substitute for visiting the users in their work environment, but it will be helpful.

Once a Contextual Task Analysis is conducted on a given user population, this analysis can be reused to develop a related product for the same user group

Also, bear in mind that once a Contextual Task Analysis is conducted for a given user population, to some extent, this analysis can be reused on any project that is developing a related product for the same user group. Thus, once it's done, the shortcut on subsequent projects is simply to reuse the Contextual Task Analysis from the previous project. This can work, for example, when a Contextual Task Analysis covered a given user job or role quite extensively, and the project only automated part of their job or role. On subsequent projects that will automate more of the same job or role, a great deal of the Contextual Task Analysis might be reusable. Comstock and Duane (1997b) describe an example in which user profiles and task analyses from previous projects that were aimed at providing a user group with component tools were reused to provide input to the design of a new product that integrated all previous components. They based their new product design completely on user profile and task analysis data that already had been collected and documented.

WEB NOTES

The problems of doing a Contextual Task Analysis for a Web site or application are very like those of doing one for a vendor company: the users may not be accessible or even known, and the work being automated may not currently performed by intended users. This doesn't mean a Contextual Task Analysis cannot be done.

A Contextual Task Analysis for a Web site or application might focus more on what people want or need than on how they currently perform tasks. You can often get help from marketing personnel to identify and get access to potential users. You can do a Contextual Task Analysis of average people doing personal tasks at home, such as catalog ordering, planning travel, or buying a new car (see, e.g., Dray and Mrazek 1996). You can also, after the fact, solicit task-related information from the Web site: create a feedback page and use feedback to update and maintain a Web site as well as to build new related Web sites and applications.

SAMPLE WORK PRODUCTS AND TEMPLATES

The following sample work products and templates for the Contextual Task Analysis task are offered here:

- Contextual Observation/Interview Data Collection—Template with Sample Data
- Sample Work Environment Analysis
- Sample Task Analysis Document
- Sample Task Scenarios
- Sample First Pass at Current User Task Organization Model
- Obtain Current User Task Organization Model—Template for Task Sorting Exercise
- Sample Current User Task Organization Model

CONTEXTUAL OBSERVATION/ INTERVIEW DATA COLLECTION— TEMPLATE WITH SAMPLE DATA

This template can be used for data collection in any contextual observation/ interview. The sample data is adapted from a property processing task in a metropolitan police department. In this sample, a police officer brings in a prisoner with property to process.

Stationhouse Contextual Observation/Interview Data Collection

Actor (User)	Trigger	Use Case (Task)	Task Scenario Sequence	Errors, Problems, Comments
Police officer	Arrest	Fill out property forms for all property associated with an arrest (in this case a domestic assault).	1. Respond to 911 call. 2. Pick up perpetrators and take property (knife, bag of marijuana) into custody. 3. Report to station commander at police station. 4. Write up property summary so station commander can make entry in station log. 5. Secure prisoner. 6. Store property in locker. 7. Fill out arrest paperwork, obtain arrest number. 8. Contact district attorney. 9. Dispose of prisoner (must be done within two hours of arrest).	Police officer may do this type of task only four times per year. Use Case may currently take two to six hours to complete. High frequency of missing data, incorrect data, missing forms. Very high frequency of interrupts and distractions during task.
	Property clerk interrupts with question regarding a previous property form.	Make corrections to a previous property form.	1. Look up previous incident in station log by date and police officer name. 2. Trace info from station log to property log. 3. Get info from property log, and supply it to property clerk so property form can be corrected.	High frequency of missing info in station log. High frequency of missing info in property log.
	(Return to arrest task.)	(Continue filling out property forms from arrest.)	10. Retrieve property from locker. 11. Back to station commander to get property forms and property packaging. 12. Fill out draft property form. 13. Back to station commander to approve draft property form.	High frequency of missing numbers. Property forms drafted before typed due to high level of errors and difficulty correcting typewritten forms.

SAMPLE WORK ENVIRONMENT ANALYSIS

This sample is adapted from excerpts from a document describing the work environment in the local police stations of a metropolitan police department.

Stationhouse Work Environment Analysis

The police station environment is described in terms of both its physical characteristics and the sociocultural environment, which is a distinct subculture within the overall police department "corporate culture." Both the physical and sociocultural work environments have specific implications for the design of user interfaces to computer systems that will be used within that environment, and these are highlighted in indented text and set off by rules above and below.

Physical Work Environment

While the exact physical layout of each local police station is different, there are important commonalities.

Open layout: With the exception of the arrest room and the property closet, which are distinct rooms with ceiling-height walls and in some cases doors, all areas are part of a large open room, defined only by desks and low walls. Even in the arrest room, there can be a lot of traffic coming and going. Thus there is almost no privacy, potentially a high volume of noise, and constant distractions and interruptions.

A software user interface in such an interrupt-driven, noisy, and distracting environment must add minimal cognitive load to the user's job. Thus, the interface needs to be very intuitive and easy to understand and use. There need to be

◆ effective attention-getting cues to highlight key information,
◆ a means to suspend an activity and pick it up again, perhaps after completing another task altogether,

"Stationhouse Work Environment Analysis," cont. next page

"Stationhouse Work Environment Analysis," cont.

◆ plenty of context information to help users keep track of their tasks between interruptions, and

◆ lots of support for the limited capacity of human short-term memory for transient information.

Oppressive atmosphere: In general, the police station buildings are fairly old, and they look it. The interiors, especially when compared to a typical business office, can at best be described as gloomy, dismal, and run-down. Wall color tends to be dark and neutral, adding to the gloomy atmosphere. The walls are plastered with miscellaneous notices and reminders, mostly reflecting time pressures (e.g., "arrest info must be entered on-line within one hour") and ominous demands to follow rules and procedures in order to avoid penalties of various kinds (e.g., "do not allow prisoners to use the water fountain," "be sure to check the prisoner for potential weapons").

There are few if any windows, and the police station is lit with bright, harsh overhead lighting. Some police stations are air-conditioned and some are not. On one of our site visits a station commander commented that "everyone is especially tense as it is so hot." In another, a radio was playing during our whole visit, adding to the already noisy environment.

The station commander's desk is raised up from floor height and tends to be an area of central focus in the police station. Its size, height from floor level, and a metal bar surrounding it all create a distance between the station commander and anyone approaching the station commander's desk, which seems to emphasize the authority of the station commander's rank within the police station. Although there seems to be an adequate amount of work space in this area, there is usually a good deal of activity around the area, with people shuffling back and forth behind the desk, and prisoners and police officers repeatedly approaching the front of the desk to interact with the station commander. The tension surrounding the station commander's desk is palpable, even in the quieter moments in the police station. The station commander has a high-accountability, highly stressful job, and this, combined with the constant yet erratic and unpredictable arrival of police officers with prisoners and numerous other complex problems, seems to permeate the general atmosphere of the police station, which can be described as stressed, pressured, tense, and at times chaotic. Station commanders appear to be sullen and not terribly positive, due to the stressful nature of their jobs.

Human performance tends to degrade under stressful, high-pressure conditions. Poor lighting and air can also affect performance. This again means that

◆ The user interface to any system used in this environment must provide lots of cognitive, perceptual, and motor support.

In addition, the interface can be made more attractive and appealing by using

◆ light colors,
◆ pleasant graphics, and
◆ a positive, helpful (rather than demanding and penalty-oriented) tone.
◆ Adding guide/tip facilities to a software program may reduce the number of times users need to ask someone what to do, especially since the someone is probably the station commander who has the most to do and most responsibility.

In sum, in the typical police station, the appearance of the interior is dark, run-down, and cluttered, the lighting is harsh and artificial, and the air is close and sometimes very hot. The noise level can be high, the work areas are cramped and cluttered, and the overall atmosphere is tense and high-pressure at best, chaotic and sometimes riotous at worst.

These conditions most likely have a general impact on morale and certainly will have an impact on cognitive functioning, which in

"Stationhouse Work Environment Analysis," cont. next page

"Stationhouse Work Environment Analysis," cont.

turn impacts productivity and effectiveness. The user interface must be carefully designed to

◆ mitigate the natural and possibly extreme degradations of human performance under these conditions.

Sociocultural Work Environment

Almost all the upper-level staff in this organization have worked up through the ranks. Organizations where this is true tend to have fairly static cultures, because workers absorb the culture when they come in at low levels and then perpetuate the culture as they rise up into managerial positions. Change in such corporate cultures is usually slow and resisted, and can often only come from strong leadership at the top of the organization in the person of someone who has come from outside the organization.

The observations made here are thus most likely based on historical factors, rather than on the philosophy and style of the current management. It is not our intention to be critical of or make recommendations for change regarding either the physical environment or the corporate culture—this is beyond both our expertise and the scope of this project. We make these observations simply because any computer system will be introduced in the context of both the physical and sociocultural environment, and these factors will heavily influence its reception and usage. We cannot change the environment, but by being aware of it, we can design the user interface to any on-line system in a way that best addresses the unique requirements of its users in their environment.

Low teamwork: One main factor in the sociocultural environment is the natural hostility and distrust between police officers and prisoners. This seems to be exacerbated by an apparent lack of trust and support between—and even within—ranks within the police department. Everyone is under a great deal of stress and pressure, and trying to avoid responsibility for errors and problems. The relationship between ranks seems to be authoritarian and status conscious, rather than supportive and teamwork oriented. There is high turnover, and to add to this, there is shift rotation among police officers and station commanders. These in turn mean that a culture of teamwork is not readily fostered. In addition, everyone is usually extremely busy with his or her own overload of responsibilities, leaving little time or energy to support one another.

In many organizations, users look to each other for help in learning and mastering new computer systems on the job. We probably cannot assume this will happen here due to the factors above. This in turn means that the user interface:

◆ should be as self-explanatory as possible, and
◆ should have built into it as many of the business rules as possible, so that users need minimal help to use it successfully even if they use it infrequently.

To summarize, this seems to be a sociocultural environment in which (especially compared with a professional business environment) office morale is low, negative pressure and stress is high, teamwork is not fostered, the only reward is escape, and perfect performance is demanded of workers under conditions that seem almost specifically designed to impede performance. In addition, staff have had mostly negative experiences—if any—with automation to date.

◆ Ease of use,
◆ ease of learning, and
◆ task and user orientation

in any system user interface in this environment will be critical to its success.

SAMPLE TASK ANALYSIS DOCUMENT

This sample is adapted from excerpts from two sections of a Task Analysis document describing the current task flow and its weaknesses for processing property in the local police stations of a metropolitan police department. In the next section I separately offer sample Task Scenarios, which would also be included in the Task Analysis document.

Stationhouse Task Analysis

Purpose and Structure of This Document

This document presents a user-oriented perspective and analysis of the tasks that will be automated by the application. The functional spec describes processes and activities in traditional systems analysis terms. Here we are describing user tasks from the perspective of the people performing those tasks in their actual work environment.

Whereas the formal description of abstract and general processes and activities in the functional spec documents the way things should be done and how they are done when everything goes smoothly and correctly, here we focus on real-life instances of tasks and highlight where things can go wrong or don't work the way the worker needs them to in order to perform his or her job effectively. This focus is key to meeting user interface design requirements for this system and ensuring that the functionality provided best supports the real-life tasks users will perform with the new application in their real work environment.

This document thus presents an analysis of the tasks to be automated from a user interface design perspective. Direct implications for user interface design are highlighted in indented text and set off by rules above and below.

Analysis of Current Work and Tasks

In this section, we make general observations from our contextual observations/interviews regarding the user tasks being automated, highlighting problem areas, bottlenecks, and opportunities for improvement, where the design of the user interface can have an impact.

Broad range of task complexity: The complexity of the property processing task can vary significantly. One police officer told us she once had to complete twelve separate property forms for a single incident; another time she saw an officer come into the police station with fifteen large bags of narcotics and related materials associated with a single incident, all of which had to be logged on property forms. By contrast, we watched another police officer come in with no prisoners and a single piece of property to process: a spent shell from a handgun. Certain property types, such as automobiles, guns, and cash, always entail quite a few complex forms, while others involve only simple paperwork.

The user interface must keep simple transactions simple but make complex transactions possible.

High degree of interrupts during tasks: The property processing tasks are subject to a high level of interruptions. In the case of the police officer, the source of interruptions may be prisoners, other police officers in the arrest room, other aspects of processing an arrest besides property, or having to leave the arrest room to gather data for the property forms, for example, to check an auto for information that needs to be included on the property form.

A software user interface in such an interrupt-driven, noisy, and distracting environment must add minimal cognitive load to the user's job. Thus, the interface needs to be very intuitive and easy to understand and use. There need to be

◆ effective attention-getting cues to highlight key information;
◆ plenty of context information on the screen at all times, so that if users are distracted, when they turn their attention back to the screen, they can quickly reconstruct where they were and what they were doing and carry on;
◆ lots of support for the limited capacity of human short-term memory for transient information;
◆ multitasking, so that users can suspend one on-line task, start another, and then return to the first task without loss of work or context.

SAMPLE TASK SCENARIOS

Task Scenarios represent concrete, detailed, real, and typical work tasks a user might encounter in his or her job. They are drawn from and reconstructed from the contextual observations/interviews. They might represent composite scenarios made up of parts of scenarios actually observed. They are written strictly in terms of abstract user tasks and goals, and make little or no reference to software or other tools currently used to get the task done. In the parlance of OOSE, they represent *instances* of Use Cases.

The first Task Scenario is written in the format and style that would be used in the Task Analysis document. Note the use of the OOSE concept of an *extension* (in this case, an interruption). Following that is a Task Scenario that has been rewritten from the Task Analysis document to serve as a prop in a usability test.

Stationhouse Task Scenario

Task: Complete property form User: Police officer

Description: Domestic dispute—couple filing charges against each other. He beat her with a broomstick, she attacked and cut him with a knife. Someone called 911 to report the incident, and the police officer picked them up and brought them in, with the knife as evidence, a beeper for safekeeping, and a bag of marijuana, which was taken from the premises where the arrests were made.

Task Flow:

1. Police officer (PO) goes to station commander's (SC) desk with perpetrators and shows all property, filling out a summary form for the SC. SC makes entry in command log.
2. PO secures the prisoners, takes fingerprints, and checks for warrants.
3. PO stores property in her own personal locker.
4. PO writes up an arrest worksheet and Prisoner Release forms, questioning the prisoners to obtain required information.
5. PO records data from the arrest worksheet and obtains an arrest number, which she writes on her hand.
6. PO contacts the assistant district attorney (ADA), faxes arrest worksheet to ADA office.

7. PO disposes of the prisoners (she must within two hours of the arrest, or the SC will have to file a special report explaining why she did not). Property forms are not yet done, so prisoners do not get copies, as they should.
8. PO fills out a complaint worksheet.
9. PO records data from the complaint worksheet and obtains complaint numbers.
10. PO retrieves property from her locker.
11. PO returns to the desk, and she gets property forms and bags, for which she signs out on the scratch property log (in other police stations, the SC distributes the bags and property forms and keeps the scratch property log).
12. PO bags the property and enters the relevant property form number on each bag.
13. PO fills out property form worksheets (optional).
14. PO takes bags and property form worksheets to SC for checking (optional).
15. PO types up the property forms herself, recording the arrest number, complaint number, and bag numbers, and also types up a letter of transmittal for the narcotics, a Controlled Substance Analysis form, a Domestic Incident form, and a Medical Treatment form (with a great deal of repeated header info on all forms).
16. PO takes all forms to the SC for approval. He checks especially all the cross-referencing of numbers (arrest number, complaint numbers, property form numbers, bag numbers), signs off, takes copies of forms, and makes entries on scratch property log and in station log.
17. PO seals all bags and attaches property forms.
18. PO disposes of all property and property forms: narcotics in a locked narcotics locker, other property in property closet.

Task Closure: This scenario took from 1 p.m., when the arrests were made, until almost 4 p.m. to process.

To support this task, the user interface should

- eliminate all redundant entry of data, such as information about the arresting police officer, prisoners, incident; and
- facilitate the cross-referencing between such things as the complaint, the arrest, the property forms, and the property bags.

Insurance Task Scenario

Enter application data on-line for a new insurance policy for an existing customer and handle two customer phone calls.

The phones are quiet, there are no sales agents around, so you decide to enter data in an on-line application form for a new policy that has been sitting in your in-basket. Humphrey Bogart, an existing client, has applied for a new insurance policy.

All Humphrey Bogart's information is available on-line, and you don't need to reenter any of it, you just need to complete an on-line application form.

Procedure

1. Get a new policy application started for Humphrey Bogart, and start filling in all the necessary information to complete the application.
2. The phone rings, and you answer it. Lauren Bacall is calling to report a change in address. She gives you a policy number. You need to suspend your data entry task and locate Lauren Bacall's information to make changes.
3. When you find Lauren Bacall's record, check to see if she has any business that includes other people, such as family members. Since she does, ask her if their addresses will be changing as well. She says yes. Make the changes as she specifies.
4. Wrap up with Lauren Bacall and hang up. Return to the application you were in the middle of for Humphrey Bogart. Complete this application.
5. The phone rings, and it is John Wayne asking to cancel a policy. He does not have his policy number. Look him up.
6. When you find his record, you note that he has several policies. Ask him if he wants to cancel just one or all. He says all. He is in financial difficulties and says he cannot afford to keep any of his policies. Tell John Wayne that you have all the necessary information and that his sales agent will be contacting him soon.

SAMPLE FIRST PASS AT CURRENT USER TASK ORGANIZATION MODEL

This sample is adapted from part of a design team's original task hierarchy for the customer support function in an insurance company. In this illustration, the text beneath the boxes represents the basic user tasks identified from the contextual observations/interviews. The text in boxes represents the hierarchy of groups developed by the design team, with labels they created—again, all based on the contextual observations/interviews. (For simplicity of the example, not all groups or low-level tasks are included.)

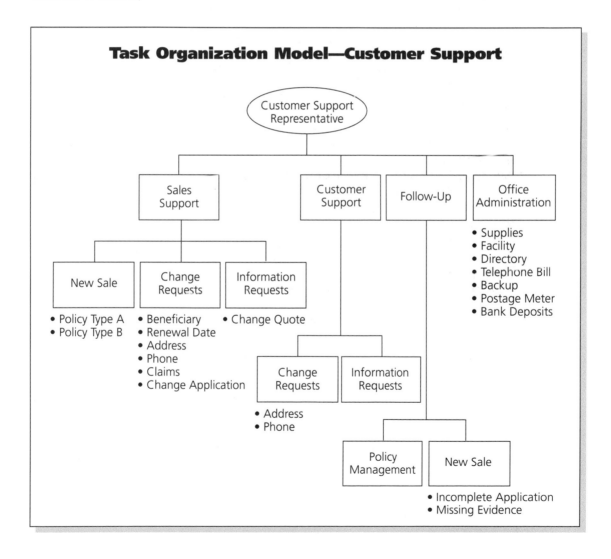

OBTAIN CURRENT USER TASK ORGANIZATION MODEL—TEMPLATE FOR TASK SORTING EXERCISE

The housekeeping task is a useful analogy for explaining to users what is expected of them in the task sorting exercise.

Task Sorting Exercise—Housekeeping Analogy

Imagine you are a housekeeper. Say we are designing your house and deciding where to store all your housekeeping tools and supplies in a way that best supports your job as housekeeper. Suppose we listed all your basic housekeeping tasks and asked you to organize them into groups, so we could better understand how to design your house and store your tools where you would find them and access them quickly.

Housekeeping Tasks—
A Random Ordering of Lowest-Level Tasks

Vacuum furniture (e.g., couches)
Serve beverages
Wash floors
Rinse dishes
Combine ingredients for cooking
Wash rugs/towels in washing machine
Sweep floors
Set the table
Cook prepared food

Polish furniture
Clear the table
Vacuum floors and rugs
Put meal on table
Wash pots and pans
Dust
Mix up ingredients for cooking
Wash fixtures (sinks, toilets, tubs)
Serve food from table
Put dishes in dishwasher

With your (the end user's) input, we hope to end up with something like the task hierarchy shown on page 119. If we had never done house-keeping ourselves, and we didn't consult you, the task expert, we might have come up with an organization that didn't support your work at all and made it unnecessarily tedious and difficult. Imagine how unusable the household would be if instead of organizing your house along the lines of the hierarchy below, we put your pantry in your attic, stored your dishes in the cellar, or placed your dishwashing liquid in a bathroom closet along with other types of cleaning liquids! Something analogous to this usually happens, unfortunately, in the way we organize functionality in software applications, because as developers, we don't really understand the work users are doing. We organize according to some logic, but it usually isn't according to user logic or actual work organization.

This hierarchy of housekeeping tasks shows both task organization groupings and tools supporting tasks (in parentheses) that should be kept together.

Housekeeping Tasks Hierarchy

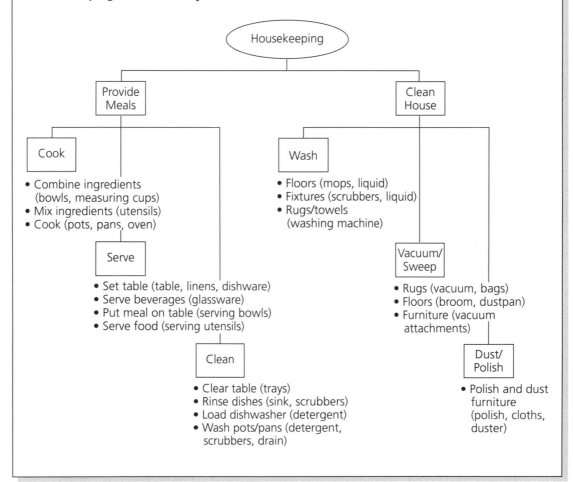

SAMPLE CURRENT USER TASK ORGANIZATION MODEL

This sample of part of one user's task hierarchy is adapted from the customer support function in an insurance company. In the model illustrated here, the text beneath the boxes represents the low-level tasks presented to the user, each task on a separate index card. The bold text in boxes represents the groups that one user formed from the low-level tasks, with labels they suggested. (This hierarchy represents a partial set of the functionality required by a customer support rep. For simplicity of the example, not all groups or low-level tasks are included.)

Note how this hierarchy is different from the one generated by the design team (see the earlier section Sample First Pass at Current User Task Organization Model). For example, the design team organizes all types of changes (e.g., Address, Beneficiary) under the category "Change Requests" within the category Sales Support. Meanwhile, this *user* distinguishes between those changes that have to do with customer information and those that relate to policy details, but locates both types of changes under the category "Customer Support" rather than "Sales Support." As it turns out, customer support staff can make simple changes to customer information on their own, but more complex paperwork and approvals are required for policy changes. Thus, these are two distinct categories of tasks to users. And even though requests for these types of changes often come from customers via sales agents, this user still regards them as reflecting customer support.

Similarly, the *design team* lumps all Office Admin tasks in one group, while this *user* distinguishes between Daily and Occasional office tasks. It turns out that different people are assigned to these types of tasks, so again, this is a meaningful distinction to users.

The *designers* imagine a category unto itself called "Follow-Up," where incomplete tasks of all types (e.g., Incomplete App) are all located; while this user considers follow-up activities as belonging with the original task type with which they are associated.

Finally, note that the user regards New Sales (entering data in new policy applications) as its own category, whereas the designers see this as a subcategory of Sales Support, a very different perception.

One important thing to note in comparing this *user's* task organization model with the designers' first pass at a task organization model is that for any set of low-level tasks, there may be a large number of very different *logical* task organizations possible, but there will only be a small number of rather similar ones that will make sense to users, given their current work models. A traditional systems analysis will uncover all the low-level tasks, but it typically does not ensure that the task organization most consistent with the Current User Task Organization Model will be presented to the user. That is the point of a Contextual Task Analysis.

Also note that this user's model is most likely not exactly the same as other users' models, although in most cases, there will be a lot of similarity across individual users' models. As part of step 11 (Obtain Current User Task Organization Model) in the Contextual Task Analysis technique described in this chapter, recall that you consolidate all the sampled users' task organization models and generate one model in the same format that captures as many commonalities as possible. Then, in a later task in the lifecycle—Work Reengineering—this consolidated user model will be reengineered (see Chapter 7).

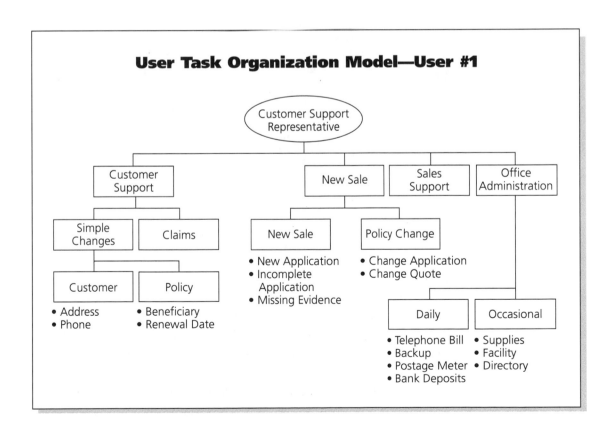

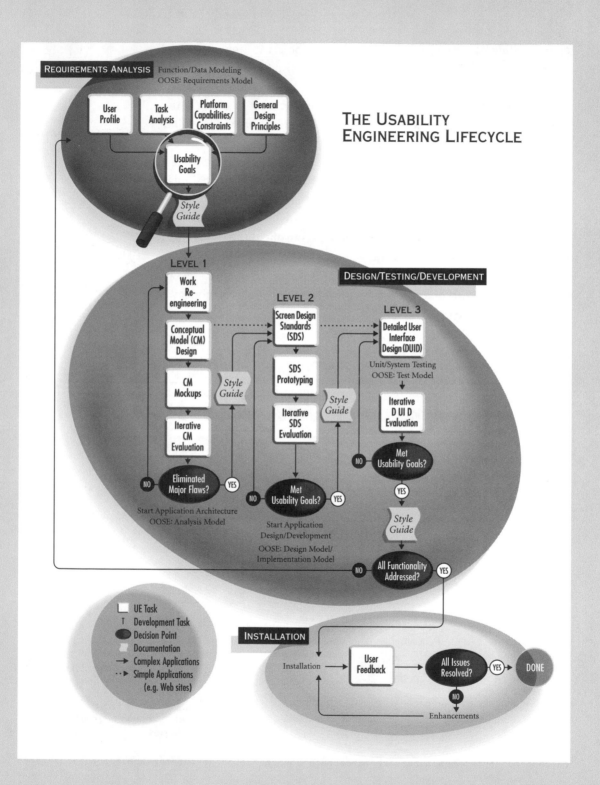

THE USABILITY
ENGINEERING LIFECYCLE

4

*Usability Goal
Setting*

*Specific usability
goals help to focus
user interface
design efforts by
giving designers
something concrete
to aim for and to
assess their design
ideas against*

PURPOSE

Most engineering processes involve setting and iterating towards specific—and usually objective and measurable—goals, established and
agreed upon early in the project. It is universally understood in the engineering disciplines that to reach a satisfactory end result on any engineering project, the project team must establish and agree upon clear
goals and then work towards accomplishing them. Usability Engineering
is no different. In the words of Wixon and Wilson (1997):

> Those goals which are clear and precise will command resources and mind-
> share. Vague and imprecise goals are often declared "met" when time and
> money have run out. One of the reasons attributes like "time to market" and
> "reliability" (eliminating bugs) play such a major role in the development
> process is that they have "metrics" that are clearly defined. Usability "bugs"
> can be just as severe as reliability bugs and should be treated with the same
> quantitative respect.

Establishing usability goals on a development project serves two primary purposes. First, specific, articulated usability goals help to focus
user interface design efforts during the design process by giving designers something concrete to aim for and something concrete to assess their
design ideas against as they generate and consider them. For example, if
all designers understand and agree that ease of use for experienced users
is much more important than ease of learning for novices, design efforts
can focus on alternatives that seem most likely to provide ease of use—
that is, speed and efficiency. Usability goals should thus drive all user

123

interface design decisions. In fact, designing *without* clear goals in mind is "making a blind choice" (Wixon and Wilson 1997).

Usability goals should drive design. They can streamline the design process and shorten the design cycle

Related to the fact that usability goals should drive design, I would add that they can also streamline the design process and shorten the design cycle. Most software developers and user interface designers have experienced endless user interface design meetings, where designers argue heatedly over design options. These meetings can go on for hours, days, and even months, when there are no shared, agreed upon usability goals focusing the design effort. Designers argue from the perspective of their best known (or imagined) or favorite type of user, even when multiple types of users will ultimately use the product. If each designer argues for design options that support a different user type, no one reaches agreement. Much time is wasted, and the most aggressive and persistent designers win design decisions, whether or not their ideas best serve the entire user population.

By contrast, agreement on design alternatives usually takes much less time and energy if all designers share a common and accurate picture of the total user population (which comes from the User Profile), a common and accurate model of the work and work environment (which comes from the Contextual Task Analysis), and they agree upon clear goals that best serve this total population doing these tasks in this environment. Thus, usability goals can save time in the overall project lifecycle as well as ensure better design for the intended user population. Even if usability goals are never tested and used as acceptance criteria, they serve a useful purpose during design.

Quantitative usability goals serve as acceptance criteria during usability evaluation

The second purpose of usability goals is to serve as acceptance criteria during usability evaluation, especially towards the end of the design process. Design efforts are iterated with evaluation until evaluation indicates that established usability goals are satisfactorily met. That is, usability goals establish criteria for when an iterative design and evaluation cycle should end and the team can move on either to the next level of design and evaluation or to development. Related to this, usability problems revealed during evaluation can be prioritized according to whether they relate to usability goals or not. When resources are limited, problems that relate directly to identified goals can be given top priority, and problems that do not relate directly to identified goals can be put on the back burner (Wixon and Wilson 1997). Thus, usability goals drive the evaluation process as well as the design process.

In particular, usability goals are used as evaluation criteria when conducting the Iterative Detailed User Interface Design Evaluation task and also during the Iterative Screen Design Standards Evaluation task. For example, a team might have established a goal stating that a certain key transaction should not take more than thirty seconds for an experienced user to accomplish. Design and evaluation of the interface to this transaction during Iterative Detailed User Interface Design Evaluation (or during Iterative Screen Design Standards Evaluation if that transaction is prototyped in this task) would then proceed until evaluation showed that, on average, experienced users could perform that transaction within this time.

Additionally, Wixon and Wilson (1997) point out that resistance on the part of a development manager or team to setting and committing to usability goals at this stage in a project should be interpreted as a red flag, indicating a fundamental lack of commitment to Usability Engineering. In such cases, usability experts who have any choice in the matter should consider offering their services elsewhere. You want to invest your energy where you are more likely to have an impact and a successful experience that will help promote Usability Engineering further in your organization (for more on promoting the Usability Engineering Lifecycle, see Chapter 18).

DESCRIPTION

Usability goals are based on the User Profile and the Contextual Task Analysis, as well as on general business goals. Thus, here we see another example of how the output of previous tasks feeds directly into later tasks in the Usability Engineering Lifecycle. In particular, certain usability goals will be appropriate for some types of users and tasks, but not others. For example (Wixon and Wilson 1997), ease-of-learning goals will not be a high priority for complex products where highly educated users will get extensive training and will use the product frequently, such as space shuttle software or air traffic control systems. For these products, ease-of-use goals will take priority. Conversely, ease-of-learning goals will be important for users of products where training is nonexistent and frequency of use is low, such as information kiosks in hotels. Refer to the Sample Work Products and Templates sections of Chapters 2 and 3 for more examples

Usability goals are based on the User Profile and the Contextual Task Analysis, as well as on general business goals

of how User Profile and Contextual Task Analysis data suggest specific usability goals.

Usability goals can also be derived from marketing groups, competitive analysis, technical support groups, or just informed opinion (Wixon and Wilson 1997). They then drive all user interface design decisions and provide the criteria for acceptance testing, particularly during Iterative Detailed User Interface Design Evaluation, but also to some extent during Iterative Screen Design Standards Evaluation.

Usability goals fall into several categories, the broadest of which are qualitative usability goals and quantitative usability goals. Quantitative goals can be further broken down into ease-of-use goals and ease-of-learning goals. Note that within these broad categories of goals, many specific goals could be formulated in any given category. Examples are given in the following discussion.

QUALITATIVE USABILITY GOALS

Qualitative usability goals are general unquantified goals that guide design

The general goals that guide design, which are not quantified, are **qualitative usability goals**. For example, qualitative goals might be

◆ The design must support users working in a high-interrupt environment, with lots of context information on screen to remind users where they are when they get distracted.

◆ The design must support very infrequent users of a very complex task. Thus, it must be self-explanatory and easy to learn and remember, incorporating as many business rules as possible and leading users by the hand through the task so they need not remember details of proper procedure between uses.

Qualitative goals are extremely useful in guiding initial design efforts. In the above examples, these goals would be drawn directly from the User Profile and the Contextual Task Analysis.

Comstock and Duane (1996) provide an excellent case study illustrating how high-level, qualitative usability goals were formulated based on user profiles and task analyses, and how these goals then influenced product design. Their goals were meant to drive high-level system architecture design for a whole family of related networking software products, rather than specific product design. They recorded their goals in a document they called "The Declaration of System Usability." Examples of their goals are paraphrased here:

- The system should integrate people's tasks, as opposed to integrating underlying technology.
- The system should recognize a person, independent of his or her individual accounts on different components of the whole system.
- The system should facilitate group operations.
- Using the system should not require knowledge of the underlying technology.
- Over releases, the system should hide changes that are not relevant to users' tasks.
- The system should provide consistency across components.

In their case study, Comstock and Duane also point to the importance of getting buy-in on the usability goals from all relevant managers before development begins. They offer interesting examples of how their agreed upon usability goals influenced the design of a number of products in the product family they were intended to support.

Quantitative Usability Goals

As useful as qualitative goals are, it is difficult to determine whether they have been met in a final design, precisely because they are so broadly stated and are not quantified. Thus, they cannot be used directly as acceptance criteria during usability testing. By contrast, **quantitative usability goals** are objective and measurable. Thus, they can serve as acceptance criteria during usability evaluation. Examples of quantitative goals might be

Quantitative usability goals are objective, measurable, and can serve as acceptance criteria during usability evaluation

- Experienced users (defined as users who have performed the transaction five times in a training session) should take no longer than two minutes on average to transcribe data from a certain paper form to a certain on-line data entry form.
- Novice users (defined as first-time users) should take no longer than three minutes to fill in a certain on-line subscription form.

Note in both examples that not only has a transaction time been quantified, but also "novice" and "expert" users have been defined. This level of specificity is necessary if assessing the interface against the goals during testing is to have any real validity. Also note that, in the first example, an ease-of-use goal has been quantified. In the second, an ease-of-learning goal has been quantified. **Ease-of-use goals** focus on the use of the product by experienced users who have been trained on how to use

Ease-of-use goals focus on the use of the product by users who have had product training and who use it frequently enough to maintain expert performance

Ease-of-learning goals focus on the use of the product by first-time users, users still in the learning process, or infrequent users

the product (either through training programs or self-training on the job) and use it frequently enough to maintain expert performance. Ease of use is generally defined as the potential speed, efficiency, and flexibility an interface offers to an experienced user.

By contrast, **ease-of-learning goals** focus on the use of the product by first-time users, users still in the learning process, or users who have been trained but use the product so infrequently that they may forget how to use it between uses. Ease of learning is roughly defined as the length and slope of the learning curve for users who have not yet reached expert levels of usage.

Relative goals refer to users' experience on the product under design relative to their experience on a benchmark, such as a competitor's product, a previous release, or the manual process for the same task

All quantitative usability goals (both ease-of-use and ease-of-learning goals) can be formulated as either absolute goals or relative goals. **Absolute goals** are those that have an absolute quantification, for example, a specific number of seconds or minutes per task or a specific number of errors per task or transaction. Both the ease-of-use and the ease-of-learning goals in the previous examples represent absolute goals. **Relative goals** refer to users' experience on the product under design relative to their experience on some benchmark, such as a competitor's product, a previous release of a product, or the manual process for doing the same task. Examples of relative goals might be

- Experienced users (defined as users who have performed the transaction five times in a training session) should take less time on average transcribing data from a certain paper form to a certain on-line data entry form on release 2 as compared to release 1.
- Novice users (defined as first-time users) should fill in a certain on-line subscription form faster and with fewer errors on application X than on any of the top five competitors' applications.

All quantitative usability goals (both ease-of-use and ease-of-learning goals) can also be formulated as either performance goals or preference/satisfaction goals. **Performance goals** quantify actual user performance while using a product to perform a task. The usual measures are time (to complete a task or learn a task) and errors (both number and type). All the preceding examples of quantitative goals are performance goals, and all employ the performance measure of task (or transaction) time.

Preference/satisfaction goals are also quantifiable. **Preference goals** aim at a clear user preference among alternative interfaces based on some level of experience with them. **Satisfaction goals** aim at a certain level of satisfaction with a particular interface. Although these types of goals measure subjective reactions, rather than objective performance, they are nevertheless quantifiable. Preference is clearly quantifiable—the user makes a choice. Satisfaction can be measured along a scale, for example, a 5-point scale ranging from "Not at all satisfied" to "Extremely satisfied." An example of a *satisfaction* goal might be

◆   Novice users (after first-time use with no prior training) must rate their satisfaction with the ease of learning of the interface as a 4 ("Very satisfied") on average, given a 5-point scale where 1 is "Not at all satisfied" and 5 is "Extremely satisfied."

Preference goals aim at a clear user preference among alternative interfaces. Satisfaction goals aim at a certain level of satisfaction with a particular interface

Note that this goal, besides being a satisfaction goal, is also a quantitative goal, an ease-of-learning goal, and an absolute goal. An example of a similar goal that is relative, rather than absolute, might be

◆   On average, novice users (after first-time use with no prior training on both applications) must give a higher satisfaction rating to this application interface, based on ease of learning, relative to the interface of our key competitor's comparable application.

Although, at first glance, performance and preference/satisfaction goals may seem redundant, objective measures of performance and preference/satisfaction do not often correlate. That is, if you measure users' performance on two different user interfaces to the same functionality, and then ask the users to give a preference (or rate relative satisfaction), they are just as likely to prefer (or express more satisfaction with) the interface on which they performed poorly as the one on which they performed well. Similarly, when users are tested on two interfaces—one they designed themselves (so one might presume they would prefer) and one designed by usability experts—they will often perform better on the one designed by the usability experts. Users' subjective reactions simply do not always correlate with their objective performance.

Objective measures of performance and preference/ satisfaction do not always correlate

What this means is that we should never assume that if we achieve performance goals, users will be satisfied or prefer our interface; and we should never assume that if we meet preference/satisfaction goals, we will have optimized performance. Instead, we need to consider the importance of both preference/satisfaction and performance goals independently, consider which are more important to the overall success of the product, and include them both if they seem equally important.

Many different metrics can be used to phrase performance goals. These include (Wixon and Wilson 1997) but are not limited to

◆ Time to complete a task
◆ Time to complete a task after a specified time away from the product
◆ Number and type of errors per task
◆ Number of errors per unit of time
◆ Number of navigations to on-line help or manuals
◆ Number of users making a particular error
◆ Number of users completing a task successfully

Whiteside, Bennet, and Holtzblatt (1988) suggest that quantitative goals be phrased at four levels:

◆ **Current level of performance (or satisfaction):** measured either in the manual process or with the current or competitive product and used as a benchmark to help set minimum acceptable levels for the planned product
◆ **Minimum acceptable level of performance (or satisfaction):** Used during iterative evaluation and redesign to determine when to stop iterating
◆ **Target level of performance (or satisfaction):** Used to drive and focus the design effort (actual expected level)
◆ **Optimal level of performance (or satisfaction):** Used as a target for the long term, say, over product releases; what should be possible if time, money, and other conflicting agendas were not considered

SCOPE AND PRIORITY OF GOALS

Goals can refer to performance or satisfaction regarding functions from completing a simple transaction to accomplishing a complex task involving many separate transactions

Goals can refer to performance or satisfaction regarding a narrowly defined product function, such as completing a simple transaction; or they can be broadly defined and refer to something like accomplishing a complex task involving many separate transactions. You must decide on the *scope* of your usability goals to best support your project. If your project is to develop a completely new product, broad task-oriented goals will probably be most useful. If you are designing enhancements to a product in response to specific user requests, narrow feature-oriented goals may be more appropriate.

Wixon and Wilson (1997) stress the importance of setting quantitative goals that walk the fine line between being so lenient as to be meaningless and so ambitious as to be unrealistic. This is something of an art and takes a certain amount of experience to master. They also point out that Usability Goal Setting should be a highly collaborative effort involving all project stakeholders, including users, user or customer management, product development managers, designers and developers, marketing staff, quality assurance staff, technical support staff, and technical writing staff. Collaboration among all these people on the Usability Goal Setting task not only helps ensure that the balance between what is important for product success and what is technically feasible is found and expressed through the usability goals, but also creates buy-in to the goals within the team and across all project stakeholders.

Usability goals, once formulated, must be prioritized. It is easy to simply list all imaginable and admirable usability goals for a project; it is hard to achieve them all. Thus, you should consider which are most likely to contribute to overall product success if met and give these the highest priority. Lower-priority goals can be identified and achieved if possible, but not at the expense of high-priority goals and not if they add excessive time and cost to the project.

Lower-priority goals can be identified and achieved but only if they don't overshadow high-priority goals or add excessive time and cost

Hix and Hartson (1993) suggest that it is wise to introduce an organization to Usability Engineering techniques by defining a few clear goals that can be easily tested and attained with minimal resources. This will help establish the feasibility and utility of Usability Goal Setting and make it easier to convince project managers to incorporate this task on future projects. Wixon and Wilson (1997) further suggest that too many goals can make testing too complex and/or time consuming and thus impractical, and so again, the number of goals should be limited. I would add that they pertain primarily to quantitative goals that you intend to use as acceptance criteria during testing. Even in organizations that are immature with respect to Usability Engineering, you should place no limits on qualitative goals, which are used primarily to drive and focus the design process, as described earlier in the Purpose section.

Whatever usability goals emerge should always be documented (ultimately, in the product Style Guide—see Chapter 14) and referred to during design (although they should be prioritized, as discussed here). A good rule of thumb is that on a given project, quantitative goals should be formulated from a small subset of high-priority qualitative goals.

SCHEDULING AND INTEGRATION WITH OTHER TASKS

The Usability Goal Setting task fits into the overall Usability Engineering Lifecycle in the following ways:

◆ This task is based on the previous two tasks—User Profile and Contextual Task Analysis. Goals are drawn directly from the output of these two tasks to address user and task requirements (see the Sample Work Products and Templates sections of Chapters 2 and 3 for examples of how goals are extracted directly from data from these tasks) and also from more general identified business goals for the project as a whole.

◆ More specifically, some quantitative goals in the Usability Goal Setting task might be based directly on Task Scenarios identified in the Contextual Task Analysis task.

◆ Goals identified and prioritized in the Usability Goal Setting task should drive all user interface design. Thus, they feed directly into all user interface design tasks: Work Reengineering, Conceptual Model Design, Screen Design Standards, and Detailed User Interface Design tasks.

◆ Goals identified and prioritized in this task also provide acceptance criteria for iterative usability evaluation. Thus, they feed directly into design evaluation tasks: Iterative Screen Design Standards Evaluation and Iterative Detailed User Interface Design Evaluation.

◆ Both quantitative and qualitative goals identified and prioritized in the Usability Goal Setting task are documented in the product Style Guide.

The Usability Goal Setting task fits into the underlying software development methodology in the following ways:

◆ This task can *parallel, overlap,* or *follow* development of the Requirements Model in the Analysis phase of OOSE (or function and data modeling in the requirements phase of a traditional rapid prototyping methodology).

◆ This task (along with all other Usability Engineering Lifecycle Requirements Analysis tasks) should precede development of the

Analysis Model in the Analysis phase of OOSE (or the application architecture design in a traditional rapid prototyping methodology).

Roles and Resources

In the Usability Goal Setting task, the usability roles might participate as follows:

Task leader: The Usability Engineer should take the lead role in this task.

Other resources: The User Interface Designer should participate heavily in identifying, quantifying, and prioritizing usability goals. Involvement by other team members, as well as other project stakeholders (e.g., managers, marketers, customers, tech support staff), is highly desirable. Input and final endorsement by project and user management is crucial.

Sample Technique— A Step-by-Step Procedure

I recommend carrying out the following steps with as much involvement as you can recruit from project stakeholders, such as users and user management, developers and development management, marketing, quality assurance, technical support, and technical writing staff.

❶ **Refer to the User Profile.** Many usability goals may be revealed in the User Profile. For example, if it is found through the User Profile that a healthy majority of users are frequent users of Microsoft Windows applications, one goal might be to follow the Windows user interface standards as closely as possible in the new application user interface (but see Chapter 8 on Conceptual Model Design). In another example, if the User Profile reveals that a significant number of users will be from diverse cultures, as might be the case when designing a Web application, it will be an important goal to design a user interface free of cultural assumptions.

In general, the User Profile will help not only to identify the relative importance of ease-of-learning versus ease-of-use goals but also the relative importance of performance versus preference/satisfaction goals. For example, if it is found that a target user population will have an extremely low frequency of use (e.g., only three or four times per year or once in a lifetime), it should be clear that ease-of-learning goals are key and ease-of-use goals not relevant at all. Similarly, if it is found that a user population is particularly hostile towards and resistant to new computer systems, their initial subjective reaction to a new product may be crucial to ultimate acceptance and productive usage. In this case, preference/satisfaction goals would have a high priority and should be included along with performance goals. All goals suggested by the User Profile should be thus identified. For more examples of how the User Profile data defines usability goals, refer to the Sample Work Products and Templates section of Chapter 2.

❷ **Refer to the Contextual Task Analysis.** The Contextual Task Analysis output will suggest usability goals related to the work environment and job context. For example, in a work environment that is noisy and subject to constant interruptions, an important usability goal might be to provide plenty of on-screen context information so that users can reorient quickly after they are distracted. In another example, say that users will perform a variety of tasks, each requiring some (possibly overlapping) set of data or information. A usability goal should be to tailor interfaces (displays of sets of data or information) for each identified task, rather than building a set of displays with all the data and information in one generic organization and requiring users to navigate through many such displays to gather all data or information pertinent to a given task.

In addition, the Contextual Task Analysis will have identified key user tasks or Use Cases, and these can serve to identify the units of work on which to base quantitative goals. For example, in an insurance application, say the Contextual Task Analysis identified making a policy holder's address change as a common and typical task for customer support staff. It could then be used to formulate an ease-of-use goal such as "After performing their first five address changes, users should, on average, be able to navigate to the correct screen and perform a typical address change in no more than thirty seconds."

For more examples of how the Contextual Task Analysis data defines usability goals, refer back to the Sample Work Products and Templates section of Chapter 3.

❸ **Research business goals.** Very often, user interface goals should reflect basic business goals. Better user interfaces can help sell more products and decrease costs in customer support, documentation, packaged training, and even in development and maintenance—all basic business goals of any vendor company (see Chapter 20 and Bias and Mayhew 1994). Similarly, for internal development organizations, better user interfaces can increase user productivity and decrease costs in training, customer support, and development and maintenance. Thus, identifying and quantifying usability goals can often be based directly on identifying and quantifying basic business goals.

The business organization sponsoring a development project will usually have general goals for the project that can easily translate into usability goals. For example, in a vendor organization trying to increase market share, marketing staff may have conducted customer surveys or focus groups and gained insight into what users want and what might make them choose a new product over a comparable competitor's product. Perhaps potential customers have complained about high training costs, long learning curves, poor documentation, and/or low productivity on current products. These might be translated into relative performance and preference goals relating to increased ease of learning/training and increased ease of use as compared to existing and competitive products.

In an example from an internal development organization, one client organization told me the purpose of a certain development effort was to increase the volume of customer service transactions handled daily by 10 percent without increasing the current level of customer service staff. Because current volumes of transactions were known, this could easily be translated directly into an absolute, ease-of-use, performance goal for a representative transaction on a new customer service application.

④ **Identify and draft qualitative usability goals.** Study in the first three steps will reveal a number of qualitative usability goals. Write drafts of these goals as you find them during the first three steps. You will document them more thoroughly in step 7.

⑤ **Prioritize usability goals.** The User Profile, the Contextual Task Analysis, and the basic business goals will all help identify important and useful usability goals to include. They also lend insight into which usability goals are most important to the overall success of the project, which are only somewhat important, and which would be nice to achieve but are not crucial. As noted earlier, it is easy to enumerate a long list of generic and specific usability goals for a project but often very difficult to achieve them all. Product development teams need to come up with priority classifications that work for them. Here is one possible priority classification:

1 = Required for release
2 = Important if not excessively expensive or time consuming to achieve
3 = Desirable but only if low cost

For example, a User Profile and Contextual Task Analysis might suggest that both ease of learning and ease of use are important to different subsets of users. But one subset of users might be more important than another, or there might simply be more of them, and so both types of goals should be included but might be prioritized accordingly.

⑥ Formulate quantitative usability goals. Some qualitative goals identified in step 4 will lend themselves to quantification, and some will not. For example, a goal relating to general productivity (i.e., ease of use) can usually be quantified by defining a specific user task and then quantifying hoped-for performance on that task. But a goal regarding support for an interrupt-driven work environment by providing plenty of on-screen context information is, while not impossible, somewhat harder to quantify.

In this step, you identify those goals from step 4 that are relatively high in priority *and* seem easily quantifiable. Then you select specific tasks that represent them and formulate quantified goals. For example:

◆ After performing their first five address changes, users should, on average, be able to navigate to the correct screen and perform a typical address change in no more than thirty seconds.

Common measures used in quantified usability goals include

◆ Average *expert time* to perform a benchmark task or set of tasks
◆ Average number of *expert errors* in performing a benchmark task or set of tasks
◆ Average number of *expert keystrokes* to perform a benchmark task or set of tasks
◆ Average *novice time* to learn a benchmark task or set of tasks
◆ Average *novice trials* to learn a benchmark task or set of tasks
◆ Average number of *novice errors* in learning a benchmark task or set of tasks
◆ Average *novice satisfaction rating* for ease of learning
◆ Average *expert satisfaction rating* for ease of use

❼ **Document prioritized usability goals.** Both qualitative and quantitative usability goals should always be documented (ultimately, in the product Style Guide—see Chapter 14) and distributed to all team members. The relative priority of different goals should be clearly indicated. Designers should refer to them constantly during design and testing tasks. For samples of documented and prioritized usability goals, see the Sample Work Products and Templates section later in this chapter.

❽ **Conduct user/management review.** Ideally, users and management have been involved in all the steps so far. At the very least, usability goals formulated and documented as described above should be reviewed with project management—and with user management in the case of internal development organizations—to achieve consensus and buy-in. Establishing universal commitment to usability goals at the management level early in the development lifecycle can go a long way towards staying on track on the Usability Engineering Lifecycle down the road (see, e.g., Comstock and Duane 1996).

I have too often conducted usability tests and found serious usability flaws in the middle of a project, only to be told that it was too late to make changes. If usability goals are endorsed as minimum acceptance criteria up front by project and user management, and *then* usability testing reveals that those goals have not been met, it is likely that time and budget will be found to continue the iterative design/test cycle until the goals are met. When no goals are established up front (or when usability experts form goals but fail to get user and management commitment to them), it is too easy to point to the schedule and budget and decide that it is too late to fix things.

❾ **Establish benchmark data for relative quantitative goals.** When you choose to cast a usability goal as relative rather than absolute, you must establish benchmark data on the product or process to which the new product will be compared. For instance, if you have identified as a usability goal that first-time users of a new on-line service must be able to subscribe and log in faster and with fewer errors than they can on any of the top three competing on-line services, you must measure user performance on this task on each of the three competing products to identify the performance level you have to beat.

Establishing benchmarks is accomplished with a method virtually identical to running a usability test (see Chapters 10, 13, and 16). It is fairly labor intensive and should not be done until management has approved the usability goals.

LEVEL OF EFFORT

Table 4.1 gives a sample level of effort for the Usability Goal Setting task. The work effort will vary widely depending on the complexity of the product. This sample represents a moderately complex product and includes the benchmarking step, which is costly and not always necessary.

Table 4.1
Level of effort—Usability Goal Setting

Usability Time		User/Management Time	
Step	Hrs	Step	Hrs
Refer to User Profile	6		
Refer to Contextural Task Analysis	6		
Research business goals	12	Research business goals	6
Draft qualitative goals	12		
Formulate quantitative goals	6		
Prioritize usability goals	6		
Document prioritized goals	24		
User/management review	8	User/management review	16
Establish benchmark data	90	Establish benchmark data	24
Total	170	Total	46

ALTERNATIVE TECHNIQUES— A REVIEW

Usability Goal Setting is a fairly straightforward task. I have not encountered in the literature any approaches that vary significantly from the one described here.

SHORTCUTS

On simple projects small in scope, or on projects in which you have come on board late or where resources are scarce, it's still important to establish usability goals to guide design and testing. Nevertheless, acceptable short-cuts in these situations include less extensive research to determine goals and less formal documentation of goals. You could make good handwritten notes to yourself, get management buy-in on goals through a face-to-face meeting, and then develop qualitative goals further just before beginning design tasks and quantitative goals more thoroughly during the appropriate usability evaluation task. Establishing benchmark data for relative goals can be time consuming, so focus on absolute goals instead to save time.

WEB NOTES

In many cases when designing Web sites or applications, ease-of-learning/ remembering goals will be more important than ease-of-use goals, due to the infrequency of use. Many users will not visit a given Web site daily, and many often visit a site only once. Ease of navigation and maintaining context will usually be very important qualitative goals for Web sites and applications.

With Web sites or applications, ease-of-learning goals are often more important than ease-of-use goals

Web designers need to be aware when formulating quantitative performance goals that system response time will limit and impact user performance, and system response time will vary enormously depending on the users' platforms. In many cases of Web site or application design, relative quantitative goals may be appropriate (e.g., it must take no longer to make travel reservations on the Web site than it does with a travel agent by phone).

SAMPLE WORK PRODUCTS AND TEMPLATES

This section offers samples of what usability goals might look like and a template for quantitative usability goals. The following tools and templates are included:

◆ Sample Qualitative Goals
◆ Quantitative Goals Template
◆ Quantitative Goals Template with Sample Data

SAMPLE QUALITATIVE GOALS

The sample goals described here are adapted from those for a project developing a property management application to be used in a metropolitan police department. In reading them, note that the text in italics highlights the User Profile and Contextual Task Analysis data from which they were drawn.

Stationhouse Usability Goals

Support Task Interruptions

In the *noisy, stressful, and distracting work environment* in a typical police station, users will *frequently be interrupted* while performing property management tasks, sometimes by other competing tasks, sometimes by unexpected events, unpredictable prisoners, and so on. The user interface must constantly maintain enough context on the screen so that when users' attention is temporarily drawn away from their property management tasks, they can reorient quickly, and continue their task without errors and without having to back up or repeat any work.

Structure Work Tasks and Guide the User through Them

Because of the *extreme infrequency of use* and the *extreme complexity of the tasks*, the user interface should not require that users remember the correct sequences of steps to complete a property entry task. Instead, it should

- Allow users to define and stay focused on their immediate task goal (e.g., complete a property entry task)
- Guide users through tasks correctly and completely, based on minimal task/goal definitions provided by the users and relying minimally on user knowledge and memory
- Provide lots of support for users to remember and follow required policies and procedures

Provide Information Views Tailored to Specific Users and Tasks

This interface should avoid the common practice of providing general displays that, in theory, support many users and tasks. Users in the police station work environment have *minimal cognitive resources available* to perform property management tasks, due to the *distracting environment* and *demanding and multiple roles* they are playing. This means the application itself must do as much of the information processing as possible, leaving as little as possible up to the user. One way to do this is to tailor different views of information to optimize the performance of specific users performing specific tasks. For example, police officers, station commanders, and property clerks might all require different views of a property invoice.

QUANTITATIVE GOALS TEMPLATE

The following template can be used to record quantitative usability goals.
You would fill in only those fields relevant to a particular goal.

Usability Goals

Goal #: _____

Task: _____

Operational Definitions
Expert: _____
Novice: _____
Learn: _____
Satisfaction: _____

Priority Definitions
1 = _____
2 = _____
3 = _____

Ease-of-Learning Goals

Priority	Measure	Goal
	Novice Time	
	Novice Trials	
	Novice Errors	

Ease-of-Use Goals

Priority	Measure	Goal
	Expert Time	
	Expert Errors	

Satisfaction Goals

Priority	Measure	Goal
	Expert	
	Novice	

QUANTITATIVE GOALS TEMPLATE WITH SAMPLE DATA

The following template is filled in with sample data describing several types of usability goals for the user interface to a log-on procedure to an application.

Usability Goals

Goal #: __1__

Task: __Log on with security__

Ease-of-Learning Goals

Priority	Measure	Goal
	Novice Time	
1	Novice Trials	3
	Novice Errors	

Operational Definitions

Expert: __Third trial__
Novice: __First two trials__
Learn: __Error-free performance__
Satisfaction: __1=very unsatisfactory__
__4=neutral, 7=very satisfactory__

Ease-of-Use Goals

Priority	Measure	Goal
1	Expert Time	≤ 7 sec.
1	Expert Errors	0

Priority Definitions

1 = __Required for release__
2 = __Important if not too ##__
3 = __Desirable if easy__

Satisfaction Goals

Priority	Measure	Goal
3	Expert	6
3	Novice	5

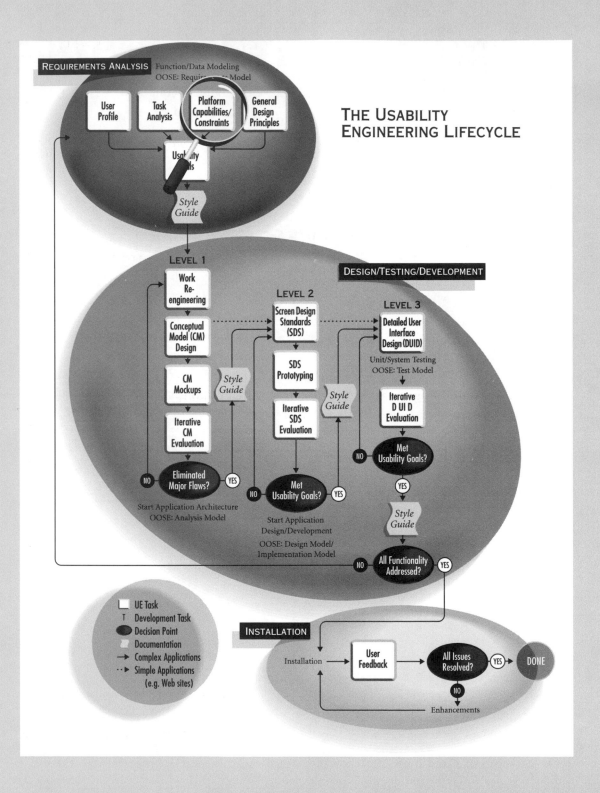

THE USABILITY
ENGINEERING LIFECYCLE

5

Platform Capabilities and Constraints

PURPOSE

The purpose of the task discussed in this chapter is to define the user interface–related capabilities and constraints of the hardware and software platform for a product. The hardware and software platform places a whole set of constraints on user interface design options. Obviously, User Interface Designers need to know what design options are and are not available to them before they start designing. In addition, they need to distinguish between user interface capabilities that are possible but not easy, and those that are specifically facilitated by chosen development tools. Sometimes approaches to user interface design are technically possible, but not justifiable given development and maintenance costs.

Many User Interface Designers are company employees who are developing software for users in typical office environments. A majority of them are designing for the current Microsoft Windows platform, which is already installed on the workstations of all users who will use their software. For these designers, defining the platform capabilities and constraints for a new application is straightforward: the platform is Windows, and they are already quite familiar with the Windows user interface standards, capabilities, and constraints. There is no need to research and formally document platform capabilities and constraints.

Each time a new version of Windows comes out, however, this task becomes relevant again, as designers must get up to speed on what new user interface standards, capabilities, and constraints are introduced by

The hardware and software platform places a set of constraints on user interface design options

145

*Even if the basic
platform is a
familiar version of
Microsoft Windows,
designers must also
be familiar with
relevant secondary
tools and platforms
that may impact
the use of Windows
capabilities*

the revised platform. Even so, Windows usually comes with fairly good documentation of user interface standards, so reviewing this documentation is often all that is required.

On the other hand, even if the basic platform is Windows, and designers are familiar with the current version, they must also be familiar with other relevant secondary tools and platforms that may impact the use of basic Windows capabilities and constraints. For example, two Windows development projects building with two different development tools (e.g., Visual Basic and PowerBuilder), may have slightly different capabilities and constraints. These types of development tools usually further constrain the Windows platform, rather than add capabilities to it. In addition, even when the operating system is Windows, if you are building an application based on another basic tool, such as a database package, do not assume that all Windows capabilities and standards will apply. You must research and understand the specific capabilities and constraints of these additional tools.

Finally, as hardware evolves, new user interface capabilities are introduced, such as multitasking, better response times, and greater modem speed and bandwidth. Designers must keep up with these changes and their implications in order to take advantage of new and more powerful user interface capabilities.

For other designers, the Platform Capabilities and Constraints task becomes more formal and more important. As an independent consultant, for example, I often work on projects where the platform is Windows, but I also work on projects with specialized platforms that I have never encountered before, usually much more constrained than today's GUI platforms. I have worked on several different kinds of computer-based factory equipment, including manufacturing robots and product testing equipment, and also on medical and scientific equipment, such as medical monitors and data collection instruments. Software applications for these products must be designed around the constraints of unique hardware, unique operating systems, and unique development tools. When I come in as a consultant, I usually know nothing about these platforms, which makes this task indispensable. Often the platforms are very constrained, with small, text-only, monochrome displays, limited memory and processing speed, and little in the way of development tools.

Even designers who are full-time employees working within, say, the medical or manufacturing industry do not have the advantage of such universal platforms and standards as do those who design and develop basic business software for Windows. Designers working in these industries may find they must learn very different platforms if they change companies or even if they simply move between product divisions within a single company. There simply are no universal hardware or software platforms with user interface standards in these industries.

Thus, there will always be cases in which designers find themselves about to design for a software application that will be based on a hardware and software platform they know little or nothing about. In these cases, the designer needs to recognize this task in the Usability Engineering Lifecycle, budget time and money for it, and be sure it is carried out. If designers are familiar with the capabilities and constraints of the predetermined hardware and software platform(s), they can avoid pursuing design directions that are neither feasible nor cost effective.

DESCRIPTION

There are many platform constraints and capabilities that will define the scope of product user interface possibilities. Rather than enumerating them all, I offer a list of sample capabilities/constraints, ranging from the most basic to the more specific. Remember that some capabilities may be possible but expensive in terms of development and maintenance time.

- ◆ Display size (e.g., 1 line by 72 characters versus 17-inch diagonal display)
- ◆ Bit-mapped versus character-based display
- ◆ Color (and number of colors) versus monochrome display
- ◆ Input devices (keyboard, mouse, joystick, trackball, touchscreen, etc.)
- ◆ System speed (in MHz)
- ◆ Modem speed
- ◆ Windowing or not
- ◆ Independently controllable/updatable window panes or not
- ◆ Multitasking or not
- ◆ Special effects (3-D, reverse video, blinking, video, animation, sound, etc.)
- ◆ GUI control tool set (list boxes, tabled list boxes; single-line input fields, multiline input fields, etc.)

Designers working in some industries may find they must learn very different platforms if they change companies or even move between product divisions within a company

There will be cases in which you are basing an application on an unfamiliar hardware and software platform, so be sure to recognize this lifecycle task, budget time and money for it, and be sure it is carried out

Whenever designers doubt the feasibility of a design direction, they should meet with developers before they spend too much time following that design direction

Usually, at this point in the Usability Engineering Lifecycle, you would gather capabilities and constraints at the level of those listed as examples above. Much more specific capabilities and constraints may come up later during the different levels of the design process. Designers need to keep in close touch with developers to make sure their user interface designs can be implemented easily and cost effectively on the chosen platform. Whenever designers are in doubt about a design direction, they should meet with developers to determine its feasibility. Answering most feasibility questions up front before starting design will save time in the design process later.

Some of you may question my placement of this task in the overall Usability Engineering Lifecycle. Surely, hardware and software platforms should be selected after software design. Indeed, in an ideal world the appropriate way to proceed would be first to research user requirements, then design a software user interface that would optimally meet those requirements, and only then select a hardware and software platform that would support and facilitate the development of that software user interface. This would indeed optimize the user interface; unfortunately, even if you could make a strong cost-justification case that this would be the right thing to do, this simply would not fly for organizational and/or political reasons. And in many cases, the cost cannot be justified, because intended users already have platforms on their desks running many other applications that they use and need.

My placement of this task in the overall Usability Engineering Lifecycle reflects this fact of life—in most cases, software under development must, for practical and/or political reasons, run on existing platforms. All we can do as User Interface Designers is take into account the user interface–related capabilities and constraints of the existing platform and treat them as just another requirement that must be juggled along with user characteristics, task characteristics, market forces, budgets, schedules, and so on.

In my thirteen-plus years of consulting, I have experienced only two cases where hardware and software platforms were chosen on the basis of software user interface requirements (see the War Story in this section). This is why I do not describe a general Usability Engineering Lifecycle in which application user interface design drives hardware and software platform design. Instead, I offer a process that assumes application user interface design will be constrained by previously made choices of hardware and software platforms.

W A R   S T O R Y

WHEN THE HARDWARE
IS THE PROBLEM

I have had that rare experience in my consulting practice in which I convinced a client to radically alter their hardware and software platform to accommodate the application user interface requirements. The product under development was a new version of a software application that ran on a hardware product already in the marketplace—a robot used in manufacturing plants. The robot itself participated in an assembly-line process, and the software allowed users whose job it was to monitor the largely automated manufacturing process to set operating parameters for the robot and troubleshoot when problems arose. Problems could in fact arise in several different components of the robot and other equipment interfacing with the robot. During operation the robot collected data that could be reviewed to pinpoint the source of any malfunctions.

My client brought me in to address complaints from customers and users about how difficult it was to learn and use the robot software. In fact, the software was in turn severely limited by the hardware platform, which provided a one-line, text-only, monochrome display area. Through this tiny peephole, users had to navigate through and interpret large amounts of abstract, numerical data to pinpoint the source of malfunctions or even just inefficient operation. Because the software was so difficult to learn and use, users tended to troubleshoot inefficient operation by trial and error, resetting operating parame-

ters each time and wasting manufacturing materials in the process. My client was hoping I could provide them with insights into how to make the software easier to understand and use.

I spent three days with my client management and project team trying to understand their product and its software user interface. Well into the third day, I was still confused and had developed no clear mental model of what the product did or how to use it through the software user interface. To their credit, my client began to see that if a professional, experienced consultant could not understand their software, they couldn't reasonably expect hourly wage workers with no more than a high school education and zero computer literacy to understand it.

Throughout our discussion about their product, they explained the tedious navigation through lots of numerical data that was required for the user to determine something simple, such as that a particular hose was plugged up or that a container was out of material. I found myself asking them repeatedly: "Why can't the system know that and simply tell the user? Why does the user have to do the analysis to figure that out; why can't the computer do the analysis for them?" After hearing that enough times, it began to dawn on my client that, in fact, this was entirely possible. But it would require building new intelligence into their hardware and also providing a very different sort of output device than their current one-line display. In the end, we all concluded that there was no way to significantly

cont. next page

cont. from previous

improve their software user interface without radically changing their hardware platform. They then decided not to proceed with my help to change their software, but instead to go back and completely rethink their hardware. I had succeeded in one way, but a potential project had failed to materialize!

However, a year later I heard from them again. They had fixed the hardware and were now ready for my input on their hardware and software user interface design. Part of the interface I designed was an LED display on the robot itself, which presented a schematic of the robot and all its components plus some crucial interfacing equipment. When a malfunction occurred or the robot began operating outside optimal ranges, lights on the schematic pinpointed the location of the problem. Then a small screen (although larger than their original one-liner) allowed users to access more specific data about the identified problem that helped them solve it.

In the end, user requirements defined the type of user interface that would improve performance, and the hardware and software platform was adapted to allow that software user interface. About six months after the new product was introduced to the market, my client wrote to thank me for my input and let me know that the product was selling much better than the earlier one and that customers and users had given it rave reviews.

In another example from my consulting practice, I was hired to perform a cost-benefit analysis to determine whether replacing a large number of older, character-based dumb terminals already on users' desks with modern, bit-mapped, intelligent workstations would pay off. My analysis showed that the cost of replacing 1,500 workstations could clearly be justified in a fairly short time by the bottom-line value of increased user productivity, decreased training costs, decreased user support costs, and other usability benefits achieved from adopting a higher-end workstation. Again, user requirements drove software user interface design requirements, which in turn drove the choice of hardware and software platform.

SCHEDULING AND INTEGRATION WITH OTHER TASKS

The Platform Capabilities and Constraints task fits into the overall Usability Engineering Lifecycle in the following ways:

◆ This task can be performed anytime before the beginning of the design process in the Design/Testing/Development phase. It is independent of any other Requirements Analysis tasks.

◆ If there are multiple platforms, and/or designers are unfamiliar with their capabilities and constraints, results of this task should be documented in the product Style Guide, where they will serve as context and also rationale for design.

◆ User interface design capabilities and constraints identified in this task feed directly into all user interface design tasks (the Conceptual Model Design, the Screen Design Standards, and the Detailed User Interface Design) by defining the scope of possibilities for these design issues.

◆ Prototyping tools used in the design process (during Conceptual Model Mock-ups and Screen Design Standards Prototyping) must be chosen to adequately simulate the capabilities and constraints of the ultimate hardware and software platform.

The Platform Capabilities and Constraints task fits into the underlying software development methodology in the following ways:

◆ This task can occur anytime after the choice of platforms is made but must occur before development of the Analysis Model in the Analysis phase of OOSE (or the application architecture design in a traditional rapid prototyping methodology), which in turn is driven in part by user interface design decisions premised on the results of the Platform Capabilities and Constraints task.

ROLES AND RESOURCES

In the Platform Capabilities and Constraints task, the usability roles might participate as follows:

Task leader: The User Interface Designer should take the lead role in this task.

Other resources: Usability Engineers can assist in this task by providing already documented platform capabilities and constraints if they have been prepared for previous projects, or by helping a User Interface Designer inexperienced in this task to structure the task and documentation. Technical staff will need to be consulted to identify platforms, to clarify capabilities and constraints, and to validate documented findings.

SAMPLE TECHNIQUE— A STEP-BY-STEP PROCEDURE

Step 1 should always be performed for this task, but all subsequent steps are necessary only if more than one platform is identified and/or if all User Interface Designers are not already familiar with the user interface–related constraints and capabilities of the platform(s).

❶ **Identify all relevant aspects of all hardware and software platforms.** Interview project management and technical staff to identify platforms. There may be a single platform or multiple platforms. Workstations (including input devices), operating systems, and development tools all need to be identified. All parts of the platform introduce constraints and capabilities.

❷ **Review any platform documentation.** Some platform components come with documentation of user interface standards, or at least user interface tools and capabilities. If any exist, read them to gain a basic understanding of user interface–related platform constraints and capabilities.

❸ **Interview technical staff.** For further clarification, identify appropriate technical staff, interview them, and ask questions about user interface–related platform constraints and capabilities.

❹ **Document Platform Capabilities and Constraints.** This is not important when designers are already familiar with a platform. However, it becomes particularly important if multiple designers are assigned to the project and not all of them are familiar with the platform, and/or if there are multiple platforms with different capabilities and constraints. In the latter case, specifically identifying commonalities and differences between platforms will help you take advantage of commonalities and formulate strategies for dealing with differences. As much user interface consistency as possible across platforms (while maintaining consistency *within* platforms) is desirable, both to accommodate users and to streamline development and maintenance. Where capabilities and constraints differ significantly, approaches to interface design should still maximize similarity as much as possible.

One exception to this rule is that when platforms differ widely in *basic* capabilities, it is not necessarily optimal to design for the lowest common denominator. To give an extreme example, if some users have dumb terminals, while others have intelligent workstations, you obviously would not design an interface based on the dumb terminals, ignoring the capabilities of the higher-end workstations to achieve across-platform consistency. When differences between platforms are this extreme, the best course is to design two different interfaces, each taking maximum advantage of capabilities, and incorporate similarities between the interfaces wherever possible.

But when, for example, you have two different platforms with subtly different capabilities and constraints—such as Windows 3.1 and Windows 95, or Windows 95 and OS/2, or Windows 95 and Macintosh—maximizing consistency and similarity (without violating within-platform standards) is desirable. To achieve this, you need to study in detail the capabilities and constraints of all platforms. Documentation specifically identifying similarities and differences between the platforms will facilitate the design process.

W A R   S T O R Y

UNDERSTAND YOUR PLATFORM CONSTRAINTS

I once encountered an interesting case highlighting the importance of understanding platform capabilities and constraints when dealing with multiple platforms. A client had an existing product installed at a customer site, and they were updating the product based on a new version of the database platform. In addition, they were implementing the same product on an intranet, tied into the same database but presented through a browser-based user interface. Users were expected to use the intranet version while out in the field and the PC-based version while in the home office. In this case, we had to compare the user interface capabilities and constraints of a traditional software platform with a browser platform and create commonalities where we could. We approached this by setting up a common navigational structure (i.e., Reengineered Task Organization Model—see Chapter 7) and then creating similar Conceptual Model Designs (see Chapter 8) that followed analogous sets of design rules but used different controls based on the differing platform standards and capabilities.

❺ Validate documented Platform Capabilities and Constraints. To validate the documented Platform Capabilities and Constraints, you simply need feedback from appropriate technical staff. Probably the best way to do this is to distribute the documentation to appropriate technical staff for review, and then hold a meeting to discuss their feedback. Then make changes as necessary to the documentation to finalize it.

LEVEL OF EFFORT

Table 5.1 gives a sample level of effort for the Platform Capabilities and Constraints task. The work effort will vary widely depending on the number and complexity of the platforms and designers' and usability experts' familiarity with them. This sample represents a case of a single, relatively simple but unfamiliar platform.

Table 5.1
Level of effort—Platform Capabilities and Constraints

Usability Time		Developer Time	
Step	**Hrs**	**Step**	**Hrs**
Identify HW/SW platform(s)	4	Identify HW/SW platform(s)	4
Review platform documentation	12		
Interview technical staff	6	Interview technical staff	6
Document Platform Capabilities and Constraints	16		
Validate Platform Capabilities and Constraints	6	Validate Platform Capabilities and Constraints	6
Total	44	Total	16

Alternative Techniques— A Review

Establishing Platform Capabilities and Constraints is a straightforward task. I have not encountered in the literature any approaches to it that vary significantly from the one described here.

Shortcuts

In organizations in which a small number of platforms are in use, and designers are already familiar with them, this task can be skipped altogether—it is in effect already done. When resources and schedules are tight, formal documentation can be skipped, but at least informal notes should be prepared and passed around to all designers. More reliance can be placed on constant communication with developers during design to check design ideas against technical feasibility, with less effort spent on upfront establishment and documentation of all capabilities and constraints.

Web Notes

Unlike many other Usability Engineering Lifecycle tasks, the Platform Capabilities and Constraints task will often be more complicated when designing a Web site or application compared with designing traditional software applications. This is because (with the exception of some intranet applications) designers usually have to assume a potentially very large number and wide variety of hardware and software platforms. Internet users' platforms will vary in at least the following ways (see also Forsythe, Grose, and Ratner. 1998 ch. 12, 16):

- Screen size and resolution
- Modem speed
- Browser capabilities vary by vendor and version, for example:
  - controls available through the browser (versus provided within the site or application)
  - browser interpreters (e.g., version of HTML, Java)
  - installed helper applications or plug-ins (e.g., multimedia players)

User Interface Designers for the Web need to design for the expected range of platform capabilities and constraints. For example, one common technique is to have a control at the entry point to a Web site or application that allows users to choose between a graphics mode or text mode. Thus, users with slow modems can turn off any graphics that seriously degrade download time and see an alternative text-only version of the site or application. Similarly, many Web sites or applications that require specific helper applications or plug-ins are now designed to allow immediate downloading and installation of these tools. Unfortunately, the user interface for downloading and installing them is still often not very friendly, but providing the capability is a step in the right direction.

In general, Web designers need to be aware that if they take full advantage of all the latest Web capabilities, many users will find their Web site or application unusable. Care needs to be taken to provide alternative interfaces for users with lower-end platforms.

SAMPLE WORK PRODUCTS AND TEMPLATES

One template is offered here: Platform Capabilities and Constraints Template with Sample Data.

PLATFORM CAPABILITIES AND CONSTRAINTS TEMPLATE WITH SAMPLE DATA

The template records specific capabilities and indicates whether they are present in the platform. Capabilities in the first column are filled in according to what is learned about the platform. Data in the remaining columns indicates exact capabilities and constraints. This example is based on a specialized, simple platform for a piece of manufacturing equipment with a software-based operator user interface.

XYZ Platform Capabilities and Constraints

Platform: XYZ Platform

Capability	Supported	Possible with Effort	Not Possible
Display size	40 characters, 6 lines		
Bit-mapped			X
Color			X
Input devices	Alphanumeric keypad, cursor keypad		
Windowing			X
Multitasking			X
Special effects	Bold, caps, reverse video, straight lines		

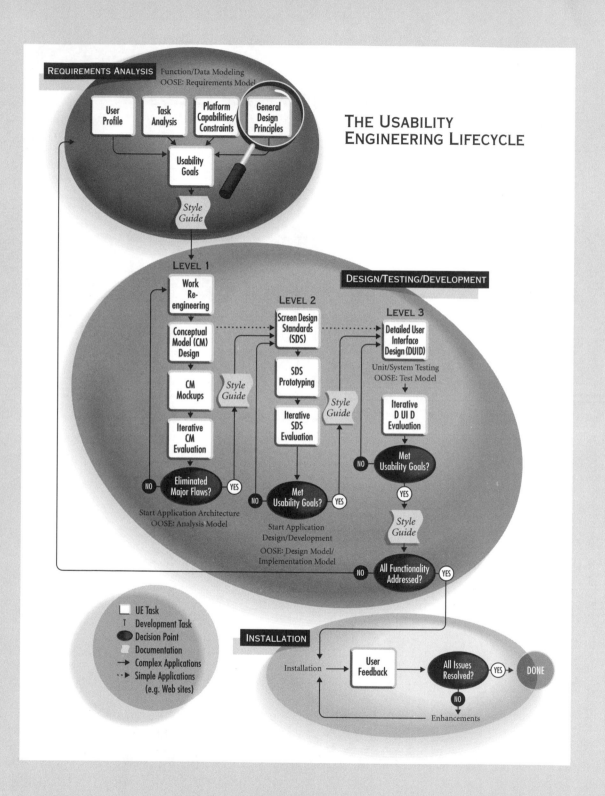

General Design Principles

PURPOSE

The purpose of the General Design Principles task is to identify and review general user interface design principles and guidelines that may be applicable to the design of the product user interface during the Design/Testing/Development phase, which comes next in the Usability Engineering Lifecycle. More than twenty years of research and case studies on software user interface design are documented in the literature. In addition, much of this research has been synthesized into general design principles (see, e.g., Mayhew 1992) that are applicable across a broad range of user, task, and technology platform types.

General design principles are not a substitute for product-specific requirements analyses and iterative usability evaluation. Rather, they work together with requirements analyses to provide guidance for the first pass at design at levels 1, 2, and 3. Then iterative evaluation is employed to validate and refine initial design ideas. When applied together, requirements analyses and general design principles can significantly shorten the iterative cycle of design and evaluation by helping to generate a better first pass at design. For example, one well-known general design principle is to be cautious in the use of color as a fundamental cue (particularly in the use of red and green) if the user population is heavily male. This is because men have a relatively high incidence of color blindness, especially red-green color blindness. You may have your User Profile information regarding gender but not be familiar with this general design principle. Or you may be familiar with this particular design principle but not know how many of your users

General design principles work together with requirements analyses to provide guidance for the first pass at design at levels 1, 2, and 3

159

On projects in which analysis tasks are difficult, you can fall back on general design principles to guide your first pass at design

will be men. You need to combine the User Profile information and the general design principle to achieve optimal design.

On the other hand, when requirements analysis tasks are particularly difficult, you can at least fall back on general design principles to guide your first pass at design. For example, as an outside consultant, I am often called upon to assist in the design process, or provide a Heuristic Evaluation or expert review of a prototype design (see Chapter 10), but simply am not allowed the time and/or budget to conduct user requirements analyses in any detail. In these cases, I fall back on general design principles to guide my design advice. I am willing to do this because I know even advice based only on general design guidelines can make a significant contribution. But I always point out to my clients the value of requirements analysis tasks in the hope that on future projects they will plan the time and budget to perform these tasks.

Recall that, in general, user interface design can be greatly improved and facilitated by four general strategies that summarize the overall Usability Engineering Lifecycle:

- Conducting a thorough requirements analysis
- Applying known general design principles and guidelines
- Approaching user interface design through a structured process
- Employing iterative usability testing

Because much is known about good interface design, it is simply inefficient and ineffective not to tap into this body of knowledge

Gathering and using available and applicable general user interface design principles is a key part of the overall Usability Engineering Lifecycle. Because much is known about good interface design, it is simply inefficient and ineffective *not* to tap into this body of knowledge.

DESCRIPTION

In this task you pull together sources of general design principles that might be relevant to your product, so they are readily available, and you review them so they are fresh in your mind. Potential sources of general design principles are listed here, and specific examples are recommended in the section Sample Technique—A Step-by-Step Procedure later in the chapter.

- High-level Style Guides (e.g., platform, corporate, or product family— see also Chapter 14)
- Books on general user interface design principles and guidelines
- Course materials from classes on user interface design principles

◆ References reporting findings from research studies and case studies on user interface design issues, such as professional journals, professional society publications, conference proceedings, and internal research reports

If there is a centralized Usability Engineering organization within a company, one useful role for this organization is to maintain a library, which could include the types of resources identified above. Such a centralized organization might also be responsible for producing and disseminating high-level Style Guides and for providing courses on general user interface design principles and guidelines. In addition, professional Usability Engineers (see Chapters 1 and 21 for definitions of all Usability Engineering roles) working within a centralized Usability Engineering organization are usually familiar with and up-to-date on user interface design principles and guidelines. They can serve as internal consultants to designers on specific projects. If there is no centralized Usability Engineering organization, it is up to the designers on each project team to find and use sources of general design principles, including outside consultants.

Different general user interface design principles will apply to the different levels of design identified in the Usability Engineering Lifecycle. That is, principles may relate to design issues at the Conceptual Model Design, Screen Design Standards, or Detailed User Interface Design levels. As you read Chapters 8, 11, and 15 on each of those design tasks, it should be clear to you which level of design different guidelines apply to.

SCHEDULING AND INTEGRATION WITH OTHER TASKS

The General Design Principles task fits into the overall Usability Engineering Lifecycle in the following ways:

◆ This task can be conducted anytime during the Requirements Analysis phase of the Usability Engineering Lifecycle. Sources should be pulled together and reviewed before the design tasks in the Design/Testing/Development phase begin.

◆ The sources identified and reviewed in the General Design Principles task will be regularly referred to during each level of design, that is, during the Conceptual Model Design, Screen Design Standards, and Detailed User Interface Design tasks.

- ◆ Results of this task are used in conjunction with all output from the Requirements Analysis tasks to take first passes at design at each level.
- ◆ Unlike most other lifecycle tasks, results of this task are not documented in the product Style Guide.

The General Design Principles task fits into the underlying software development methodology in the following way:

- ◆ This task can occur anytime before development of the Analysis Model in the Analysis phase of OOSE (or the application architecture design in a traditional rapid prototyping methodology), which in turn is driven in part by user interface design decisions.

ROLES AND RESOURCES

In the General Design Principles task, the usability roles might participate as follows:

Task leader: The User Interface Designer should take primary responsibility for gathering and reviewing written resources and for arranging schedules and budgets for the involvement of inside or outside consultants during the design process.

Other resources: If there is a centralized Usability Engineering organization, the Usability Engineers from this organization may provide actual resources, in terms of a library or internal consultants, or they may direct User Interface Designers to resources, including outside consultants.

SAMPLE TECHNIQUE— A STEP-BY-STEP PROCEDURE

The technique offered here consists of two steps in conducting a literature review.

❶ **Review any relevant high-level Style Guides.** The Usability Engineering Lifecycle for the design and development of a particular product involves developing a set of standards, or *product Style Guide*, for that specific product (see Chapter 14). Distinct from this, there may be other higher-level Style Guides previously developed, such as *platform, corporate,* and *product family* Style Guides.

For example, a corporate Style Guide is meant to provide design guidance and "look and feel" standards that will be applied across all products developed within the organization. A corporate Style Guide is much more general than a product Style Guide. It might include some actual standards that should always be followed regardless of the particulars of the product, but standards at this level are usually limited to design techniques that ensure a common corporate "look," such as logos or company colors. Corporate Style Guides more often include general principles and guidelines meant to alert designers to issues that should be addressed and to provide guidance in deciding how to address them, but falling short of dictating particular standards.

If such a corporate Style Guide exists, obtain a copy, review it, and follow it to the extent possible when developing the product Style Guide. It provides yet another source of general design principles and guidelines relevant to the product under development. Platform and product family Style Guides can be consulted for the same purpose.

❷ **Locate and review other resources offering general design principles.** Some specific books and other publications are listed here to get you started. Gather relevant sources and make them accessible to all designers during the Design/Testing/Development phase that comes next.

- ◆ Books on general user interface design principles and guidelines:
  - *The Design of Everyday Things,* by Donald Norman
  - *Designing User Interfaces for International Use,* by Jakob Nielsen
  - *Developing User Interfaces,* by Deborah Hix and H. Rex Hartson
  - *Envisioning Information* and *Visual Explanations,* by Edward Tufte
  - *The Essential Guide to User Interface Design: An Introduction to GUI Design Principles and Techniques,* by Wilbert Galitz
  - *The GUI Style Guide,* by Susan Fowler and Victor Stanwick
  - *The Icon Book,* by William Horton
  - *Principles and Guidelines in Software User Interface Design,* by Deborah J. Mayhew
  - *Readings in Human-Computer Interaction: Towards the Year 2000,* edited by Ronald Baecker, Jonathan Grudin, William Buxton, and Saul Greenberg

- ◆ Professional journals:
  - *Human Factors* (Human Factors and Ergonomics Society)
  - *Behaviour and Information Technology* (Taylor & Francis)

- *Interacting with Computers* (Lawrence Erlbaum Associates Publishers)
- *Human-Computer Interaction* (Butterworth-Heinemann)

◆ Professional society publications:
  - *Interactions* (ACM SIGCHI)
  - *Ergonomics in Design* (Human Factors and Ergonomics Society)
  - *Common Ground* (Usability Professionals' Association)
  - SIGCHI Bulletin (ACM SIGCHI)

◆ Conference proceedings:
  - ACM SIGCHI Annual Conference
  - Human Factors and Ergonomics Annual Meeting
  - Interact (annual conference sponsored by IFIP)
  - Annual conference of the Usability Professionals' Association

◆ Other general resources:
  - Course materials
  - Internal research reports

In addition, designers should consider and arrange for inside and/or outside Usability Engineering consultants to be available as sources of general design guidelines during the design process.

LEVEL OF EFFORT

Table 6.1 gives a sample level of effort for the General Design Principles task. The work effort will vary widely depending on how familiar designers already are with user interface design principles and guidelines, and what resources are readily available. The table represents a relatively simple situation in which there is already a corporate Style Guide, there is a centralized Usability Engineering organization with a well-stocked, organized library of resources available to designers, and designers are already somewhat familiar with user interface design principles and guidelines.

Table 6.1
Level of effort—General Design Principles

Usability Time

Step	Hrs
Identify/review high-level Style Guides	12
Locate/review other resources	16
Total	28

ALTERNATIVE TECHNIQUES— A REVIEW

An interesting experimental automated tool for incorporating general guidelines in design is described in Malinowski and Nakakoji (1995). They embedded a knowledge database of design guidelines into a development environment for a particular application. When designers were working on the interface with the development tool, the knowledge base interrupted to point out a violation of a user interface design guideline (e.g., menu items should be ordered consistently across different invocations of the menu). Designers could consider the advice and choose to ignore it or conform to the noted guideline by changing their design. If they ignored it, they were provided with a mechanism for capturing their design rationale, so violations of guidelines were consciously made and justified in a permanent record.

It is hard to judge this tool from just reading about it, but the idea of incorporating general user interface design guidelines into design and development tools seems promising. Nichols and Ritter (1995) also report building an automated design tool that incorporates known user interface design guidelines. Their tool generates aliases for command language command names, based on well-researched guidelines for command language design. Their tool also assesses the resulting set of command aliases by subjecting them to a model of human performance called the keystroke model (Card et al. 1983). Although an interesting idea, their tool is limited

Although there have been a number of attempts to automate the incorporation of general user interface design principles into design, no generally applicable, validated, and usable tool has yet emerged

to supporting this one very simple aspect of user interface design and thus is not generally applicable for supporting designers.

A number of attempts to automate the incorporation of general user interface design principles into design have been reported in the literature over the years, but no generally applicable, validated, and truly usable tool has yet emerged. For the time being, we are left with the "low-fidelity" technique of acquiring a knowledge base of usability guidelines in the traditional way through the literature, or by hiring someone who already has this knowledge to be a part of the design team.

SHORTCUTS

To cut this task short, simply limit the scope of gathering and reviewing available literature. Other shortcuts are to hire temporary user interface design consultants who can either provide design guidance based on knowledge of established design principles and guidelines or offer courses on user interface design to project teams as they start the design phase of projects.

WEB NOTES

Most general software user interface design principles and guidelines will be directly applicable to Web site and application design, but bear in mind some things that make designing for the Web a little different:

◆ Response times are slower and less predictable on the Web, limiting what design techniques are practical.

◆ There are no existing user interface standards for the Web.

◆ Browsers and users, rather than designers and developers, control much of the appearance of Web content.

◆ Web users are mainly discretionary and infrequent, increasing the need for "walk up and use" interfaces.

◆ The Web is a huge and fluid space with fuzzy boundaries between sites. There is thus an increased need for navigational support and a "sense of place."

These differences are not quantitative, but a matter of degree. Currently, Web platforms simply place more constraints on designers than do traditional platforms. Designing for the Web is somewhat like designing for traditional software twenty years ago.

SAMPLE WORK PRODUCTS AND TEMPLATES

Rather than offer samples here, I refer you to the references for this chapter at the end of the book. Also, sample design principles and guidelines are given in the chapters on design—Chapters 8, 11, and 15.

II

Design/Testing/Development

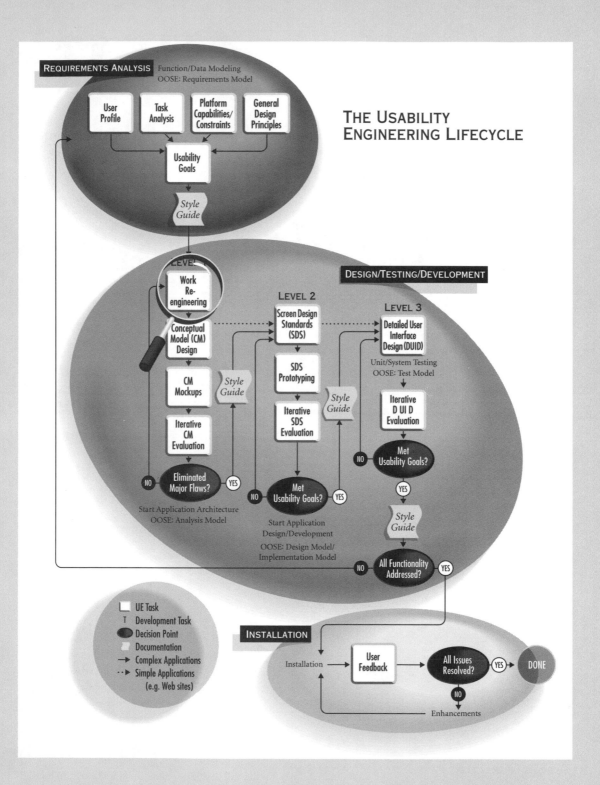

THE USABILITY
ENGINEERING LIFECYCLE

REQUIREMENTS ANALYSIS Function/Data Modeling
OOSE: Requirements Model

User Profile
Task Analysis
Platform Capabilities/ Constraints
General Design Principles

Usability Goals

Style Guide

LEVEL

DESIGN/TESTING/DEVELOPMENT

Work Re-engineering

LEVEL 2

LEVEL 3

Conceptual Model (CM) Design

Screen Design Standards (SDS)

Detailed User Interface Design (DUID)

Unit/System Testing
OOSE: Test Model

CM Mockups

Style Guide

SDS Prototyping

Style Guide

Iterative D UI D Evaluation

Iterative CM Evaluation

Iterative SDS Evaluation

NO

Met Usability Goals?

NO

Eliminated Major Flaws?

YES

NO

Met Usability Goals?

YES

YES

Start Application Architecture
OOSE: Analysis Model

Start Application Design/Development
OOSE: Design Model/ Implementation Model

Style Guide

NO

All Functionality Addressed?

YES

UE Task
T Development Task
Decision Point
Documentation
→ Complex Applications
‥▶ Simple Applications (e.g. Web sites)

INSTALLATION

Installation → User Feedback → All Issues Resolved? → YES → DONE

NO

Enhancements

7

Work Reengineering

PURPOSE

In a previous task, Contextual Task Analysis, you obtained several models of how users as a group *currently* think about, do, and talk about the work you are automating. First, you extracted a Current User Task Organization, which described how users organize all their low-level tasks. This model is most often a hierarchy, but can take other forms (see Chapter 3). The model includes terminology that users currently use to name tasks and task groupings. You also obtained Task Scenarios describing actual procedures for accomplishing tasks as they are currently done. If your project is following the OOSE methodology, at this point you also have a collection of documented Use Cases, formulated by consolidating data from individual Task Scenarios, which describe generalized procedures for tasks as they are currently done. These models correspond roughly to the development of the Requirements Model in the Analysis phase of OOSE (see Jacobson et al. 1992, 156–74), and you will recall the parallels between OOSE concepts (Actors and Use Cases) and Usability Engineering concepts (user categories and Task Scenarios).

It is important to understand here that the purpose of the Contextual Task Analysis is not to understand current work practice so as to simply mimic it in product design. In the words of Button and Dourish (1996), you want to ". . . align system design not so much with the details of *specific working practices*, as with the details of the *means by which such working practices arise and are constituted*."

The Contextual Task Analysis identifies the underlying goals of users' work practices, the general task organization and sequence models through which they work, and the work environment—all elements that will inform and direct your design efforts

You conduct the Contextual Task Analysis to understand the underlying goals of users' work practices and procedures, the general task organization and task sequence models through which they understand and carry out their work tasks, the physical and sociocultural environment in which they conduct their work, and so on. These things do not dictate design; rather they inform and direct your design efforts, including Work Reengineering. Thus, your first real step in the design process is to "reengineer" these current user work models. This task corresponds roughly to the development of the Analysis Model during the Analysis phase in OOSE (see Jacobson et al. 1992, 174–200).

The purpose of reengineering current work models is to meet the following goals:

1. Realizing the power and efficiency that automation makes possible
2. Reengineering work to more effectively support business goals
3. Minimizing retraining by having the new product tap as much as possible into users' existing task knowledge, and maximizing efficiency and effectiveness by accommodating human cognitive constraints and capabilities within the context of their actual tasks

General business goals were translated into usability goals in the Usability Goal Setting task and will now directly drive Work Reengineering

Recall that general business goals were translated into explicit usability goals in the Usability Goal Setting task (see Chapter 4). These usability goals will now directly drive the work model reengineering that is the focus of this task.

Traditionally in software development methods (and to some extent also in OOSE), the focus is on the first goal listed above, and some of the second goal and most of the third are lost, because designers never thoroughly understand the current work. A great deal of work reengineering occurs in software design, and only some of it serves the first two goals. Much of it is unnecessary and results in training and usage burdens on the user. In the words of Button and Dourish (1996):

> . . . the introduction of technology designed to support "large-scale" activities while fundamentally transforming the "small-scale" detail of action can systematically undermine exactly the detailed features of working practice through which the "large-scale" activity is, in fact, accomplished.

At this point in the whole Usability Engineering Lifecycle, you have not only a clear understanding of how users currently think and work but also much insight into the usability requirements the work environment and user analyses demand from your product. So you can factor the third goal in with the first two in a more balanced fashion. Starting with the Current User Task Organization Model, and the Task Scenarios and Use Cases, you make changes only where necessary to specifically achieve goals 1 and 2. You end up with a Reengineered Task Organization Model and Reengineered Task Sequence Models.

The reengineered work models then become the basis for your user interface design. In particular, the Reengineered Task Organization Model provides the first piece of your "user interface architecture," which as a whole includes an underlying organizational and navigational structure (the Reengineered Task Organization Model), plus a set of conventions regarding the presentation of that structure (the Conceptual Model Design). The Reengineered Task Sequence Models will define the underlying flow upon which the Detailed User Interface Design for specific tasks will be based.

Note that the Reengineered Task Organization Model and Reengineered Task Sequence Models, although they are certainly an aspect of design, are not, strictly speaking, user interface design. Note that for any single Reengineered Task Organization Model, there are an infinite number of possible Conceptual Model Designs, or *visual* presentations of the functionality organized in the Reengineered Task Organization Model. Getting the Reengineered Task Organization Model right is key, and separating it from Conceptual Model Design will greatly facilitate the overall design process by untangling the issues of organization and presentation. This distinction will become clearer through examples given in Chapter 8. Also, this distinction corresponds roughly to the distinction in OOSE between the Analysis Model, which is platform/implementation independent, and the Design Model, which assumes particular platforms, tools, and implementation approaches. Similarly, the reengineered work models are independent of any particular interface approach, such as GUIs, voice interfaces, and character-based interfaces, while the user interface design assumes a particular interaction style and specifies how its components are used to present the underlying reengineered work models.

Getting the Reengineered Task Organization Model right is key

DESCRIPTION

In the Work Reengineering task, you perform the following basic steps:

◆ Reengineer the Current User Task Organization Model and the Task Scenarios and Use Cases.
◆ Validate and refine the Reengineered Task Organization Model and the Reengineered Task Sequence Models.
◆ Document the Reengineered Task Organization Model and the Reengineered Task Sequence Models.

Reengineer the current work models only to exploit the power of automation and achieve identified business goals

You reengineer the current work models explicitly to achieve the goals of exploiting the power of automation and achieving identified business goals, but other than changes specifically for these two purposes, you do not make changes to existing models. In this way, you address all three goals described in the previous section. Then you take the reengineered work models back to your end users and validate them. (A specific exercise is offered later for validating the Reengineered Task Organization Model.) Finally, you document the reengineered work models (ultimately, in the product Style Guide), so that they can be communicated and adhered to as you move forward into user interface design tasks.

SCHEDULING AND INTEGRATION WITH OTHER TASKS

The Work Reengineering task fits into the overall Usability Engineering Lifecycle in the following ways:

◆ This task is driven directly by the Contextual Task Analysis task and also takes into consideration output from the User Profile.
◆ In particular, the Reengineered Task Organization Model generated in this task is based on the Current User Task Organization Model derived from the Contextual Task Analysis, and the Reengineered Task Sequence Models generated in this task are based on the Task Scenarios extracted from the Contextual Task Analysis.
◆ Work model reengineering in this task is also driven directly by goals established in the Usability Goal Setting task.

- The Reengineered Task Organization Model and Reengineered Task Sequence Models from this task are documented in the product Style Guide.
- The Reengineered Task Organization Model from this task will provide the foundation for the Conceptual Model Design.
- The Reengineered Task Sequence Models from this task will provide the foundation for Detailed User Interface Design.

The Work Reengineering task fits into the underlying software development methodology in the following ways:

- This task should *follow* development of the Requirements Model in the Analysis phase of OOSE (or function and data modeling in a traditional rapid prototyping methodology), as it is based on these analyses of current work practice.
- In particular, Use Cases in the Requirements Model of OOSE help drive the Reengineered Task Sequence Models in this task.
- This task should *precede* or *parallel* development of the Analysis Model in the Analysis phase of OOSE (or the application architecture design in a traditional rapid prototyping methodology), which in turn is driven partly by user interface design decisions that will be based on the reengineered work models.

ROLES AND RESOURCES

In the Work Reengineering task, the usability roles might participate as follows:

Task leader: The User Interface Designer should take the lead role in this task.

Other resources: Any and all project team members who have participated in the User Profile and Contextual Task Analysis tasks should participate and provide input and feedback during the Work Reengineering task. The Usability Engineer should participate as well to provide direction and feedback. Users participate especially in the reengineered work model validation exercises, but they could also participate more actively in the process of work reengineering.

SAMPLE TECHNIQUE—
A STEP-BY-STEP PROCEDURE

❶ **Reengineer the Current User Task Organization Model and Task Scenarios.** In a software application, you typically do not wish simply to mimic the current work organization, be it paper based or an older software application. But neither do you want to unnecessarily force users to learn entirely new ways of thinking about and doing their work. Instead, you want an application and user interface that represents a compromise or trade-off between the three goals of work reengineering listed earlier.

Let's assume you have documented the actual current task organization and task sequences users use to accomplish their tasks (the Current User Task Organization Model and Task Scenarios). If you analyze this organization and these processes in terms of their underlying *goals*, you can often see opportunities for reducing work and streamlining work processes. Exploiting these opportunities in product design may result in an automated system that significantly changes work practices, but this is justified, when it will not only help meet the general goal in automation of increasing productivity, but also help meet specific usability goals identified in the Usability Goal Setting task. We recognize and accept that some retraining will be required in order to achieve the potential benefit of automation.

For example, consider the use of "styles" in a word processor. This concept has no analogy in the manual world of typewriters. So word processor user interfaces had to present a whole new concept that was not familiar to typewriter users. Nevertheless, there is much else in a word processor that is reminiscent of the manual (typewriter) world. Thus, the analogy to the manual world is helpful, but opportunities to exploit the power of automation are not lost.

In any automation project, some reengineering is intended to exploit the power of automation, and some reengineering is intended to further specific business goals. Typically, however, there is some reengineering that adds no real value to the application, simply because designers do not understand the user's work and tasks. Even in the course of designing automated tools, it is common to miss important requirements and fail to support key aspects of users' work. Ramey, Rowberg, and Robinson (1996, 8–13) give an example of a task analysis of physicians performing diagnostic radiology. Many ways of interacting with images (e.g., pointing, scanning, marking), which would have undoubtedly been missed by traditional systems analy-

WHO'S AFRAID OF AUTOMATION?

When performing a task analysis for a project to automate property management in a metropolitan police department, my project team observed that police officers currently had to fill out a large number of forms by hand or typewriter, and a great deal of the information recorded repeated across forms. In this application, rather than simply putting all the current forms on-line and requiring the same redundant data entry, we redesigned the forms so that only unique data would need to be entered on different forms.

Also, police officers had to remember what forms were necessary, given the circumstances under which property was taken in, and what fields on generic forms did or did not need to be filled in. Clearly, the application should ask the police officer for some basic details about the circumstances and then present only the required fields for those circumstances. In these two ways, the application would present a very different process to the users than what they were currently used to, but the change required in the users' mental model of their task would be outweighed by the productivity and usability benefits that would eventually (after retraining) be realized. So we consciously made the decision to depart from the Current User Task Organization Model and the current task sequences represented in the Task Scenarios.

sis approaches, were observed and built into the system. Without features supporting these interactions, users would have been forced users to work differently and find all manner of work-arounds to accomplish their goals. You want to eliminate this inadvertent type of reengineering while accomplishing reengineering that has real value. This is what you are trying to do by starting out with current user work models as a base and only altering them when real value is added.

The Sample Work Products and Templates section later in the chapter provides an example of a Reengineered Task Organization Model and gives references for examples of Reengineered Task Sequence Models.

❷ **Validate and refine the Reengineered Task Organization Model and Reengineered Task Sequence Models.** Authors of work modeling techniques emphasize the importance of validating the reengineered work models with actual end users as well as user representatives (see Jacobson et al. 1992; Wood 1996; Holtzblatt and Beyer

W A R   S T O R Y

KEEPING BOTH THE CUSTOMER
AND USER HAPPY

You will encounter other circumstances in which you know the way users currently think about and do their work must change to accommodate more specific business goals beyond simple increases in productivity. For example, in one insurance company, the customer support function concentrated on individual policies. All current software applications allowed lookup by policy number, but there was no way to see what other policies a customer owned when looking at one of their policies.

A specific business goal was defined to refocus customer support staff on *customers*, so that even when looking at a specific policy, they had easy access to all other policies owned by that customer. This would allow the staff to provide

better customer service by noting that customers had other policies when they called in to change a beneficiary (or change an address or cancel a policy) and asking them whether they wanted these changes applied to other policies. It would also allow staff to support the sales agent function by making suggestions for products that might complement the customer's whole portfolio.

My team's compromise was to create an interface that was customer centered—allowing and encouraging lookup directly by customer—while maintaining lookup by policy number. When users did a lookup by policy number, however, they also saw all customer information, including a list of the customer's other policies. This realized the business goal of shifting the user's focus to the customer, while allowing users to think and work in ways that were familiar.

1996). I have used the following technique to validate the Reengineered Task Organization Model that emerges from step 1. I prefer something like this technique to simple walk-throughs of models with users whenever possible, as it goes beyond simply asking users to understand and approve the model. Instead, it tests their performance while actually using the model.

Perform the exercise with two to five users of *each* major user type (Actor). Make sure these users have not participated in past task analysis exercises. You want unbiased responses and data from new users in order to expand the total sample of users having input into the task analysis.

◆ Make up index cards with the labels of all groups and subgroups from the Reengineered Task Organization Model derived in step 1 of the sample technique.

◆ Make up index cards with all low-level tasks.

◆ Recruit two to five users of each major user type (Actor) and schedule them for one to two hours each.

◆ For each user, lay out the group and subgroup label cards, and ask her or him to sort all the low-level task cards into the defined hierarchy.

◆ After running all users, reconcile the overall hierarchy to capture the most common expectations across users about how low-level tasks fall into groups and subgroups.

Recognize that some deviations from the Reengineered Task Organization Model that users come up with are expected and can be ignored, because they represent current ways of doing things that are being intentionally reengineered for good reason (see step 1).

The technique I use to validate the Reengineered Task Sequence Models is simply to walk through them with several representative users to make sure they make sense and no important aspects or variations of tasks have been missed.

❸ Document the Reengineered Task Organization Model and Reengineered Task Sequence Models. Document the final task hierarchy or Reengineered Task Organization Model (see the Sample Work Products and Templates section for an example). This will be incorporated into the first pass at a Conceptual Model Design in the next lifecycle task. Also document the Reengineered Task Sequence Models (see Beyer and Holtzblatt 1998; Hackos and Redish 1998, for examples). These will be used as the basis for Detailed User Interface Design, some of which occurs in the Screen Design Standards task and the rest of which occurs in the Detailed User Interface Design task.

All reengineered work models are ultimately included in the product Style Guide (see Chapter 14).

LEVEL OF EFFORT

Table 7.1 gives a sample level of effort for the Work Reengineering task. The work effort will vary widely depending on the complexity of the product. This sample represents a simple to moderately complex product, with two analysts/designers participating.

Table 7.1
Level of effort—Work Reengineering

Usability Time (two staff sharing all tasks)		User Time	
Step	Hrs	Step	Hrs
Reengineer work models	48		
Validate work models	24	Validate work models	18
Document work models	16		
Total	88	Total	18

ALTERNATIVE TECHNIQUES— A REVIEW

Two excellent books on task analyses offer many useful ideas related to this task. Beyer and Holtzblatt (1998) offer techniques for obtaining and then reengineering work models. Although their scope is wider than mine (their focus is on reengineering entire enterprises and then identifying opportunities for automation, while mine is limited to completely designing already identified and scoped products), some of their work models can be adapted and used within the Usability Engineering Lifecycle. Their "User Environment Design" is in some ways similar to what I refer to as the Reengineered Task Organization Model, although wider in scope, and their Sequence Models are very similar to Use Cases and to what I refer to as Reengineered Task Sequence Models. They also suggest a technique they call a "User Environment Design Walkthrough" for validating their User Environment Design. Hackos and Redish (1998) also offer a whole book on task analysis techniques, which provides some ideas on using task analysis data in design, including reengineering work models.

Rosson and Carroll (1995) report on an interesting experimental design tool that attempts to support Work Reengineering and user interface design and at the same time tightly integrate these tasks with implementation tasks in the context of object-oriented development. With this tool, designers start with Task Scenarios from the Contextual Task Analysis task and use these to identify strengths and weaknesses in the current work process. Work is then reengineered and user interface design is begun around this analysis of Task Scenarios. Developers use the same tool collaboratively to reason from the same Task Scenarios and interface design ideas and start generating object classes and object behaviors—the basis of object-oriented designs and the components of object-oriented implementation models. New Task Scenarios covering different aspects of usage are added, and work flow and interface design ideas, as well as implementation models, evolve and become more and more general and applicable across all usage situations. Thus, the Task Scenarios generated in the Contextual Task Analysis are used both to keep a focus on real user tasks and usage situations during user interface design and to support the analysis of implementation issues and the construction of implementation models.

Although focusing design on specific Task Scenarios may seem to be a bottom-up approach that could result in inconsistency across the user interface design, Rosson and Carroll point out that, in fact, the object-oriented approach to implementation naturally forces you to look for abstractions and generalities and opportunities for consistency and reuse. And, they point out, as long as designers make it their agenda to look for and exploit opportunities for consistency (see Chapters 8 and 11 for definitions of consistency), a bottom-up approach has the advantage of avoiding abstractions early on and keeping the focus on concrete usage scenarios. The object-oriented approach to implementation also naturally supports the identification of opportunities to better support user tasks with the powers of automation. Another advantage noted by Rosson and Carroll is that because of the parallel and tightly integrated development of both user interface design and implementation design, the inevitable trade-offs between usability issues and implementation constraints are highlighted early and can be rationally addressed.

Rosson and Carroll's tool is experimental and only applies to the development of Smalltalk applications. However, the more general approach their tool represents—that of Task Scenarios driving Work Reengineering and interface design; the tight coupling of interface design and implementation design; and the implied close and ongoing collaboration of users, designers, and developers—is one from which we can all learn.

SHORTCUTS

One shortcut to the Work Reengineering task would be abbreviating or skipping the validation exercise, hoping you will catch problems with work flow in the several rounds of usability evaluation you will be doing during the user interface design process that comes next in the lifecycle. Another would be skipping formal documentation of the reengineered work models, keeping good notes that you will incorporate as you begin design level 1, Conceptual Model Design. Taking these shortcuts can save time and resources on simple projects, small in scope, but is not advised on large, complex projects where evaluation at each level and good documentation will pay off in the long run.

WEB NOTES

Sometimes you are actually engineering—rather than reengineering—work, because your Web site or application supports "work" unlike anything most of the intended users currently do (e.g., you may be deciding on the structure for an information space users previously were unable to

---

WAR STORY

THE INFORMATION YOU NEED IS YOURS TO FIND

One of my clients had two purposes in mind when building a Web-based application to help their users track work resources, such as supplies and equipment. They wanted to be able to keep track of these resources and find them when needed, and also to justify budget plans for future years based on resource usage in the current year. As it happened, the user organization did not previously track work resources, and so a new job was being introduced at the same time as the software tool to facilitate the job. You might think that since users were not formally tracking the resources, we couldn't do a task analysis. However, since they were currently using the work resources, we could observe the way they found and used them, as well as how they named them, talked about them, and thought about them. This would give us important insights into how to model the organization and procedures through which users would record and track the resources in a software user interface.

access). Nevertheless, you can still do a Contextual Task Analysis to discover users' needs and desires and can base your initial work organization on this analysis.

In most cases, even when a particular job is not currently being done, something highly related to that job is being done. This can be the focus of a Contextual Task Analysis and can then feed into Work Reengineering. In addition, once an initial release of a Web application is in production, you can perform another Contextual Task Analysis to discover how the application is being used and where it breaks down, and use these insights to reengineer the underlying work models for later releases. And, just as you do when designing traditional software, you can still validate your reengineered work models empirically, as described in the earlier section Sample Technique—A Step-by-Step Procedure.

Even when one job isn't currently being done, another highly related job may be being done

SAMPLE WORK PRODUCTS AND TEMPLATES

One sample is offered here: a Sample Reengineered Task Organization Model. For examples of how to formulate and specify reengineered task flows (what I call Reengineered Task Sequence Models), see Beyer and Holtzblatt (1998) and Hackos and Redish (1998).

SAMPLE REENGINEERED TASK ORGANIZATION MODEL

The model offered on page 185 is adapted from the customer support function in an insurance company. It is based on the Sample Current User Task Organization Model offered in the Sample Work Products and Templates section of Chapter 3. In the model illustrated here, regular text represents the basic user tasks, which have not changed from previous task organization models generated by designers (see the Sample First Pass at Current User Task Organization Model offered in the Sample Work Products and Templates section of Chapter 3) and users (see the Sample Current User Task Organization Model). Bold text in boxes represents the new hierarchy and grouping of those tasks. (This hierarchy represents a partial set of the functionality required by customer support staff. For simplicity of the example, not all groups or low-level tasks are included.)

This model was obtained by starting with the Current User Task Organization Model, that is, the model that captured the commonalities across the work models obtained from individual users. Then some changes were made to this composite users' model, but only to reengineer their tasks to meet business goals and exploit the power of automation.

Note that this organization of low-level tasks differs both from the designers' original hierarchy and from the hierarchy generated by a single user. Customer and Policy changes are distinguished, but at a higher level in the hierarchy than was the case in the user model. New Sale gets its own category, on the same level as Customer and Policy tasks, and all follow-up activities related to New Sales are included in this category. Claims becomes its own high-level category, and Office is subdivided as the users indicated. Note that this model is fairly close to the Current User Task Organization Model, with changes only to reduce the depth of the hierarchy and to reflect a desired focus on the customer. In a validation exercise, users had little or no trouble finding tasks in this hierarchy.

Note that this is the third distinct task organization model offered for the same set of basic user tasks (the first was generated by designers in an attempt to define functionality, and the second was generated by an individual user during a task analysis exercise). This illustrates the important fact that there are often many logical ways to organize a set of low-level tasks or functions. At this point in this example, the project team believes they have discovered the best organization to meet the three goals stated earlier:

1. Realizing the power and efficiency that automation makes possible
2. Reengineering work to more effectively support business goals
3. Minimizing retraining by having the new product tap as much as possible into users' existing task knowledge, and maximizing efficiency and effectiveness by accommodating human cognitive constraints and capabilities within the context of their actual tasks

Now they are in a strong position to proceed to the next task in the lifecycle, Conceptual Model Design.

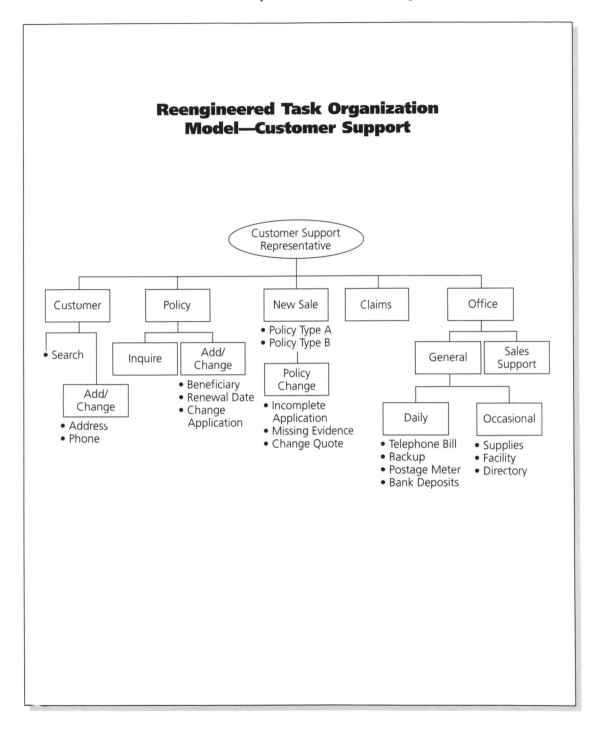

Reengineered Task Organization Model—Customer Support

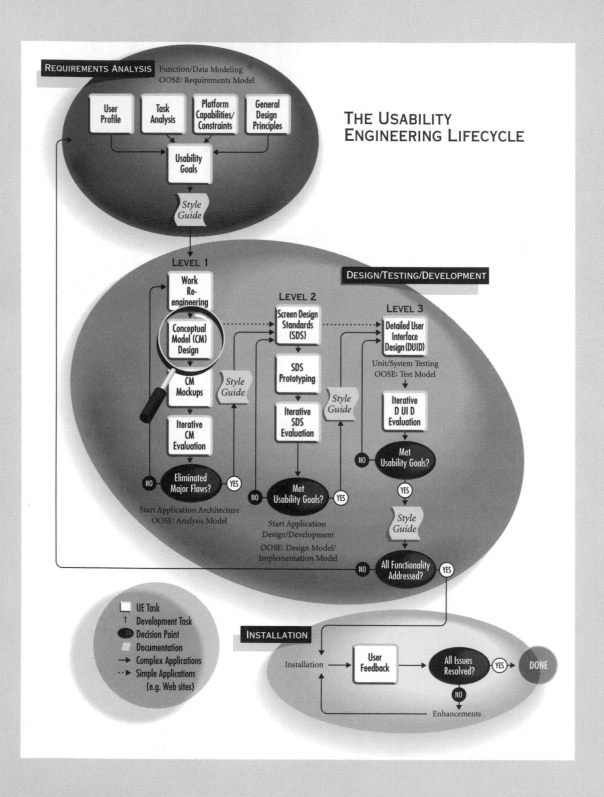

THE USABILITY
ENGINEERING LIFECYCLE

REQUIREMENTS ANALYSIS Function/Data Modeling
OOSE: Requirements Model

User Profile

Task Analysis

Platform Capabilities/ Constraints

General Design Principles

Usability Goals

Style Guide

LEVEL 1

DESIGN/TESTING/DEVELOPMENT

Work Re-engineering

Conceptual Model (CM) Design

CM Mockups

Iterative CM Evaluation

Eliminated Major Flaws?   NO   YES

Start Application Architecture
OOSE: Analysis Model

LEVEL 2

Screen Design Standards (SDS)

SDS Prototyping

Iterative SDS Evaluation

Style Guide

Met Usability Goals?   NO   YES

Start Application Design/Development

OOSE: Design Model/ Implementation Model

LEVEL 3

Detailed User Interface Design (DUID)

Unit/System Testing
OOSE: Test Model

Iterative D UI D Evaluation

Met Usability Goals?   NO   YES

Style Guide

Style Guide

All Functionality Addressed?   NO   YES

UE Task
T Development Task
Decision Point
Documentation
→ Complex Applications
··▶ Simple Applications (e.g. Web sites)

INSTALLATION

Installation → User Feedback → All Issues Resolved?   YES → DONE

NO

Enhancements

Conceptual Model Design

PURPOSE

I find it useful to divide the process of actual user interface design into three levels. In level 1, Conceptual Model Design, I design high-level presentation rules that map to the Reengineered Task Organization Model generated in the Work Reengineering task. In level 2, I design lower-level rules for screen design (Screen Design Standards), and in level 3, I design the complete Detailed User Interface Design, based on the rules generated, refined, and validated in levels 1 and 2. This chapter presents level 1 design issues, while Chapters 11 and 15 present level 2 and 3 design issues, respectively.

The Reengineered Task Organization Model generated in the Work Reengineering task becomes the foundation for the product user interface design. It provides the underlying structure and organization of the total "user interface architecture," which also includes a set of conventions regarding the presentation of that structure (the Conceptual Model Design and the Screen Design Standards). Detailed User Interface Design is then premised on and driven by this user interface architecture.

For any single Reengineered Task Organization Model, there are an infinite number of possible Conceptual Model Designs, or visual presentations of the functionality organized in the model. Getting the Reengineered Task Organization Model right is a key step, and separating it from Conceptual Model Design greatly facilitates the overall design process by untangling the issues of organization and presentation. Also, this distinction corresponds roughly to the distinction in OOSE between the Analysis Model, which is platform/implementation independent, and

The interface design process is divided into three levels: Conceptual Model Design, Screen Design Standards, and Detailed UI Design

187

the Design Model, which assumes particular platforms, tools, and implementation approaches (see Jacobson et al. 1992). Similarly, the Reengineered Task Organization Model is independent of any particular interface approach, such as GUIs, voice interfaces, and character-based interfaces, while the Conceptual Model Design assumes a particular visual and interaction style and specifies how its components are used to present the underlying Reengineered Task Organization Model. OOSE is particularly weak on specifying when and how to approach user interface design, but the approaches defined in this and later design chapters in this book fill in these missing pieces and tie into OOSE rather well.

The purpose of this task in the overall Usability Engineering Lifecycle is to take the Reengineered Task Organization Model and use it as the foundation for Conceptual Model Design, the first real step in user interface design. In turn, the purpose of a Conceptual Model Design is to define a coherent, rule-based framework that will provide a unifying foundation for all the detailed interface design decisions to come.

Within any interactive product they encounter, users have a tendency to look for a unifying model—a set of rules that allows them to reduce the full complexity of a product to a smaller set of information to learn and remember. Such a "mental model" helps them learn the product more quickly, use it more efficiently and effectively, and predict product behavior in novel situations (see Mayhew 1992, ch. 3, for a detailed discussion of user mental models and how they drive the need for a Conceptual Model Design).

A good Conceptual Model Design, as an aspect of user interface design, in turn facilitates users' development of a good user mental model of the product by tapping into the ways people most naturally think, reason, and learn. It also reinforces the Reengineered Task Organization Model, which organizes functionality in a way that best supports the specific work being automated.

DESCRIPTION

From this point on, this chapter focuses on designing software applications in particular (as opposed to other kinds of interactive products), and examples are based on current standard GUI platforms such as Microsoft Windows, Apple Macintosh, and IBM OS/2. I chose this general platform through which to discuss and illustrate the idea of a Conceptual Model Design in user interface design simply because it is so common and because I expect most if not all my readers to be familiar with it. However, the principles behind the notion of a Conceptual Model Design are very general, and Conceptual Model Designs can be designed for very different technology platforms with very different capabilities. I have, for example, designed Conceptual Models for Web applications as well as for factory equipment whose interface consisted mostly of knobs, dials, and LED displays. The idea of *a set of presentation rules that consistently present categories of functional components*—that is, the idea of a Conceptual Model—can be very generally applied.

The principles behind a Conceptual Model Design are general. Conceptual Models can be designed for different platforms with different capabilities

Although Work Reengineering might be thought of as an aspect of design, it is really the design of the organization of functionality, independent of any particular presentation. In Conceptual Model Design, which is the first pass at actual user interface design work, we consider only the highest level of user interface design and make such decisions as

◆ Whether to design a product-process-oriented Conceptual Model
◆ How to define products or processes
◆ How to present products or processes
◆ What rules to follow for the use of window types
◆ How to define major displays and the navigational pathways between them

These design issues are discussed in detail in the chapter's Sample Technique—A Step-by-Step Procedure section and illustrated through examples in the Sample Work Products and Templates section.

The Conceptual Model Design will be based on the organization of functionality represented in the Reengineered Task Organization Model and also on the output from all Requirements Analysis tasks. Initially in this task, you begin a process of design and evaluation to *iteratively* develop the final Conceptual Model Design. In particular, you will be generating several sketchy alternative Conceptual Model Designs, which you will then subject to objective evaluation through the Conceptual Model Mock-ups and Iterative Conceptual Model Evaluation tasks described in the next two chapters. Your initial Conceptual Model Designs will be based on small, representative pieces of the total product functionality. Also, only high-level presentation and navigation issues are considered and designed. There will be little, if any, real content to any particular display in your designs, and at this point you are not at all concerned with screen layout and design. For example, in your initial Conceptual Model

Your initial Conceptual Model Designs will be based on small, representative pieces of the total product functionality

Optimally, generate and discuss at least several competing Conceptual Model Designs, with two or three selected for initial testing

Designs for a typical GUI, parts of the menu bar would be designed to represent navigational pathways, and the major types of windows that come up would be identified and named but not filled in with any content.

Optimally, at least several competing Conceptual Model Designs should be generated and discussed, with two to three selected for initial testing. The final alternatives should be chosen to represent important trade-offs that cannot be resolved based on the Requirements Analysis data gathered to date. For example, designers may not be sure whether one metaphor works better than another, or they may be struggling with some trade-offs between ease of use and ease of learning. Models representing alternatives that vary on these dimensions can be devised, and these can be compared in the Iterative Conceptual Model Evaluation task (see Chapter 10) that comes later.

In approaching the design process in this task, sketch out how Conceptual Model Design ideas would come to life in the context of several Task Scenarios generated in the Contextual Task Analysis

In approaching the design process in this task, you should make use of the Task Scenarios generated in the Contextual Task Analysis task. As you think up and try out Conceptual Model Design ideas, sketch out right away how they would come to life in the context of several specific Task Scenarios. That is, take your generic ideas about Conceptual Model Design *rules* and play them out through particular Task Scenarios. This will give you immediate feedback on how your Conceptual Model Design will actually be experienced by users in typical usage situations.

Note the combination of top-down and bottom-up approaches to design in this process. You use the low-level, concrete Task Scenarios to keep you thinking in concrete, realistic terms about users' work. However, as you generate design ideas through which to present this functionality, you are constantly looking for the generalities, the opportunities for consistency, the rules, that will make the interface coherent and predictable across usage situations (Rosson and Carroll 1995).

SCHEDULING AND INTEGRATION WITH OTHER TASKS

The Conceptual Model Design task fits into the overall Usability Engineering Lifecycle in the following ways:

◆ The Conceptual Model Design may (or may not) be premised on a standard platform conceptual model (e.g., Microsoft Windows, Apple Macintosh).

- This task is based upon the Work Reengineering task (it defines the presentation of the organization and structure that were established in that task), and it takes into consideration all data gathered in the Requirements Analysis tasks, including general design principles.
- The Conceptual Model Design will be constrained by the Platform Capabilities and Constraints.
- This task will feed directly into the next two tasks, in which mock-ups are constructed and usability evaluation is planned and iteratively executed, ultimately resulting in a fairly stable Conceptual Model Design.
- Ultimately, the Conceptual Model Design will be documented in the product Style Guide.
- All Screen Design Standards and Detailed User Interface Design will be designed in the context of the validated Conceptual Model Design.
- The Conceptual Model Design will be continuously refined and updated in response to all later usability evaluation tasks.

The Conceptual Model Design task fits into the underlying software development methodology in the following ways:

- This task should *follow* the development of the Requirements Model in the Analysis phase of OOSE (or function and data modeling in a traditional rapid prototyping methodology), as it is based on the Reengineered Task Organization Model, which in turn is based upon analyses of current work practice.
- This task should *precede* or *parallel* the development of the Analysis Model in the Analysis phase of OOSE (or the application architecture design in a traditional rapid prototyping methodology), as the application architecture should be designed to support the Conceptual Model Design of the user interface.
- In OOSE, while exactly where and how user interface design is accomplished is quite vague, it is specified as part of the development of the Analysis Model in the Analysis phase.
- Eventually, the Conceptual Model Design can be incorporated into application documentation and training. Describing the rules of the Conceptual Model Design explicitly will facilitate learning and remembering the user interface.

ROLES AND RESOURCES

In the Conceptual Model Design task, the usability roles might participate as follows:

Task leader: The User Interface Designer should take the lead role in this task.

Other resources: Any and all project team members who have participated in the User Profiles, Contextual Task Analysis, and Work Reengineering tasks should participate and provide input and feedback. The Usability Engineer should participate as well, to provide direction and feedback. Users can also participate (see Chin, Rosson, and Carroll 1997; Bloomer, Croft, and Wright 1997; Malinowski and Nakakoji 1995).

SAMPLE TECHNIQUE— A STEP-BY-STEP PROCEDURE

This section provides some structure to the process of Conceptual Model Design, which is an inherently creative activity, by identifying the major design issues that must be addressed and offering some discussion and examples of these issues. First though, I offer some general advice about the design process. In the technique discussed here, I assume no automated design tools.

◆ Design in a small team of two to six people. All designers should have participated in at least parts of the Contextual Task Analysis (see Chapter 3) and Work Reengineering (see Chapter 7) tasks.

◆ Start with a decision on whether to approach the design as product or process oriented (see step 1 below) and with a clear identification of products or processes to be presented. This decision should emerge somewhat naturally from the Contextual Task Analysis and Work Reengineering tasks.

◆ Based on results from all Requirements Analysis tasks to date, start generating alternative ways of representing either the application product(s) or the different levels of processes in the process hierarchy.

◆ Keep focused on high-level navigation and presentation, but delve into details when necessary just to test high-level ideas and get a more concrete feeling for the consequences of a high-level design idea.

◆ When unresolvable trade-offs arise, start codeveloping alternative models to represent the trade-offs.

◆ Split into smaller subgroups to flesh out the alternative models selected for further study.

Although the following design issues to be addressed are numbered, it is not necessary to consider and make these decisions in the implied order. It is only important that all these issues are ultimately considered and explicitly addressed in the designs that are defined.

❶ **Define the Conceptual Model as either product or process oriented.** A **product-oriented** model will best fit an application in which there are clear, identifiable *work products* that users individually create, name, and save. Examples of product-oriented applications include Microsoft Word, Excel, and PowerPoint. In each case, the main point of the application is to allow users to create, modify, and maintain documents (products) of different types (e.g., documents, spreadsheets, presentations). If a product-oriented model is selected, a standard Conceptual Model is available on each GUI platform (e.g., Microsoft Windows, Apple Macintosh).

A **process-oriented** model will best fit an application in which there are no clearly identifiable primary work products. In these applications, the main point is to support some work process. Information may be stored and retrieved, but usually all users have access to the same information—they are not creating individual work products such as documents. Examples of process-oriented applications include those that support customer service, plant floor management, inventory tracking, or financial management. There are no industry-standard models for process-oriented applications, so you must generate your own. You can usually do so using the tool sets available for standard GUIs.

Examples of both product- and process-oriented Conceptual Model Designs are offered in the Sample Work Products and Templates section later in the chapter.

❷ **Clearly identify products or processes.** In a product-oriented model, this means identifying what the primary *product(s)* of the application will be and what *tools* users will need to build those primary products. (Tools are sometimes user-unique *products,* although secondary ones.) For example, in a word processing application, the primary product is a document, and one example of a tool would be predefined document styles or formats. In a spreadsheet application, the primary product is a spreadsheet, and one example of a tool would be the standard equations that are typically provided. In a software and hardware inventory program, a primary product might be a procurement form, and one tool might be a list of vendor contacts.

In a process-oriented model, the task hierarchy or Reengineered Task Organization Model defines the processes and subprocesses of the application.

❸ Design presentation rules for products or processes. In a product-oriented model, this means deciding how primary products and tools (including secondary products) will be represented on the screen. A small set of consistently followed rules should dictate the presentation of all primary and secondary products and tools.

In a product-oriented GUI interface, almost everything presented to users can be classified as one of three things: *products,* which are entities that users would think of as things or products that they can create, name, and save; *tools*, which are objects supplied by the system that users might use in building products; and *actions*, which users can perform in order to create and modify products. There are in turn two types of products (things users create, name, and save): *primary products*, which are the main point of the application, and *secondary products*, which users may create to use as a tool in building or modifying the primary products.

For example, in the Microsoft Windows and Apple Macintosh Conceptual Models (which are both inherently product oriented), the presentation rules are that primary products are represented as icons at the desktop level (and as labeled items in a list box in the Open dialog box within the application), and secondary products are presented through an interaction involving the menu bar pull-downs and dialog boxes. This can be seen in Microsoft Word, where documents are presented as icons on the desktop, but styles created, named, and saved by the user are presented in a list box in a dialog box invoked by the Style action in a menu bar pull-down. Similarly, in Microsoft Excel, spreadsheets are represented as icons at the desktop level, but standard equations (tools) are presented in a list box in a dialog box invoked by the Function action in the menu bar.

If you are designing a product-oriented Conceptual Model and choose to follow a standard GUI Conceptual Model, to be consistent with the standard model, primary work products should always be cast as icons at the operating system or desktop level. Products that users may create, name, and save but are really secondary products, representing tools for building primary products, should always be presented through a list in a dialog box invoked by initiating some action from the menu bar pull-down within the application. Thus, for example, in a software and hardware inventory application, procurement forms would be presented as icons on the desktop, but vendor contacts would be presented in a dialog box invoked from the menu bar.

The rationale for these conventions is as follows. They result in an application Conceptual Model that is consistent with the inherent generic, platform Conceptual Model of current GUI platforms, and that inherent generic model is a good one to follow. Too many icons at the desktop level, representing a variety of types of things, have several undesirable effects in an interface: their very number can confuse users, they fail to help users know where to begin and how to structure their tasks, and they often result in poor organization of functionality and tedious navigation through the interface to accomplish typical tasks. Limiting the use of icons to represent only primary products, and casting everything else consistently as tools for building those products, accomplishes a variety of goals: it makes an interface simpler and less cluttered on first encounter, it focuses the user's attention on the right thing right away (i.e., the primary product they are working to create), and it often streamlines interaction by making all the necessary tools readily available without ever having to "leave" the primary product. These are good reasons to follow a standard GUI Conceptual Model in your applications when they are inherently product oriented.

In a process-oriented model, on the other hand, you start with the process hierarchy (the Reengineered Task Organization Model) generated in the Work Reengineering task and define rules for how each level in the hierarchy will be visually represented. For example, perhaps a tab metaphor is being considered, and first-level processes in the hierarchy are represented as tabs, second-level processes as menu bar picks within tabs, and third-level processes as pull-downs from menu bar picks (see the Sample Work Products and Templates section). Or, in a more Microsoft Windows–like model, first-level processes might be presented as grouped selections in the hierarchy invoked from the Start button, second-level processes might be presented as menu bar picks within an application window, and third-level processes as pull-downs from the menu bar. The basis of the Conceptual Model is that all processes or tasks at a given level in the Reengineered Task Organization Model will always be presented in a similar, if not identical, manner.

See the Sample Work Products and Templates section for example rules for product- and process-oriented Conceptual Models.

❹ **Design rules for windows.** In both product- and process-oriented Conceptual Model Designs, there should be rules for the use and behavior of windows for different kinds of displays. In today's standard GUI Conceptual Models (e.g., Microsoft Windows, Apple Macintosh), which are all inherently product oriented, a simple set of rules defines when to use the several different kinds of available windows (see the Sample Work Products and Templates section). If you are designing a product-oriented application that follows a current standard GUI Conceptual Model, follow these rules, both for consistency's sake and because they contribute to a simple and powerful Conceptual Model Design. You will find these rules documented in your current platform Style Guide.

For example, for Microsoft Windows 95, the rules can be summarized as follows. First, *primary windows*, which can be "minimized" and represented as icons (items on a task bar), are reserved for presenting folders, applications, and primary products (e.g., word processing documents, graphics documents, spreadsheet documents). Folders, applications, and primary products, in turn, will always and only be presented in primary windows. Primary windows generally have a special icon in the title bar for closing or minimizing them to their iconic (or task bar) form, and they are resizable, movable, and scrollable. They are also typically modeless systemwide, meaning that the user can move to another document window or application window without closing down the current application or current document window.

In addition, it is highly advisable to define document windows as "children" of application windows, so that they share the application window's menu bar. This minimizes the number of menu bars on the screen at any given time and reduces errors and confusion that occur when multiple menu bars are present.

Second in the set of rules for Windows 95, dialog boxes, which cannot be minimized, are used to display any details of an action initiated from the menu bar, including the creation and selection of secondary products. Dialog boxes should usually be movable but not resizable or scrollable. They present fixed displays, and allowing resizing or scrolling would mean allowing the user to obscure important information or fields, including the push buttons for navigating out of them. In most cases dialog boxes should probably also be *modal* within the application, meaning that within the application, users can only move to another already open dialog box or primary window by closing down the dialog box that currently has focus (usually via the Cancel and OK push buttons). This prevents the user from getting "lost" in a series of dialog boxes and losing track of the relationships between dialog boxes in a sequence.

Finally, *message boxes* are always presented in secondary windows, which may be movable but are almost always modal within an application, nonresizable, and nonscrollable. They are used for presenting read-only messages to users, including error and warning messages.

Primary and secondary windows are visually distinguished by different window decorations, particularly in the title bar. In addition, different background colors could be consistently used to help the user quickly distinguish among application, document, dialog box, and message box windows.

In a process-oriented model, a set of rules for windows should also be defined, but it will be different from the rules for a product-oriented Conceptual Model. For an example, see the Sample Work Products and Templates section.

❺ Identify major displays. Decide generally how functionality and information will be divided across individual displays, each of which (in a GUI) will be presented in a distinct window according to the rules for windows laid out in step 4. For example, in Microsoft Word, a product-oriented application, one major display is the document. According to the standard GUI Conceptual Model's rules for windows, it is always displayed in a primary window. Then a number of displays presented in dialog boxes (secondary windows) represent major types of actions that can be performed on documents, such as print, spellcheck, and apply style.

At this point in design, window content can be left out, and only the primary window or dialog box titles need be included. When selecting an action from the menu bar would lead to a dialog box, only key dialog boxes need to be identified. Actions that do not result in taking the user to another window (e.g., Cut, Paste) also do not need to be identified at this point. During later design tasks, you can decide exactly what content will go in all the different identified windows and how it will be laid out, how many related dialog boxes are necessary or desirable to complete a given action, and what the total set of actions will be.

❻ Define and design major navigational pathways. Here you define all the different pathways by which the user can move between displays. (For example, in Microsoft Word, users can navigate directly from any document window to the Styles dialog box, the Print dialog box, and so on.) And you define the interaction for following each pathway. (For example, in Word, users follow certain paths through the menu bar and pull-downs to get to dialog boxes.) In a product-oriented model that follows a standard GUI model, *initiating* actions is done via the menu bar, pull-downs, and dialog boxes, while *completing* actions and returning to documents is done through push buttons within dialog boxes.

Even in process-oriented GUIs, much of designing navigational pathways might involve designing a menu bar, pull-down, and dialog box structure (although process-oriented models might *not* involve menu bars at all and could use alternative controls for navigation, such as push buttons).

This step is often a matter of taking a high-level pass at the application menu bar and its pull-downs, and identifying choices that are relevant to navigation through the interface. Again, at this point the focus is on overall structure, organization, and navigation, not on screen content or design, or actions at the level of screen editing.

❼ Document alternative Conceptual Model Designs in sketches and explanatory notes. Suppose you are documenting a product-oriented Conceptual Model Design following a standard GUI model. First, draw (by hand) two screens, one representing how the application and its associated documents will be represented on the desktop (although icon detail need not be designed at this point) and the other representing the open application and one or more open document windows within it. On the latter, include the menu bar in the application window. On a separate piece of paper, enumerate all the pull-down choices identified so far, representing where they will appear relative to standard menu bar/pull-down choices (e.g., File, Open). On additional pieces of paper, depict major typical pathways between primary windows, dialog boxes, and message boxes. Separately, document the rules (e.g., for presentation of products/processes, for use of windows) that are illustrated in your drawings. See the Sample Work Products and Templates section for several examples of how to document Conceptual Model Design.

Remember that Conceptual Model Design is iterative and may be modified not only during later iterations of this and the following two tasks in the lifecycle but also during later tasks addressing detailed design. The *spirit* of the rules and guidelines described in steps 1–6, however, should always be maintained, even though the actual design decisions may change and evolve over the course of the project.

And, because change is inevitable over iterations, I do not recommend any formal documentation during early iterations of this task. Doing so will take a significant effort, and updating such documents after iterations of testing will take more effort. The tedium of updating various specifications created with independent documentation tools that do not support cross-referencing will prove such an effort that it is likely to discourage further iterations (Sumner 1995). Do your work by hand at this point in the process. It is much easier to throw away and redo hand-drawn design ideas than formally documented design ideas.

Sorely lacking in the Usability Engineering field are good design specification tools that make it easy to document design ideas in different formats (e.g., text, graphics, flowcharts, tables) but in a linked manner so that they can be easily and consistently updated during iterative design. It is important to support and encourage change and evolution of design ideas at this point. There will be an appropriate time for formal documentation later, when the Conceptual Model Design is relatively stable. Ultimately, validated Conceptual Model Design will be formally documented in the product Style Guide, where more formal illustrations will be appropriate.

LEVEL OF EFFORT

Table 8.1 gives a sample level of effort for the Conceptual Model Design task. The work effort will vary widely depending on the complexity of the application, and this sample represents a simple to moderately complex application, with two analysts/designers participating.

Table 8.1
Level of effort—Conceptual Model Design

Usability Time
(three staff working as a team in meetings)

Step	Hrs
Design products/processes	48
Design rules for windows	36
Identify major displays	36
Define navigational pathways	36
Document design	48
Total	204

ALTERNATIVE TECHNIQUES— A REVIEW

You might consider involving users in this and later design activities as active collaborators. It has been shown (Chin, Rosson, and Carroll 1997; Bloomer, Croft, and Wright 1997) that given properly structured techniques, users can be invaluable and effective team members during design. Technologists are necessary to propose practical technological solutions, and usability experts have a general understanding of human cognition and user interface design skills, but only users really understand the work being automated. Their input and direction during the design process can streamline the overall Usability Engineering Lifecycle by making sure initial design ideas make sense even before they are subjected to structured usability evaluation.

Malinowski and Nakakoji (1995) also offer ideas on drawing users into active participatory design through a tool that allows users to tailor a default user interface, receive feedback if they violate any built-in user interface design principles while tailoring, document their redesign rationale if they choose to ignore the design advice, and transmit their redesign and rationale automatically back to designers who are responsible for updating the user interface design in later releases. This approach has the advantage of soliciting user feedback in a structured way while they are actively engaged in real work. It has two drawbacks, however. It does not involve users during the initial design process, and it is a "high-fidelity" technique, requiring fairly sophisticated software that must be tailored to each individual application.

Malinowski and Nakakoji also highlight the need for application domain knowledge during design. I focus on collecting this type of knowledge during the Contextual Task Analysis task, but others strongly advocate having users actively participate in the design process as a way to ensure this knowledge drives the design process. Malinowski and Nakakoji offer a simple example of how these two types of knowledge— user interface design expertise and task domain knowledge—must be integrated to make good design decisions: "For example, . . . the . . . rule: 'pop-up menus need to be ordered semantically consistent'. User interface designers needed to know which operations are semantically corresponding to each other in this specific domain."

Rather than rely on the Contextual Task Analysis alone to generate all task information that will be needed during design, proponents of participatory design suggest that having users actively collaborate during the design tasks will better ensure that knowledge of the task domain will be incorporated into the design.

In theory, I am a strong believer in the concept of participatory design. It is consistent with the general notion of the cross-functional project team discussed in some detail in Chapter 1. In practice, however, at least in my experience as a consultant, it is hard enough to get developers involved in Usability Engineering tasks, and harder yet to get access to users just for observations during task analysis and as test users during usability testing. It is very difficult to get user managers to support heavy involvement of users on a development project because it takes too much time away from users' jobs and also because managers consider product design to be the job of product developers, not users. Often it is difficult to get a client in the development organization to support me in recruiting users to participate in this way. However, I would encourage you to experiment with these promising techniques whenever possible.

A final note on alternative techniques: some researchers are developing experimental automated design tools (see, e.g., Rosson and Carroll 1995), but none are yet generic and commercially available.

Some proponents of participatory design suggest that having users actively collaborate during the design tasks will ensure that their knowledge of the task domain will be incorporated into the design

Shortcuts

On very small and simple projects, it may not be necessary to formally document the Conceptual Model in the product Style Guide even after it is stabilized through iterative testing and redesign, although good notes summarizing design rules—even if they are only handwritten—will always be important. Also on such projects, all three design levels might be collapsed into one round of iterative design and testing. Nevertheless, the Conceptual Model must always be explicitly designed and validated.

Web Notes

The Conceptual Model Design is equally important in Web site and application design as in traditional software design. Most Web sites and applications will be process-oriented, in that they will simply support navigation through information or completion of work processes rather than allow users to create, name, and save individual work products. A Conceptual Model Design for a Web site might typically include rules that would cover the consistent presentation of

- Site title/logo (location and presentation)
- Panes (e.g., for highest-level links, context information, page content)
- Links at different levels of the site organization
- Links versus other actions (e.g., "Submit")
- Links versus nonlinks (e.g., illustrations)
- Inter- versus intrasite links
- Visual cues that indicate:
  - where the user currently is in the site organization
  - which pathway the user came down in the site organization to where he or she currently is
  - whether the user is currently pointing at a link or other control

Also note that in Web design, the role of User Interface Designer can be split effectively between two kinds of specialists: Usability Engineers and graphic designers. The Usability Engineers can design the Reengineered Task Organization Model and Reengineered Task Sequence Models as described in Chapter 7, and also can define the need for consistent cues as given above. Then, graphic designers might be more qualified to design the visual presentation of these work models and abstract requirements for consistent cues. Unlike in most traditional software, there is a high need in Web design for such things as corporate branding, marketplace differentiation, and appropriate image. These things fall within the skill set of graphic designers, but are not skills usually found in User Interface Designers of more traditional software.

On very simple Web site or application projects, it will not be necessary to formally document the Conceptual Model Design, and testing may even be collapsed across all three design levels in the Usability Engineering Lifecycle. Nevertheless, the Conceptual Model must be explicitly designed and validated.

SAMPLE WORK PRODUCTS AND TEMPLATES

The following sample work products and templates are offered here:

- Standard GUI Conceptual Model—Product-Oriented
- Sample Conceptual Model Design—Product-Oriented
- Sample Conceptual Model Design—Process-Oriented

STANDARD GUI CONCEPTUAL MODEL—PRODUCT-ORIENTED

What follows is a description of a particular standard GUI Conceptual Model (Microsoft Windows 95), as realized in a particular application: a version of Microsoft Word. Many if not most commercial Microsoft Windows and Apple Macintosh applications follow a very similar model. The model specification here is not exhaustive and complete, but it covers the major aspects of the Conceptual Model Design of the Word application and thus represents the level of design work that might be done in this task in the Usability Engineering Lifecycle. It is organized according to the design steps for this task, as laid out in the Sample Technique—A Step-by-Step Procedure section.

The Standard GUI Conceptual Model

1. Define the Conceptual Model as either Product- or Process-Oriented.

The conceptual model for Microsoft Word is product-oriented.

2. Clearly Identify Products or Processes.

There is one type of primary product: a document. There is at least one type of secondary product—styles—and there likely will be others.

3. Design Presentation Rules for Products or Processes.

Primary products (documents) are represented at the desktop or operating system level as large icons with labels. They are also represented within the application through the Open dialog box as labeled small icons in a list box.

    The only other entities represented as icons at the desktop level are folders and applications.

"The Standard GUI Conceptual Model," cont. next page

"The Standard GUI Conceptual Model," cont.

Sample Desktop Folder Window

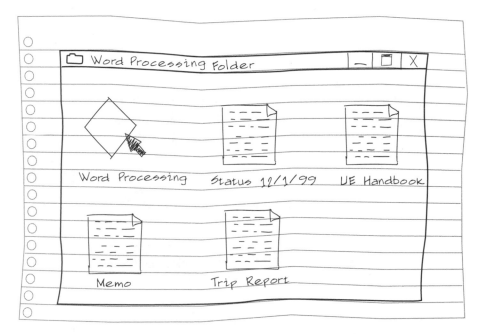

The user may have created and saved any number of documents. The user might also have created a folder at the desktop level and in it stored the application and all associated documents. If not, then the application would be stored somewhere in the Start button hierarchy, and the documents would be stored on directories in the Windows Explorer.

Double-clicking on the application icon at the desktop or operating system level opens the application in a primary window, and an empty, untitled product (document) in a primary window within it.

Double-clicking on a product (document) icon from the operating system or desktop level opens the application window and a product (document) window displaying that product (document).

Secondary products, such as styles, are presented as labels in a list box within a dialog box accessed through the menu bar.

Sample Application Window

4. Design Rules for Windows.

Only applications and products (documents) are presented in primary windows—all other displays are presented in dialog boxes.

Document windows always and only present a particular product (document).

Only the application window has a menu bar and a status/message line—document windows, dialog boxes, and message boxes do not have menu bars.

The application window is full screen by default, but resizable and movable.

Product (document) windows by default fill all available space within the application window, but are resizable and movable.

Application and product (document) windows never contain push buttons, but may include ribbons, rulers, and toolboxes.

"The Standard GUI Conceptual Model," cont. next page

"The Standard GUI Conceptual Model," cont.

Sample Dialog Box

All other windows are contained within the application window, between the menu bar and status lines (they are "child" windows of the application window).

Product (document) windows are modeless, resizable, movable, and scrollable.

Dialog boxes are usually application modal, unresizable, movable, and unscrollable.

Dialog boxes present dialogs related to acting on the contents of an application or document window.

Dialog boxes may contain controls such as radio buttons, check boxes, list boxes, and drop-down combo boxes.

The application menu bar is not available within a dialog box. All actions are provided through push buttons.

Pop-up message boxes are usually modal, unsizable, unmovable, and unscrollable.

Message boxes are used to present warning, error, and information messages.

The application menu bar is not available within a message box. All actions are provided through push buttons.

5. Identify Major Displays.

Product (document) windows display the contents of particular primary products (documents). A number of different *views* of any given product (document) are available, including Normal, Header and Footer, and Outline.

Dialog boxes allow users to define actions to be performed on products (documents) or the contents of products (text, styles, graphics etc.)

Major dialog boxes include:

Open	Formatting dialog boxes
Save As	(e.g., font, paragraph, columns)
Document Layout	Spellcheck
Page Setup	Thesaurus
Replace	Insert Table

6. Define and Design Major Navigational Pathways.

Users navigate between primary products (documents) by clicking on open windows, selecting window names from the Window menu bar pull-down, or selecting currently closed products (documents) through the Open dialog box.

All actions that can be performed on products (documents) or the contents of products (text, graphics, styles, etc.) are presented through the menu bar and its pull-downs. Shortcuts (e.g., mouse shortcuts, keyboard shortcuts, or toolbar icon shortcuts) for menu picks may be available for *some* actions, but the menu bar contains *all* actions. Some actions occur instantly upon selection from the pull-down, for example, Save, Close, Print Preview, Cut, Paste. Others require selections from a pop-up dialog box to be completely defined.

Had Microsoft Word been developed according to the Usability Engineering Lifecycle, the following might have been a first pass at identifying and grouping main actions that result in navigation to other displays. All other actions—for example, those that allow the user to edit

"The Standard GUI Conceptual Model," cont. next page

the contents of a particular product (document)—would have been identified and designed at a later stage in the overall design process defined by the Usability Engineering Lifecycle. The navigation that occurs upon invoking the identified actions is described below the illustration of the menu bar and its pull-downs. This initial design would likely have been modified and would certainly have been added to as design proceeded to lower levels of detail.

All pull-down choices followed by ellipses (. . .) lead to a dialog box or boxes. A dialog box or a sequence of cascading dialog boxes always ultimately return focus to the product (document) window from which they were invoked.

Ultimately, **New, Open, Save As,** and **Subscribe To** open new document windows and transfer focus to them. All of them first present the user with a dialog box. The picks under **Windows** will refer to other currently open document windows, and selecting one transfers focus directly to it.

The **Close** action closes a document window and returns focus to the previously active document window if there was one, or to the application window if no other document windows are open. **Quit** closes the application and all its currently open document windows, returning the user to the desktop.

Sample Menu Bar with Pull-Downs

	MENU BAR DESIGN			
File	Edit	View	Format	Tools
New		Normal		Spelling...
Open...		Outline		Grammar...
Close		Page Layout		Thesaurus...
Save	Glossary...		Style...	
Save As...		Header...		Calculate
Print...		Footer...		
Quit	Subscribe To...		Preferences...	

Glossary provides access to tools (in this case, to secondary products) that allow users to create, name, save, and apply text strings. Glossary entries are presented via a list box in a dialog box. **Subscribe To** links a portion of one document to a portion of another, so that changes to one are always immediately reflected in the other. Interaction with dialog boxes and a second document window occurs during the process of linking.

Normal, Outline, and **Page Layout** all leave focus in the current document window, but directly change the format of its contents.

Header and **Footer** invoke dialog boxes that present and allow editing of document headers and footers. Upon completion, focus is returned to the document window.

Styles provides access to tools (in this case, to secondary products) that allow users to create, name, save, and apply formatting and styles (e.g., margin settings, font and point size defaults) to the current document. A single dialog box allows users to create, name, and save new styles and to select and apply existing styles via a list box. Upon completion, focus is returned to the document window.

Preferences allows users to set various document or view settings to default values. These settings are presented through a cascading sequence of dialog boxes. They immediately take effect on the document window from which the action was invoked, when the last dialog box is "OK'ed."

Spell, **Grammar,** and **Thesaurus** allow users to check spelling or grammar in their document and consult a thesaurus for synonyms, and these actions are presented through dialogs conducted in dialog boxes. Upon completion, focus is returned to the document window.

Calculate allows users to type an arithmetic expression in a document, select it, and evaluate it. The result of the calculation is presented in the status line of the application window. The current document window maintains focus.

The execution or cancellation of actions defined within dialog boxes is invoked by push buttons in the action dialog box.

The application menu bar is not available within a dialog box. All actions within and navigating out of the dialog box are provided through push buttons.The application menu bar is not available within a message box. All actions are provided through push buttons.

SAMPLE CONCEPTUAL MODEL DESIGN—PRODUCT-ORIENTED

This sample illustrates how the generic Conceptual Model Design inherent in the previous example could be applied to a potential car dealership application. This application lends itself well to a product-oriented Conceptual Model.

Conceptual Model—Car Dealership Application

The application is represented as an icon on the desktop and also in the Start button hierarchy.

There is only one type of primary product: a worksheet. Worksheets are represented as icons at the desktop level: the user might store existing worksheets in a user-created folder. Worksheets can also be found in

Sample Desktop Folder Window

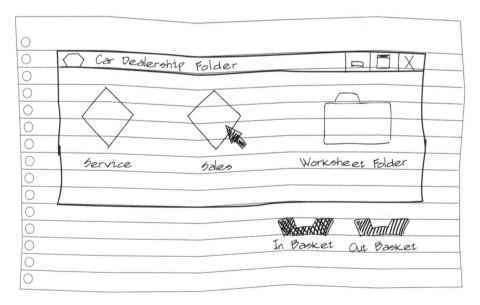

the Windows Explorer, and they are represented within the application through the Open dialog box as labeled small icons in a list box.

Double-clicking on the application icon at the desktop level opens the application in a primary window and an empty, untitled worksheet in a primary window within it. Double-clicking on a worksheet from the desktop level opens the application and the selected worksheet.

Secondary products, including the catalog, customers, and a stock list, are presented in a dialog box accessed through the menu bar.

This design also follows all the rules for windows identified in the previous section.

This design consistently follows the generic, standard GUI Conceptual Model, in which primary products are the only application entities at the desktop or operating system level, and everything else is presented as a tool within the application.

Sample Application Window

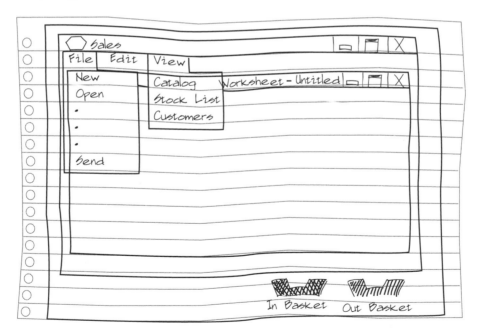

SAMPLE CONCEPTUAL MODEL DESIGN—PROCESS-ORIENTED

Imagine a customer service application for a utility company, such as an electric company or a phone company. Such an application has no primary product that users uniquely create, name, and save as the main focus of their interaction with the application. Instead, there is just one big shared database, containing customer account information that users add to and access. Thus, the industry-standard, product-oriented model demonstrated in the previous two samples would not apply. We need a Conceptual Model Design that is a set of presentation rules, but a different one—a process-oriented one.

Assume that the hierarchy of work processes for this application (that is, the Reengineered Task Organization Model) is as follows:

UTILITY CUSTOMER SERVICE

Service Requests

    Change Service

    Cancel Service

    Install New Service

        Add Customer Info

        Select Service

        Check Credit

        Quote Rate

        Schedule Install

Billing Questions

    View Bill

    Change Bill

    Sales—Offer Service Options

Maintenance Requests

    Report Problem

> Schedule Maintenance
>
> View Maintenance History

Info Requests

> Show Services
>
> Show Products
>
> Show Installation Procedures

Here is a possible design presenting these work processes through a process-oriented Conceptual Model:

Conceptual Model—Utility Customer Service

Application Window

"Conceptual Model—Utility Customer Service," cont. next page

The presentation rules followed in this design are as follows (this design is not complete; it simply provides some examples of components of a process-oriented model).

The overall application is represented as a tab metaphor. *Highest-level processes* (e.g., billing questions, maintenance requests) are represented by tabs, and each tab represents a work space for that process. The tabbed work space includes a main window where that process is carried out, plus two "common windows," where tools common across all highest-level processes are maintained.

Second-level subprocesses are represented by selections in the menu bar within each tab, and *third-level subprocesses* by selections in pull-downs from the menu bar.

Structured subprocesses are controlled through dimming of subprocesses in pull-downs (until earlier subprocesses are completed, later subprocesses are dimmed out and unselectable).

Completed subprocesses are designated with a check mark.

Common activities available across highest-level processes (i.e., Customer, Calculator) are presented as separate, dedicated windows within the tabbed work spaces.

All windows are dialog boxes—that is, they cannot be minimized. They are all unresizable and unscrollable, but are movable and modeless. The main dialog box represents subprocesses, and it changes contents as the user moves through the subprocesses in sequence to complete a given subprocess and process.

Different windows have different background colors. Note that the active tabbed workspace itself is dark gray, the main subprocess dialog box is white, and all common dialog boxes are light gray.

Now see how a second application, Money Management, could be cast in the same Conceptual Model Design—that is, could follow the same set of rules. The process hierarchy (or Reengineered Task Organization Model) in this case is as follows:

MONEY MANAGEMENT

    Investments

        (Portfolios, Securities, Positions)

    Income/Expense

        (Spend, Deposit, Transfer, etc.)

    Financial Planning

        (Ins./Ret., College, Refinancing)

    Taxes

        Self-Employed

            Business Profit/Loss

                8829: Bus./Home

                4562: Depr./Amort.

                C: Profit/Loss

            SE: Self-Emp. Tax

            F: Farm Profit/Loss

        Itemized Deductions

            A: Itemized Deductions

        Tax Computation

            B: Int./Div. Income

            D: Cap. Loss/Gain

            E: Supp. Income

            5329: IRA Income

            1040: Tax Comp

Here is how the functionality would be presented if it followed the same process-oriented Conceptual Model as the customer service application:

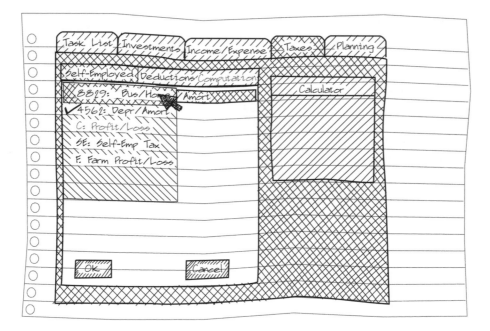

Notice how similar it looks to the customer service application. This is because it is following the same Conceptual Model, although in this case it is not the standard GUI Conceptual Model (e.g., Microsoft Windows, Apple Macintosh); it is a made-up process-oriented model.

Remember that a Conceptual Model Design, whether product or process oriented, whether industry standard or of your own design, is a set of rules about how to consistently present categories of functional components, and adhering to a defined Conceptual Model Design creates consistency and predictability within and across applications that follow that model.

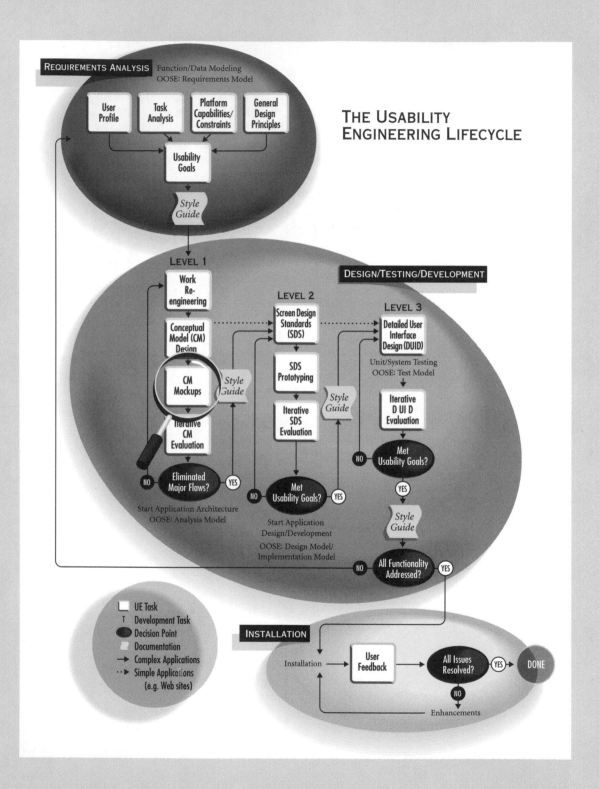

9

Conceptual Model Mock-ups

PURPOSE

There are several reasons to build Conceptual Model Mock-ups:

◆ The main point of Conceptual Model Mock-ups is to support formal evaluation of the Conceptual Model Design(s) generated in the *previous* task, in the Iterative Conceptual Model Evaluation task that comes *next*. Evaluation at this earliest stage of design means that you will not invest a lot of time designing without knowing whether you are on the right track.

◆ Comparing alternative Conceptual Model Designs in the Iterative Conceptual Model Evaluation task that comes next allows you to select the best model to move forward with and gives you more insight into the design issues represented in the alternative models that could not be resolved based on Requirements Analysis data alone.

◆ Recruiting users to evaluate very early, very high-level design ideas (in the Iterative Conceptual Model Evaluation task) helps to continue the ongoing, highly iterative process of understanding and addressing user requirements. An ongoing give-and-take between designers and users is simply a more effective approach than a monolithic approach in which Requirements Analysis is carried out exhaustively, followed by complete detailed user interface design.

Evaluation at this earliest stage of design helps you determine if you are on the right track before you invest a lot of time in design

219

DESCRIPTION

Conceptual Model Mock-ups will include representative pieces of the total product functionality, and only broad presentation and navigation design ideas

Optimally, two or three out of numerous Conceptual Model Designs should be selected for Conceptual Model Mock-ups and should represent important trade-offs that cannot be resolved with Requirements Analysis data alone

You are building the mock-ups to support evaluation of the general Conceptual Model Design rules you generated in the previous task. Thus, the Conceptual Model Mock-ups will only include small, representative pieces of the total product functionality. Also, only high-level presentation and navigation issues, as described in the previous chapter, are included in the mock-ups. There will be little, if any, real content to any particular display in the mock-ups, and at this point you are not at all concerned with screen layout and design. In a typical GUI, parts of the menu bar would be included in the Conceptual Model Mock-up to represent navigational pathways, and the major types of windows would be identified and named but not necessarily filled in with any detailed content.

Optimally, numerous competing Conceptual Model Designs would have been generated in the previous task, with two to three selected for implementation as Conceptual Model Mock-ups and initial evaluation. The final alternatives should be chosen to represent important trade-offs that cannot be resolved based on Requirements Analysis data alone. For example, you may not be sure whether one potential metaphor works better than another, or you may be struggling with some ease-of-use versus ease-of-learning trade-offs. Conceptual Model Mock-ups can be constructed to represent alternative Conceptual Model Designs that vary on these dimensions, and these can be compared in the Iterative Conceptual Model Evaluation task that comes next.

If a good prototyping tool and a proficient prototyper are available, the Conceptual Model Mock-ups can be realized as simple running prototypes ("high-fidelity" mock-ups). If not, then paper-based foils ("low-fidelity" mock-ups) will more than suffice. There is strong evidence to suggest that low-fidelity mock-ups are just as effective in revealing design flaws as high-fidelity mock-ups, at least at this early stage of design and perhaps later as well (Virzi et al. 1996).

A usability test of a running prototype is usually easier to conduct than a usability test of a paper-based foil, simply because it requires less intervention by the testers. But an important advantage of paper-based foils is that designers tend to be more objective about and less invested in designs represented on paper than designs constructed as prototypes. It is simply easier to throw away paper than to throw away hardware or software prototypes! They are also, of course, cheaper and quicker to produce.

SCHEDULING AND INTEGRATION WITH OTHER TASKS

The Conceptual Model Mock-ups task fits into the overall Usability Engineering Lifecycle in the following ways:

◆ This task is based directly on the previous task, Conceptual Model Design. Alternative models generated in that task are implemented as paper mock-ups or simple running prototypes.

◆ This task will then feed into the next task, Iterative Conceptual Model Evaluation, where the Conceptual Model Designs they represent will be evaluated through some technique such as formal usability testing.

The Conceptual Model Mock-ups task fits into the underlying software development methodology in the following ways:

◆ This task should *follow* the development of the Requirements Model in the Analysis phase of OOSE (or function and data modeling in a traditional rapid prototyping methodology), as it is represents Conceptual Model Design ideas generated from requirements analyses.

◆ This task should *precede* or *parallel* the development of the Analysis Model in the Analysis phase of OOSE (or the application architecture design in a traditional rapid prototyping methodology), as this task is part of the process of refining a Conceptual Model Design, which should in turn drive the design of the system architecture.

ROLES AND RESOURCES

In the Conceptual Model Mock-ups task, the usability roles might participate as follows:

Task leader: The User Interface Designer should take the lead role in this task.

Other resources: Any and all project team members who have participated in the Requirements Analysis task, as well as in the Work Reengineering and Conceptual Model Design tasks, should participate and provide input and feedback. The Usability Engineer should participate as well to provide direction and feedback. If running prototypes are planned, a proficient prototyper should be recruited to build them. Users might also participate in this task in the overall design process (see, e.g., Bloomer, Croft, and Wright 1997).

SAMPLE TECHNIQUE— A STEP-BY-STEP PROCEDURE

❶ Select the functionality. Select a small subset of functionality to feature in a mock-up, based on the most important issues, and based on variations in Conceptual Model Designs that you want to directly test and compare. Wixon and Wilson (1997) point out some good criteria for selecting functionality for mock-up and testing:

◆ Parts that all users will use
◆ New features with high visibility
◆ Features with mission-critical outcomes, even if infrequently used
◆ Older features that have been updated
◆ Parts of the product interface that the team has concerns about
◆ Features involving safety or liability concerns
◆ Features that will be highlighted in marketing efforts

❷ Sketch the user interface design. For the functionality selected in step 1, sketch the exact design for the mock-up. Include screen design detail only when it seems essential to establish enough context for the user to understand each step in the process of navigating through the interface. In most cases, you can just put some explanatory text in parentheses in empty windows to explain the general purpose of the window (see the example mock-up in the Sample Work Products and Templates section later in the chapter). In some cases, you may want to lay out some display content, and this is fine; just remember that detailed screen design is not your main focus at this time and there will be opportunities to focus on those details later.

❸ Build mock-ups. Either construct paper-based mock-ups, or implement the design as a simple running prototype. If you use paper, use one piece of paper to represent the screen. Separate pieces can represent specific windows, dialog boxes, and pull-down menus, which can be overlaid on the "screen" and on each other, simulating interaction.

If you implement the design(s) as a simple running prototype, focus on live navigation, with little or no screen design and processing of data input.

LEVEL OF EFFORT

Table 9.1 gives a sample level of effort for the Conceptual Model Mock-ups task. The work effort will vary widely depending on the complexity of the product and the fidelity of the mock-ups. This sample represents a simple to moderately complex application involving two analysts/designers and the development of two separate mock-ups built as running prototypes.

Table 9.1
Level of effort—Conceptual Model Mock-ups

Usability Time (2 staff, one a prototyper)

Step	Hrs
Select functionally	8
Sketch design(s)	24
Prototype designs	48
Total	80

ALTERNATIVE TECHNIQUES— A REVIEW

The main variation across techniques for constructing Conceptual Model Mock-ups is in the relative fidelity of the mock-ups. Virzi and colleagues (1996) point out a number of dimensions of mock-up fidelity, including

- **Breadth of features**: the number of features the mock-up supports
- **Degree of functionality**: the extent to which the details of operation are complete
- **Similarity of interaction**: how similar interactions with the mock-up are to interactions with the final product (e.g., a simulated vs. actual touchscreen interaction)

◆ **Aesthetic refinement**: how realistic displays are (e.g., colors, graphic design)

They note that low-fidelity mock-ups, such as paper-based foils, can have extensive breadth of features and a high degree of functionality, even if they are low on similarity of interaction and aesthetic refinement. Their comparison of low- and high-fidelity mock-ups found that when the main point is to identify major problems (as is the case here), rather than to collect accurate timing data, low-fidelity mock-ups were as sensitive (i.e., revealed as many problems and the same types of problems) as high-fidelity mock-ups, as long as comparable breadth of features and degree of functionality were included. The researchers do note that high-fidelity mock-ups are necessary for some things, such as taking accurate timing data (important down the line in Iterative Detailed User Interface Design Evaluation—see Chapter 16) and specifically evaluating aspects of physical interaction or aesthetic refinement.

SHORTCUTS

Paper-based foils can be considered a shortcut method for building mock-ups, as compared to running prototypes. Also, in very simple products, you might consider skipping the iterative evaluation of the Conceptual Model Design at this point (and thus skipping this mock-up task), and combine it with a single round of iterative evaluation when all three design levels are complete.

When resources are extremely tight, or no formal usability testing can be conducted for other reasons, at least have a Heuristic Evaluation or review of your mock-ups conducted by a user interface design expert (see Chapter 10) before proceeding.

WEB NOTES

In very simple Web sites and applications, you might consider skipping the creating and testing of the Conceptual Model Design mock-ups at this point in the lifecycle, and conduct iterative evaluation and redesign only after all three levels of design are complete. In complex Web sites and applications, however, you may want to independently evaluate the Conceptual Model Design(s) and then collapse design levels 2 and 3 for prototyping and evaluation.

Instead of paper foils or throwaway prototypes, in the case of Web sites and applications, the "mock-ups" can simply be partially coded products, for example, pages, panes, and navigational links with minimal page content detail.

SAMPLE WORK PRODUCTS AND TEMPLATES

One sample is offered here: Sample Conceptual Model Mock-up.

SAMPLE CONCEPTUAL MODEL MOCK-UP

The following Conceptual Model Mock-up is based on a travel application to be used by anyone at home on a personal computer. Users should

Desktop Folder Window

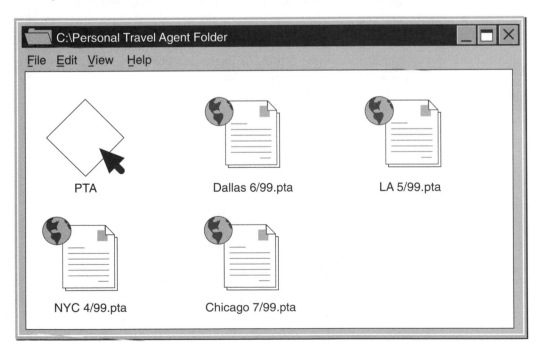

be able to find information and make their own travel reservations. It represents a product-oriented Conceptual Model Design and follows the standard GUI Conceptual Model described in Chapter 8. Primary products are "Trips," which include all kinds of reservations related to a given trip (air, hotel, car, etc.).

Also included would be partially complete pull-downs from each menu selection. Note that there is no screen design detail, only an identification of major displays and navigational pathways between them. Also note, however, that empty windows contain text that, during evaluation, will help users understand generally what function is to be performed in the window. Users will need this minimal context to make sense of the high-level mock-up.

Application and Document Windows

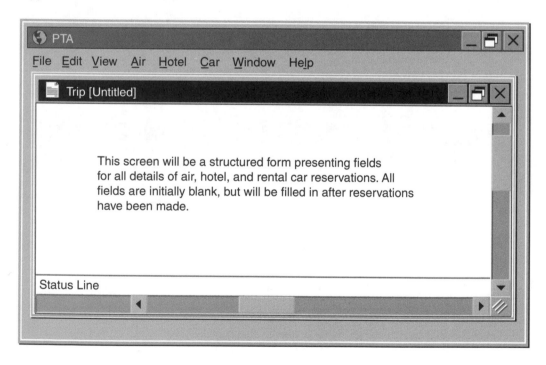

Pathway of Dialog Box Windows

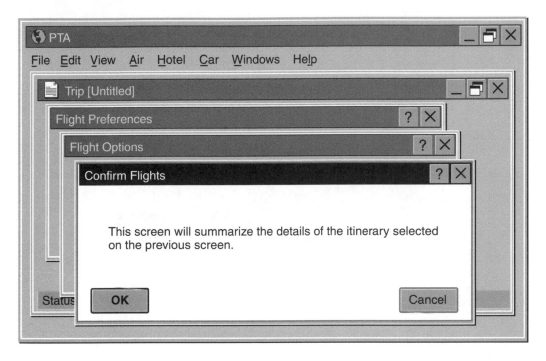

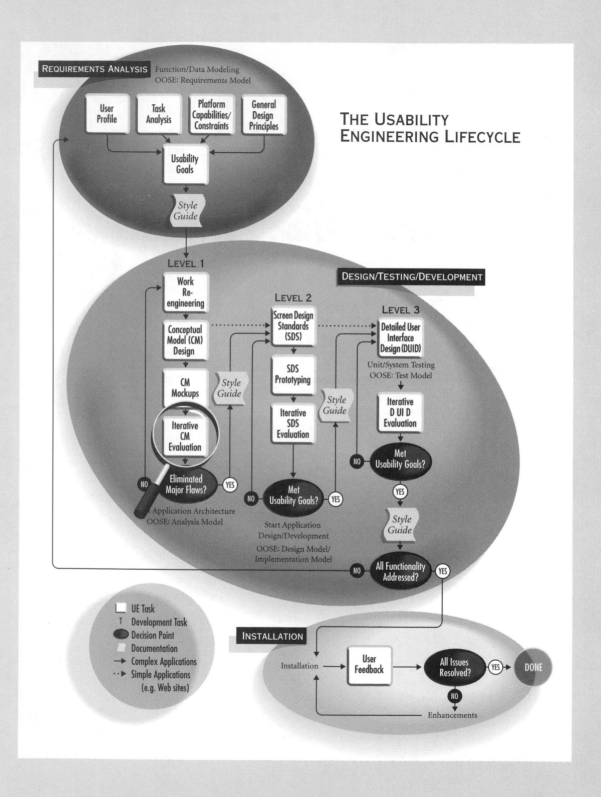

THE USABILITY
ENGINEERING LIFECYCLE

REQUIREMENTS ANALYSIS Function/Data Modeling
OOSE: Requirements Model

User Profile
Task Analysis
Platform Capabilities/ Constraints
General Design Principles

Usability Goals

Style Guide

LEVEL 1

Work Re-engineering

Conceptual Model (CM) Design

CM Mockups

Style Guide

Iterative CM Evaluation

Eliminated Major Flaws?   NO   YES

Application Architecture
OOSE: Analysis Model

DESIGN/TESTING/DEVELOPMENT

LEVEL 2

Screen Design Standards (SDS)

SDS Prototyping

Iterative SDS Evaluation

Style Guide

Met Usability Goals?   NO   YES

Start Application Design/Development

OOSE: Design Model/ Implementation Model

LEVEL 3

Detailed User Interface Design (DUID)

Unit/System Testing
OOSE: Test Model

Iterative D UI D Evaluation

Met Usability Goals?   NO   YES

Style Guide

All Functionality Addressed?   NO   YES

UE Task
T   Development Task
Decision Point
Documentation
→   Complex Applications
⇢   Simple Applications (e.g. Web sites)

INSTALLATION

Installation → User Feedback → All Issues Resolved?   YES → DONE

NO

Enhancements

10

Iterative Conceptual Model Evaluation

*The Iterative
Conceptual Model
Evaluation task
uses formal tech-
niques that are
much more objec-
tive than simply
asking for feedback
from users*

PURPOSE

The purpose of the Iterative Conceptual Model Evaluation task is to get some quick and early feedback on the usability of the Conceptual Model Design mock-ups generated in the previous two tasks. Formal evaluation techniques are much more objective and effective than just doing a demo and asking for subjective feedback from users.

Iterative design and evaluation can be efficiently and effectively conducted at a time when no major investment or commitment in detailed design or code has been made to any particular user interface design. Changes are thus simple and easy to make in response to findings. Refining the Conceptual Model Design through Iterative Conceptual Model Evaluation before either Detailed User Interface Design or development have begun minimizes costly revisions to completed designs or code. Spending resources now on usability evaluation saves resources in the long run by minimizing modifications to design or code during development and after implementation.

DESCRIPTION

The first decision to make is whether a given evaluation will focus on ease of learning or ease of use. Whether one or the other or both (in different evaluations) will be studied depends on the usability goals established during the Usability Goal Setting task. One technique for evaluation is *formal usability testing*. For each iteration, three to ten representative

Timing data will not be accurate at this point, as users will be thinking out loud

users (depending on factors such as diversity of users and number of iterations anticipated) should run through a set of core, high-frequency, realistic test tasks. Testing should be conducted in the users' actual work space if possible (as opposed to a usability lab or area away from their normal work environment). To test for ease of learning, minimal instruction should be given, or a one- or two-page "manual" provided. To test for ease of use, adequate training and practice should be provided to simulate expert usage. The testing should be videotaped, if possible, for data collection backup and presentation purposes. Error data should be collected, and users should be asked to "think out loud" as they work. Timing data is not typically collected in this early evaluation task. Timing data will not be accurate now, due to asking users to think out loud; and testing against specific, quantitative usability goals will be the focus of later evaluation tasks.

Error data and other observations are summarized to isolate major problem areas, and the Conceptual Model Design is redesigned to "engineer out" these identified problems. The revised design must then be retested to confirm that problems have been eliminated and to ensure that new ones have not been introduced. Design and testing should be carried out iteratively until all major identified problems at the Conceptual Model Design level have been eliminated.

The general steps for each iteration of testing include

◆ Plan the test and develop supporting materials.
◆ Run the test users and collect data as specified in the test plan.
◆ Analyze and interpret the data and formulate redesign recommendations.

At the end of each test, steps are

◆ Modify the Conceptual Model Design(s).
◆ Modify the Conceptual Model Mock-up(s).
◆ Modify the test plan and materials.

That is, you iterate back through the previous two tasks in the lifecycle and then return to this one. Iteration is terminated when all identified major problems have been eliminated, and a single Conceptual Model Design is optimized.

Scheduling and Integration with Other Tasks

The Iterative Conceptual Model Evaluation task fits into the overall Usability Engineering Lifecycle in the following ways:

◆ This task is based directly on the previous two tasks, Conceptual Model Design and Conceptual Model Mock-ups. The mock-ups, which represent alternative Conceptual Model Designs, are submitted to formal, objective evaluation techniques in this task. The Conceptual Model Design is then redesigned, realized in another mock-up, and reevaluated in an iterative fashion.

◆ Usability goals from the Usability Goal Setting task are consulted to determine whether a given evaluation will focus on ease of learning or ease of use and also to help formulate test tasks.

◆ When using the formal usability testing technique, the User Profiles will drive the selection of test users and provide direct input to the design of the pretest questionnaire.

◆ Test tasks used in conducting this task are adapted from Task Scenarios from the Contextual Task Analysis task.

◆ When the Conceptual Model Design is stabilized at the end of the final iteration of this task, it feeds directly into later design tasks (Screen Design Standards and Detailed User Interface Design) and is ultimately documented in the Style Guide.

The Iterative Conceptual Model Evaluation task fits into the underlying software development methodology in the following ways:

◆ This task should *follow* development of the Requirements Model in the Analysis phase of OOSE (or function and data modeling in a traditional rapid prototyping methodology), as it is evaluating Conceptual Model Design ideas generated from requirements analyses.

◆ This task should *precede* or *parallel* development of the Analysis Model in the Analysis phase of OOSE (or the application architecture design in a traditional rapid prototyping methodology), as this task is part of the process of refining a Conceptual Model Design, which should in turn drive the design of the system architecture.

ROLES AND RESOURCES

In the Iterative Conceptual Model Evaluation task, the usability roles might participate as follows:

Task leader: The Usability Engineer should take the lead role in this task.

Other resources: The User Interface Designer should participate as an assistant in both planning and executing the evaluation. Other team members can participate as assistants as needed, and all should participate as observers. In the formal usability testing technique, users will participate as test users, and they can also provide valuable input to the design of the test tasks.

SAMPLE TECHNIQUE— A STEP-BY-STEP PROCEDURE

The technique offered here for Iterative Conceptual Model Evaluation is formal usability testing. It can be divided into two phases: planning and preparing for testing and conducting the tests.

PLANNING AND PREPARING

Just as with other Usability Engineering Lifecycle tasks, *planning and preparing* for usability testing should be a highly collaborative activity, involving not only Usability Engineers and User Interface Designers (see Chapters 1 and 21 for definitions of all Usability Engineering roles), but also project management, developers, and user and/or marketing staff. As Wixon and Wilson (1997) point out, if these other stakeholders are not involved in preparing the test plans and committed to carrying them out, it will be easy for them to discard any results that point to serious problems requiring extensive rework.

❶ **Decide on ease of learning/ease of use focus for the test.** Based on the User Profile and the usability goals, first decide whether an ease-of-learning or ease-of-use test will be conducted. In the former, novice test users are recruited, only minimal introduction and instruction are provided, and the focus is on discovering how easy to learn the product user interface is for the first-time, minimally trained user. In the latter, users must be trained and expertise simulated, so that measures of efficiency of expert use can be obtained.

❷ **Decide on user and task focus for the test.** Identify the type and range of users to be included in the test. You might decide to focus on one category of potential users considered to be "high-priority" users (e.g., in a police department application to manage property, they might be police officers) or to sample broadly from all potential categories of intended users (e.g., police officers, property clerks, station commanders). Once you have chosen a group of users to focus on, be sure to sample representatively *within* the overall group, so that no sampling bias is introduced into the data. For example, if you know computer literacy varies widely in the population of users, include both computer-naive and computer-literate test users in your sample. The User Profiles and usability goals will provide some direction in making sampling decisions.

Make a list of specific user characteristics and skill levels that must be included in the test sample, indicating the total numbers of users to be tested and the relative numbers of each characteristic and skill level to be included.

Next, identify the general types of *tasks* to focus on. Usually these should be core, high-frequency tasks and/or tasks of most importance to the business. For example, in the police department application, typical tasks might include simple property entry tasks, complex property entry tasks, returning property to owners, and transferring property out of the police station.

Wixon and Wilson (1997) offer some suggestions for where to focus testing:

◆ Features that all users will use
◆ New features with high visibility
◆ Features with mission-critical outcomes, even if infrequently used
◆ Older features that have been updated
◆ Parts of the product interface that the team has concerns about
◆ Features involving safety or liability concerns
◆ Features that will be highlighted in marketing efforts

❸ **Design test tasks.** The Contextual Task Analysis will have yielded some Task Scenarios appropriate to adapt for use in testing. Recruit an experienced end user to help design the detailed tasks for the test. Write task descriptions in a format that can be handed directly to test users, read, and easily understood. Make tasks as realistic as possible. Estimate how long it will take the slowest user to complete all preliminary activities, all test tasks, and any posttest questionnaires. A good rule of thumb is not to exceed two hours total time. Any longer than this is both tiring to users and a long time to ask them to leave their work.

Wixon and Wilson (1997) distinguish between two types of tasks—"results based"and "process based." In a *results-based* task, users are given a description (or picture) of the desired end result of a task, then given a starting point on the mock-up and asked to achieve the result. Users must structure the approach to the task themselves. By contrast, in a *process-based* task, the steps or subgoals for achieving the overall goal of a task are outlined for the user (in task terms, not in user interface–specific terms). Both types of tasks have their pros and cons. Results-based tasks might be more realistic, because they better reflect real usage. That is, users normally have a goal in mind and no predefined structure to help them achieve that goal. But it can be very difficult to collect data that can be easily summarized across users in this type of task, precisely because users will approach a problem in many unique ways. Process-based tasks force users to structure a task in one common way, allowing the tester to collect comparable data across users more easily as well as to test specific aspects of the interface. The trade-off is that such tasks may not represent real usage situations well.

I tend to use process-based tasks, because I am assured of getting feedback (and comparable feedback across all test users) on the specific aspects of the interface I am concerned with at any particular level of testing (see, e.g., the Sample Test Task and Data Collection Sheet Template with Sample Data, in the Sample Work Products and Templates section later in the chapter). However, it might make sense to use results-based tasks during Iterative Conceptual Model Evaluation, as they might provide a better sense of how users respond to the overall *framework* of the design in a more realistic usage situation. Then, once you are fairly confident about the overall approach to the task and pathways through the interface that users might choose on their own, process-based tasks could be used at later levels of design and testing, where the focus is on more specific, detailed aspects of the interface.

Wixon and Wilson (1997) also point out that in a given test session, where multiple test tasks are presented to users, the tasks can be either completely *independent* of one another or *dependent*—that is, the user must successfully complete one task before moving on to the next. Again, there are advantages and disadvantages to each. Dependent tasks are often more realistic, but if users get stuck on one, they may have difficulty doing any others. Independent tasks don't have this drawback, but they may be less realistic.

Usually, I use a mixture of dependent and independent tasks. I use whole tasks that, because they are process based, are in fact a set of subtasks completely dependent on one another (see the Test Task in the Sample Work Products and Templates section). But I also use a number of overall tasks in a testing session, and I tend to make these completely independent of one another. In designing tasks of any type, I try to be sure that the tasks are as realistic as possible (that is, they represent real and typical work tasks that the product is intended to support), but also exercise all the parts of the interface that I am concerned with testing at a given stage in the design process.

Most commonly, users will be tested one at a time. Some testers, however, have found it useful to test users in pairs and have them work together on tasks (see, e.g., Comstock 1983). Users working together naturally tend to "think out loud" while they are working, and sometimes richer data can be gathered this way.

A sample test task is given in the Sample Work Products and Templates section later in this chapter. Another is given in the Sample Work Products and Templates section (see Sample Task Scenarios) of Chapter 3 on Contextual Task Analysis.

❹ Design the test and develop test materials. Plan the exact sequence of events for the test. A single test session should take somewhere between one and three hours. Less than one hour is usually not enough time to go through all procedures and collect meaningful data, and over three hours is usually too tiring for test users and testers alike. Then develop all supporting materials. See the Sample Work Products and Templates section for examples of each of the items described below.

- **Observer briefing:** Instructions for designers, developers, and any others who plan to observe the test sessions: information about how to schedule an observation; requests not to interrupt or interfere in any way during the testing. Hand this out to potential observers before the test sessions.
- **Welcome:** A general statement of purpose and an expression of appreciation for the test user's participation. Hand this out along with the introduction and training materials at the beginning of the test session.
- **Introduction:** A description of how the test session will be administered, so the test user knows what to expect and what will be expected of him or her. This should always include a comment on the fact that it is the *interface* that is being tested, rather than the *user*, to put the test user at ease and reduce tension and performance anxiety. Hand this out along with the welcome and training materials at the beginning of the test session.
- **Pretest questionnaire:** A set of questions about test user characteristics that will help in the interpretation of data. Questions should poll job role and

experience, skill levels, demographics, and attitudes towards technology, and can be drawn directly from the User Profile. Hand this out to each test user for completion before commencing the test.

◆ **Training:** If this is an ease-of-learning (rather than an ease-of-use) test, no explicit instructions or training are provided, just a brief conceptual description of the functionality represented in the mock-ups and enough background to get the test user started on exploring the mock-ups. For an ease-of-use test, training should be complete. Walk the user through all aspects of application usage, and provide enough practice to simulate expert usage. Training can be written and handed out along with the welcome and introduction materials or conducted by the tester at the beginning of the test session.

◆ **Video permission form:** If you plan to videotape the test sessions, it is important to get permission from users to do so. It is best to get this permission in writing, and you can prepare a standard form for this.

◆ **Test tasks:** Tasks to perform on the mock-ups, handed out one a time to the test users. These are the actual test situations during which you collect data. Test users first read through the instructions for a task and may refer back to them at any time while carrying out the task.

◆ **Data collection sheets:** Log errors and record other observations during each test task. Record user comments when this seems helpful for data interpretation. You need to design data collection sheets in advance to provide a format for collecting and documenting this data. Test sessions may also be videotaped so that any data missing from the sheets can be recovered. Videotapes also can be useful to present test results to audiences that were unable to observe during testing.

◆ **Posttest questionnaire:** These collect some *subjective* reactions of the test users to the mock-ups. Mainly objective *performance* measures are collected during the test sessions. Here you can ask for subjective reactions as well as suggestions for improvement in specific areas.

◆ **Data analysis summaries:** Typically, in usability testing at this point in the lifecycle, the goal is primarily to reveal any basic, glaring flaws in design at the Conceptual Model Design level, rather than to fine-tune the interface to meet usability goals, which will be addressed in later tasks. Therefore, the main data of interest are errors, points of confusion, and users' introspection into their own thought processes as they learn and use the application. Most simply, a copy of the data collection sheet can be used to tally the number and type of errors across test users for each step. Then a table of "Problems and Proposed Solutions" can be prepared.

❺ Design and assemble the test environment. For products that will be used in a typical, quiet office environment, testing can be successfully conducted in a usability lab. If a lab is not available, locate a room where the testing can take place. In either case, try to set it up to resemble the typical user's real work area as much as possible. Bring in a workstation, furniture, plants, a coffee maker, and so on. Whenever possible, however, but at least for products that will be used in more unusual work environments (e.g., police stations, hospital operating rooms), testing should be carried out in the actual intended work environment.

Arrange video cameras as unobtrusively as possible (on the ceiling is ideal). Two cameras are optimal, with their images integrated on a single tape. Focus one on the computer screen and the other on the user's face. Make chairs available for observers where they can see but are not hovering around the user. Make sure the prototype database is populated with appropriate data to support the test tasks. Plan and arrange for any additional personnel required to support the testing, such as camera operators, data recorders, and people to conduct posttest questionnaires so the experimenter can move on to the next test user.

❻ Recruit/schedule pilot test users. Recruit and schedule one, two, or three "pilot" users. Make sure they are as representative of the actual target user population as the final test users will be.

❼ Run pilot test. Run the pilot users through the test procedure as a way of "debugging" the test procedure and all supporting materials. Do not bother to analyze the data, and do not include it in the final data analysis. Simply observe where materials and procedures need to be changed to increase clarity of instructions and accuracy of data collection.

Wixon and Wilson (1997) list some specific things that pilot testing can help ascertain:

◆ A running prototype is actually in working order with all necessary data loaded.

◆ All supporting materials are ready.

◆ All observation and data collection methods are working.

◆ All planned tasks can be accomplished in the planned time period.

◆ Time is allotted to reset the mock-up between test users.

◆ All observers understand the ground rules for observation.

❽ **Revise test procedures and materials.** Make any necessary changes to procedures and materials as a result of step 7.

❾ **Recruit/schedule test users.** Consult the description of test users specified in step 2. Consult with the business customer to discuss where test users might be recruited. For each iteration, three to ten representative users (depending on factors such as diversity of users and number of iterations anticipated) should run through the test.

Do not underestimate the time and resources it might take to recruit appropriate test users (Wixon and Wilson 1997). The effort required will depend on such things as whether users are in-house or outside the company, whether outside users are from an installed base or will be brand-new customers, how large the potential pool of users is, how pressed for time users are in their work, where they are located relative to the testing site, and how valuable their time is (you may have to pay people to participate). Techniques to use when it is hard to recruit users for any of these reasons include conducting remote testing (see the Alternative Techniques—A Review section later in the chapter), recruiting through the Internet, providing large incentives, and hiring outside search firms to recruit test users (Wixon and Wilson 1997). Ehrlich and Rohn (1994) suggest from experience that recruiting outside users can take anywhere from half an hour to six hours *each*.

Add half an hour to the planned length of a test session (see step 3), and schedule users no closer together than this interval. This leaves time for users who are late, who take longer than expected, and so on. It also leaves time to reset the mock-ups, complete any note taking on the data collection sheets, and give the testers a break!

Finally, allow for occasional no-shows. You can reduce no-shows by reminding users a day before their scheduled test session, and you can sometimes arrange to have backup test users who can step in if someone fails to show (Wixon and Wilson 1997).

CONDUCTING THE TESTS

Actually conducting usability testing involves the following five steps.

❶ **Run the test and collect data.** Run the test users through the testing procedure as planned and scheduled, videotaping if possible and collecting data on the data collection sheets. Assign numbers to test users in the order they are tested, and code all related test materials from a given user with that number.

- First present the welcome. Reading it to the user from a script is best, to ensure consistent presentation across users and also to establish communication and rapport with the user.
- Collect the pretest information using the prepared questionnaire. This information is mainly for documenting user characteristics that might help explain the user's behavior in the testing (e.g., job type, experience level with computers/GUIs) and for comparing the users who participate in the mock-up testing with the overall User Profile of the target audience to establish that you have a representative sample of users.
- Read the introduction to the user from a script. Ask if he or she has any questions.
- For an ease-of-learning test, hand the user the training materials to read, or read them to the user, and then answer any questions that are *not* questions about how the interface works. Tell the user to keep the training materials and refer to them anytime during the test. For an ease-of-use test, conduct the training one-on-one from a prepared script, providing opportunities for hands-on practice.
- If mock-ups representing alternative designs are being compared, be sure to randomize the order in which the mock-ups are presented across users, so that the order does not influence your results. Sometimes learning can be transferred from one mock-up to the next, which may falsely suggest that the later ones are easier. Conversely, sometimes learning on the earlier mock-ups causes interference in learning the later ones, falsely suggesting that the earlier ones are easier. Only if a given mock-up shows optimal performance *regardless of order* is the effect valid. Ideally, be sure that equal numbers of users experience the mock-ups in each possible order, and be sure all users experience all mock-ups. If this would require too many users, at least be sure each mock-up is experienced first and last with at least one user.
- Hand the user the first test task, and let her or him read it through completely before starting. Again, answer any questions that do not relate directly to how the interface works.
- During the testing, it is very important not to lead the user in any way, or give away any information about how the interface works, as this would invalidate the data being collected. This is not easy to do, especially if users cannot remember not to ask inappropriate questions. It often takes a certain amount of experience conducting usability tests before testers are able to consistently

inhibit their natural instinct to instruct and help. Testers should carefully limit their comments and questions to understanding what the user is doing and why, never giving away what to do next or how to accomplish something. If users become absolutely stuck and have no idea what to do, the tester should provide the minimum amount of information necessary to get the user moving again.

◆ As you work with users during this level of design and testing, encourage them to think out loud while they interact with the mock-up. If they do not, ask them questions constantly about why they are doing what they are doing, what they expect will happen, how they interpret what happened, and so on. At this stage you are most interested in errors and sources of confusion and in getting insight into how the design of the mock-up may be contributing to them. Taking accurate timing data is not a priority. At later levels of design and testing, when you are testing for the achievement of specific performance goals, you will not intervene so much as users work, as this would invalidate your timing data.

◆ Collect data on the data collection sheets all through the testing for each test task. Ideally, two separate testers are involved, one managing and facilitating the testing and one recording the data. Videotaping is not necessary for adequate data collection but can be done if you want to show it to some audience that cannot be present at the actual test sessions. It also provides a backup if recorded data is lost or difficult to interpret later. If you do use videotaping, bear in mind Mackay's (1995) guidelines for ethical use, summarized in Chapter 3.

◆ Complete all planned test tasks with a given mock-up before moving on to the next mock-up. Use the same test tasks for all mock-ups.

◆ When all test tasks have been completed with all mock-ups for a given user, collect the posttest information using the prepared questionnaire. Ask the user the prepared questions verbally, and record the answers on the form. The main purpose of the posttest questionnaire is to solicit *subjective* feedback from the user. When comparing multiple mock-ups, this is where you ask users which they would prefer, and get them to explain why. This can then be compared with their actual performance on the different mock-ups.

❷ **Summarize data.** Collate and summarize the data as planned—for example, number of errors per task, types of errors per task, and collections of user comments after particularly common errors.

Wixon and Wilson (1997) offer a list of possible ways to summarize data, which I paraphrase below. Note that you can summarize data across all tasks, if the tasks take users through the same functionality and interface, or across individual tasks, if they exercise different parts of the functionality and interface. In most cases, you will be summarizing across all test users, or perhaps across important subgroups of users.

◆ Number of times each particular problem was experienced
◆ Amount of time spent in errors versus in productive work
◆ Number of users experiencing a given problem
◆ Total number of errors of all types for a particular task

In the Sample Work Products and Templates section, I offer a sample Data Analysis Sheet that shows a tally of all errors made on a step-by-step basis *across all users* during a particular task. From this summary, I could have further summarized the data in all the above ways except the timing summary.

I usually find simple data summaries such as these completely sufficient. I agree with Wixon and Wilson (1997) and Dumas and Redish (1993) that in most cases, inferential statistical analysis of data is not appropriate in an engineering environment. Often testers are not experienced in these techniques, and audiences for test results (e.g., developers and designers) are not experienced in interpreting statistical results anyway. Furthermore, sample sizes are usually too small, and other necessary assumptions for statistical analysis (e.g., random sampling, normal curves) are not met. For all these reasons, I almost never use inferential statistics for data summary and analysis when doing usability testing in a product development context.

More sophisticated ways of summarizing data, such as Pareto Charts and Impact Analysis Tables, can be useful in some situations. Impact Analysis Tables offer a way to weight the relative severity of identified problems, and Pareto Charts allow you to identify the subset of all identified problems that account for the main impact on usability. If you are interested in learning how to use these data summary techniques, I refer you to Wixon and Wilson (1997).

❸ **Analyze/interpret data.** Focus on areas where the data seems to indicate a problem (high frequency of errors, a common confusion), and try to interpret these problem areas by analyzing what it is about the interface that might account for them. You will be focusing on problems at the Conceptual Model Design level, but you may also uncover problems with screen design issues (if you have included any screen design detail in your mock-ups), which you can hold and address during later design tasks (i.e., Screen Design Standards and Detailed User Interface Design).

❹ **Draw conclusions/formulate recommended design changes.** Draw conclusions about the specific sources of identified problems, and formulate recommended design changes to eliminate these problems. Recommendations might include a prioritization of problems as well as a prioritization of solutions. Problem areas can be ranked according to their impact on usability, and solutions can be ranked on how expensive they would be to implement. Problems with high impact on usability that have cheap solutions can be given highest priority, followed by problems with high impact but expensive solutions. Lowest in priority would be problems with low impact but expensive solutions. In turn, problem impact can be assessed in different ways, such as number of users affected, amount of time wasted over a problem, whether a problem caused total paralysis or just wasted time, and the number of times users tended to experience a given problem. (Wixon and Wilson 1997).

In the Sample Work Products and Templates section, I offer a sample "Problems and Solutions" chart as a way to summarize recommendations. Wixon and Wilson (1997) suggest a more detailed chart in which, for each identified problem, they assign:

◆ A severity ranking
◆ An assessment of impact on user performance
◆ Alternative solutions
◆ A recommended solution
◆ An estimated cost of the recommended solution
◆ A status that reports whether the project team decides to fix, defer, or ignore the problem

A simple chart like mine will probably suffice when a team is working closely together on all aspects of design and implementation. Wixon and Wilson's more detailed chart will be useful when project team members are dispersed and working independently, and thus thorough, clear, and detailed documentation is more crucial to communication within the team.

Finally, it can be very useful for usability practitioners to track the number of problems they identify in testing and the number of those that actually get addressed (either immediately fixed, or at least planned for the next release) across projects, as a concrete measure of their contribution to the development organization (Wixon and Wilson 1997). This can help down the line when trying to win (or just maintain!) funding and resources from management, and when trying to "sell" Usability Engineering services to other projects in the development organization.

❺ **Document/present results.** When project team members cannot be present during testing, put together presentation props and clips from the videotapes and present the results orally whenever possible. Video clips can be very effective in communicating usability test results, but preparing them is labor intensive. Nielsen (1993a) reports that it takes three to ten hours to prepare one hour of video clips.

At least document the results in a report, which should have an executive summary (high-level description of identified problems and recommended changes) as well as a more detailed summary of data, interpretations, and recommended design changes. Wixon and Wilson (1997) suggest soliciting feedback on the usability of your test reports from their intended audiences (e.g., project team members, management, those responsible for fixing identified usability problems) and refining them in response to this feedback. Eventually you will develop a "template" format that you can reuse. Simple language and lots of illustrations, lists, and tables will enhance your report.

As pointed out elsewhere in this book, documentation in general has varying importance depending on the project and organizational factors, such as size, complexity, and timetable of a project, and on the level of maturity of an organization with respect to Usability Engineering. Although there is often resistance to documentation (see Wixon and Wilson 1997), in my opinion, documentation usually serves an important function but is not *sufficient* as the main form of communication. It is important as a memory aid, a communication aid, and a historical record, but it should not be used as a primary form of communication within project teams.

Remember that usability testing often reveals problems and flaws in design. Usually you should not distribute reports outside the project team without the permission of project management. There are exceptions to this of course. I know of one internal Usability Engineering organization that got its start precisely by conducting a usability test late in the development cycle of a project and then sharing the results with upper management. This did not endear them to the project team, who were forced to pull their product back after announcing its impending release and rework it significantly due to usability flaws revealed in the testing. But it did call attention to the importance of usability and the value of Usability Engineering, and it resulted in support and funding from upper management to establish and grow a Usability Engineering department within the company.

LEVEL OF EFFORT

Table 10.1 gives a sample level of effort for the Iterative Conceptual Model Evaluation task. The work effort for this task will vary widely depending on the technique chosen and on the complexity of the product. This sample represents usability testing of a moderately complex product, with two testers participating.

Note that the level of effort is estimated for a *first iteration test*. Certain steps will take less time in later iterations, specifically the first four, which involve designing and developing the test procedure and materials. Once a basic test procedure and test materials are developed and debugged, they can be reused across iterations. The only changes required are those that involve tailoring materials to the redesigned mock-up.

Table 10.1
Level of effort—Iterative Conceptual Model Evaluation

Usability Time

Step	Hrs
Design/develop the test tasks/materials	32
Design/assemble test environment	8
Run pilot test	8
Revise test tasks/materials	8
Run test/collect data	32
Summarize/interpret data, draw conclusions	16
Document/present results	40
Total	144

These days, it is possible to conduct usability testing remotely via networking, the Internet, and video conferencing

ALTERNATIVE TECHNIQUES— A REVIEW

These days, it is possible (via networking, the Internet, and video conferencing) to conduct usability testing *remotely*, that is, to have the testers and test users separated by space and even time. These remote techniques also support conducting testing in the user's natural work environment.

A number of possible remote testing techniques are reviewed by Hartson and his colleagues (1996), and four of them are briefly described here:

◆ **Remote-control evaluation:** The user's computer (in the user's work environment) and the tester's computer (in a remote usability lab) are connected via the Internet or via commercially available software and a phone line. The tester can view (and videotape) the user's inter-action in real time on the user's own computer and communicate with the user during testing, as is done in more traditional testing. Or the tester can have usage data collected automatically by other spe-cialized software installed on the user's computer.

◆ **Video conferencing:** A remote tester can view the user's interaction on the user's own computer in his or her own work environment on video-conferencing equipment, communicating with the user simul-taneously by phone.

◆ **Instrumented remote evaluation:** Software monitors, which collect usage data, are installed on the user's computer. This data is then packaged and sent over a network (e.g., the Internet) to the testers for analysis.

◆ **Semi-instrumented remote evaluation:** In this technique, users are trained to identify usability problems during their normal usage of an application. The application has a function built in through which the user "tags" the context of their problem. The application records the system state when the user invokes this tagging function and then prompts the user to record a description of the problem, either writ-ten or verbal. The package of system state and user comments is then forwarded to testers over a network (e.g., the Internet).

Studies testing the effectiveness and validity of some of these remote techniques show that they each have their own particular drawbacks, but nevertheless seem to show promise (Hartson et al. 1996). Remote testing has the potential advantages of

◆ Allowing testers access to widely dispersed user populations
◆ Eliminating travel time and costs for users or testers
◆ Minimizing scheduling problems by not requiring testers to be pres-ent (in time or space) during testing
◆ Allowing users to be tested in their natural work environment

In many of the above techniques, training, instructions and pre- and posttest questionnaires can be administered via email or a Web site.

Nielsen and Mack (1994) provide instructions on how to execute a number of usability evaluation techniques that are alternatives to formal usability testing

In their book *Usability Inspection Methods* (1994), Nielsen and Mack provide instructions on how to execute a number of usability evaluation techniques that are alternatives to formal usability testing as described in the sample technique in this chapter. In all these techniques, rather than have representative users perform tasks on a mock-up, various kinds of staff such as usability experts, but also developers, users, and marketers, attempt to evaluate the potential usability of a given user interface design, identify usability flaws, and generate redesign solutions to them, based on a design specification or a prototyped design. In brief, the techniques covered in this excellent book include

◆ **Heuristic Evaluations:** Usability experts review a design based on their knowledge of human cognition and general user interface design guidelines.

◆ **Guideline reviews:** An interface is inspected for adherence to some list of general user interface guidelines.

◆ **Pluralistic walk-throughs:** Users, developers, and usability experts step through a design together based on a test task, discussing usability issues as they arise.

◆ **Consistency inspections:** Representatives from the user interface design teams from different products within a product family inspect the design of a new product user interface to ensure consistency across the product family.

◆ **Standards inspections:** An expert in the relevant user interface standard (e.g., MS Windows 95) checks an interface design for adherence to those standards.

◆ **Cognitive walk-throughs:** The analyst simulates a user's problem-solving process at each step in carrying out a task scenario on a given user interface design to analyze it for usability successes and failures. This technique does not require a usability specialist (see, e.g., John and Packer 1995).

◆ **Formal usability inspections:** This is a group process very similar to code inspections, except it is oriented towards identifying and resolving usability issues.

When used in the context of the Usability Engineering Lifecycle, these alternative evaluation techniques can be premised on the various Requirements Analysis tasks that precede the design and evaluation tasks. And they can be carried out by specialists skilled at least in user interface design, if not in Usability Engineering in general. They will be more effective as alternative evaluation techniques when used in this context than when used in isolation from Requirements Analysis data.

Besides providing thorough instructions on how to carry out these various techniques, Nielsen and Mack's book offers data comparing them to each other and to usability testing on a number of criteria. Generally speaking, they all have their strengths and weaknesses. Based on my own experience, I believe there is no substitute for formal usability testing, but I have used some of these techniques successfully when resources are not available for usability testing. And the techniques can be combined for more effective evaluation. For example, consistency inspections and/or standards inspections could be combined with Heuristic Evaluations or cognitive walk-throughs to evaluate a single interface, not only for general usability but also for compliance with product family and platform design standards.

Inspection techniques can be useful when resources are not available for formal usability testing

If you are a usability practitioner and are asked to perform a Heuristic Evaluation as a substitute for a usability test, Sawyer, Flanders, and Wixon (1996) offer some good advice on how best to have an impact. They are usability practitioners at Digital Equipment Corporation, where, as part of strategic planning for the Usability Engineering function at DEC, they came up with a way to measure the impact of their Heuristic Evaluations. They now use this measure to help plan the use of their limited resources most effectively and to provide feedback to management on their performance. Their approach to maximizing the impact of a Heuristic Evaluation includes the following:

◆ Offer a written proposal to your "client" stating exactly what parts of the product you will inspect and which aspects of usability you will assess (e.g., Style Guide compliance, visual design, on-line help).

◆ Provide your client with documentation describing the design principles on which you will base your inspection.

◆ Produce a written report clearly enumerating problems found. For each problem identified, provide specific principles violated, a relative rating of severity, and a specific, detailed redesign solution.

◆ Require (up front as part of your "contract" with your client) that, for each problem identified in your report, your client state in writing whether and when they will fix the problem, whether they will use your recommended solution or not, and if they will not address a problem, why not.

Another way to bypass usability testing is to employ formal computational models of human performance to predict performance on specific designs

This approach works in their organization—that is, they have a measurable impact on products, and other usability practitioners can learn from their experience.

Another way to bypass usability testing is to evaluate design ideas by employing formal computational models of human performance to predict performance on specific designs. The idea behind this approach is that a fairly simple model of human perceptual, cognitive, and motor processing from which you can compute or predict performance in given circumstances can substitute for running tests with actual users. While some studies have shown that these models can predict simple expert performance times fairly accurately, they do not shed light on ease-of-learning issues or reveal sources of errors and confusion very well. Also, such models do not take into account the rich variations in work situations, task types, and user characteristics—all of which are known to significantly impact user performance. In addition, you don't learn anything new about users and designs in general by performing computations with a model; every usability test I run is a rich learning experience that goes beyond simply learning about a particular design. Finally, in my experience, computational models are not nearly as compelling to designers and developers as usability tests of actual users. Though I have not found them particularly useful, they do offer a possible shortcut that is better than no evaluation at all. If you are interested in learning more about these models and how to use them for design evaluation, I recommend Kieras, Wood, and Meyer (1995) and Bellotti and colleagues (1995).

Shortcuts

One way to cut down on the labor of running iterative usability testing is to have the entire team participate fully in the whole process. If all team members are present during an entire testing session, you can skip steps 2–5 of *conducting* the test, as described in the Sample Technique—A Step-by-Step Procedure, and simply convene the whole team right after testing to analyze results and generate redesign ideas (Wixon and Wilson 1997). Analysis can be done as a team activity using "affinity diagrams" or card sorting (see Chapter 3), two similar techniques that involve recording individual data points (in this case errors or user comments) on cards or self-sticking notes and then sorting them into related groups.

You won't have documentation for historical purposes or to communicate results outside the team in this approach, but it can cut down dramatically on time, allowing more iterations of testing in shorter time frames and at less expense.

When resources are extremely tight, or no formal usability testing can be conducted for other reasons, at least have a Heuristic Evaluation or review of your design conducted by a usability expert before proceeding. See all of the books listed under Jakob Nielsen for this chapter in the References and especially Nielsen and Mack (1994), whose book describes eight different methods for "usability inspections," including Heuristic Evaluations.

For very simple products, you might consider skipping the iterative evaluation of the Conceptual Model Design at this point, and combine it with a single round of iterative evaluation when all three design levels are complete.

WEB NOTES

In relatively simple Web sites and applications, it might be more practical to combine the three levels of the design process into a single level, where Conceptual Model Design, Screen Design Standards, and Detailed User Interface Design are all sketched out, in sequence, before any evaluation proceeds. Then a single process of design and evaluation iterations can be carried out. In this case, evaluation must address all levels of design simultaneously. This is practical only if the whole product is fairly simple, which Web sites and applications often are. Remember that even if Detailed User Interface Design is drafted before any evaluation commences, it is still crucial to consider all the same design issues that arise in the Conceptual Model Design and Screen Design Standards tasks when conducting design and evaluation in a three-level process.

In Web sites and applications of intermediate complexity, the first design level, Conceptual Model Design, might be conducted as described. Then one additional process of iterative design and evaluation could be carried out combining Screen Design Standards and Detailed User Interface Design. Also, in the case of Web site or application design, mock-ups can simply be partially coded Web sites or applications (for example, browser panes and navigational links, but little page context), rather than paper foils or throwaway prototypes.

Remote testing (see the Alternative Techniques—A Review section) is also particularly well suited to testing Web sites and applications.

SAMPLE WORK PRODUCTS AND TEMPLATES

This section contains samples of what each of the recommended supporting materials for a formal usability test might look like (see the section Sample Technique—A Step-by-Step Procedure). All are adapted from a project developing a property management application for use in a large city police department. The following are included:

- Sample Observer Briefing
- Sample Welcome
- Sample Introduction
- Sample Pretest Questionnaire
- Sample Training Materials
- Sample Video Permission Form
- Sample Test Task
- Data Collection Sheet Template
- Sample Posttest Questionnaire
- Data Summary Sheet Template with Sample Data
- Data Analysis Sheet Template with Sample Data

SAMPLE OBSERVER BRIEFING

Observer Briefing

You are invited and encouraged to observe part of the Property Application usability test.

Although we will be videotaping the testing, and then collating and summarizing the results, there is nothing like being present at the testing to really understand the users' responses to your design. The videotaping cannot capture all there is to see; occasionally comments are made that are not intelligible on the tape; and the summarized data does not give you a real sense of what the users' experiences were like.

Thus, we very strongly encourage you to attend as much as you can, within the limits of your own schedule and the guidelines below.

The testing will take place (dates), at (location). Test users and observers are scheduled at the times shown on the attached document.

Ordinarily in a usability lab, users and observers are separated by one-way glass, so users are unaware of observers. This minimizes the pressure and anxiety test users may feel about being observed. Since we do not have such facilities, in order that your observation be least disruptive and stressful to the test users, we ask that you observe the following simple guidelines:

1. Please schedule your observations in advance through (contact person and phone number or email address). We will be limiting the number of observers at any time to (a number, ideally no more than four). If you suddenly have some time free, we certainly encourage you to check and see if you can observe, but do not count on being able to schedule observation time at the last minute.
2. Having people come and go during testing would be distracting and disruptive to our test users, so please arrive at least a few minutes before a given test user is scheduled to begin, and plan on staying until that user has finished.
3. It is especially important that you do not talk at all during the testing, either among your fellow observers or to the user. Only the study administrator, (name), will be talking with the test users. We must tightly control everything that is said to each user during testing. Please remember that your only role is to observe. You are welcome to take notes for any reason if you wish. Please also refrain from moving around the room. We want to minimize any distractions for the test users.

   In the event of a question about the application or what it does that (name of test administrator) would like to answer but can't, she or he may turn to the developers or business customers in the observer audience for help. In this case only, we would appreciate your input, but please listen closely to how (name of test administrator) asks you to respond to the question and follow his or her direction.

Thank you in advance for your cooperation with these simple guidelines. We look forward to having you sit in on the usability testing, and to hearing your insights afterwards, as we consider the results and think about implications for redesign.

SAMPLE WELCOME

Welcome

Welcome to the **Property Application USABILITY STUDY!**

We are conducting this study for the **Property Application project team.** The Property Application project team is building the Property Application to **support personnel in the police stations and warehouses as they take in, track, transfer,** and **dispose of property.**

The Property Application project team is currently in **the earliest stages of designing the Property Application "user interface"**—that is, what you will see in the future on your Property Application workstation screen and how you will interact with it to accomplish property management tasks.

We have **chosen you carefully** to participate in this study because we believe you represent one of the most important types of potential users of the Property Application. We want to get your feedback and input on the team's initial design ideas.

Your participation will be extremely useful to the Property Application team in designing the Property Application user interface to best meet your needs as a potential user.

SAMPLE INTRODUCTION

Introduction

The main **purposes of the Property Application** are to

◆ Eliminate redundant data entry
◆ Eliminate the need to learn and remember complex policies and procedures
◆ Reduce errors
◆ Speed up the processing of property

What you will see in this study is a mock-up of **ONLY PART** of the whole Property Application. In our mock-up, we have only addressed one specific property management task: **property entry, done by police officers.**

What you will see in the mock-up is **one possible user interface** (that is, a set of screens and ways of interacting with them) for this task on the Property Application.

Your participation in this study will take about two hours. It will be conducted in three steps.

First, some information will be given to you, and some information taken from you. This **Introduction** is part of the information we need to give you. In addition, you will soon be given some very brief application **"training."**

We also need to gather a little information about you, to help us interpret your feedback on the mock-up. You will be asked to fill out a **short questionnaire**.

Second, after we have exchanged information, we will give you a **specific, realistic property entry task** and ask you to try to **carry it out using the Property Application mock-up**. This step is explained in more detail below.

Third, after performing these tasks on the mock-up, we will ask you to fill **out another questionnaire** about your experience with and reactions to the mock-up, to get some additional feedback and input from you.

Before giving you our questionnaire and brief application training, here is a little more information about the format of Step Two, where you will be trying to use the mock-up.

During this step in our study, we will ask you to try to perform a **set of specific, realistic tasks** that the application can help you to do. We will **observe and make notes** as you try to carry out these tasks on the mock-up. We will be **videotaping** as well.

You may feel like you are taking a test, and that your performance is being measured. Knowing you are being observed and videotaped is bound to make you feel a bit nervous and under pressure!

In fact, however, it's very important that you understand that **we are not studying you**—we are studying the design of the user interface to the Property Application. **We expect you to make mistakes and get confused**, because although we will give you some very brief and general training about the mock-up, you will have had absolutely no specific training on how to use it and, in fact, will never have seen any of it before.

When you do make mistakes or get confused, **this is actually useful, valuable feedback for us**, as it suggests where the mock-up is not as

"Introduction" cont. next page

"Introduction" cont.

easy to understand and learn as it might be. By observing where a whole group of users like yourself make mistakes and get confused, we can learn both how we might improve the design and what to focus on in training. So please relax and try not to feel anxious about your performance.

As you try to perform the tasks, we would like to ask you to do three things:

1. Try to **work efficiently**, but not at the expense of accuracy. Imagine you are trying to use the application for the first time to get real work done. Try to work at the pace you would work in that situation.

2. **Please think out loud** as you try to do each task. Tell us what you are going to try and why, what you think will happen, what you think terms or symbols you encounter mean, what terms you would have expected to be used and would have understood more readily, and what you are confused about. This will help us to better understand what is and isn't intuitive and clear about the mock-up.

3. Initially, we will not interfere or tell you how to do anything. You may ask questions, as this will help us understand where the user interface is confusing. **However, please understand that we will not answer most questions.** Please try to figure things out on your own, as if you were really at work and no one else was available to help you. We will intervene and help you out only when you get absolutely stuck and cannot go on.

To recap, you will next do the following:

◆ Fill out a questionnaire.
◆ Receive the brief application training.
◆ Do some real tasks on the mock-up.
◆ Fill out a final questionnaire.

If you have **any questions**, please feel free to ask them now.

Again, thank you for your participation!

SAMPLE PRETEST QUESTIONNAIRE

Questions in the sample pretest questionnaire can be taken directly from
the User Profile questionnaire (see Chapter 2).

Pretest Questionnaire

ITERATION : _____

LOCATION: _____

USER NAME: _____   USER NO.: _____

DATE: _____   TIME: _____

FACILITATOR: _____ DATA COLLECTOR: _____

We need to know a little about you in order to best interpret and analyze your reactions to the user interface mock-up we will be asking you
to use. Please answer the following questions.

1. Check the **job title** that best describes your current primary job:
   - _____   **Police Officer**
   - _____   **Station Commander**
   - _____   **Property Clerk**
   - _____   **Other** (please describe) _____

2. How would you describe your **experience level** in your current
   job title?
   - _____   **Less than three months**
   - _____   **Three months to six months**
   - _____   **More than six months but less than one year**
   - _____   **One year to three years**
   - _____   **More than three years but less than five years**
   - _____   **Five years or more**
   - _____   **Other** (please describe) _____

"Pretest Questionnaire" cont. next page

"Pretest Questionnaire" cont.

3. Are you:
   _____ **Male**
   _____ **Female**

4. **How old** are you?
   _____ **18–25**
   _____ **26–40**
   _____ **41–55**
   _____ **over 55**

5. Do you wear **glasses or contact lenses**?
   _____ **No**
   _____ **Yes** (Please describe your vision problem and correction method, for example, nearsighted, farsighted; bifocals, contact lenses.) _____

6. Are you **color blind** in any way?
   _____ **No**
   _____ **Yes** (please describe) _____

7. Describe your **educational background**:
   _____ **High school** (attended but did not graduate)
   _____ **High school degree**
   _____ **Trade or vocational school degree** (beyond the high school level)
   _____ **College** (some course work but no degree)
   _____ **College degree** (for example, B.A., B.S., Associate College degree)
   _____ **Graduate school** (some course work but no degree)
   _____ **Graduate school degree** (for example, M.A., M.S., Ph.D., Ed.D.)
   _____ **Other** (please explain) _____

8. What is your level of **typing skill**?
   _____ **"Hunt and peck"** typist (less than 15 words per minute)
   _____ **Moderately skilled** touch typist (between 15 and 50 words per minute)
   _____ **Highly skilled** touch typist (greater than 50 words per minute)

9. In the last six months, how **frequently** have you had to **enter property**—that is, fill out property forms?

_____ **Not at all** (in the last six months)

_____ **Infrequently** (more or less monthly)

_____ **Frequently** (more or less weekly)

_____ **Very frequently** (more or less daily)

_____ **Other** (please explain) _____

10. In the last six months, how **frequently** have you had to **check/approve a property form**?

_____ **Not at all** (in the last six months)

_____ **Very infrequently** (only a few times)

_____ **Infrequently** (more or less monthly)

_____ **Frequently** (more or less weekly)

_____ **Very frequently** (more or less daily)

_____ **Other** (please explain) _____

11. Do you have any **experience** (on or off the job) **using the Microsoft Windows operating system?**

_____ **No**

_____ Yes—but **only Windows 3.1**

_____ Yes—but **only Windows 95**

_____ Yes—**both** Windows 3.1 and Windows 95

12. How would you describe your general **level of expertise** in using Microsoft **Windows applications** such as Word, Excel, and/or Power-Point (on either Windows 3.1 or Windows 95)?

_____ **None** (I have never or only briefly used a Windows application.)

_____ **Low** (I use at least one Windows application but only occasionally.)

_____ **Moderate** (I use at least one Windows application but do not consider myself an expert.)

_____ **High** (I consider myself an expert user of two or more different Windows applications.)

_____ **Other** (please describe) _____

"Pretest Questionnaire" cont. next page

"Pretest Questionnaire" cont.

13. How would you describe your general level of **computer experience**?

_____ **None** (I have never used a computer.)

_____ **Low** (I have used only one or two software applications.)

_____ **Moderately low** (I have learned and used between three and ten different software applications.)

_____ **Moderately high** (I have learned and used more than ten software applications but have no programming skills.)

_____ **High** (I have used more than ten different software applications and have some programming skills.)

_____ **Other** (please describe) _____

THANK YOU!

SAMPLE TRAINING MATERIALS

Training

In our **mock-up,** only one specific property management task is supported: **property entry**, done by police officers.

Please note that the **mock-up is very sketchy.** It is not a real application. It is mostly a facade of displays and does very little actual processing of input data. Therefore, not everything will work exactly as it would on the real Property Application. For example, the mock-up will not always save and "remember" your previous input, and we will be "faking" your bar code scanner and touchscreen input.

Certain basic property entry procedures will change with the introduction of the Property Application.

1. There will no longer be multiple property forms for a single incident, such as an arrest. Instead, there will be **a single electronic**

record in which all property taken in a single event (such as an arrest) will be documented and detailed. The advantages of this are, for example, that information such as arresting officer identification, which currently is entered many times on many different forms, need only be entered once. This also means that all property, whether it is evidence, safekeeping, or found property, can go in a single record. Separate forms (again requiring redundant data entry of certain common information) according to property type and destination are no longer required.

2. Because property entry on the Property Application is electronic, somewhat like word processing, **the need for draft forms goes away**. It is always easy (at least up until the point of final Station Commander approval) to edit any information you have entered regarding property. The Property Application will allow users the option of either

♦ first entering a brief description of each property item, to create a sort of checklist of property, and then later going in and adding all the required detailed information for each property item, or

♦ completing all required information for each property item, one at a time.

Some Basic Information about How to Use the Property Application

A few general rules of interaction apply over and over again in the mock-up.

1. One primary way of interacting with the Property Application mock-up is to use the bar code scanning device provided with each workstation. On many Property Application screens, you will **start or complete tasks by scanning a bar code.** For example:

♦ To **enter your user ID**, scan in the bar code from your ID badge.

♦ To **enter property** in the Property Application, scan in the bar code from the security envelope you are putting the property in.

♦ To **find a piece of property** in the Property Application, scan in the bar code from the security envelope containing the property, or from the paper receipt for that property.

"Training" cont. next page

"Training" cont.

We do not actually have an active bar code scanner on our mock-up. However, we would like you to pretend we do! Please use the inactive bar code scanner whenever this seems like the appropriate way to interact with the mock-up, and we will make the mock-up respond to your input as if it had actually detected your scanner.

2. Another **primary way of interacting** with the Property Application **is by touching symbols or controls right on the Property Application screens**. The Property Application workstation screens will respond to the touch of your finger. For example:

◆ To **initiate an action** represented by a push button on the screen, touch the push button.

◆ To **type in something** such as a name or address, first touch the place on the screen where you want to type, then type.

◆ To **fill in a text area by selecting from a pick list**, touch the down arrow button to the right of the text area, then touch your choice. If you cannot see your choice, touch the scroll arrow buttons to scroll the pick list.

◆ To **edit a text area**:
either touch it, and it will highlight so you can type over the current text, or
touch the right arrow button to the right of the text area, and then edit the display that comes up.

◆ To **select from a pick list**:
Radio buttons: touch the circle to the left of your choice.
Check boxes: touch the square to the left of your choice.
List boxes: touch your choice (touch the scroll arrow buttons if you cannot currently see your choice).

We do not actually have an active touchscreen on our mock-up. However, we would like you to pretend we do! Please touch the screen whenever this seems like the appropriate way to interact with the mock-up, and we will make the mock-up respond to your input as if it had actually detected your touch.

That is everything we want to tell you before you try the mock-up! We hope you enjoy the rest of this study. Again, thank you very much for your participation! Just let us know when you have finished reading this document.

SAMPLE VIDEO PERMISSION FORM

Video Permission

I give my permission to be videotaped as I participate in the Property Application usability study on __/__/__ at _____.
I understand that it is the mock-up that is being tested, rather than my performance, and that this tape will be used for research purposes only to support the development of the Property Application user interface, and will not be used in any way to assess my job performance or job qualifications.

_____
Print Name

_____
Signature

SAMPLE TEST TASK

These can usually be adapted directly from the Task Scenarios developed in the Contextual Task Analysis task (see Chapter 3). For another example, see "Sample Task Scenarios" in the Sample Work Products and Templates section of Chapter 3.

Test Task 1

Enter Property

Enter property taken from two prisoners picked up together in a car, one charged with Driving While Intoxicated and the other with Disorderly Conduct and Resisting Arrest.

    You have just come into the station with two men you picked up in a car that was weaving down the road. You are charging the driver, from whom you took a quart bottle of rum, with Driving While Intoxicated

"Test Task 1" cont. next page

"Test Task 1" cont.

(DWI). The passenger, who caused trouble during the arrest of the driver, is being charged with Disorderly Conduct and Resisting Arrest.

You approach the Station Commander's desk and first take all property from each prisoner. At this time, the Station Commander will make appropriate entries in the Station Log. The Station Commander will also give you a set of appropriate security envelopes for the property. When that is complete, you will take your prisoners, property, and envelopes down to the arrest processing area. First, you will secure the prisoners in the jail cell. Then, for each prisoner, you will (as described below in detailed steps):

◆ Take each piece of property and put it in the appropriate type of security envelope.
◆ Enter a brief description of each security envelope and its contents into the Property Application.
◆ Print out a receipt for all property from the Property Application, to be given to the prisoner.

After entering brief descriptions of all property from the arrest, and generating receipts for your prisoners, you will then go back and enter the required detailed information about all property from the arrest in the Property Application. Do this in the following steps:

1. Starting from the Main Menu, take the necessary steps to get to the screen on which you will describe all the property taken from—and then produce a receipt for—Prisoner 1: **John Doe**, charge = **DWI**. Assume that the complaint number for this arrest is **12345**.

2. Now that you are on the appropriate screen for entering property for Prisoner 1, first enter the bottle of rum, which you took at the time of the arrest as evidence:

    One **quart bottle of rum**, taken as arrest evidence, (put in a medium security envelope)

3. Now take all the prisoner's personal effects, which you are taking for safekeeping, put them in appropriate security envelopes, and enter them into the Property Application:

    All of the following can go together in a Medium Security Envelope:
    Two **house keys**
    One **brush**
    Eight **miscellaneous papers**
    One **wallet**

In a Night Deposit Bag, put:
$300 in U.S. currency

4. When all the above property has been entered into the Property Application, produce a property receipt for Prisoner 1, John Doe, charge = DWI.

You have now completed entering the description of property for Prisoner 1, John Doe, and provided him with a receipt. You are now ready to enter the property taken from your second prisoner.

5. From where you are now in the Property Application, get to the screen on which you will describe the property you have taken from—and produce a receipt for—Prisoner 2: **Scott Walker,** charge = **Disorderly Conduct** and **Resisting Arrest.**
6. Now that you are on the appropriate screen, enter the property taken off the prisoner for safekeeping.

In a single Medium Security Envelope, put:
One **beeper**
Two **house keys**
Four **miscellaneous papers**
One **pencil**
One **wallet**

In a Night Deposit Bag, put:
$5,000 in U.S. currency

7. Finally, enter the **car** (which the passenger claims is his), which you will hold for safekeeping. Obviously, you don't put a car in a Security Envelope. Instead, you get a bar coded sticker, which you will later go out and affix to the car. Also, you cannot completely describe the car yet, as you must inspect it to get all the information that will be required in the Property Application. But you can enter a brief description of it and look ahead to see what information is required.
8. Now produce a property receipt for Prisoner 2, Scott Walker, charge = Disorderly Conduct and Resisting Arrest.

You have now completed entering the property for Prisoner 2, Scott Walker, and have provided him with a receipt. Both prisoners now have receipts, and the Property Application has a listing of all property taken during this arrest.

"Test Task 1" cont. next page

9. Just after you hand Scott Walker, Prisoner 2, his receipt, the first prisoner, **John Doe**, pulls a **comb** out of his pocket and starts combing his hair. You must take the comb from him and add it to the collection of his safekeeping property in the Medium Security Envelope. Now, enter this new property item in the appropriate place in the Property Application.
10. Now you frisk both prisoners again, to make sure you have not missed any additional property, and find some **change (3 quarters)** in the pocket of the second prisoner, **Scott Walker**. You must take it and add it to the Night Deposit Bag containing his other cash. Now, update the Property Application to reflect the new total amount of cash taken from Scott Walker, Prisoner 2.
11. Now imagine you have completed entering information about all property from this arrest except the complete information about the car. **Get out of the Property Application.**

Now imagine that you go back out to the car to attach the property bar code to it and to gather information you will need to describe the car in the Property Application. While there, you do a routine follow-up check and find a hidden compartment inside the dashboard containing 50 vials of suspected crack and a .22 caliber automatic. You bring these items back into the Station Commander, who enters them in the Station Log. Prisoner 2, Scott Walker, owner of the car, admits to owning both items. The Station Commander advises you to make the following changes to your initial Property Application entries. Starting from the Main Menu:

12. Add two additional charges against Prisoner 2, **Scott Walker: Criminal Possession of a Weapon** and **Criminal Sale of a Controlled Substance.**
13. Change the category of the **car** taken from Prisoner 2, **Scott Walker,** to **Evidence.**
14. Take the currency **($5,000.75)** taken from Prisoner 2, **Scott Walker,** out of its Night Deposit Bag (it has not yet been sealed), stamp it, change its category in the Property Application to **Evidence,** and put it in a new Medium Security Envelope.
15. Take the **beeper** from Prisoner 2, **Scott Walker,** out of its Security Envelope (which contains other items and has not been sealed yet), change its category in the Property Application to **Evidence,** put it in a new Medium Security Envelope. Leave the remaining items in the original Security Envelope.

16. Enter the 50 vials of **narcotics** belonging to Prisoner 2, **Scott Walker,** in the Property Application, putting it in a Narcotics Envelope. It is arrest **evidence.**
17. Enter the .22 caliber automatic **handgun** belonging to Prisoner 2, **Scott Walker,** in the Property Application, putting it in a Medium Security Envelope. It is arrest **evidence.**
18. Produce a new **receipt** for Prisoner 2, **Scott Walker,** to reflect the items you have added since you printed him a receipt earlier.
19. Produce a new **receipt** for Prisoner 1, John Doe, to reflect the items you have added since you printed him a receipt earlier.
20. You are done! **Get out of the Property Application.**

DATA COLLECTION SHEET TEMPLATE

Data Collection Sheet—Task 1

ITERATION : _____

LOCATION: _____

USER NAME: _____   USER NO.: _____

DATE: _____   TIME: _____

FACILITATOR: _____   DATA COLLECTOR: _____

Enter Property

Enter property from two prisoners picked up together in a car, one charged with Driving While Intoxicated, and the other with Disorderly Conduct and Resisting Arrest.

"Data Collection Sheet—Task 1" cont. next page

"Data Collection Sheet—Task 1" cont.

Do this in the following steps:

1. Starting from the Main Menu, take the necessary steps to get to the Property Application screen on which you will describe all the property taken from—and then produce a receipt for—Prisoner 1: **John Doe**, charge = **DWI**. Assume that the complaint number for this arrest is **12345**.

Correct steps	Correct?		Errors/Comments
	Y	N	
Touch "New Incident" push button on Main Menu			

Fill in "New Incident" dialog box:
    Scan ID
    PIN
    12345
    Arrest
and touch OK button			

Fill in "Property Taken From" dialog box:
    John Doe (touch Add button)
    Prisoner
    DWI (touch Add button)
and touch OK button			

2. Now that you are on the appropriate screen for entering property for Prisoner 1, first enter the bottle of rum that you took at the time of the arrest as evidence:

   One **quart bottle of rum**, taken as arrest evidence, (put in a Medium Security Envelope)

Correct steps	Correct?		Errors/Comments
	Y	N	
Scan new envelope bar code Touch OK button			
Select "Arrest Evidence" Touch Description button Touch OK button			

3. Now take all the prisoner's personal effects, which you are taking for safekeeping, put them in appropriate security envelopes, and enter them into the Property Application:

   All of the following can go together in a Medium Security Envelope:

   Two **house keys**
   One **brush**
   Eight **miscellaneous papers**
   One **wallet**

Correct steps	Correct?		Errors/Comments
	Y	N	
Touch New Envelope button OR Scan new envelope			
Select "Safekeeping" Touch Description button Touch OK button			

SAMPLE POSTTEST QUESTIONNAIRE

Posttest Questionnaire

ITERATION : _____

LOCATION: _____

USER NAME: _____   USER NO.: _____

DATE: _____   TIME: _____

FACILITATOR: _____   DATA COLLECTOR: _____

Please answer the following questions by indicating the number that best expresses your feelings and opinion. **Please give any comments** that would help us better understand your answer. Please be candid! Your real reactions will be very helpful to us as we try to refine and improve the user interface to the Property Application user interface.

14. Although we only showed you a mock-up of one very small part of the planned functionality of the Property Application, based on this experience, please tell us how **useful** you think the Property Application will be in your job. (Circle the number that best expresses your opinion.)

```
1            2            3            4            5
|------------|------------|------------|------------|
```
Not Useful   Very Useful

Comments?

15. Based on your experience with the Property Application mock-up, **how willing would you be to use** the Property Application? (Circle the number that best expresses your opinion.)

```
1            2            3            4            5
|------------|------------|------------|------------|
```
Not Willing   Very Willing

Comments?

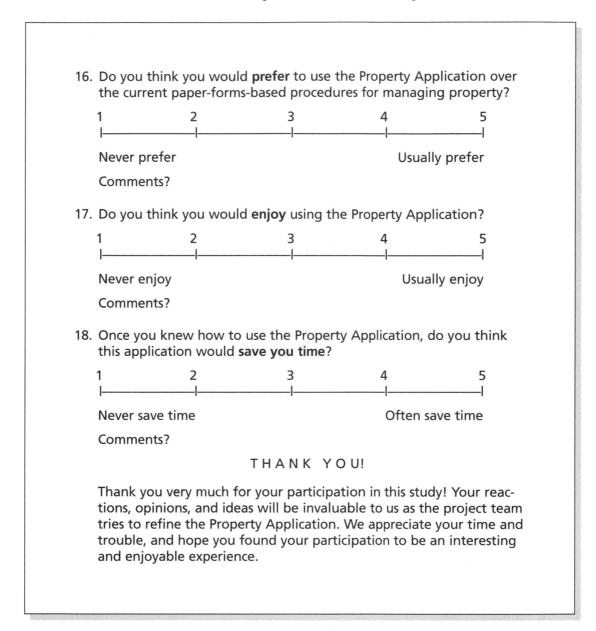

16. Do you think you would **prefer** to use the Property Application over the current paper-forms-based procedures for managing property?

```
1              2              3              4              5
|──────────────|──────────────|──────────────|──────────────|
Never prefer                                      Usually prefer

Comments?
```

17. Do you think you would **enjoy** using the Property Application?

```
1              2              3              4              5
|──────────────|──────────────|──────────────|──────────────|
Never enjoy                                       Usually enjoy

Comments?
```

18. Once you knew how to use the Property Application, do you think this application would **save you time**?

```
1              2              3              4              5
|──────────────|──────────────|──────────────|──────────────|
Never save time                                   Often save time

Comments?
```

THANK YOU!

Thank you very much for your participation in this study! Your reactions, opinions, and ideas will be invaluable to us as the project team tries to refine the Property Application. We appreciate your time and trouble, and hope you found your participation to be an interesting and enjoyable experience.

DATA SUMMARY SHEET TEMPLATE WITH SAMPLE DATA

To prepare a Data Summary Sheet, simply use a blank copy of the Data Collection Sheet, and summarize data across test users in the Errors/Comments column. In this column "CM" indicates a Conceptual Model Design issue, and "SD" indicates a screen design issue. The numbers in parentheses after each error description indicate which test users, by number, made this error, and thus you can also see how many users made each error by the number of user numbers listed.

Data Summary Sheet

1. Starting from the Main Menu, take the necessary steps to get to the screen on which you will enter a brief description of all the property taken from—and then print a receipt for—**Prisoner 1**: John Doe, charge = DWI. Assume that the complaint number for this arrest is 12345.

Correct steps	Correct?		Errors/Comments
	Y	N	
Touch "New Incident" push button on Main Menu			CM-Touched "Transfer Property" (6)

Fill in "New Incident" dialog box:
    Scan ID
    PIN
    12345
 	
    Arrest
			SD-Typed in ID/KB navigation (1,4,6,9)
			
			SD-Trying to type in drop-down (6)

and touch OK button			SD-Confusing Incident Type with Charge (1,4)

Fill in "Property Taken From" dialog box
 	
    John Doe (touch Add button)
 	
    Prisoner
    DWI (touch Add button)
and touch OK button
			SD-Confused by Add/Remove (1,2,8,9)
			
			CM-Tried to enter both prisoners (4)
			
			SD-Trying to type in drop-down (6)
			SD-Confused by "Person Type" (10)

DATA ANALYSIS SHEET TEMPLATE WITH SAMPLE DATA

This is a summary of the problems tallied in the Data Summary Sheet just shown, with suggestions on how the design might be changed to eliminate each problem.

Data Analysis

Problems	Solutions
1. Cue to scan seems insufficient (up to 4 subjects in 13 of 17 potential scan interactions).	- Have push buttons, such as "Find Property," "Enter Property," that bring up dialog boxes prompting to scan—directly scanning can be a shortcut, noted in secondary pop-up message dialog boxes. - In dialog boxes, let scan fields have a dialog box widget (leader dots) that brings up dialog box prompting to scan, with pop-up notice of shortcut to scan directly when cursor in field.
2. Users just don't get the "Property Group" concept or icon/controls.	- Icons need to look more like interactive controls - Better wording on buttons and in dialog boxes - Maybe people icon on buttons and visuals in dialog boxes - People names in context area (vs. title bar) - More prominent people names on icons - More salient cues tying icon to Group window
3. Users ignore Quantity field (almost universal)—and when they get it later, still enter wrong quantity when multiple items in one envelope.	- Provide more specific options in Property Category pull-down (e.g., radio). - Somehow allow multiple line items per envelope at high-level entry (maybe "Enter Property" button with dialog box can solve this by allowing to rescan envelope adding to—but then need way for shortcut. - I guess rescanning existing envelope could allow you to add something to it. - Relocate in line, so not confused with line number on traditional form. - Maybe include system-generated line numbers, as this is what some thought QTY field was. - Better label of QTY field.

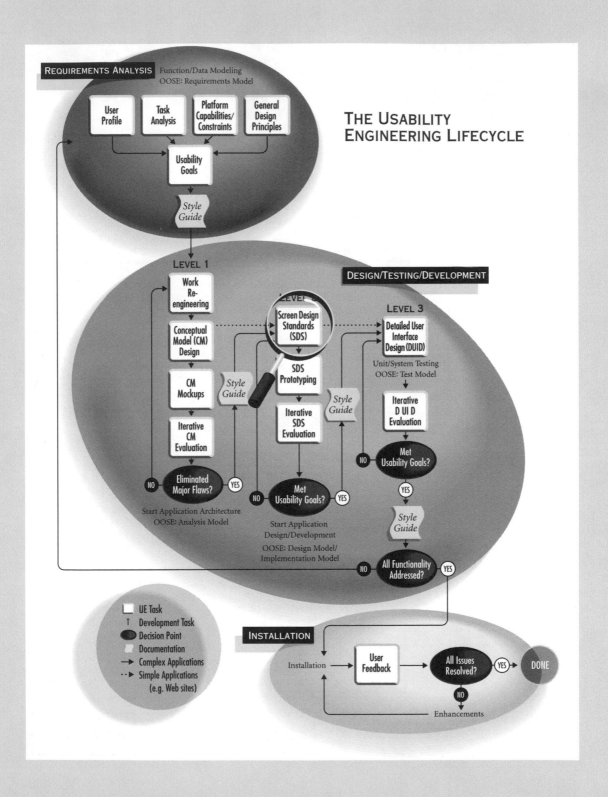

THE USABILITY
ENGINEERING LIFECYCLE

REQUIREMENTS ANALYSIS Function/Data Modeling
OOSE: Requirements Model

User Profile · Task Analysis · Platform Capabilities/ Constraints · General Design Principles

Usability Goals

Style Guide

LEVEL 1

Work Re-engineering

Conceptual Model (CM) Design

CM Mockups

Iterative CM Evaluation

Eliminated Major Flaws? NO YES

Start Application Architecture
OOSE: Analysis Model

DESIGN/TESTING/DEVELOPMENT

LEVEL 2

Screen Design Standards (SDS)

Style Guide

SDS Prototyping

Iterative SDS Evaluation

Met Usability Goals? NO YES

Start Application Design/Development
OOSE: Design Model/ Implementation Model

LEVEL 3

Detailed User Interface Design (DUID)

Unit/System Testing
OOSE: Test Model

Style Guide

Iterative D UI D Evaluation

Met Usability Goals? NO YES

Style Guide

All Functionality Addressed? NO YES

UE Task
T Development Task
Decision Point
Documentation
→ Complex Applications
⋯▸ Simple Applications (e.g. Web sites)

INSTALLATION

Installation → User Feedback → All Issues Resolved? YES → DONE
NO
Enhancements

11

Screen Design Standards

PURPOSE

Just as the purpose of Conceptual Model Design is to ensure consistency and simplicity in *high-level user interface design*, the purpose of Screen Design Standards is to ensure consistency and simplicity in *detailed design* across all displays within a product interface, as well as across other products used by the same users. Consistency contributes not only to ease of learning and remembering but also to ease of use. Users expect consistency (see Mayhew 1992, ch. 3) and will make errors where inconsistencies occur. Standards articulated before Detailed User Interface Design begins make achieving consistency in design simpler and more efficient.

Screen Design Standards also ensure quality, when the standards are based on the User Profiles, Contextual Task Analysis, Usability Goal Setting, and General Design Principles tasks, as outlined in previous chapters. Finally, standards can reduce time and cost in both development and maintenance in two ways: they allow for development of reusable code, and different designers working on the same product or product family do not have to "reinvent the wheel" in the design process.

DESCRIPTION

In this task you define and document a set of Screen Design Standards to be followed by all displays and interactions with them. Some of your standards will be adopted directly, or adapted, from any platform user

Some of your standards will be adopted or adapted from any platform user interface standards you may choose to follow

273

interface standards you may choose to follow, and you can simply refer to the platform Style Guide (e.g., Microsoft Windows, Apple Macintosh) where appropriate. Others (and in many cases most) will be unique to your product, and these you will base on information gathered in Requirements Analysis tasks, including the General Design Principles task (see, e.g., Mayhew 1992).

Examples of screen design issues that should be standardized include

◆ Use of controls (e.g., check boxes, option buttons, list boxes, combo boxes, push buttons)
◆ Location and format of standard display components (e.g., title bar, status line, display body, control and navigation controls, action controls)
◆ Terminology
◆ Use of color
◆ Use of type fonts and styles
◆ Pointing device interactions and keyboard shortcuts
◆ Type, location, format, and wording of messages and on-line instructions

Validated Screen Design Standards are documented in the product Style Guide and applied during Detailed User Interface Design

Screen Design Standards will be followed as actual screens are designed and prototyped during the Screen Design Standards Prototyping task, and then they will be refined and validated through iterative Screen Design Standards Evaluation. Validated Screen Design Standards are later documented in the product Style Guide and applied during Detailed User Interface Design.

SCHEDULING AND INTEGRATION WITH OTHER TASKS

The Screen Design Standards task fits into the overall Usability Engineering Lifecycle in the following ways:

◆ Some Screen Design Standards might be adopted or adapted from a platform Style Guide (e.g., Microsoft Windows, Apple Macintosh). Others will be unique, and these will be tailored to the product based on information gained from Requirements Analysis tasks.

- Screen Design Standards are designed in the context of the Conceptual Model Design.
- General Design Principles should also drive the drafting of Screen Design Standards.
- Screen Design Standards will be constrained by the Platform Capabilities and Constraints.
- Screen Design Standards are refined and validated through the Screen Design Standards Prototyping and Iterative Screen Design Standards Evaluation tasks that follow.
- Validated Screen Design Standards are ultimately documented in the product Style Guide.
- The validated Screen Design Standards, along with the validated Conceptual Model Design, will ultimately drive all Detailed User Interface Design.
- The Screen Design Standards will be continuously refined and updated in response to all later usability evaluation tasks.

The Screen Design Standards task fits into the underlying software development methodology in the following ways:

- This task can *parallel* or *follow* development of the Analysis Model in the Analysis phase of OOSE (or the application architecture design in a traditional rapid prototyping methodology), as it will most likely not have any significant effect on the design of the application architecture.
- This task can *parallel* development of the Design Model in the Construction phase of OOSE (or module design in a traditional rapid prototyping methodology), as screen design details usually will not have an effect on high-level code design.
- This task should *precede* development of the Implementation Model in the Construction phase of OOSE (or code development in a traditional rapid prototyping methodology), as Screen Design Standards will drive Detailed User Interface Design, which in turn will be coded.
- The Screen Design Standards can eventually be incorporated into any product documentation and training (Screen Design Standards, like the Conceptual Model Design, facilitate documentation and training by reducing the complexity of a product user interface to a small number of consistently followed standards).

ROLES AND RESOURCES

In the Screen Design Standards task, the usability roles might participate as follows:

Task leader: The User Interface Designer should take the lead role in this task.

Other resources: Any and all project team members who have participated in the Requirements Analysis tasks, the Work Reengineering task, and the Conceptual Model Design task should participate in this task and provide input and feedback. The Usability Engineer should participate as well to provide direction and feedback. Users can also participate as active design participants (see Chin, Rosson, and Carroll 1997; Bloomer, Croft, and Wright 1997; Malinowski and Nakakoji 1995).

SAMPLE TECHNIQUE— A STEP-BY-STEP PROCEDURE

The Screen Design Standards for a product may be based in part on a platform Style Guide (e.g., Microsoft Windows, Apple Macintosh) and should simply make direct references to it wherever appropriate to avoid redundancy. Only detail unique to the product (e.g., specialized data or other screen elements) need be explicitly designed and documented.

Screen Design Standards based on today's GUI platform standards can be grouped into the following categories:

◆ Control standards
◆ Product/process window standards
◆ Dialog box contents standards
◆ Message box contents standards
◆ Input device interactions standards
◆ Feedback standards

The steps here are simply a matter of drafting a set of standards within each of these categories. For products *not* based on today's GUI platforms, Screen Design Standards would need to be categorized in some similar way, and then steps in this design task would involve drafting standards with each category.

❶ **Draft control standards.** Current GUI platforms offer a variety of controls through which you can offer actions to, and solicit input from, users. Examples of such controls include option buttons, check boxes, list boxes, and spin boxes (see your platform Style Guide for a complete list of all controls and how they operate). For any given field, often more than one of these controls would work, but platform standards generally do not dictate when to choose one control over another.

You can achieve consistency within your design by following a set of standards for the use of controls. Consider the following set of controls, applied to fields from different screens in a catalog order application. You can probably see immediately that this first layout is poor, but do you know why?

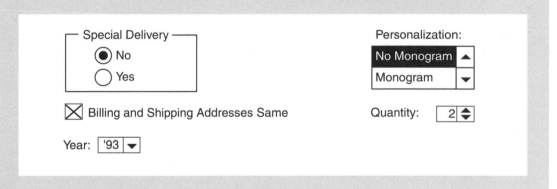

Each control *functions* perfectly well, given the input being solicited from users. However, there is no particular reason, and no consistency, behind these choices for controls.

If you consider all the fields, you will notice that they fall into two types: some offer simple binary yes/no or on/off choices, and the others present numerical ranges.

Now consider the control choices, based on these two types, and notice the clear lack of consistency:

◆ Simple On/Off or Yes/No:

Special Delivery	=	Option buttons
Address	=	Check box
Personalization	=	List box

◆ Simple Numerical Range:

Quantity	=	Spin box
Year	=	Drop-down

Next, consider an alternative set of controls for these same fields:

The control choices here can be categorized as follows:

◆ Simple On/Off or Yes/No:

Special Delivery	=	Check box
Address	=	Check box
Personalization	=	Check box

◆ Simple Numerical Range:

Quantity	=	Spin box
Year	=	Spin box

Now you can see there is a simple set of standards operating: if the field is a simple on/off or yes/no question, use a check box; if it presents a numerical range, use a spin box.

Once they perceive the standards, users can work through the interface quickly and efficiently. If they are looking for a particular field and know generally what type it is (e.g., a simple yes/no question), users can scan for the field (in this case they would scan for check boxes). Also, if they encounter a new field for the first time (say, a spin box), they might more quickly comprehend what is expected of them in the field (in this case, they will understand immediately that they are to select from a numerical range).

The Sample Work Products and Templates section later in the chapter offers a sample set of standards for control use. It is not meant to be *the* set of standards, or even a *recommended* set of standards, but merely an example of what a set of control standards might look like. You will need to tailor a set of control use standards that meets your own unique product requirements.

❷ **Draft product/process window standards.** Depending on whether your Conceptual Model Design is product or process oriented (see Chapter 8), you will have windows that represent *products* (e.g., a worksheet in a car sales application) or *processes* (e.g., a new service request in a customer service application). You will want to design a set of standards for the layout and design of these types of displays, and you can document these standards with a template. For example, in the car sales application, the worksheet may be a form with a standard set of fields arranged in a particular order, represented by a particular set of controls (which follow the general standards for controls designed in step 1), with particular captions, and so on. Empty, untitled worksheets that the user starts with, as well as created and saved worksheets, will then always follow these layout standards.

❸ **Draft dialog box standards.** In the generic, standard (product-oriented) GUI Conceptual Model, dialog boxes are generally used to complete actions initiated through the menu bar, and they present fill-in forms. In a process-oriented Conceptual Model of your own design, dialog boxes may serve this and/or other purposes. In any case, part of the Conceptual Model Design will be a set of standards for the use of different kinds of windows, which will dictate, in part, what dialog boxes will be used for. Here, you will establish a set of standards for the consistent design of the contents of dialog boxes. These might include such things as standards for designating required versus optional fields and read-only versus editable fields, locating and titling push buttons, and so on. A sample set of dialog box standards are offered in the Sample Work Products and Templates section.

❹ **Draft message box standards.** Message boxes are usually read-only. You might have a set of standards for indicating different types of messages, such as error, warning, and status messages; a set of standards for the placement, and consistent syntax and format of message wording; as well as standards regarding the use, placement, and labeling of push buttons.

❺ **Draft input device interaction standards.** Here you will identify all input devices and design standard interactions for them. These might include the meanings of different mouse buttons or different numbers of mouse clicks, keyboard shortcuts (i.e., accelerator keys), and so on.

❻ **Draft feedback standards.** These standards define how you will consistently provide certain types of feedback. Depending on your product functionality, you may want to provide feedback on such things as selection, task completion, active process or product, and status. You can link visual cues (e.g., color, highlighting, blinking, shape, size) to types of feedback in a set of feedback standards. For example, you might use a small set of colors to indicate the status of something, or highlighting to indicate selection, or cursor shape to indicate task in progress versus task completion.

❼ **Document all draft standards.** All Screen Design Standards should be written down and illustrated. Pictures are worth a thousand words when it comes to Screen Design Standards specifications. An example of a standard "in action" is much easier to understand than an abstract description.

Initially, paper sketches and handwritten notes are all that are necessary. Because change is inevitable over iterations, I do not recommend any formal documentation in early iterations of this task. Unlike the examples in the Sample Work Products and Templates section (which are meant to illustrate final, validated standards), do not take the time and effort to draw and write design ideas on formal tools such as graphics software and word processors. Doing so will take a significant effort, and updating such specifications after each iteration of evaluation will take additional effort. The tedium of updating various specifications created with independent specification tools that do not support cross-referencing will prove such an effort that it is likely to discourage further iterations (Sumner 1995).

As mentioned in Chapter 8, the Usability Engineering field lacks good design specification tools that make it easy to document design ideas in different formats (e.g., text, graphics, flowcharts, tables) but in a linked manner so that they can be easily and consistently updated during iterative design. It is important to support and encourage change and evolution of design ideas early in the design process. It is much easier to throw away and redo hand-drawn design ideas than formally documented design ideas. Ultimately, validated Screen Design Standards will be formally documented in the product Style Guide (see Chapter 14), where more professional illustrations and typewritten text will be appropriate.

WAR STORY

ESTABLISHING INTERACTION AND FEEDBACK STANDARDS

In one application I worked on, one of the main input devices was a bar code scanner. Users used the scanner to enter new information about bar coded items and to search for information already entered about bar coded items. In the interaction standard we designed, whenever bar code scanning was appropriate, the screen included a push button representing the appropriate action (e.g., search, enter), and when it was pressed, a dialog box appeared with an input field prompting for a scan of a bar code. Alternatively, using the bar code scanner independently of the push buttons was also valid, and this could be used as a shortcut.

We designed these two standard alternative uses of the scanner because we discovered in early testing that without the push button as a prompt, novice users rarely figured out that they could simply scan to initiate an action. Once they understood this, they eventually preferred to bypass the push button and simply scan. We were then consistent across the interface in *always* providing a well-labeled push button where scanning was a valid action, but also always accepting scanning directly.

In another example from the same application, we displayed a small set of related objects as icons and also displayed the contents of one object at a time in a nearby window. We used background color in the icons to indicate which object was currently "opened" and being displayed in the nearby window. We also used some shape and color cues in the detail of the icons to give status information regarding the contents of the object, so users did not have to open each object to get basic information about its contents. Again, these were standards that we established early and then followed consistently throughout our user interface design.

LEVEL OF EFFORT

Table 11.1 gives a sample level of effort for the Screen Design Standards task. The work effort will vary widely depending on the complexity of the product. This sample represents a simple to moderately complex product with two analysts/designers participating.

Table 11.1
Level of effort—Screen Design Standards

Usability Time (two usability staff working as a team)

Step	Hrs
Draft control standards	12
Draft product/process window standards	32
Draft dialog box standards	32
Draft message box standards	8
Draft input device interaction standards	16
Draft feedback standards	24
Document all draft standards	56
Total	180

ALTERNATIVE TECHNIQUES— A REVIEW

Participatory design (in which users participate as active members of the design team) and automated design tools both represent alternative techniques for the Screen Design Standards task. I refer you to the discussion in the Alternative Techniques—A Review section of Chapter 8.

SHORTCUTS

There is no way to get around the need for Screen Design Standards. The only way to reduce effort on this task is to skip formal documentation. On the other hand, the evaluation effort following this task can be reduced by collapsing all three design levels (or at least levels 2 and 3) into one, and running just one round of iterative evaluation on a complete Detailed User Interface Design. This is only advised for projects involving very simple products, and if you do this, you still need to design and follow a set of Screen Design Standards even if you don't evaluate them separately from other design issues.

WEB NOTES

Screen Design Standards are just as important and useful in Web design as in traditional software design. Besides the usual advantages of standards discussed elsewhere in this chapter, in a Web site they will help users maintain a sense of place within a site, as your site standards will probably be different from those (if any!) on other sites.

Web design techniques (both good and bad) tend to be copied. Perhaps other Web designers will copy your Screen Design Standards! And perhaps someday, we will have a set of universal Web Screen Design Standards supported by Web development tools, not unlike Microsoft Windows and Apple Macintosh standards. This would contribute greatly to the usability of the Web, just as the latter standards have done for traditional software.

Perhaps someday we will have a set of universal Web Screen Design Standards supported by Web development tools

SAMPLE WORK PRODUCTS AND TEMPLATES

The following sample work products and templates are offered here:

- Sample Control Standards
- Sample Dialog Box Standards

SAMPLE CONTROL STANDARDS

Following is a sample set of standards defining which GUI controls to use to represent different types of menu fields in dialog boxes. Remember, it is not *the* set of standards, or even a *recommended* set; it is meant to illustrate what such a set of standards might look like. You will need to tailor a unique set of standards to meet the requirements of your product.

Control Standards

Menu Contents	Control
Navigational actions	Push buttons
Small number/choose one/fixed list	Option buttons
Small number/choose many/fixed list or yes/no, on/off	Check boxes
Large number or variable list/scarce screen space or to reduce clutter	Drop-down list box
Large number or variable list or choose many	Standard list box
Variable input	Text box
Very long lists/scarce screen space	Drop-down combo box
Very long lists	Standard combo box
Numbers or sequential lists	Spin button

SAMPLE DIALOG BOX STANDARDS

The following template is designed to illustrate a set of Screen Design Standards for dialog boxes. The standards illustrated in the dialog box template are listed with it.

For purposes of this publication, I've indicated shades of gray for the sample's standard colors. In practice, you should take advantage of the contrasting colors available to you.

Dialog Box Standards

◆ Always use medium gray (or, for example, cyan) as dialog box background color
◆ Match title to the menu bar selection that brought it up, left-justified in the title bar
◆ Create vertical groups of logically related fields
◆ Within field groups, left-align captions, left-align fields, try to minimize white space between captions and fields (through careful labeling), use first-letter caps for all main words in captions, include a colon immediately following each caption

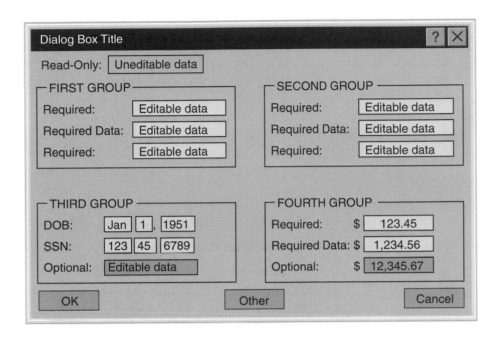

◆ Use group boxes, embed all-caps titles in upper left of group box (do not use all caps anywhere else)
◆ Order groups left to right, top to bottom according to natural order or expected frequency of use
◆ Use white space to set off and reinforce groups
◆ Right-justify or decimal-align numbers and currency *upon display* (allow left-justified input)
◆ Always place OK push button at lower-left edge, Cancel push button at lower-right edge, any other push buttons evenly spaced in between (push buttons are dark gray)
◆ Never use scroll bars in dialog boxes
◆ Background colors for fields:
  Read-only—medium gray (or, for example, cyan)
  Required—white (or, for example, yellow)
  Optional—dark gray (or, for example, gray)
◆ Use consistent labels for common fields
  SSN (Social Security Number)
  DOB (Date of Birth)
◆ Use consistent display format for all dates: Jan 1, 2000 (or Jan 1)

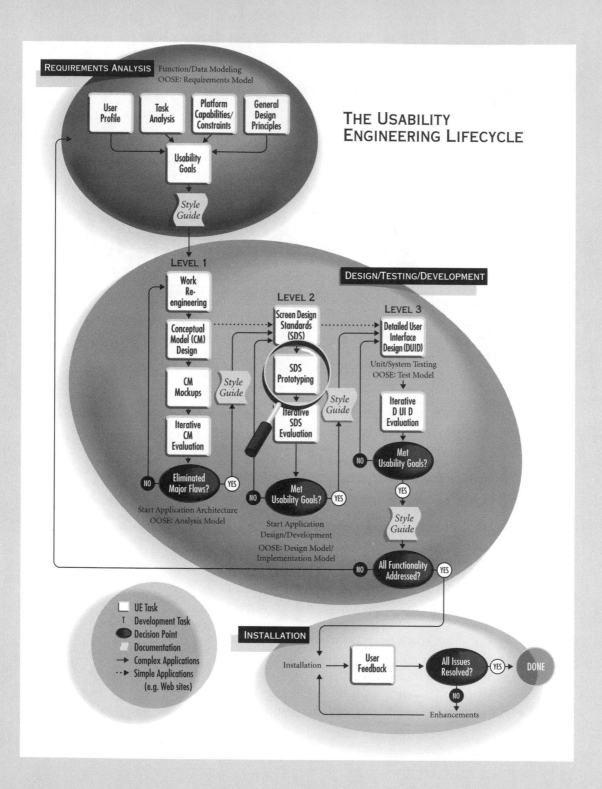

THE USABILITY ENGINEERING LIFECYCLE

REQUIREMENTS ANALYSIS Function/Data Modeling
OOSE: Requirements Model

User Profile

Task Analysis

Platform Capabilities/Constraints

General Design Principles

Usability Goals

Style Guide

LEVEL 1

DESIGN/TESTING/DEVELOPMENT

Work Re-engineering

Conceptual Model (CM) Design

CM Mockups

Iterative CM Evaluation

Style Guide

LEVEL 2

Screen Design Standards (SDS)

SDS Prototyping

Iterative SDS Evaluation

Style Guide

LEVEL 3

Detailed User Interface Design (DUID)

Unit/System Testing
OOSE: Test Model

Iterative D UI D Evaluation

NO   Eliminated Major Flaws?   YES

Start Application Architecture
OOSE: Analysis Model

NO   Met Usability Goals?   YES

Start Application Design/Development

OOSE: Design Model/Implementation Model

NO   Met Usability Goals?   YES

Style Guide

NO   All Functionality Addressed?   YES

UE Task
T   Development Task
Decision Point
Documentation
→   Complex Applications
⋯▸   Simple Applications (e.g. Web sites)

INSTALLATION

Installation → User Feedback → All Issues Resolved?   YES → DONE

NO

Enhancements

12

Screen Design Standards Prototyping

PURPOSE

There are several reasons to build Screen Design Standards Prototypes at this point in the Usability Engineering Lifecycle:

◆ The main point of Screen Design Standards Prototyping is to support the evaluation of the Screen Design Standards, generated in the *previous* task, in the Iterative Screen Design Standards Evaluation task that comes *next*. Feedback at this early stage of design means that designers will not invest a lot of time designing without knowing whether they are on the right track.

◆ Asking users to evaluate early high-level design ideas (in the prototype evaluation task that comes next) helps to continue the ongoing, highly iterative process of understanding and addressing user requirements. A continuous give-and-take between designers and users is a more effective approach than a monolithic approach in which Requirements Analysis is carried out exhaustively, followed by complete detailed design.

◆ The evaluation of the prototypes designed and built in this task provides feedback not only on the general Screen Design Standards generated in the previous task, but also on the specific detailed design to the small subset of product functionality embodied in a particular prototype.

◆ Because this task builds on all the earlier tasks in the lifecycle, it also serves to broaden the scope of evaluation of the Conceptual Model Design to new subsets of functionality and new users and user categories.

287

DESCRIPTION

The first step in this task is to select a subset of the total product functionality for prototyping. To do this, you will need to consider a variety of factors. One goal is to select the smallest subset of functionality that will exercise the largest number of Screen Design Standards drafted in the previous task. These standards will be evaluated in the next task.

Unlike the Conceptual Model Mock-ups, prototypes include complete functional and user interface detail for the selected subset of functionality

Using the Conceptual Model Design and the Screen Design Standards as guides, a simple paper-and-pencil sketch is made of all screens required to represent the selected functionality. Unlike in the mock-ups designed and built in the Conceptual Model Mock-ups task, complete functional and user interface detail is specified for the selected subset of functionality. Recall that the Screen Design Standards generated in the previous task specified general standards for the design of such things as dialog boxes. Here, the prototype will contain the *detailed design* of all actual dialog boxes (for example) in the subset of functionality being prototyped.

Again, as in the Conceptual Model Mock-ups task (see Chapter 9), you can choose either low-fidelity (paper) or high-fidelity (live, on-line) prototypes. Virzi and colleagues (1996) provide strong evidence that low-fidelity prototyping can be just as effective as high-fidelity prototyping, even at this stage in the Usability Engineering Lifecycle. Other research (Cantani and Biers, 1998; Uceta et al., 1998) supports this finding. And it is cheaper and faster to produce. If you choose to go with low-fidelity prototyping, all the necessary foils for conducting the evaluation in the Iterative Screen Design Standards Evaluation task can be prepared from the paper-and-pencil specification.

Low-fidelity prototyping can be just as effective as high-fidelity prototyping—and it is cheaper and faster to produce

If you go with a high-fidelity prototype, you can informally present the paper specification to a prototyper. A formal specification is unnecessary at this point. The designer(s) can simply provide verbal direction to the prototyper as he or she builds the prototype based on the paper sketches. A high-fidelity prototype should be fully interactive, in that users can enter data in fill-in fields and make selections, look up sample information, and navigate through functionality via menu choices, dialog boxes, and so on. However, the prototype need not be *functionally* complete, in that it need not be supported by complete databases or actually process all user input.

With the right high-fidelity prototyping tool, the prototype can become the implemented user interface code. In other words, the right tool allows the interface built with the tool eventually to be integrated directly with application code. This can be risky, however, as prototypes tend to be somewhat sloppily built, precisely because they are prototypes and are expected to change significantly over iterations. Also, if a prototype is considered to be an evolving product, rather than a throwaway experiment, there is often more pressure to go with it as is. It is usually wise to get agreement up front among all project stakeholders to consider a prototype just that—a throwaway prototype. Then the group won't resist changes indicated by evaluation and won't waste time on carefully revising the prototype code after every iteration.

Depending on the complexity of both the product functionality and the set of Screen Design Standards being prototyped, you might build and evaluate multiple prototypes. This would be the case if one prototype and evaluation process simply could not address all key Screen Design Standards generated in the previous task. In this case, you would repeat this task and the next one (Iterative Screen Design Standards Evaluation) for each separate prototype. Recall also that for each separate prototype, these tasks are carried out iteratively (design, prototype, test, redesign, prototype, retest, etc.). This is done until all identified problems are eliminated and *quantitative* usability goals developed in the Usability Goal Setting task seem to be within reach.

Depending on the project's complexity, you might build and evaluate multiple prototypes

SCHEDULING AND INTEGRATION WITH OTHER TASKS

The Screen Design Standards Prototyping task fits into the overall Usability Engineering Lifecycle in the following ways:

◆ The user interface design implemented as a prototype in this task is based on the Conceptual Model Design and the Screen Design Standards generated in previous tasks.

◆ The user interface design implemented as a prototype in this task and the Screen Design Standards it is based on will be constrained by the Platform Capabilities and Constraints.

- The user interface design implemented as a prototype in this task is also based on General Design Principles.
- The prototyped user interface design and the supporting Conceptual Model Design and Screen Design Standards are refined through iterative evaluation and redesign as described in the next task (Iterative Screen Design Standards Evaluation) until all major problems are eliminated and the quantitative goals established in the Usability Goal Setting task seem within reach.

The Screen Design Standards Prototyping task fits into the underlying software development methodology in the following ways:

- This task can *parallel* or *follow* development of the Analysis Model in the Analysis phase of OOSE (or the application architecture design in a traditional rapid prototyping methodology), as Screen Design Standards will most likely not have any significant effect on the design of the application architecture.
- This task can *parallel* development of the Design Model in the Construction phase of OOSE (or module design in a traditional rapid prototyping methodology), as screen design details usually will not have an effect on high-level code design.
- This task should *precede* development of the Implementation Model in the Construction phase of OOSE (or code development in a traditional rapid prototyping methodology), as Screen Design Standards will drive Detailed User Interface Design, which in turn will be coded.

ROLES AND RESOURCES

In the Screen Design Standards Prototyping task, the usability roles might participate as follows:

Task leader: The User Interface Designer should take the lead role in the design and specification of the prototype. If a low-fidelity (paper) prototype is chosen, the User Interface Designer can prepare this prototype.

Other resources: Any and all project team members who have participated in the Requirements Analysis tasks and the Work Reengineering, Conceptual Model Design, and Screen Design Standards tasks should participate and provide input and feedback on the prototype design specification. The Usability Engineer should participate as well to provide direction and feedback. An experienced prototyper, who may or may not be the User Interface Designer, would build a high-fidelity prototype.

SAMPLE TECHNIQUE— A STEP-BY-STEP PROCEDURE

This task is carried out in three straightforward steps, as follows:

❶ **Select functionality to be prototyped.** Select the subset of total product functionality to be prototyped, based on the issues of most concern and interest. Exactly which functionality to prototype should be driven by a variety of factors, including:

   ◆ Functions that will exercise the maximum number of Screen Design Standards drafted in the previous task
   ◆ Functions considered to be core—the most fundamental and frequently used
   ◆ Functions whose interface is considered most likely to be problematic
   ◆ Functions considered to be most representative of the full functionality
   ◆ Functions most likely to be executed in a sequence

❷ **Prepare an informal paper-and-pencil specification.** Take the selected subset of product functionality and specify the detailed user interface design for it with informal paper-and-pencil sketches of actual screens. The design should follow the Conceptual Model Design and the Screen Design Standards generated in previous tasks. In the case of a typical GUI, informal sketches would be made of

   ◆ Windows/dialog boxes including detailed content and layout
   ◆ Action controls (e.g., menu bars and pull-down menus, push buttons) including exact labeling and organization
   ◆ User interactions and pathways through the interface to selected product functionality
   ◆ Messages (status, error, warning, etc.) that could be invoked by varying user input

❸ **Build the specified prototype.** In the case of low-fidelity prototyping, paper foils to support the evaluation that comes next are prepared (see Chapter 9). In the case of high-fidelity prototyping, the designated prototyper builds the prototype according to the specified design. The designer(s) communicate the design to the prototyper with the informal paper specification and through ongoing verbal direction.

LEVEL OF EFFORT

Table 12.1 gives a sample level of effort for the Screen Design Standards Prototyping task. The work effort will vary widely depending on the complexity of the selected functionality to design and prototype and the chosen fidelity for the prototype. This sample represents a simple to moderately complex, high-fidelity prototype, with two designers and one prototyper participating. This sample also assumes that a running prototype was built in the Conceptual Model Mock-ups task and that the high-fidelity prototype is used as the basis for this more detailed one.

Table 12.1
Level of effort—Screen Design Standards Prototyping

Usability Time (two designers, one prototyper)

Step	Hrs
Select subset of functionality	8
Prepare paper-and-pencil spec	64
Build prototype	80
Total	152

ALTERNATIVE TECHNIQUES— A REVIEW

The main variation across techniques for constructing Screen Design Standards Prototypes is in the relative fidelity of the prototypes. Virzi and colleagues (1996) discuss the dimensions of prototype fidelity, and their ideas are discussed in the Alternative Techniques—A Review section of Chapter 9.

SHORTCUTS

As noted, low-fidelity prototypes (paper mock-ups) can save time and resources relative to high-fidelity prototypes (running, interactive prototypes). See Chapter 9 for more discussion on low- and high-fidelity prototypes. On projects developing very simple products, you might consider skipping the iterative evaluation of the Screen Design Standards at this point (and thus skipping this prototyping task as well), and combining it with a single round of iterative evaluation when design levels 2 and 3— or even all three design levels—are complete.

Low-fidelity prototypes can save time and resources relative to high-fidelity prototypes

When resources are extremely tight, or no usability testing can be conducted for other reasons, at least have a Heuristic Evaluation or review of your design conducted by a usability expert (see Chapter 10) before proceeding.

WEB NOTES

For very simple Web sites and applications, you might consider skipping the prototyping and evaluation of the Screen Design Standards at this point in the lifecycle, and conduct iterative evaluation and redesign only after all three levels of design are complete. For Web sites of medium complexity, you could conduct level 1, and then collapse levels 2 and 3 into one iterative design and evaluation process.

Instead of paper foils or throwaway prototypes, in the case of Web sites and applications, the prototypes can simply be partially coded products, such as selected pages, panes, and navigational links, now with complete page content detail.

SAMPLE WORK PRODUCTS AND TEMPLATES

One sample is offered here: a Sample Screen Design Standards Prototype.

SAMPLE SCREEN DESIGN STANDARDS PROTOTYPE

The following illustration shows part of a Screen Design Standards Prototype. You will notice, on the dialog box in the foreground, that all the Screen Design Standards for dialog boxes given in the Sample Work Products and Templates section in Chapter 11 are being followed. Imagine that all the dialog boxes you see in the background also follow these same standards. Having users perform tasks that take them through this set of dialog boxes, in the evaluation task that comes next, will test these general standards as well as the entire detailed design of the prototyped user interface to this subset of product functionality.

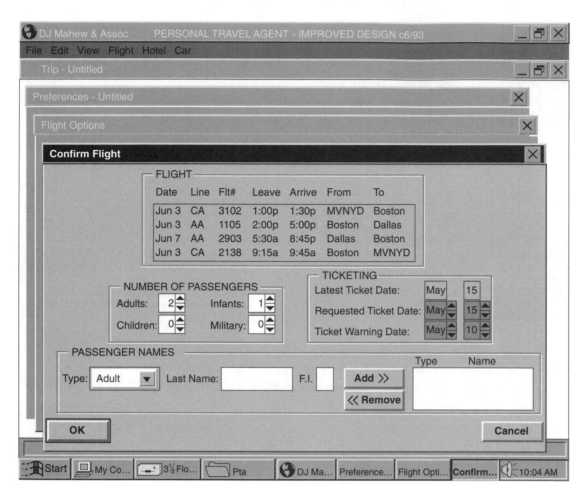

Screen Design Standards

◆ Always use light gray (or, for example, cyan) as dialog box background color
◆ Match title to menu bar selection that brought it up, left-justified
in the title bar

- Create vertical groups of logically related fields
- Within field groups, left-align captions, left-align fields, try to minimize white space between captions and fields (through careful labeling), use first-letter caps for all main words in captions, include a colon immediately following each caption
- Use group boxes, embed all-caps titles in upper left of group box (do not use all caps anywhere else)
- Order groups left to right, top to bottom according to natural order or expected frequency of use
- Use white space to set off and reinforce groups
- Right-justify or decimal-align numbers and currency upon display (allow left-justified input)
- Always place OK push button at lower left edge, Cancel push button at lower-right edge, any other push buttons evenly spaced in between (push buttons are same gray as background)
- Never use scroll bars in dialog boxes
- Background colors for fields:
    Read only—light gray (or, for example, cyan)
    Required—white (or, for example, yellow)
    Optional—medium gray (or, for example, gray)
- Use consistent labels for common fields
    SSN (Social Security Number)
    DOB (Date of Birth)
- Use consistent display format for all dates: Jan 1, 2000 (or Jan 1)

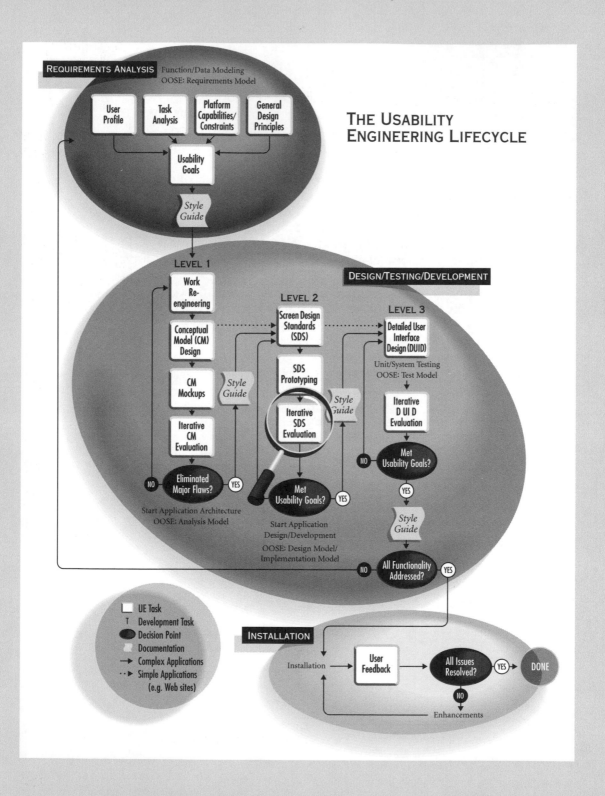

THE USABILITY
ENGINEERING LIFECYCLE

REQUIREMENTS ANALYSIS   Function/Data Modeling
OOSE: Requirements Model

User Profile
Task Analysis
Platform Capabilities/ Constraints
General Design Principles

Usability Goals

Style Guide

LEVEL 1

DESIGN/TESTING/DEVELOPMENT

Work Re-engineering

LEVEL 2

LEVEL 3

Screen Design Standards (SDS)

Detailed User Interface Design (DUID)

Conceptual Model (CM) Design

SDS Prototyping

Unit/System Testing
OOSE: Test Model

CM Mockups

Style Guide

Style Guide

Iterative DUID Evaluation

Iterative CM Evaluation

Iterative SDS Evaluation

Met Usability Goals?   NO

NO   Eliminated Major Flaws?   YES

Met Usability Goals?   YES

YES

Start Application Architecture
OOSE: Analysis Model

Start Application Design/Development

OOSE: Design Model/ Implementation Model

Style Guide

All Functionality Addressed?   NO   YES

UE Task
T   Development Task
Decision Point
Documentation
→   Complex Applications
∙∙▸   Simple Applications (e.g. Web sites)

INSTALLATION

Installation → User Feedback → All Issues Resolved?   YES → DONE

NO

Enhancements

Iterative Screen Design Standards Evaluation

PURPOSE

The purpose of the Iterative Screen Design Standards Evaluation task is to get some quick and early feedback on the usability of the prototypes designed and built in the previous two tasks, which represent both general Screen Design Standards and the detailed design of a subset of product functionality. Valuable objective feedback can be obtained from the formal techniques in Iterative Screen Design Standards Evaluation.

Iterative design and evaluation can be efficiently and effectively conducted at a time when no major investment or commitment in detailed design or code has been made to any particular interface design. Changes are thus simple and easy to make in response to findings. Refining the Screen Design Standards and detailed design of prototyped functionality through Iterative Screen Design Standards Evaluation before either Detailed User Interface Design or development is begun means that costly revisions to completed designs or code are minimized. Spending resources now on usability evaluation saves resources in the long run by minimizing modifications to code during development and after implementation.

DESCRIPTION

Planning and carrying out Iterative Screen Design Standards Evaluation is very similar overall to planning and carrying out Iterative Conceptual Model Evaluation as described in Chapter 10. There are some important differences however:

297

◆ The purpose of Iterative Conceptual Model Evaluation is to validate Conceptual Model Design, while the purpose of Iterative Screen Design Standards Evaluation is to validate Screen Design Standards and the detailed design of subsets of product functionality.

◆ Whereas Conceptual Model Mock-ups can be paper-based foils or superficial running prototypes, Screen Design Standards Prototypes should usually be complete, detailed, and fully interactive running prototypes.

◆ Test tasks used for Iterative Conceptual Model Evaluation are quite broad and fairly unstructured, as only the Conceptual Model is being evaluated; whereas test tasks used for Iterative Screen Design Standards Evaluation are much more formally structured, detailed, and specific.

◆ Whereas you rarely try to collect timing data during Iterative Conceptual Model Evaluation, you can collect and usefully interpret at least rough timing data during Iterative Screen Design Standards Evaluation.

The first decision to make is whether an evaluation will focus on ease of use or ease of learning

Just as in Iterative Conceptual Model Evaluation, the first decision to make is whether a given evaluation will focus on ease of learning or ease of use. Whether one or the other or both will be studied will depend on the usability goals established during Usability Goal Setting.

Again, one technique for evaluation is formal usability testing. For each iteration, three to ten representative users (depending on factors such as diversity of users and number of iterations anticipated) should run through a set of core, high-frequency, realistic test tasks. Testing should be conducted in the users' actual work space if possible (as opposed to a usability lab or area away from their normal work environment). To test for ease of learning, minimal instruction should be given, or a one- or two-page "manual" provided. To test for ease of use, adequate training and practice should be provided to simulate expert users.

The testing should be videotaped, if possible, for data collection backup and presentation purposes. Error data should be collected, and users should be asked to "think out loud" as they work. Timing data can also be collected, but the main purpose here is not to test against ultimate usability goals, but to identify major problems in the Screen Design Standards and the detailed design represented by the prototype interface. Timing data will not be accurate now, due to asking users to think out loud, but it will give a crude indication of how close to meeting quantitative usability goals the current design iteration is. You will focus on goal testing in a later evaluation task.

Error data and other observations are summarized to isolate major problem areas, and the Screen Design Standards and detailed design for prototyped functionality are redesigned to "engineer out" these identified problems. The revised design must then be retested to confirm that problems have been eliminated and to ensure new ones have not been introduced.

The general steps for each iteration of testing include

◆ Plan the test and develop supporting materials.
◆ Run the test with users and collect data as specified in the test plan.
◆ Analyze and interpret the data and formulate redesign recommendations.

At the end of each test, steps are

◆ Modify the Screen Design Standards.
◆ Modify the prototype.
◆ Modify the test plan and materials.

Iteration is terminated when all identified major problems have been eliminated and quantitative usability goals seem within reach. Screen Design Standards are then documented in the product Style Guide Development task, which comes next.

Iteration is terminated when all major problems are eliminated and quantitative usability goals seem within reach

Scheduling and Integration with Other Tasks

The Iterative Screen Design Standards Evaluation task fits into the overall Usability Engineering Lifecycle in the following ways:

◆ This task is based directly on the previous two tasks. The Screen Design Standards Prototypes, which represent Screen Design Standards, are submitted to objective evaluation techniques in this task and redesigned and retested in an iterative fashion.
◆ Usability goals from the Usability Goal Setting task are referenced to determine whether a given evaluation will focus on ease of learning or ease of use, and also to help formulate test tasks.

◆ When using the formal usability testing technique, the User Profiles will drive the selection of test users and provide direct input to the design of the pretest questionnaire.

◆ Test tasks are adapted from Task Scenarios developed in the Contextual Task Analysis task. They can also be adapted from test tasks used in the Iterative Conceptual Model Evaluation task. The test tasks in this task need to be narrower and more specific, however, in order to effectively test the greater level of design detail at this level of design.

◆ When Screen Design Standards are stabilized at the end of the final iteration of this task, they—along with the Conceptual Model Design—are documented in the product Style Guide Development task. Then they feed directly into the Detailed User Interface Design task.

The Iterative Screen Design Standards Evaluation task fits into the underlying software development methodology in the following ways:

◆ The Iterative Screen Design Standards Evaluation task can *parallel* or *follow* development of the Analysis Model in the Analysis phase of OOSE (or the application architecture design in a traditional rapid prototyping methodology), as Screen Design Standards will most likely not have any significant effect on the design of the application architecture.

◆ The Iterative Screen Design Standards Evaluation task can *parallel* development of the Design Model in the Construction phase of OOSE (or module design in a traditional rapid prototyping methodology), as screen design details usually will not have an effect on high-level code design.

◆ The Iterative Screen Design Standards Evaluation task should *precede* development of the Implementation Model in the Construction phase of OOSE (or code development in a traditional rapid prototyping methodology), as Screen Design Standards will drive Detailed User Interface Design, which in turn will be coded.

Roles and Resources

In the Iterative Screen Design Standards Evaluation task, the usability roles might participate as follows:

Task leader: The Usability Engineer should take the lead role in this task.

Other resources: The User Interface Designer should participate as an assistant in both planning and executing the evaluation. Other team members can participate as assistants as needed and should participate as observers. In the formal usability testing technique, users will participate as test users.

Sample Technique—A Step-by-Step Procedure

The technique offered here, as in Chapter 10, is formal usability testing. It can be divided into steps in planning and preparation and steps in conducting the tests.

Planning and Preparation

Planning and preparing for a prototype usability test of Screen Design Standards is almost identical to planning and preparing for the usability testing which is conducted during the Iterative Conceptual Model Evaluation task. Refer to Chapter 10 for a detailed outline of the steps. Here, I provide quick reviews and/or point out any important variations in the steps required in this task, given its focus on a different level of design detail.

❶ **Decide on ease-of-learning/ease-of-use focus for the test.** Based on the User Profiles and the usability goals, first decide whether an ease-of-learning or ease-of-use test will be conducted. In this task, you focus on the ease of learning or ease of use of the Screen Design Standards drafted in the previous task.

❷ **Decide on user and task focus for the test.** Identify the type and range of users to be included in the test. You might decide to focus on one category of potential application users considered to be "high-priority" users (e.g., in a police department application for managing property intake, they might be police officers) or to sample broadly from all potential categories of intended users (e.g., police officers, property clerks, station commanders, etc.).

You could either continue to test the same high-priority users tested in the Iterative Conceptual Model Evaluation task or take this opportunity to sample from another major category of users who were not represented in the previous evaluation. Bear in mind that the prototype, while representing Screen Design Standards, will also embody the Conceptual Model Design, and so this testing task could also be an opportunity to widen the test of the Conceptual Model Design to other important categories of users.

In any case, you should usually avoid using the same test users who participated in previous testing if at all possible, for two reasons. First, users already familiar with an earlier version of the design will not provide as good a test of ease of learning as first-time users. Also, ease-of-use tests might be affected if users are confused by aspects in the new design that are different from the design they previously used. Second, you should not lose the opportunity to test as many individual users as possible. The larger your total sample of users throughout all levels of testing, the more representative it will be.

Once a group of users is selected, identify the general types of *tasks* to study. Usually these should be core, high-frequency tasks, and/or tasks of most importance to the business. For example, for the police department application, typical tasks might include simple property entry tasks, complex property entry tasks, returning property to owners, and transferring property out of the station.

❸ Design test tasks. Test tasks can be adapted from the Task Scenarios generated in the Contextual Task Analysis task and also from test tasks developed for the Iterative Conceptual Model Evaluation task. Recruit an experienced end user to help design the detailed tasks for the test. Write task descriptions in a format that can be handed directly to test users, read, and easily understood. Make tasks as realistic as possible.

Remember that test tasks must be written in language that refers only to user goals, not to aspects of the user interface and how to achieve those goals on it. See the Sample Work Products and Techniques sections of Chapters 3 and 10 for samples of test tasks.

Test tasks in Iterative Screen Design Standards Evaluation must be more detailed and specific than those used in Iterative Conceptual Model Evaluation, in order to provide data on aspects of more detailed design issues. Test tasks for evaluating the Conceptual Model focused mainly on the user's grasp of the overall structure of the product and interactions for navigating through it. Test tasks in this usability test need to test users' comprehension of detailed aspects of screen design. Thus, they need to be tasks that require users to correctly complete detailed transactions on individual screens, not just navigate efficiently through the correct screens.

❹ **Design the test and develop test materials.** Plan the exact sequence of events for the test. Plan for testing sessions to take somewhere between one and three hours. Develop all supporting materials, including

- Observer briefing
- Welcome
- Introduction
- Pretest questionnaire
- Training
- Video permission form
- Test tasks
- Data collection sheets
- Posttest questionnaire
- Data analysis summaries

See the Sample Work Products and Templates section of Chapter 10 for examples of each of these materials.

❺ **Design and assemble test environment.** For products that will be used in a typical, quiet office environment, testing can be successfully conducted in a usability lab. If a lab is not available, locate a room where the testing can take place. Try to set it up to resemble the typical user's real work area as much as possible. Bring in a workstation, furniture, plants, a coffee maker, and so on. Whenever possible, but especially for products that will be used in more unusual work environments (e.g., police stations, operating rooms), testing should be carried out in the actual work environment.

⑥ Recruit/schedule pilot test users. Recruit and schedule two or three "pilot" users. Make sure they are as representative of the actual target user population as the final test users will be. Again, recruit users who have not participated in any previous testing.

⑦ Run pilot test. Run the pilot users through the test procedure as a way of "debugging" the test procedure and all supporting materials. Simply observe where materials and procedures need to be changed to increase clarity of instructions and accuracy of data collection.

⑧ Revise test procedure and materials. Make any necessary changes to procedures and materials as a result of step 7.

⑨ Recruit/schedule test users. Consult the description of test users specified in step 2. Consult with the business customer to discuss where test users might be recruited. Plan to include between three and ten users per iteration, depending on such factors as the diversity of users and the number of iterations anticipated.

The test session should last between one and three hours. Add half an hour to the planned length of a test session (see step 3), and schedule users no closer together than this interval.

CONDUCTING THE TESTS

Actually conducting this usability test of Screen Design Standards is almost identical to conducting the usability testing that focused on Conceptual Model Design, and again, you are referred to Chapter 10 for details. Here, I provide quick reviews and/or point out any important variations.

❶ Run the test and collect data. Run the testing procedure as planned and scheduled, videotaping if possible and collecting data on the data collection sheets. First present the welcome, and collect the pretest information using the prepared questionnaire. Read the introduction to the user from a script, conduct any training, and present the test tasks. During the testing, it is very important *not* to lead the user in any way, or give away any information about how the interface works, as this would invalidate the data being collected.

While users interact with the prototype, encourage them to talk out loud, and if they do not, ask them questions constantly about why they are doing what they are doing, what they expect will happen, how they interpret what happened, and so on. You can also take some timing data here, just to get a rough idea of whether you are within striking distance of your performance goals. But do not, at this stage, limit user introspection in order to collect valid timing data. You will miss too much important data. Instead, as suggested by Wixon and Wilson (1997), take rough timing data that includes when user introspection starts and stops. Later, you can subtract talking time estimates out of overall task times. This will not yield highly accurate timing data, but that is not your main interest at this time anyway. Another way to do this is to perform the testing with minimal interaction with the user, collect timing data and videotaping the testing session. Then, immediately after, review the videotape with users and ask them to think about what was going through their mind as they performed different parts of the task, made errors, got confused, and so on. This will yield more accurate timing data, but less accurate introspection data, as our memories of our thought processes are not always accurate. However, either of these two approaches will at least give you a ballpark idea of whether you are close to meeting quantitative performance goals, without sacrificing the collection of the introspection data that you really need at this point.

All through the testing for each test task, collect data on the data collection sheets. When all test tasks have been completed for a given user, collect the posttest information using the prepared questionnaire.

❷ **Summarize data.** Collate and summarize the data as planned—for example, number of errors per task, types of errors per task, a collection of user comments after some particularly common error, and possibly rough timing data, keeping in mind that the "thinking aloud" encouraged in this phase of testing means the timing data does not reflect usage times in the real world.

❸ **Analyze and interpret data.** Focus on areas where the data seems to indicate a problem (high frequency of errors, a common confusion, very long average task time), and try to interpret these problem areas by analyzing what might account for them. You will be focusing mostly on insight into the usability of general Screen Design Standards. But you may also uncover new Conceptual Model Design problems, which you will need to go back and address, or problems with aspects of detailed design not directly related to general Screen Design Standards, which you can address in the next design task, Detailed User Interface Design.

❹ **Draw conclusions and formulate recommended design changes.** Draw conclusions about the specific sources of identified problems, and formulate recommended design changes to eliminate these problems.

❺ **Document and present results.** Whenever possible, but especially when all team members cannot be present during testing, put together presentation props and clips from the videotapes and present the results orally. At least document the results in a report, which should have an executive summary (a high-level description of identified problems and recommended changes) as well as a more detailed summary of data, interpretations, and recommended design changes.

LEVEL OF EFFORT

Table 13.1 gives a sample level of effort for the Iterative Screen Design Standards Evaluation task. The work effort will vary widely depending on the complexity of the application and on the evaluation technique chosen. This sample represents a moderately complex application and the formal usability testing technique with two testers participating.

Note that this sample level of effort is for a first iteration test. Certain steps will take less time in later iterations—specifically the first four, which involve designing and developing the test procedure and materials. Once a basic test procedure and test materials are developed and debugged, they can be reused across iterations. The only changes required are those that involve tailoring materials to the changed prototype design.

Table 13.1
Level of effort—Iterative Screen Design Standards Evaluation

Usability Time

Step	Hrs
Design/develop the test tasks/materials	32
Design/assemble test environment	8
Run pilot test	8
Revise test tasks/materials	8
Run test/collect data	32
Summarize/interpret data, draw conclusions	16
Document/present results	40
Total	144

Alternative Techniques— A Review

Remote usability testing; alternatives to formal usability testing such as Heuristic Evaluations, consistency inspections, and the like; and applying formal computational models of human performance, are all alternative techniques that can be applied in the Iterative Screen Design Standards Evaluation task. These techniques are all discussed in detail in the Alternative Techniques—A Review section of Chapter 10. I refer you to that section for review.

Shortcuts

Again, as in Iterative Conceptual Model Evaluation, having the whole project team participate in the formal usability testing technique can eliminate the need for the documentation and communication steps.

When resources are extremely tight, or no formal usability testing can be conducted for other reasons, at least have a Heuristic Evaluation or review of your design conducted by a usability expert before proceeding. Also, employing formal computational models as an evaluation technique can help (see Chapter 10).

For very simple products, you might consider skipping the iterative evaluation of the Screen Design Standards at this point, and combining it with a single round of iterative evaluation when design levels 2 and 3—or even all three design levels—are complete.

WEB NOTES

In relatively simple Web sites and applications, it might be more practical to combine the three levels of the design process into a single level, in which Conceptual Model Design, Screen Design Standards, and Detailed User Interface Design are all sketched out, in sequence, before any evaluation proceeds. Then a single process of design and evaluation iterations can be carried out. In this case, evaluation must address all levels of design simultaneously. It is important to remember that even if Detailed User Interface Design is drafted before any evaluation commences, it is still crucial to consider all the same design issues that arise in the Conceptual Model Design and Screen Design Standards tasks when conducting design and evaluation in a three-level process.

In Web sites and applications of intermediate complexity, design levels 2 and 3 (Screen Design Standards and Detailed User Interface Design) might be combined into a single process of design and evaluation iterations to validate them simultaneously.

Remote usability testing (see the Alternative Techniques—A Review section of Chapter 10) can be particularly useful when testing Web sites and applications.

Instead of paper foils or throwaway prototypes, in the case of Web sites and applications, the prototypes can simply be partially coded products, for example, selected pages, panes, and navigational links, now with complete page content detail.

Sample Work Products and Templates

The sample work products and templates offered for the Iterative Conceptual Model Evaluation task also serve as sample work products and templates for the Iterative Screen Design Standards Evaluation task, so they are not repeated here. I refer you to Chapter 10 for the following materials relevant to this task:

- Sample Observer Briefing
- Sample Welcome
- Sample Introduction
- Sample Pretest Questionnaire
- Sample Training Materials
- Sample Video Permission Form
- Sample Test Task
- Data Collection Sheet Template with Sample Data
- Sample Posttest Questionnaire
- Data Summary Sheet Template with Sample Data
- Data Analysis Sheet Template with Sample Data

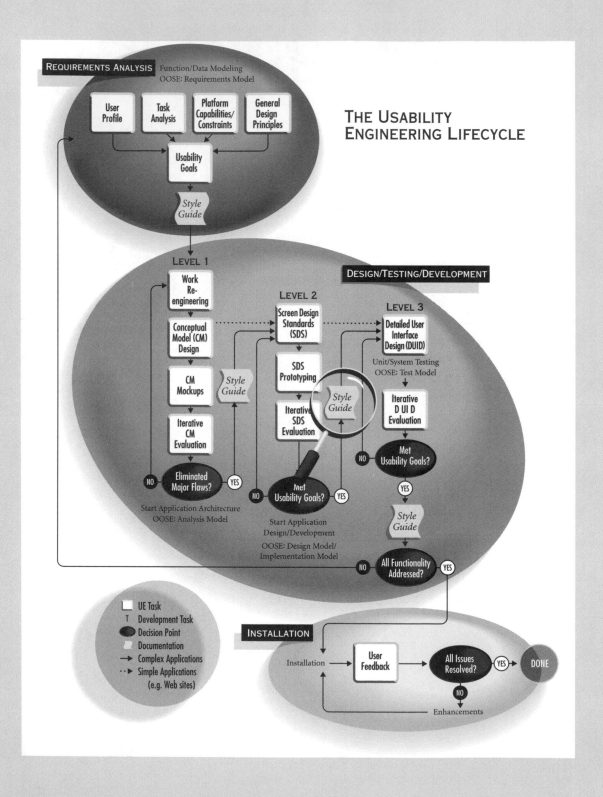

THE USABILITY
ENGINEERING LIFECYCLE

REQUIREMENTS ANALYSIS Function/Data Modeling
OOSE: Requirements Model

User Profile
Task Analysis
Platform Capabilities/ Constraints
General Design Principles

Usability Goals

Style Guide

LEVEL 1

DESIGN/TESTING/DEVELOPMENT

Work Re-engineering

Conceptual Model (CM) Design

CM Mockups

Iterative CM Evaluation

Style Guide

NO Eliminated Major Flaws? YES

Start Application Architecture
OOSE: Analysis Model

LEVEL 2

Screen Design Standards (SDS)

SDS Prototyping

Iterative SDS Evaluation

Style Guide

NO Met Usability Goals? YES

Start Application Design/Development

OOSE: Design Model/ Implementation Model

LEVEL 3

Detailed User Interface Design (DUID)

Unit/System Testing
OOSE: Test Model

Iterative DUID Evaluation

NO Met Usability Goals?

YES

Style Guide

NO All Functionality Addressed? YES

UE Task
T Development Task
Decision Point
Documentation
→ Complex Applications
··▸ Simple Applications (e.g. Web sites)

INSTALLATION

Installation → User Feedback → All Issues Resolved? YES → DONE

NO

Enhancements

14

Style Guide Development

PURPOSE

The purpose of this task is to bring together in a single document all previous Requirements Analysis and user interface design work products relevant to a particular product. As you can see in the lifecycle chart at the beginning of this chapter, you actually start developing the contents of the product Style Guide earlier in the lifecycle than is implied by its placement in the order of the chapters in this book. However, this seemed like the best place to stop and describe it, as this is the point at which you would finally complete its contents.

It is useful and important to document the Usability Engineering Lifecycle work products along the way for several reasons:

- Especially on projects with long development cycles, it is too easy to forget information and design decisions across time unless they are well documented. Also, documentation ensures that information is not lost and tasks don't have to be redone in the common event of staff turnover.
- Especially on complex projects in which great volumes of requirements analysis information are gathered and many design decisions are made, it is too difficult for designers to keep all this information in mind. They need documentation to which they can constantly refer, making sure all requirements analysis data is actually applied to design, and all design decisions are actually implemented.

311

◆ Especially on projects with large project teams and a lot of division of labor, documentation is an important means of communication across people and groups. It is essential if team members are geographically dispersed.

◆ The product Style Guide documents Conceptual Model Design and Screen Design Standards. The purpose of these standards is to ensure consistency and quality across the product user interface during Detailed User Interface Design, which in turn will improve product usability.

◆ Much of the work on a specific project can often be reused on later projects that have similar functionality and the same or similar users. Documentation from one project can thus be reused on later projects, minimizing effort on those later projects.

The product Style Guide documents intended user interface standards for designers and developers to follow during Detailed User Interface Design and development

One of the primary purposes of the product Style Guide is to document and communicate intended user interface standards to designers and developers so they will follow them during Detailed User Interface Design and development. It also contains the rationale behind the standards (i.e., the Requirements Analysis data) to help motivate designers and developers to follow the standards consistently and as intended.

DESCRIPTION

In general, Style Guides can be produced at different levels with different scopes. Different levels and scopes, from highest to lowest, include

◆ **Platform Style Guide:** Scope is all products built on a given platform, such as Apple Macintosh, Microsoft Windows, IBM OS/2, OSF Motif.

◆ **Corporate Style Guide:** Scope is all products built by a given company; the purpose is to give a corporate "look and feel" to all corporate products.

◆ **Product Family Style Guide:** Scope is all products built by a single company that are related in some important way, for example, aimed at a particular industry or used by a common population of users.

◆ **Product Style Guide:** Scope is a single product.

In this chapter, I am specifically referring to a *product* Style Guide, which is developed and applied during a specific product development project (for tips on developing Style Guides at other levels, see Gale 1996). The product Style Guide may draw upon the contents of any higher-level Style Guides but will contain many product-unique elements as well.

The reengineered work models, Conceptual Model Design, and Screen Design Standards, along with all the work products of all Requirements Analysis tasks, are documented in the product Style Guide. Chapters in the product Style Guide might include

◆ Introduction
◆ Overview of Product Functionality
◆ User Profiles
◆ Contextual Task Analysis
◆ Platform Capabilities and Constraints
◆ Usability Goals
◆ Reengineered Work Models
◆ Conceptual Model Design
◆ Input and Output Devices
◆ Screen Design Standards
◆ Feedback

The purpose of including all Requirements Analysis work products in the same document as design standards is to maintain and link the design rationale to the design itself. It is too easy for designers to ignore product Style Guide standards when they don't understand the research and reasoning behind the design of the standards. Including design rationale is especially important on large projects involving many people and long time frames. It is also helpful to designers when reusing past designs on new products and when carrying out maintenance and enhancements projects. Karsenty (1996) provides a case study of the importance and utility of documenting design rationale to support design specifications.

The purpose of including all Requirements Analysis work products in the same document as design standards is to maintain and link the design rationale to the design itself

A product Style Guide is not a detailed user interface specification. It summarizes the high-level Conceptual Model and a set of Screen Design Standards that should be followed as actual screens are designed during Detailed User Interface Design. These standards ensure consistency in such things as control selection, terminology, use of color and other visual cues (e.g., reverse video, bold), and location of standard screen elements such as titles and instructions. The Screen Design Standards chapter in the product Style Guide can potentially contain

Table 14.1　Three types of information contained in Style Guides

	Principles	Guidelines	Standards
Definition	General, high-level goals	General rules of thumb	Specific, customized translations
Example	Support the user's task with visual cues	Use color to code categories	Green background for status messages
Advantages	Help organize, focus design efforts	Based on research and experience, focus design	Directly applicable, tailored to users/tasks
Disadvantages	Too general, not directly applicable	Too general, require interpretation	Very specific, may not be optimal in some cases

three types of information: principles, guidelines, and standards. These vary in how specific they are, and they are differentiated in Table 14.1.

In platform, corporate, and product family Style Guides, there will be more principles and guidelines, and fewer standards. The product Style Guide, on the other hand, should contain mostly standards, translating principles and guidelines from the higher-level Style Guides into appropriate standards for the product.

SCHEDULING AND INTEGRATION WITH OTHER TASKS

The product Style Guide Development task fits into the overall Usability Engineering Lifecycle in the following ways:

◆ This task starts during the Requirements Analysis phase and *stabilizes* at the end of design level 2 (Screen Design Standards) in the Design/Testing/Development phase.

◆ While it should be relatively stable at the end of design level 2 in the Design/Testing/Development phase, the product Style Guide is an evolving document whose contents may continue to change during the rest of development and even after installation.

◆ The product Style Guide documents the results of all previous life-cycle tasks, including all Requirements Analysis work products, the validated reengineered work models, the validated Conceptual Model Design, and the validated Screen Design Standards.

◆ The product Style Guide drives Detailed User Interface Design and may continue to be refined and updated in response to the Iterative Detailed User Interface Design Evaluation and User Feedback tasks.

The product Style Guide Development task fits into the underlying software development methodology in the following ways:

◆ This task is ongoing throughout the Usability Engineering Lifecycle.

◆ Parts of the product Style Guide are developed during each phase of the underlying software development methodology prior to implementation, as indicated in the lifecycle chart at the beginning of this chapter and in the Scheduling and Integration with Other Tasks sections of each chapter.

ROLES AND RESOURCES

In the Style Guide Development task, the usability roles might participate as follows:

Task leader: The User Interface Designer should take the lead role in this task.

Other resources: The Usability Engineer can provide guidance, and other team members can participate, especially those who have been involved in Requirements Analysis tasks.

SAMPLE TECHNIQUE— A STEP-BY-STEP PROCEDURE

❶ **Document work products from all Requirements Analysis tasks.** Here is the place to bring together the output of earlier Requirements Analysis tasks, including the User Profile, the Contextual Task Analysis (including a work environment analysis, the Current User Task Organization Model, Task Scenarios, etc.), the Platform Capabilities and Constraints, and the Usability Goals. Here, also, you would document the reengineered work models.

❷ **Document the validated Conceptual Model Design.** The Conceptual Model Design may (or may not) be based on appropriate platform—and possibly corporate and/or product family—Style Guides, and the product Style Guide should make reference to those other Style Guides wherever applicable. The only detail the product Style Guide contains is detail unique to the product. See the Sample Work Products and Templates section of Chapter 8 for examples of how to document the Conceptual Model Design.

❸ **Document the validated Screen Design Standards.** The Screen Design Standards in the product Style Guide may also be based on appropriate platform—and possibly corporate and/or product family—Style Guides, and the product Style Guide should make reference to those other Style Guides wherever applicable. The only detail the product Style Guide contains is detail unique to the product. For example, the product Style Guide should list the rules that provide consistency for data or other screen elements unique to the product.

The Sample Work Products and Templates section later in the chapter contains a template representing a product Style Guide Table of Contents for a product based on a GUI platform. This sample outline offers one possible way to organize Screen Design Standards in the product Style Guide. The Sample Work Products and Templates section of Chapter 11 offers some examples of how to document Screen Design Standards.

❹ **Communicate the Style Guide.** Without proper communication, Style Guides may have no impact whatsoever. For example, if User Interface Designers (see Chapters 1 and 21 for definitions of all Usability Engineering roles) develop the Conceptual Model Design and Screen Design Standards in isolation, and then publish them in a product Style Guide hundreds of pages long, there is little hope developers will read and follow them during Detailed User Interface Design. Sometimes developers are expected to conduct Detailed User Interface Design themselves directly from a product Style Guide (as opposed to code from a Detailed User Interface Design specification provided by the User Interface Designer). In this case, I have found (see also Gale 1996) it is necessary to educate designers and developers on the benefits of standards; to develop standards collaboratively with input from users and developers; and then to provide training to other designers and developers on what the standards are and how to use prototypes that embody the standards. (For an example of using a prototype to communicate standards, see Miller 1996.) Product Style Guides also need to be presented to designers and developers as "a practical and creative tool," rather than "a set of rules" (Miller 1996).

5 **Enforce the Style Guide.** Even when product Style Guides are effectively communicated, they are not always adhered to by designers and developers who did not participate in developing them. They need to be enforced. Here, management support is key. Following the product Style Guide standards should be mandatory, and this can only be enforced by management. Your organization may need to introduce a process by which designs are submitted for review to determine whether they conform to the product Style Guide standards, and if not, the project cannot proceed to the next step until they do. There should also be an appeals process, so legitimate exceptions can be made, and standards can evolve in the face of feedback from iterative design and evaluation. Probably the best way to communicate *and* enforce product Style Guide standards at the same time is to build the standards into development tools, making it easy to conform to them and difficult to deviate from them during development.

LEVEL OF EFFORT

Table 14.2 gives a sample level of effort for the product Style Guide Development task. This task is really nothing more than documenting the results of all previous lifecycle tasks; in the level-of-effort estimates for those tasks in previous chapters, documentation efforts were already factored in. Here I have pulled out all the documentation steps from those previous tasks and consolidated them, simply to give an idea of the documentation effort as a whole. As always, the work effort will vary widely depending on the complexity of the product. This sample represents a simple to moderately complex product.

Table 14.2
Level of effort—Product Style Guide Development

Usability Time

Step	Hrs
Document User Profiles	24
Document Contextual Task Analysis	72
Document Platform Capabilities	16
Document Usability Goals	24
Document Reengineered Work Models	16
Document Conceptual Model	48
Document Screen Design Standards	56
Total	256

ALTERNATIVE TECHNIQUES—A REVIEW

Since it is a document, the product Style Guide is not an ideal tool for communicating design

Since the product Style Guide is a document, it is not an ideal tool for communicating design and design rationale. As Brown, Graham, and Wright (1998) point out, the work products of many Usability Engineering tasks, such as task analyses and user interface design, must coevolve with each other during iterative design and coevolve along with the work products of software engineering tasks such as architecture design and code. Currently we lack good tools to support this coevolution of requirements analysis, design, and development work products. Brown and colleagues report on an experimental tool that supports hypertext links between certain design and development work products—specifically, task hierarchies from a task analysis, user interface specifications, system architecture specifications, and user interface code. These links allow a designer or developer to easily see and maintain the specific connections between these work products as they coevolve, which has several benefits:

◆   Designers can more readily see and respond to the implementation implications of their designs.

◆ Developers can more easily maintain a user/task perspective as they design system architecture and code.

◆ Both designers and developers can more easily maintain an awareness of the connections between user/task requirements and design.

The field could benefit from more generic and widely available tools such as these.

In his address at the April 1998 ACM CHI conference, Shneiderman gave a hypothetical example from a medical context of an automated tool that supports in an integrated fashion what he identifies as the four phases of any kind of creative work:

◆ Collect information from an existing domain of knowledge.
◆ Create innovations.
◆ Consult with peers or mentors to refine creations.
◆ Disseminate results to contribute to the existing knowledge domain.

In this hypothetical medical system, a physician trying to diagnose and treat a patient has, all on one integrated software system, the capabilities to

◆ Consult the literature to help with a diagnosis of symptoms (collect information)
◆ Design a treatment plan (create)
◆ Consult with other specialists to get feedback and advice on the proposed treatment plan (consult)
◆ Report the results of the treatment back to the medical community (disseminate)

These general phases of creative work correspond closely to the phases and tasks in the Usability Engineering Lifecycle of

◆ Requirements Analysis (collect)
◆ Design (create)
◆ Testing (consult)
◆ Product Style Guide development (disseminate)

Analogous to Shneiderman's medical system, what we need are powerful automated tools that support us in carrying out and integrating the various tasks in the Usability Engineering Lifecycle. Currently, we simply document the work products from each task and then assume others will

Until generic and powerful automated tools are developed to support the lifecycle, we must make do with more primitive and less integrated tools such as the product Style Guide

read them, understand them, and integrate them into later tasks in both design and development. This works reasonably well when small multidisciplinary teams work closely together on all requirements analysis, design, and development tasks, but it breaks down on large projects with distinct divisions of labor according to areas of expertise. However, until generic and powerful automated tools to support the Usability Engineering Lifecycle are developed, we must make do with more primitive and less integrated tools such as the product Style Guide.

SHORTCUTS

For small, simple projects, producing a formal product Style Guide may not be important. But for projects of any complexity with large project teams and long development schedules, it is very important to do documentation of all kinds, including user interface Style Guides, for all of the reasons described earlier in this chapter.

WEB NOTES

For simple Web sites and applications, as long as good design processes and principles have been followed, documenting the design may not be necessary. For sites of intermediate complexity, at least documenting design standards is recommended. For complex Web sites—even intranet Web sites—with many designers, developers, and/or maintainers of a constantly evolving site, documenting Requirements Analysis work products and design standards is as important as it is on large traditional software projects.

SAMPLE WORK PRODUCTS AND TEMPLATES

One template for the product Style Guide Development task is offered here: the Style Guide Table of Contents Template. Refer to the Sample Work Products and Templates sections of each previous chapter for examples of documented work products that would be included in the product

Style Guide chapters. The Table of Contents template is annotated where it might not be clear from previous chapters what content is intended. This template assumes a software product based on a typical GUI platform (e.g., Microsoft Windows, Apple Macintosh).

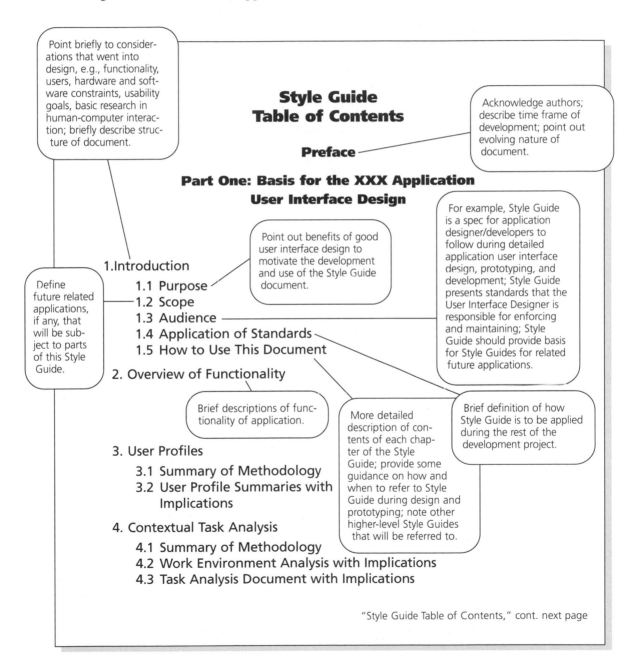

Point briefly to considerations that went into design, e.g., functionality, users, hardware and software constraints, usability goals, basic research in human-computer interaction; briefly describe structure of document.

Style Guide
Table of Contents

Acknowledge authors; describe time frame of development; point out evolving nature of document.

Preface

Part One: Basis for the XXX Application User Interface Design

For example, Style Guide is a spec for application designer/developers to follow during detailed application user interface design, prototyping, and development; Style Guide presents standards that the User Interface Designer is responsible for enforcing and maintaining; Style Guide should provide basis for Style Guides for related future applications.

Define future related applications, if any, that will be subject to parts of this Style Guide.

1.Introduction

Point out benefits of good user interface design to motivate the development and use of the Style Guide document.

  1.1 Purpose
  1.2 Scope
  1.3 Audience
  1.4 Application of Standards
  1.5 How to Use This Document

2. Overview of Functionality

Brief descriptions of functionality of application.

More detailed description of contents of each chapter of the Style Guide; provide some guidance on how and when to refer to Style Guide during design and prototyping; note other higher-level Style Guides that will be referred to.

Brief definition of how Style Guide is to be applied during the rest of the development project.

3. User Profiles
  3.1 Summary of Methodology
  3.2 User Profile Summaries with Implications

4. Contextual Task Analysis
  4.1 Summary of Methodology
  4.2 Work Environment Analysis with Implications
  4.3 Task Analysis Document with Implications

"Style Guide Table of Contents," cont. next page

"Style Guide Table of Contents," cont.

4.4 Task Scenarios with Implications
4.5 Current User Task Organization Model with Implications

5. Platform Capabilities and Constraints

5.1 Identification of Hardware Platforms
5.2 Identification of Software Platforms and Tools
5.3 Summary of Platform Capabilities and Constraints with Implications

6. Usability Goals

6.1 Qualitative Goals
6.2 Quantitative Goals

Part Two: Designing the XXX Application User Interface

7. Reengineered Work Models

7.1 Reengineered Task Organization Model
7.2 Reengineered Task Sequence Models

8. Conceptual Model Design

8.1 Identification of Products/Processes
8.2 Presentation Rules for Products/Processes
8.3 Rules for Windows
8.4 Major Displays
8.5 Major Navigational Pathways (e.g., Menu Bar)

9. Input and Output Devices

9.1 Screen
9.2 Mouse/Pointing Devices
9.3 Keyboard
9.4 Sound

> List available screen attributes from the Platform Capabilities/Constraints chapter, such as color, dimming, bold, reverse video, available typefaces, styles, and point sizes, etc., and assign rules for consistent usage; refer to higher-level (i.e., platform or corporate) Style Guides where appropriate.

> Define, for example, click, double-click, and drag for each mouse button in different contexts; refer to higher-level Style Guides where appropriate.

> Define standard uses for bell and any other sounds; refer to higher-level Style Guides where appropriate.

> Define standard uses for arrow keys, modifier keys such as Shift and Alt, and other special-purpose keys such as Enter, Home, Tab, and function keys; refer to higher-level Style Guides where appropriate.

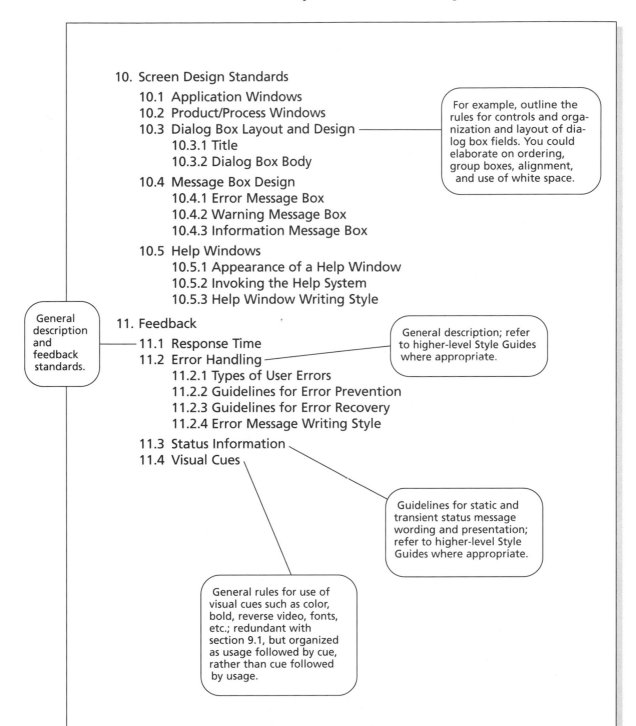

10. Screen Design Standards
    10.1 Application Windows
    10.2 Product/Process Windows
    10.3 Dialog Box Layout and Design
        10.3.1 Title
        10.3.2 Dialog Box Body

> For example, outline the rules for controls and organization and layout of dialog box fields. You could elaborate on ordering, group boxes, alignment, and use of white space.

    10.4 Message Box Design
        10.4.1 Error Message Box
        10.4.2 Warning Message Box
        10.4.3 Information Message Box
    10.5 Help Windows
        10.5.1 Appearance of a Help Window
        10.5.2 Invoking the Help System
        10.5.3 Help Window Writing Style

> General description and feedback standards.

11. Feedback
    11.1 Response Time
    11.2 Error Handling
        11.2.1 Types of User Errors
        11.2.2 Guidelines for Error Prevention
        11.2.3 Guidelines for Error Recovery
        11.2.4 Error Message Writing Style

> General description; refer to higher-level Style Guides where appropriate.

    11.3 Status Information
    11.4 Visual Cues

> Guidelines for static and transient status message wording and presentation; refer to higher-level Style Guides where appropriate.

> General rules for use of visual cues such as color, bold, reverse video, fonts, etc.; redundant with section 9.1, but organized as usage followed by cue, rather than cue followed by usage.

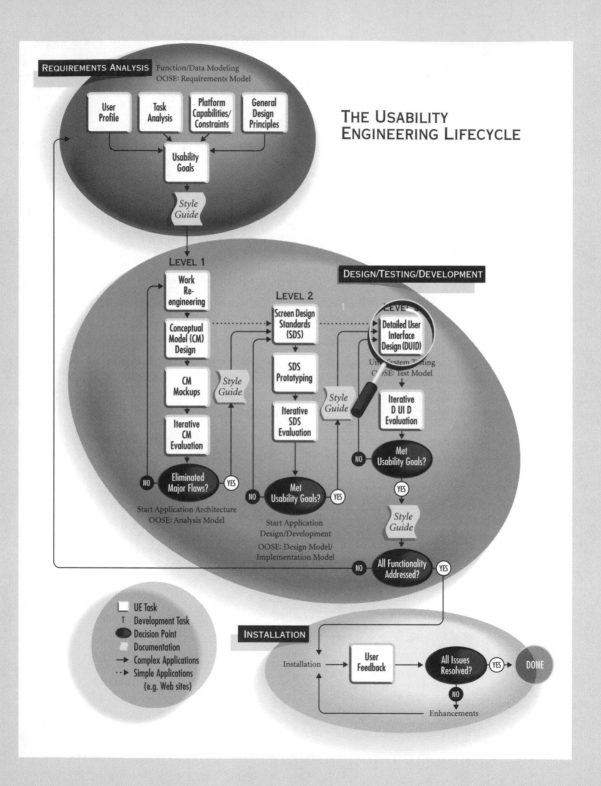

THE USABILITY
ENGINEERING LIFECYCLE

REQUIREMENTS ANALYSIS Function/Data Modeling
OOSE: Requirements Model

User Profile

Task Analysis

Platform Capabilities/ Constraints

General Design Principles

Usability Goals

Style Guide

LEVEL 1

DESIGN/TESTING/DEVELOPMENT

Work Re-engineering

LEVEL 2

LEVEL 3

Conceptual Model (CM) Design

Screen Design Standards (SDS)

Detailed User Interface Design (DUID)

Style Guide

Style Guide

Unit/System Testing
OOSE: Test Model

CM Mockups

SDS Prototyping

Iterative CM Evaluation

Iterative SDS Evaluation

Iterative D UI D Evaluation

NO

Met Usability Goals?

Eliminated Major Flaws?

YES

NO

Met Usability Goals?

YES

YES

Start Application Architecture
OOSE: Analysis Model

Start Application Design/Development

OOSE: Design Model/ Implementation Model

Style Guide

NO

All Functionality Addressed?

YES

UE Task
T Development Task
Decision Point
Documentation
→ Complex Applications
∙∙▸ Simple Applications
(e.g. Web sites)

INSTALLATION

Installation → User Feedback → All Issues Resolved? → YES → DONE

NO

Enhancements

15

Detailed User Interface Design

PURPOSE

The design of the product user interface in all its complete detail is, of course, the ultimate purpose of the whole Usability Engineering Lifecycle; all the other tasks across the lifecycle are aimed at accomplishing this task as efficiently and effectively as possible. We want more than just a complete user interface design (which will happen with or without the Usability Engineering Lifecycle); we want a complete user interface design that optimizes user performance and satisfaction, and that is created through a cost-effective development process.

DESCRIPTION

In the Detailed User Interface Design task, we define and (sometimes) document the design based on the Conceptual Model Design and the Screen Design Standards established in previous tasks, so that all pathways, displays, and interactions follow the product user interface standards developed in those earlier tasks. You will recall that aspects of the Conceptual Model Design (see Chapter 8) for a typical software GUI include

- Decision on whether to design a product- versus process-oriented Conceptual Model
- Identification of products or processes
- Rules for the presentation of products or processes
- Rules to follow for the use of window types

325

◆ Identification of major displays and the navigational pathways between them

And aspects of the Screen Design Standards (see Chapter 11) include

◆ Rules for the use of controls (e.g., check boxes, option buttons, list boxes, combo boxes, push buttons)
◆ Rules for the location and format of standard display components (e.g., title bar, status line, display body, navigation controls, action controls)
◆ Rules for terminology
◆ Rules for the use of color
◆ Rules for the use of type fonts and styles
◆ Rules for input device interactions and keyboard shortcuts
◆ Rules for the type, location, format, and wording of messages and on-line instructions

You now follow the standards previously established in all the above aspects (assuming the product is software based on a typical GUI platform) in performing the following tasks:

◆ Complete the identification of all pathways between windows, dialog boxes, and message boxes
◆ Complete the detailed design of the menu bar and/or all other action controls
◆ Complete the detailed design of the content of all windows, dialog boxes, and message boxes
◆ Complete the detailed design of all interactions with input devices

When applications are relatively simple, and/or when developers are experienced in designing and developing directly from a product Style Guide, it may not be necessary to document the complete Detailed User Interface Design in a formal way. As individual developers work on the part of the code for which they are responsible, they can simply follow the Conceptual Model Design and the Screen Design Standards as laid out in the product Style Guide. The product Style Guide will ensure consistency and adherence to the Conceptual Model Design and Screen Design Standards as long as developers understand it, follow it faithfully, and communicate effectively with one another and with the User Interface Designer (see Chapters 1 and 21 for definitions of all Usability Engineering roles) when questions, conflicts, and other issues arise.

On the other hand, when products are large and complex, project staff are dispersed, and labor is distinctly divided across specialty areas, and/or when developers are *not* experienced designing and developing directly from a product Style Guide, it may be important for the User Interface Designer to create a complete, documented, formal specification of the Detailed User Interface Design from which developers can write their code. Sometimes only this will ensure that the quality and consistency that is the whole point of all previous tasks in the Usability Engineering Lifecycle will be realized in the final product user interface.

The User Interface Designer should create a complete formal specification of the Detailed User Interface Design for developers who are inexperienced in designing directly from a product Style Guide

Scheduling and Integration with Other Tasks

The Detailed User Interface Design task fits into the overall Usability Engineering Lifecycle in the following ways:

- The Detailed User Interface Design is generated directly from the Conceptual Model Design and the Screen Design Standards documented in the product Style Guide.
- Either developers will themselves design and develop directly from the product Style Guide, or the User Interface Designer will generate a Detailed User Interface Design specification based on the product Style Guide and provide it to developers for coding purposes.
- The Detailed User Interface Design will be realized as application code and then subjected to further usability evaluation in the next task, Iterative Detailed User Interface Design Evaluation.

The Detailed User Interface Design task fits into the underlying software development methodology in the following ways:

- This task should *parallel* or *follow* development of the Design Model in the Construction phase of OOSE (or module design in a traditional rapid prototyping methodology), as screen design details usually will not have an effect on high-level code design.
- This task should *precede* development of the Implementation Model in the Construction phase of OOSE (or code development in a traditional rapid prototyping methodology), as Detailed User Interface Design is in part what will be coded in the Implementation Model.

Roles and Resources

In the Detailed User Interface Design task, the usability roles might participate as follows:

Task leader: If the product is complex, project staff are dispersed, labor is distinctly divided across specialists, and/or developers are inexperienced with designing and developing directly from a product Style Guide, the User Interface Designer should take the lead role in this task and produce a written Detailed User Interface Design specification from which developers can write their code.

On the other hand, if the product is relatively simple and/or developers are experienced with designing and developing directly from a product Style Guide, the developers themselves might design and produce detailed user interface code directly from the product Style Guide, as long as they communicate closely with one another and the User Interface Designer to resolve in a common way any questions, conflicts, and other issues that arise.

Other resources: If the User Interface Designer has produced a written Detailed User Interface Design specification for developers, the developers will code directly from this specification. On the other hand, if the developers themselves are designing and developing detailed user interface code directly from the product Style Guide, the User Interface Designer should serve as both a consultant when questions arise and a decision maker when conflicts arise. The Usability Engineer can provide input and advice when solicited by the User Interface Designer.

Sample Technique—A Step-by-Step Procedure

I present the steps for completing a Detailed User Interface Design in linear fashion, which may seem to imply a top-down approach to design at this level. However, you can approach the issues represented in these steps in any order, from addressing each issue one at a time for all functionality, to taking subsets of functionality one at a time and applying all issues to them before moving on to the next subset of functionality. Thus, my intention is not to imply a particular order, but to list all the design issues that must ultimately be addressed for all application functionality before a Detailed User Interface Design can be completed.

Also note that when Detailed User Interface Design specifications will be formally documented by User Interface Designers, each step below implies that the designer should be making design decisions and documenting them in a design specification. The design specification at this level in the design process should be primarily illustrations of displays and screen states, with text only where aspects of the design cannot be effectively illustrated through pictures alone (e.g., descriptions of interactions with input devices). When developers will design and develop directly from a product Style Guide, they must address all the issues listed in the steps below but need not document them in a specification.

❶ **Complete the identification of all pathways between windows, dialog boxes, and message boxes.** During the development of the Conceptual Model Design (see Chapter 8), you identified the main pathways between primary displays and other general display types (e.g., in Microsoft Word, from any document window, users can navigate directly to any number of dialog boxes). Now you must complete the identification of all pathways between all displays (e.g., in Microsoft Word, the pathways from a document window to all dialog boxes—Styles dialog box, Print dialog box, etc.).

❷ **Complete the design of menu bar and/or all other action controls.** Here you design the detailed presentation of all the controls that will allow users to navigate the pathways identified in the previous step, and also perform all other actions. In a product-oriented Conceptual Model Design (see Chapter 8) that follows a standard GUI model (e.g., Microsoft Windows, Apple Macintosh), initiating actions—including navigational actions—is done via the menu bar, pull-downs, and dialog boxes, while completing actions and returning to documents is done through push buttons within dialog boxes. Even in process-oriented GUIs (see Chapter 8), much of designing navigational controls might involve designing a menu bar, pull-downs, and dialog box structure.

Recall that a pass at designing menu bars and/or other action controls was made during the Conceptual Model Design task, but only a subset of primary navigational and other actions were designed in detail. Also, during Screen Design Standards (see Chapter 11) you would have designed general standards for control use and design. Now it is time to complete the detailed design of the controls representing all actions, navigational and otherwise, following the standards laid out in these two previous levels of design. This might or might not involve completing the design of a menu bar structure, but it will always involve completing the design of the presentation of all action controls, including navigational action controls.

❸ **Complete the design of content of all windows, dialog boxes, and message boxes.** Recall that during Conceptual Model Design you identified major displays and types of displays but did not design their content. Then, during Screen Design Standards, you established general standards that would be applied to all displays according to type. Also, in the process of prototyping and performing usability evaluation, you completed the detailed design of a small subset of actual displays. Now it is time to specify the detailed design of the content of all application displays, including windows, dialog boxes, and message boxes. In doing this, you refer constantly to the Screen Design Standards as documented in the product Style Guide, following them faithfully whenever they are applicable.

During Detailed User Interface Design, no Conceptual Model Design or Screen Design Standards should be violated without discussion and consensus among all project team members with responsibility and authority for user interface design. When changes to standards are agreed upon, they must be reflected in an updated product Style Guide and communicated effectively to all designers.

❹ **Complete the design of all interactions with input devices.** In step 2, the presentation of action controls was designed—for example, the exact appearance of menu bar structures, push buttons, and so on. In this step, you detail all the ways in which users can interact with these controls using optional input devices. For example, when designing an application user interface according to a standard GUI model, you may assume that users would interact with most controls through standard mouse interactions, such as single clicks, double clicks, and drag-and-drop operations. Now is the time to formally specify these interactions.

It will now also be necessary to define in detail all keyboard shortcuts (e.g., accelerator keys) for interacting with application-unique menu bar picks and other action controls. And if additional alternative input devices such as touchscreens or trackballs are to be enabled, then exactly how the user will use these devices to interact with controls must also be designed now.

When designing an interface that does not follow a standard GUI model, you cannot simply follow a set of platform standards for input device interactions with controls. Refer instead to the set of interaction standards you designed as part of the Screen Design Standards task (see Chapter 11). At that time you will have attempted to design intuitive, comfortable interactions that, as a set, provide maximum consistency and simplicity as well as ease of use from a motor standpoint. Now is the time to apply these standards and specify the particulars of all input device interactions with all display controls.

LEVEL OF EFFORT

Table 15.1 gives a sample level of effort for the Detailed User Interface Design task. The work effort will vary widely depending on the complexity of the product, and this sample represents a simple to moderately complex product.

Table 15.1
Level of effort—Detailed User Interface Design

Usability and/or Development Time

Step	Hrs
Complete identification of pathways	40
Complete design of menu bar and/or all action widgets	40
Complete design of content of all windows, dialog/message boxes	80
Complete design of input device interactions	80
Total	240

ALTERNATIVE TECHNIQUES— A REVIEW

Participatory design (in which users participate as active members of the design team) and automated design tools are two alternative techniques for the Detailed User Interface Design task. See Alternative Techniques—A Review in Chapter 8 for details.

SHORTCUTS

There is no way around it—Detailed User Interface Design has to be done, one way or another! Traditionally, it has been done without all the preceding and supporting tasks in the Usability Engineering Lifecycle, with less than optimal results, and often at much greater cost in the long run. The Usability Engineering Lifecycle, while perhaps increasing the labor before development, can significantly decrease the labor during and after development. It decreases labor during development by resulting in reusable code; and after development, it eliminates costly redesign and redevelopment that is often necessary when major usability problems are discovered after a product is released, documentation is published and distributed, and users are trained.

However, on very simple projects, you might have deferred any usability evaluation until the detailed design level. This can save time and resources on the project overall and still allow you to refine and validate all aspects of detailed design (Conceptual Model Design, Screen Design Standards, and Detailed User Interface Design) in a single round of iterative evaluation. Also on relatively simple products, and/or on projects where developers are very experienced with Usability Engineering in general and designing from product Style Guides in particular, you can skip having User Interface Designers document Detailed User Interface Design in a specification. Instead, developers can design and develop directly from the product Style Guide, following the Conceptual Model Design and Screen Design Standards as they go. User Interface Designers can review all detailed design against the product Style Guide for conformance and help developers resolve conflicts and ambiguities.

WEB NOTES

For simple Web sites or applications, designers might bypass evaluating and documenting user interface design at the Conceptual Model Design and Screen Design Standards levels, and simply prepare Detailed User Interface Design specifications directly from standards they have informally established at these earlier design levels. Developers can then code directly from these specifications.

For sites of intermediate complexity, you might conduct one process of iterative design and evaluation for levels 2 and 3.

For more complex Web sites or applications, the Conceptual Model Design and Screen Design Standards should have been completed, documented, and evaluated before this point. Then, developers can code directly from a product Style Guide or from Detailed User Interface Design specifications based on a product Style Guide and prepared by the User Interface Designer.

SAMPLE WORK PRODUCTS AND TEMPLATES

One sample is offered here: Sample from a Detailed User Interface Design Specification.

SAMPLE FROM A DETAILED USER INTERFACE DESIGN SPECIFICATION

This sample contains excerpts from the Detailed User Interface Design for an on-line travel reservations application, which happens to follow a standard GUI Conceptual Model (Microsoft Windows). Notes in parentheses are to help you understand the connections between the different excerpts from the specification. Note the use of detailed illustrations, along with text to explain interactions with screen elements. Finally, note that a Detailed User Interface Design specification describes all actual and detailed display designs and the interactions with them. This is in contrast to the product Style Guide, which describes a set of general design standards that determine to some extent how these actual displays and interactions will play out.

Personal Travel Agent Application— Detailed UI Design Specification

Following the Microsoft Windows standard, users launch the application from the desktop or operating system level. Users can store the application

"Detailed UI Design Specification," cont. next page

"Detailed UI Design Specification," cont.

itself, as well as the primary products created with it (in this case, Trips), in any way they wish in their folder structure. In the following illustration, the user has stored the application and all current primary products (Trips) in the same folder (called "Pta," for Personal Travel Agent).

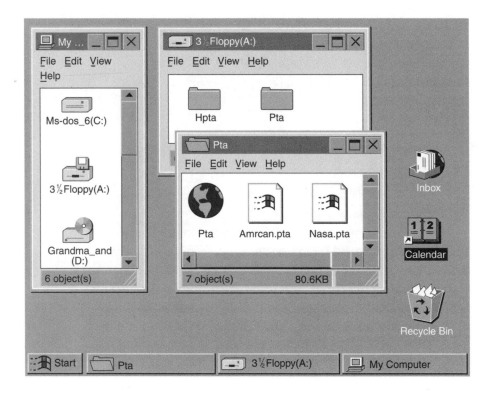

To launch the application, any standard Windows method may be used, including double-clicking with the mouse on the application icon or on any primary product (Trip) icon on the desktop. This opens the application window, with a primary product (Trip) window within it containing either an empty untitled trip or the saved trip that was double-clicked, respectively.

(Here, the specification would show the above mentioned configurations of windows.)

Only the application window contains a menu bar, and it is designed as follows. (The menu bar structure shown in this sample is not complete but would be completely specified in your Detailed User Interface Design.)

When a document (Trip) window is open:

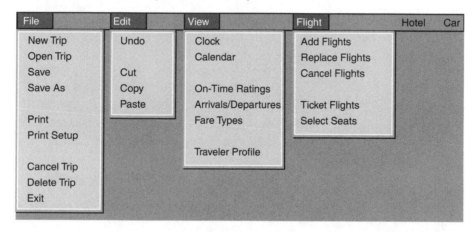

When no document (Trip) windows are open:

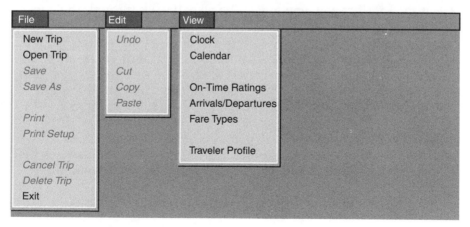

"Detailed UI Design Specification," cont. next page

"Detailed UI Design Specification," cont.

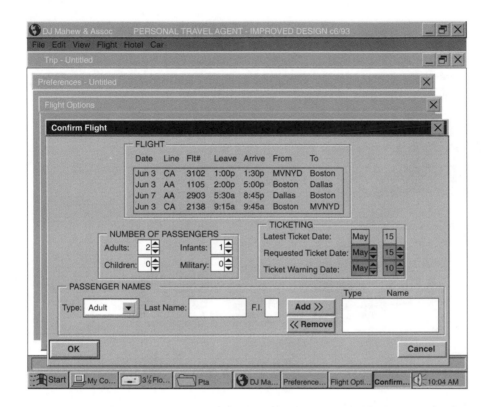

(Next the specification would describe all pathways through the application, showing the results of all possible picks within the menu bar and all displays, including the complete contents of all menu controls within each display. At some point in this complete and exhaustive specification, the illustration might look like the next illustration, showing a particular pathway initiated through the menu bar that takes the user through a set of cascading dialog boxes. Each dialog box would be illustrated in complete detail, with descriptions of how to interact with it, as in the following text).

The user fills in at least the required (light gray) fields and perhaps the optional (dark gray) ones. The controls for these fields operate in the standard Windows way.

The Passenger Type Name list box is filled in by successively filling in the Type, Last Name, and F. I. (First Initial) controls and then invoking (by any of the standard Windows methods) the Add push button. Passengers can be removed by selecting them in the Type Name list box and then invoking the Remove push button.

When all required fields are filled in, the user can click the OK button. This returns the user to the document (Trip) window, with all specified data from the dialog box sequence now filled in. If the user clicks the OK push button before all required fields are entered, a pop-up message box appears. (Here the specification would show this particular message box in an illustration and describe how to interact with it.)

At any time, the user can click the Cancel push button and return to the previous dialog box in the sequence. The menu bar is not active within the dialog box—only the push buttons are active. They are the only means of navigation out of the dialog box. The dialog box is also "modal," meaning the user cannot give focus to any other window simply by clicking on it. Again, only the push buttons within the dialog box provide navigation out of it.

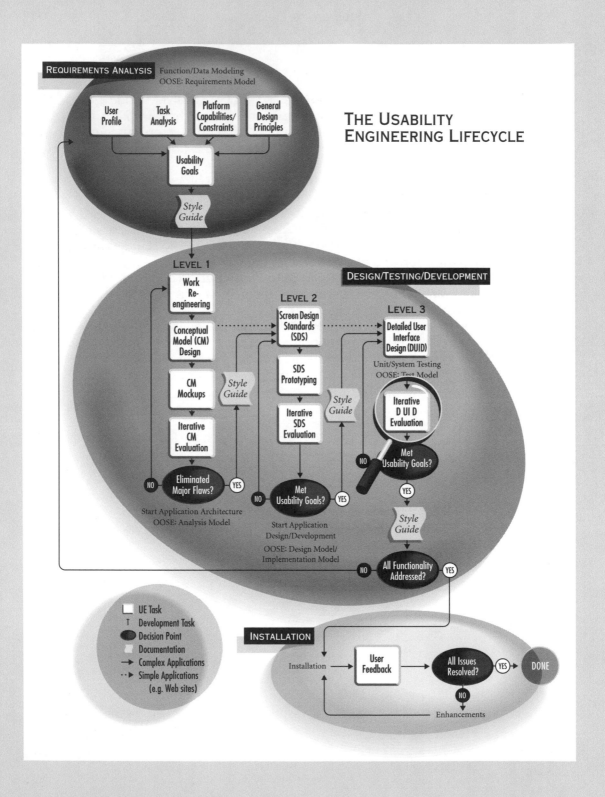

THE USABILITY
ENGINEERING LIFECYCLE

REQUIREMENTS ANALYSIS Function/Data Modeling
OOSE: Requirements Model

User Profile
Task Analysis
Platform Capabilities/ Constraints
General Design Principles

Usability Goals

Style Guide

LEVEL 1

DESIGN/TESTING/DEVELOPMENT

Work Re-engineering

Conceptual Model (CM) Design

CM Mockups

Iterative CM Evaluation

Style Guide

NO Eliminated Major Flaws? YES

Start Application Architecture
OOSE: Analysis Model

LEVEL 2

Screen Design Standards (SDS)

SDS Prototyping

Iterative SDS Evaluation

Style Guide

NO Met Usability Goals? YES

Start Application Design/Development
OOSE: Design Model/ Implementation Model

LEVEL 3

Detailed User Interface Design (DUID)

Unit/System Testing
OOSE: Test Model

Iterative D U I D Evaluation

NO Met Usability Goals?

YES

Style Guide

NO All Functionality Addressed? YES

UE Task
T Development Task
Decision Point
Documentation
→ Complex Applications
∙∙▸ Simple Applications
(e.g. Web sites)

INSTALLATION

Installation → User Feedback → All Issues Resolved? YES → DONE

NO

Enhancements

Iterative Detailed User Interface Design Evaluation

16

CHAPTER CONTENTS

PURPOSE

The purpose of the Iterative Detailed User Interface Design Evaluation task is to further refine the product Detailed User Interface Design, which was specified in the previous task based on the Conceptual Model Design and the Screen Design Standards, and which is now under development. In addition, during this evaluation task the main focus is to evaluate the final interface against usability goals (see Chapter 4), and usually (when performance goals have a higher priority than satisfaction goals), timing data is the key data being collected. Formal evaluation is much more objective than just doing a demo and asking for subjective feedback.

Because thorough evaluation of the Conceptual Model Design and the Screen Design Standards has already been conducted (see Chapters 10 and 13), evaluation at this level in most cases should reveal only simple, cosmetic problems at the detailed screen design level, rather than basic flaws at the level of general user interface standards. Such problems should be relatively easy to fix, so even though evaluation is being conducted after real code has been built, implementing design changes at this time is usually still very cost effective.

Recall that during the Conceptual Model Design and Screen Design Standards levels in the design process of the overall lifecycle, only subsets of total product functionality were designed, built, and evaluated. Thus, another purpose of this later evaluation task is simply to widen the scope of usability evaluation to cover functional areas not already evaluated in these earlier tasks.

During this evaluation task, the main focus is to evaluate the final interface against usability goals

DESCRIPTION

Planning and carrying out Iterative Detailed User Interface Design Evaluation is very similar overall to planning and carrying out Iterative Conceptual Model Evaluation, as described in Chapter 10, and Iterative Screen Design Standards Evaluation, as described in Chapter 13. There are some important differences however:

◆ The purpose of Iterative Conceptual Model Evaluation is to evaluate the Conceptual Model Design, and the purpose of Iterative Screen Design Standards Evaluation is to evaluate general screen design standards and small subsets of detailed design. By contrast, the purpose of this task is to further evaluate aspects of Detailed User Interface Design not already directly subjected to usability evaluation.

This evaluation is conducted on actual application code as it is developed

◆ Whereas Conceptual Model Mock-ups could be paper-and-pencil foils, and Screen Design Standards Prototypes were just that— potentially throwaway prototypes—Iterative Detailed User Interface Design Evaluation is conducted on actual application code as it is developed.

◆ Test tasks used for Iterative Conceptual Model Evaluation were quite broad and unstructured as only the Conceptual Model was being evaluated; whereas test tasks used for this task—much like those used for Iterative Screen Design Standards Evaluation—are much more detailed, specific, and structured because the detailed design of subsets of product functionality are being evaluated. In addition, since you are evaluating completely new subsets of the product functionality, you must use completely new test tasks.

◆ Whereas Iterative Conceptual Model Evaluation could be fairly informal and unstructured, Iterative Detailed User Interface Design Evaluation should be more formal and structured.

Timing data is the key data being collected

◆ You rarely try to collect timing data during Iterative Conceptual Model Evaluation, and you can collect and usefully interpret only rough timing data during Iterative Screen Design Standards Evaluation. During this task, the main focus is to evaluate the final interface against *quantitative* usability goals (see Chapter 4), and as performance goals usually have a higher priority than satisfaction goals, timing data is the key data being collected.

Just as in Iterative Conceptual Model Evaluation and Iterative Screen Design Standards Evaluation, the first decision you need to make is whether a given evaluation will focus on ease of learning or ease of use. Whether one or the other or both will be studied depends on the usability goals established during the Usability Goal Setting task. As before, one technique for evaluation at this level is formal usability testing. Here your main purpose is usually to collect timing data in order to test the final interface against performance goals. Therefore, users are not asked to think out loud as they work, as this will slow down performance times. Error data should also be collected.

The data is summarized to isolate major problem areas and to reveal unmet usability goals. Ideally, flaws at the Detailed User Interface Design level only will be identified, and these are usually easy and inexpensive to fix. The design must then be redesigned, recoded and retested to confirm that problems have been eliminated and to ensure new ones have not been introduced. Design and testing should be carried out iteratively until minimum acceptance criteria (usability goals) are met and all major identified problems have been eliminated.

Flaws discovered at this level are usually easy and inexpensive to fix

However, if flaws are uncovered at the Conceptual Model Design or Screen Design Standards levels, then the project team must assess the potential costs and benefits of backtracking to fix these more fundamental (and potentially more costly) problems and make a practical decision about how to proceed.

The general steps for each iteration of testing are the same as before:

◆ Plan the test and develop supporting materials.
◆ Run the test users and collect data as specified in the test plan.
◆ Analyze and interpret the data and formulate redesign recommendations.

At the end of each test, steps are

◆ Modify the Detailed User Interface Design.
◆ Modify the application code.
◆ Modify the test plan and materials.

Iteration is terminated when minimum acceptance criteria (usability goals) are met. If necessary, the product Style Guide is updated to reflect any changes in the Conceptual Model Design and/or the Screen Design Standards.

Scheduling and Integration with Other Tasks

The Iterative Detailed User Interface Design Evaluation task fits into the overall Usability Engineering Lifecycle in the following ways:

◆ This task is based directly on the previous task, Detailed User Interface Design. The product, as it is developed, is submitted to objective evaluation in this task and redesigned and reevaluated in an iterative fashion.

◆ Usability goals feed directly into this evaluation task, as this is the evaluation task in which the design is evaluated against quantitative usability goals that are used as minimum acceptance criteria.

◆ When using the formal usability testing technique, the User Profiles will drive the selection of test users and provide direct input to the design of the pretest questionnaire.

◆ Test tasks for evaluation in this task are adapted from work products from the Contextual Task Analysis. As in Iterative Screen Design Standards Evaluation, the test tasks in this task need to be narrower and more specific than those used during Iterative Conceptual Model Evaluation in order to effectively evaluate the greater level of design detail at this level of design. Also, entirely new subsets of product functionality are evaluated at this level, so test tasks that are different from those developed for Iterative Screen Design Standards Evaluation must be developed.

◆ If any Screen Design Standards or aspects of the Conceptual Model Design are revised as a result of this evaluation task, they must be updated in the Style Guide.

The Iterative Detailed User Interface Design Evaluation task fits into the underlying software development methodology in the following ways:

◆ This task should *parallel* development of the Implementation Model in the Construction phase of OOSE (or code development in a traditional rapid prototyping methodology), as the Detailed User Interface Design that is coded in the Implementation Model is being evaluated.

ROLES AND RESOURCES

In the Iterative Detailed User Interface Design Evaluation, the usability roles might participate as follows:

Task leader: The Usability Engineer should take the lead role in this task.

Other resources: The User Interface Designer should participate as an assistant in both planning and executing the evaluation. Other team members can participate as assistants as needed, but all should participate as observers. In the formal usability testing technique, users will participate as test users.

SAMPLE TECHNIQUE— A STEP-BY-STEP PROCEDURE

The steps in formal usability testing can be divided into two phases: planning and preparing for the tests and conducting the tests.

PLANNING AND PREPARATION

The planning and preparation for a product usability test focused on Detailed User Interface Design are almost identical to the planning and preparation for the usability testing conducted during Iterative Conceptual Model Evaluation (see Chapter 10) and the Iterative Screen Design Standards Evaluation (see Chapter 13). I refer you to Chapter 10 for a detailed description of the steps. Here, as in Chapter 13, I provide quick reviews and point out any important variations in those steps that are also required in this task, given its focus on a different level of design detail.

❶ **Decide on ease-of-learning/ease-of-use focus for the test.** Based on the User Profile and the Usability Goals, first decide whether an ease-of-learning or ease-of-use test will be conducted. In this testing task, you focus on the aspects of the Detailed User Interface Design that have not been directly tested in previous usability testing tasks.

❷ **Decide on user and task focus for the test.** Identify the type and range of users to be included in the test. You could either continue to test high-priority users or sample from another major category of users who were not represented in either Iterative Conceptual Model Evaluation or Iterative Screen Design Standards Evaluation. Bear in mind that the product, while representing Detailed User Interface Design, will also embody the Conceptual Model Design and Screen Design Standards, and so this testing task could also test those aspects of design with other important categories of users.

In any case, avoid using the same test users who participated in previous testing if possible, for two reasons. First, if you are doing an ease-of-learning test, using first-time users is important. The user interface may look easier to learn than it really is. If you are doing an ease-of-use test, your findings may be influenced by aspects in the new design that are different from the design users previously tested. In this case the user interface might look more difficult to use than it really is. Second, you should not lose the opportunity to test as many individual users as possible. The larger your total sample of users throughout all levels of testing, the more representative it will be.

Once you select a group of users, identify the general types of *tasks* to focus on. At this point, your goal might be to test tasks beyond the key ones already tested during either Iterative Conceptual Model Evaluation or Iterative Screen Design Standards Evaluation.

❸ **Design test tasks.** You can adapt test tasks from the Task Scenarios generated in the Contextual Task Analysis and from the test tasks developed in the Iterative Conceptual Model Evaluation. Recruit an experienced end user to help design the detailed tasks that will be used in the test.

As in Screen Design Standards Evaluation, test tasks in Iterative Detailed User Interface Design Evaluation must be more detailed and specific than those used in Iterative Conceptual Model Evaluation, in order to provide data on more detailed design issues. Test tasks at the Conceptual Model level focus mainly on the user's grasp of the overall application structure and ability to navigate through it. Test tasks in this usability test need to test users' comprehension of detailed aspects of screen design and interaction. Thus, these tasks are testing users' ability to correctly complete detailed transactions on individual screens, not just navigate efficiently to the right screen. Though this task is similar to Iterative Screen Design Standards Evaluation, you will not be able to reuse test tasks from that task because you will be testing different functionality.

 ❹ **Design the test and develop test materials.** Plan the exact sequence of events for the test, and develop all supporting materials, including

◆   Observer briefing
◆   Welcome

- ◆ Introduction
- ◆ Pretest questionnaire
- ◆ Training
- ◆ Video permission form
- ◆ Test tasks
- ◆ Data collection sheets
- ◆ Posttest questionnaire
- ◆ Data analysis summaries

See Chapter 10 for details about these materials. Recall that a test session should last between one and three hours, and three to ten test users are optimal.

❺ Design and assemble the test environment. For products that will be used in a typical, quiet office environment, testing can be successfully conducted in a usability lab if this is more convenient than testing in the user's work environment. If a usability lab is not available, locate a room where the testing can take place. Try to set it up to resemble the typical user's real work area as much as possible. Whenever possible—especially for products that will be used in more unusual work environments (e.g., police stations, operating rooms)—testing should be carried out in the actual work environment.

When usability goals are *relative*—for example, if you are comparing performance on the current product with performance on a competitive product or a manual process and have collected benchmark data on these products—every effort must be made to match all aspects of the current test situation to the benchmark testing situation. If they are not identical, any differences in performance may be due to factors such as the test environment or specific tasks used rather than the design of the product user interfaces (Wixon and Wilson 1997).

❻ Recruit/schedule pilot test users. Recruit and schedule two or three "pilot" users. Make sure they are as representative of the actual target user population as the final test users will be. Again, use different users from those who participated in previous testing.

❼ Run pilot test. Run the pilot users through the test procedure as a way to "debug" the test procedure and all supporting materials. Observe where materials and procedures need to be changed to increase clarity of instructions and accuracy of data collection.

❽ Revise test procedures and materials. Make any necessary changes to procedures and materials as a result of step 7.

❾ Recruit/schedule test users. Consult the description of test users specified in step 2. Consult with the business customer to discuss where test users might be recruited. Again, plan to have between three and ten users participate in each iteration.

CONDUCTING THE TESTS

Actually conducting this test is almost identical to conducting Conceptual Model Design testing and the Screen Design Standards testing. See Chapter 10 for a detailed description of the steps. Here again, as in Chapter 13, I provide quick reviews and point out any important variations in those steps that are also required in this task.

❶ Run the test and collect data. Run the testing procedure as planned, videotaping if possible and recording data on the data collection sheets. Remember, from step 5 in planning and preparing, when usability goals are relative, it is important that all aspects of the current test situation be identical to the benchmark testing situation.

Here is a review of the steps in the test procedure. First present the welcome and collect the pretest information using the prepared questionnaire. Read the introduction to the user from a script, conduct any training, and present the test tasks.

During the testing, *do not* lead the user in any way, or give away any information about how the interface works, as this would invalidate the data being collected. Also, remember to focus on achieving your stated performance goals. As you are most likely taking timing data, minimal intervention and discussion with the user is important so as not to invalidate timing data.

Record data on the data collection sheets all through the testing for each test task. When all test tasks have been completed for a given user, collect the posttest information using the prepared questionnaire.

❷ Summarize data. Collate and summarize the data as planned, usually by collapsing timing or satisfaction data across users.

❸ Analyze and interpret data. Focus on areas where the data shows a failure to meet minimum acceptance criteria (usability goals), and try to interpret these problem areas by analyzing what it is about the interface that might account for them. You will be focusing mostly on insight into the usability of specific screen design issues, but you may also uncover new general Screen Design Standards and Conceptual Model Design problems, which you will need to address.

❹ **Draw conclusions and formulate recommended design changes.** Draw conclusions about the specific sources of identified problems (i.e., unmet usability goals), and formulate recommended design changes to eliminate these problems.

❺ **Document and present results.** Whenever possible, but especially when all team members cannot be present during testing, put together presentation props and clips from the videotapes and present the results orally. At least document the results in a report, which should have an executive summary (high-level description of identified problems and recommended changes) as well as a more detailed summary of data, interpretations, and recommended design changes.

LEVEL OF EFFORT

Table 16.1 gives a sample level of effort for the Iterative Detailed User Interface Design Evaluation task. The work effort will vary widely depending on the complexity of the product and the evaluation technique chosen. This sample represents a moderately complex product and the formal usability testing technique with two testers participating.

Table 16.1
Level of effort—
Iterative Detailed User Interface Design Evaluation

Usability Staff

Step	Hrs
Design/develop the test tasks/materials	32
Design/assemble test environment	8
Run pilot test	8
Revise test tasks/materials	8
Run test/collect data	32
Summarize/interpret data, draw conclusions	16
Document/present results	40
Total	144

Note that the sample estimates are for a first iteration test. Certain steps will take less time in later iterations—specifically the first four, which involve designing and developing the test procedure and materials. Once you develop and debug a basic test procedure and test materials, you can simply reuse them. The only additional required changes are tailoring materials to the changed user interface design.

ALTERNATIVE TECHNIQUES— A REVIEW

As with other evaluation tasks, alternative techniques to formal usability testing that can be applied here include remote usability testing, Heuristic Evaluations and other inspection techniques, and application of formal computational models of human performance. These techniques are all discussed in detail in the Alternative Techniques—A Review section of Chapter 10.

SHORTCUTS

You can also use the same shortcuts as in Iterative Conceptual Model Evaluation and Iterative Screen Design Standards Evaluation. Having the whole project team participate in the formal usability testing technique can eliminate the need for the documentation and communication steps. On very simple projects, you might have deferred any usability evaluation (or at least design level 2 evaluation) until this design level. This can save time and resources on the project overall and still allows you to refine and validate all aspects of detailed design (Conceptual Model Design, Screen Design Standards, and Detailed User Interface Design) in a single round of iterative evaluation.

When resources are extremely tight or no formal usability testing can be conducted for other reasons, at least have a Heuristic Evaluation or review of your design conducted by a user interface design expert before proceeding. Also, employing formal computational models as an evaluation technique will help (see Chapter 10).

WEB NOTES

On projects developing relatively simple Web sites and applications, it might be more practical to combine the three levels of design into a single level, where Conceptual Model Design, Screen Design Standards, and Detailed User Interface Design are all sketched out, in sequence, before any evaluation proceeds. Then a single process of design and evaluation iterations can be carried out. In this case, Iterative Detailed User Interface Design Evaluation will be the first usability evaluation task conducted. Thus, evaluation must address all levels of design simultaneously. Remember that even if you draft the Detailed User Interface Design before any evaluation commences, you still must consider all the same design issues that arise in the Conceptual Model Design and Screen Design Standards tasks when conducting design in a three-level process.

In Web sites and applications of intermediate complexity, you might combine design levels 2 and 3, so that this will be the second and last process of Iterative Design and Evaluation.

For Web site or application design, mock-ups, prototypes, *and* application code can all simply be final code at different points of completion rather than paper foils, throwaway prototypes, and then final code.

Remote usability testing (see Alternative Techniques—A Review in Chapter 10) can be useful when testing Web sites and applications.

SAMPLE WORK PRODUCTS AND TEMPLATES

The sample work products and templates offered for the Iterative Conceptual Model Evaluation task will serve as tools and templates for the Iterative Detailed User Interface Design Evaluation task, so they are not repeated here. The materials relevant to this task are offered in the Sample Work Products and Templates section of Chapter 10.

III

Installation

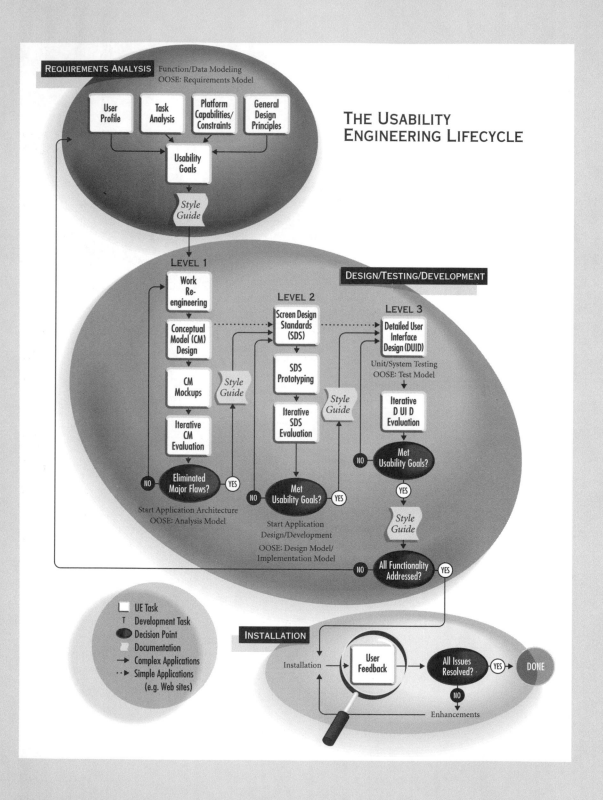

THE USABILITY ENGINEERING LIFECYCLE

REQUIREMENTS ANALYSIS — Function/Data Modeling
OOSE: Requirements Model

- User Profile
- Task Analysis
- Platform Capabilities/ Constraints
- General Design Principles

Usability Goals

Style Guide

LEVEL 1

Work Re-engineering

Conceptual Model (CM) Design

CM Mockups

Iterative CM Evaluation

Style Guide

Eliminated Major Flaws? —NO —YES

Start Application Architecture
OOSE: Analysis Model

LEVEL 2

Screen Design Standards (SDS)

SDS Prototyping

Iterative SDS Evaluation

Style Guide

Met Usability Goals? —NO —YES

Start Application Design/Development

OOSE: Design Model/ Implementation Model

DESIGN/TESTING/DEVELOPMENT

LEVEL 3

Detailed User Interface Design (DUID)

Unit/System Testing
OOSE: Test Model

Iterative DUID Evaluation

Met Usability Goals? —NO —YES

Style Guide

All Functionality Addressed? —NO —YES

Legend
- ☐ UE Task
- T Development Task
- ⬤ Decision Point
- ☐ Documentation
- → Complex Applications
- ··▸ Simple Applications (e.g. Web sites)

INSTALLATION

Installation → User Feedback → All Issues Resolved? —YES→ DONE

NO → Enhancements

17

User Feedback

PURPOSE

As you can see from looking at the Usability Engineering Lifecycle chart, the User Feedback task is conducted after a new product is installed. What could be the purpose of soliciting usability-related feedback from users at this point? There are at least four good reasons:

- To provide input to the maintenance and enhancements phase of the product lifecycle (see, e.g., Malinowski and Nakakoji 1995)
- To provide input into future releases of the product
- To provide input into the design and development of related products that will be used by the same or a similar set of users
- To learn general lessons about usability that might be applicable on any future development effort within the organization

Thus, when your project is developing a new release of a product, or a product closely related to an installed product, you could use these techniques in place of or to complement the Contextual Task Analysis techniques described in Chapter 3.

Recall also that the usability evaluation tasks carried out in each of the three levels of design in the Design/Development/Testing phase evaluated a specific level of design and expanded the general scope of evaluation across the total product functionality. It is rarely cost effective (except, perhaps with very simple products such as Web sites) to exhaustively evaluate the complete Detailed User Interface Design in all the functionality at all levels of design detail. However, you can take the opportunity to expand the scope of evaluation to new areas of functionality across design levels. Similarly, after a product is installed and has been in production for some time, you can solicit feedback on the usability of subsets of functionality not covered in any previous evaluation and apply this feedback to future efforts in any of the ways identified above.

Finally, note that in all prior evaluation tasks, you have only *simulated* expert usage in order to evaluate for ease of use. After a product has been in production for some time, there will be a pool of actual expert (or at least as experienced as they will ever get) users available, and ease-of-use evaluations can be conducted with more accuracy. Again, user feedback can feed into future efforts in any of the ways identified above.

After a product has been in production for some time, you will have a pool of actual expert users available and can conduct ease-of-use evaluations more accurately

DESCRIPTION

In this task, as in several earlier ones, you must again decide whether you are interested in ease of use or ease of learning. If you are interested in ease of learning and have focused on this aspect of usability in prior evaluation tasks, you might take this opportunity to expand your ease-of-learning evaluation to new categories of users and/or new subsets of functionality not previously evaluated. On the other hand, you might be interested in ease of use and decide to take this opportunity to conduct a more accurate evaluation than you were able to simulate prior to installation.

Next, you decide upon the timing for collecting user feedback. In an ease-of-learning evaluation, you will, of course, want to catch users during their first-time usage, or across some initial learning period. If you are interested in ease of use, and users are using the new product with a high frequency, then after perhaps three or four months you might consider them experts and be ready to solicit feedback. If they are infrequent users, you may want to wait longer to let them get up to speed before you evaluate their performance as "experts."

Finally, you decide what technique(s) to use. There are at least five to choose from: usability testing, interviews, focus groups, questionnaires, and usage studies.

A *usability testing* procedure identical to that described in Chapter 16 could certainly be employed in soliciting user feedback. The only difference is that you now have an installed product and users who are experienced using it in the context of their actual work. With this technique, you would probably be focusing on performance data, but could also solicit subjective reactions in a posttest questionnaire.

Sometimes in a real work situation, it is not possible to stop users and ask them what they are thinking about during their work (for example, a surgeon doing surgery, or a customer service representative using an application while talking to an actual customer). In such situations, one useful technique is to videotape the usage session without interrupting the user; then review the tape immediately after and ask the user to describe what was going through his or her head at each point during the interaction.

Interviews are another way of soliciting user feedback. You can conduct interviews to solicit subjective reactions from users, based on their actual experience using the product as part of their work. Interviews are conducted one-on-one. You can ask users about general satisfaction, ask them to identify particular aspects of the user interface that are problematic, and even solicit suggestions for changes. See Chapter 17's list of references at the end of the book for several published examples of using interviews.

In *focus groups*, you can get users talking about how satisfied they are with the product. You can ask questions similar to those you might ask during one-on-one interviews, but the dynamics of a group discussion should elicit different types of feedback. One advantage of both interviews and focus groups, relative to other User Feedback techniques, is that the feedback session can be relatively unstructured, allowing users to define issues. A disadvantage is that usually feedback is collected from fewer users because these techniques are relatively labor intensive.

A fourth method is to design, distribute, and analyze a structured *questionnaire* asking specific questions about product usability that elicit quantitative answers. You can usually get feedback from a much larger subset of users with this technique, compared to any of the previous techniques, but you may miss some important feedback by not asking the right questions. See the Sample User Feedback Questionnaire in the Sample Work Products and Templates section of this chapter. Also, see Chapter 17 in the References for several other published examples of using questionnaires.

In a *usage study*, you focus on identifying exactly how the product is actually being used, and then you interpret that from the standpoint of

Both interviews and focus groups allow users to define issues since the feedback sessions can be relatively unstructured. However, feedback usually is collected from fewer users because these techniques are labor intensive

If you find that certain functions or features are rarely being used, you need to ask why. If they are underused because they are hard to discover, learn, or remember, then this flags a usability problem

usability. For example, if you find that certain functions or features are rarely being used, you need to ask why. There are two possible reasons. If they are rarely or never needed, this is useful feedback, but has little bearing on usability. If they are underused because they are hard to discover, learn, or remember, then this flags a usability problem. Similarly, if you observe that usage of certain functions also frequently coincides with usage of on-line help facilities, this is a clue that there are usability problems. See Chapter 17 in the References for several published examples of using usage studies.

Your choice of technique for soliciting user feedback on installed products will depend on such things as

◆ Available resources
◆ Whether you are more interested in measures of satisfaction or performance
◆ Whether ease of learning or ease of use is more important
◆ Whether you still want to evaluate specific usability issues or you are just generally looking for any existing issues
◆ How complex the product is
◆ What kinds of evaluation and the scope of evaluation that have gone before

These factors interact in complex ways to indicate the best choice of User Feedback technique. Table 17.1 can be used to suggest possible choices depending on these factors.

In any User Feedback technique, deciding from which users to collect feedback is key. The suggestions for how to select a good sample of test users given in Chapter 10 are equally applicable in this task. I suggest you refer to the step "Recruit/schedule test users" in the Sample Technique—A Step-by-Step Procedure in that chapter and include it as a step in any User Feedback technique you choose. Also in Chapter 10, the step "Design the test and develop test materials" describes several materials useful for introducing any kind of usability study to participating users, including a welcome, introduction, and pretest questionnaire. All these materials can and should be adapted and used in all the User Feedback techniques described in the sample technique in this chapter.

Finally, note that the various techniques summarized above can be combined. It is perfectly appropriate to gather User Feedback through

Table 17.1 Selection criteria for User Feedback techniques

Technique	Product Complexity	User Sample Size	Level of Effort	Measures Performance/ Satisfaction	Measures Ease of Learning/ Ease of Use	Addresses Specific/ General Issues	Expands Scope of Evaluation
Usability testing	Simple to Complex	Small	Medium to High	Performance	Learning or Use	Specific	To More Tasks and Users
Interviews	Simple to Moderate	Small	Medium	Satisfaction	Use	Any Issues	To More Tasks and Users; From Performance to Satisfaction; From Ease of Learning to Ease of Use
Focus groups	Simple to Moderate	Medium	Low	Satisfaction	Use	Any Issues	To More Tasks and Users; From Performance to Satisfaction; From Ease of Learning to Ease of Use
Questionnaires	Simple to Complex	Large	Medium to High	Satisfaction	Use	Specific	To More Tasks and Users; From Performance to Satisfaction; From Ease of Learning to Ease of Use
Usage studies	Simple to Moderate	Small	Medium to High	Performance	Use	Specific	To More Tasks and Users; From Performance to Satisfaction; From Ease of Learning to Ease of Use

It is perfectly appropriate to gather User Feedback through several different techniques and then combine the results to draw conclusions

several different techniques and then combine the results to draw conclusions. For example, you could conduct focus groups or interviews to identify main issues, and then conduct a questionnaire to poll those issues more widely.

SCHEDULING AND INTEGRATION WITH OTHER TASKS

The User Feedback task fits into the overall Usability Engineering Lifecycle in the following ways:

◆ For a brand-new product, the User Feedback task is always the last in the Usability Engineering Lifecycle. By definition, it can only be carried out after a product is completely developed and is in production.

◆ The usability insights gained from the User Feedback task can be fed into future projects, including the maintenance and enhancements phase of the current product, new releases of the product, and the development of new but related products.

◆ User Feedback techniques can be used to complement or as substitutes for Contextual Task Analysis techniques in the case of developing new releases of existing products or new products closely related to installed products.

The User Feedback task fits into the underlying software development methodology in the following ways:

◆ In the development of brand-new products, the User Feedback task occurs after the product has been developed and installed.

◆ In the development of releases of existing products or new products closely related to installed products, the User Feedback techniques can complement or substitute for techniques in the Contextual Task Analysis task. As such, User Feedback techniques would *parallel, overlap,* or *follow* development of the Requirements Model in the Analysis phase in OOSE (or function and data modeling in the requirements phase of a traditional rapid prototyping methodology). They would *precede* development of the Analysis Model in the Analysis phase of OOSE (or the application architecture design in a traditional rapid prototyping methodology).

ROLES AND RESOURCES

In the User Feedback task, the usability roles might participate as follows:

Task leader: The Usability Engineer should take the lead role in this task.

Other resources: The User Interface Designer should participate as an assistant in both planning and executing the feedback techniques. Other team members can participate as assistants as needed, and all should participate as observers. Users will participate as the source of feedback.

SAMPLE TECHNIQUE— A STEP-BY-STEP PROCEDURE

Here, I outline the steps for the questionnaire technique of soliciting user feedback. Chapter 2 contains additional information about designing questionnaires and analyzing data from them. I highly recommend that you review that chapter as well as this section before attempting to design and administer a User Feedback Questionnaire. I also offer a Sample User Feedback Questionnaire in the Sample Work Products and Templates section of this chapter.

❶ **Develop draft questionnaire.** Hold meetings with the appropriate project team members to gather input on what usability issues should be polled in the User Feedback Questionnaire. Write draft questions and an introduction explaining the purpose and benefits of the User Feedback Questionnaire. Solicit management feedback on your draft questionnaire and make any requested or suggested changes.

❷ **Pilot/revise questionnaire.** Interview a small sample of potential questionnaire respondents by going through each question with them, checking for clarity of wording, completeness and mutual exclusivity of multiple-choice answers, and appropriateness of questions. Two to three interviewees per major user category will suffice. Revise the questionnaire to incorporate pilot feedback.

❸ **Distribute questionnaire.** In general, the response rate to mailed questionnaires is only about 10 percent. However, I have seen 100 percent response rates in some cases when in-house users will benefit from the application and management provides appropriate backing. Until your own in-house experience proves otherwise, assume a response rate of no more than 30 percent from in-house users, and no more than 10 percent from outside users.

In general, unless the total population is very large (i.e., over about 3,000), aim for a final sample of 10 percent of the total population. With in-house users, this means sending out questionnaires to a minimum of roughly 33 percent, expecting to get 30 percent of these back (with outside users you would have to send out 100 percent to expect to get 10 percent back). When user populations exceed about 3,000, as is often the case in a vendor situation, it becomes impractical to distribute and analyze questionnaires from as much as 10 percent of the total population. In these cases, aim for a final sample of at least 100 or so users from each significant user category.

Representative sampling is very important. Make sure to send questionnaires to equal numbers of each known, significant user category (e.g., physicians, nurses, technicians, receptionists—see also Chapter 2). If the first distribution does not get roughly equal returns from each category, send a second distribution to underrepresented categories.

Also sample representatively *within* each major user category. For example, in an insurance company, perhaps major user categories include clerks, managers, and claims adjusters, but there are two distinct types of claims adjusters and two types of managers, and all user types reside in different geographical locations, some of which are currently more automated than others. In this case, in the initial distribution, be sure to include equal numbers of the five categories of users, and within those categories, try to include equal numbers from the various locations and levels of automation.

Distribution can be accomplished through interoffice mail, regular mail, or electronic mail. (Don't use electronic mail if it is likely to cause a bias in response; i.e., only some users routinely use email and thus only they will get it and respond.) Make returns as easy as possible. For example, if using regular mail, include a preaddressed, stamped envelope for returns. Give a clear return deadline, but also encourage users who miss the deadline to return the questionnaire whenever they can.

❹ **Analyze data.** If using a spreadsheet, statistics package, or tailored data entry and analysis program (or just paper, pencil, and calculator), design a data entry format and analysis technique. Also plan to collate and summarize any free-form comments. As questionnaires are received, enter data as planned. When all questionnaires are returned, or upon the deadline date (perhaps allowing a grace period of several days), analyze data as planned and produce a data summary.

⑤ Draw and document conclusions. Based on the user feedback collected and analyzed in the previous steps, formulate recommendations. These might be suggestions for enhancing an existing product, redesigning a future release, or designing future related products. These recommendations should be documented so they are not lost in the time lag between the collection of user feedback and the next project that might make use of it.

See the Sample Work Products and Templates section later in the chapter for an example of a User Feedback Questionnaire study.

LEVEL OF EFFORT

Table 17.2 gives a sample level of effort for the User Feedback task. The work effort will vary widely depending on the selected technique and the complexity of the product. This sample represents the use of the questionnaire technique to solicit User Feedback on a simple to moderately complex product.

Table 17.2
Level of effort—User Feedback

Usability/Development Time		User/Management Time	
Step	Hrs	Step	Hrs
Draft questionnaire	38	Draft questionnaire	26
Pilot/revise questionnaire	14	Pilot/revise questionnaire	8
Distribute questionnaire	10	Distribute questionnaire	50
Analyze data	24		
Draw/document conclusions	24		
Total	110	Total	84

ALTERNATIVE TECHNIQUES— A REVIEW

The four alternative techniques to questionnaires for collecting User Feedback—usability tests, interviews, focus groups, and usage studies— are discussed here. Some other techniques that have been proposed in the literature are briefly reviewed as well.

USABILITY TESTS

You can use the same technique for formal usability testing described in Chapter 16 to measure the usability of the interface *after* a product has been installed and used for some time. For detailed steps in carrying out usability testing, see Chapter 10.

INTERVIEWS

There are five steps in conducting User Feedback interviews.

1. **Design interview format.** Interviews can be open-ended or highly structured. Decide whether you have specific issues you want feedback on or have no particular expectations and just want to determine what (if any) issues users have with the user interface to the product.

   If you want a fairly unstructured interview in which users identify issues, you will still want to provide some overall structure, just to get users thinking about possible issues. Sometimes when interviewed out of the context of actually using a product, users have a hard time remembering or analyzing their own reactions to the product user interface. Thus, you might have a bare-bones set of questions pointing users to general aspects of the user interface (e.g., the menu structure, the use of color, the use of labels and terminology, navigational ease) that will stimulate their memories. See also Part II of the Sample User Feedback Questionnaire in the Sample Work Products and Templates section later in the chapter for some general questions that could be used to stimulate discussion during interviews.

At the other extreme, you might be interested in user reactions to specific aspects of the user interface, and you might even be interested in quantifying their answers. For example, you might be concerned about the depth of your menu hierarchy and want to know if high-frequency, expert users are feeling frustrated by tedious navigation. In this case, you could construct something similar to a questionnaire (see the Sample Technique—A Step-by-Step Procedure section) and use it as your interview format. You can solicit a quantified reaction from users on each question and then also ask them for explanations and suggestions. For example, you could first ask a question like "Please rate the ease of navigation through the menu structure on a scale of 1 to 5, where 1 = extremely tedious and 5 = very efficient"; then ask the user to elaborate with examples from the menu structure, and offer suggestions.

2. **Design data collection forms.** For a structured interview format, you will prepare a questionnaire-like document with a multiple-choice or rating scale format for each question. Leave plenty of white space after each question so you can take notes on users' comments and explanations. For an unstructured interview format, you may just have a sheet with a list of generic issues to help jog users' memories about issues, and then simply take notes on a pad of paper during the interview.

Interviews are conducted one-on-one and should last between one and two hours

3. **Conduct interviews.** Interviews are conducted one-on-one, and you will probably need to schedule them in advance. They should usually be between one and two hours. Less won't allow you to collect much information, and more is usually too long to ask users to take time away from their work. If at all possible, conduct the interview in the user's work area, with the product up and running, so you can both point to it and discuss it. Both the context of the work area, and the running product to refer to, will help jog users' memories. Without these cues, users are likely to have trouble thinking of issues or describing and explaining them. During the interview, take notes on your data collection sheets, and also video- or audiotape if possible for a backup.

Conduct the interview in the user's work area with the product up and running, so you can both point to it and discuss it

4. **Analyze data.** If you use structured questionnaire-like interviews, answers to questions can be summarized quantitatively, and comments can also be collated and analyzed for patterns. For example, when rating scales are used to answer questions, you can tally the number of users selecting each rating on the scale and also calculate a median rating. When multiple-choice answers are provided for questions, you can compute the percentage of the total number of interviewees selecting each multiple-choice answer.

If you use an unstructured format, you must simply read through all your notes looking for common themes and common suggestions. You can still provide some simple quantitative analysis, such as citing how many interviewees raised a particular issue.

5. **Draw and document conclusions.** Based on the user feedback collected and analyzed in the previous steps, you then formulate recommendations.

FOCUS GROUPS

Conducting User Feedback focus groups is similar to interviews except for the adjustments you make in dealing with a group of users, as noted in step 3.

1. **Design focus group format.** Like interviews, focus groups can be open-ended or highly structured. Decide whether you have specific issues you want feedback on or have no particular expectations and just want to determine what (if any) issues users have with the user interface to the product.

If you want a fairly unstructured focus group that allows users to identify issues, you will still want to provide some overall structure, just to get users thinking about possible issues. Sometimes users have a hard time remembering or analyzing their own reactions to the product user interface when they are away from it. Thus, you might have a bare-bones set of questions pointing users to general aspects of the user interface (e.g., the menu structure, the use of color, the use of labels and terminology, navigational ease) that will stimulate their memories. See Part II of the Sample User Feedback Questionnaire in the Sample Work Products and

Templates section later in the chapter for some general questions that could also be used to stimulate discussion during focus groups.

At the other extreme, you might be interested in user reactions to specific aspects of the user interface (although usually in focus groups you are not looking for quantifiable answers). For example, you might be concerned about the depth of your menu hierarchy and want to know if high-frequency, expert users are feeling frustrated by tedious navigation.

2. **Design data collection forms.** For a structured focus group format, you will prepare a list of specific issues to raise and discuss. You can simply write each issue at the top of a piece of paper and leave the rest of the paper blank for note taking. For an unstructured focus group format, you may just have a sheet with a list of generic issues to help jog users' memories about their experiences with the user interface, and then simply take notes on a pad of paper during the focus group. You will want to audio- or videotape if possible to have a backup of the data.

Focus groups involve a moderated discussion among a group of users and should last between one and four hours

3. **Conduct a focus group.** As the name implies, focus groups involve a moderated discussion among a group of users. The focus group should last between one and four hours. Less won't allow you to collect much information, and more is usually too long to ask users to take time away from their work. Don't have too few or too many participants. Too few will not tap into the potential diversity of reactions and opinions across users, and too many will make discussion difficult. A good size for a focus group is between five and eight participants.

If possible, conduct the focus group in at least one user's work area, with the product up and running, so you can point to it and discuss it. Both the context of the work area, and the running product to refer to, will help jog users' memories. Without these cues, users are likely to have trouble thinking of issues or describing and explaining them. It is often less practical to arrange to conduct a focus group (as opposed to a one-on-one interview) within a work area. If work areas are small, a group might not fit. If work areas are open, a focus group may disturb other workers. If it is not

A good size for a focus group is between five and eight; if at all possible, conduct the focus group in at least one user's work area with the product running

practical to conduct a focus group in an actual work area, try to simulate the work area environment as best you can and have the product up and running in the focus group room.

In a focus group, the role of moderator or facilitator is important because he or she must manage group dynamics

In a focus group the role of moderator or facilitator is especially important because she or he must manage group dynamics. It is easy for one or two users to dominate the discussion and for subordinate users to defer to management. It is the focus group moderator's job to draw out the less talkative participants and to create an atmosphere in which everyone feels comfortable contributing and opposing opinions are encouraged. If the moderator is not successful in these aspects, a biased set of data will emerge.

A designated note taker, other than the moderator, should take notes on the data collection sheets. And it is always good insurance to have video- or audiotape as backup. The moderator will be too busy moderating to take notes.

4. **Analyze data.** If you use a structured focus group format, discussions around specific issues can be analyzed and main themes can be summarized. Specific user comments can be collated and analyzed for patterns. If you use an unstructured format, you will simply summarize the main issues that come up, along with the consensus or major disagreements relating to those issues.

5. **Draw/document conclusions.** Based on the user feedback collected and analyzed in the previous steps, you then formulate recommendations.

USAGE STUDIES

A usage study is similar in many ways to a usability test. I recommend that you review Chapter 10, the main chapter on usability evaluation, as well as the following steps before attempting to conduct a usage study.

There are two ways to collect actual usage data: random observation and software monitors

1. **Design data collection technique.** There are basically two ways to collect actual usage data: random observation and software monitors. In either case, you prepare users in advance for what you are going to do, but you actually collect data at some random, unscheduled time during their normal work hours. To prepare

users in advance, you can use all the same approaches described in Chapter 10.

When conducting random observations, you alert recruited users in advance that you will be coming by to observe anytime within a specified time range (e.g., "sometime during the third week in January"). You arrive at some unscheduled time during that range and observe for a predetermined amount of time, such as half an hour to an hour. You take handwritten notes on a previously prepared data collection sheet that lists all the functions and features for which you want to measure usage. As you observe, you simply tally the number of times you observe the user invoke that function or feature, or the total amount of time the user spent during the session using that feature or function. Thus, for random observations, the main preliminary tasks are designing your user preparation materials, deciding what features and functions to monitor, and preparing the data collection sheet to facilitate tallying the usage of those features and functions.

When using software monitors, do the same user preparation as for random observations. In this case the data is collected by an installed software monitor that is turned on at a random time for the specified amount of time. Such a monitor tallies and/or times the usage of functions and features automatically and produces a report. Thus, for software monitoring, the main preliminary tasks are designing your user preparation materials, deciding what features and functions to monitor, and designing and building the software that will monitor the usage of those features and functions.

2. **Recruit/schedule study users.** Users must be recruited. When a group of users is identified and recruited, all the user prep (e.g., introduction, welcome, prestudy questionnaire) can be administered to the whole group at one time if this is convenient. Then users are alerted to the overall time frame in which they should expect to be randomly observed or monitored.

3. **Run study and collect data.** At random times, arrive to observe a user (or activate a software monitor) and tally and/or time their usage of the predetermined features and functions. When planning

When planning observations or monitors, sample across different days of the week and different times of the day, as work patterns may vary along those time dimensions

observations or monitors, make sure to sample across different days of the week or month, and different times of the day, as work patterns may vary along those time dimensions. If you arrive at a time that seems highly uncharacteristic of normal usage (e.g., the user points out they are doing some very infrequent activity), come back at another random time.

4. **Analyze data.** Summarize the relative usage of monitored features/functions across users. This might be the average number of times users invoke a feature or function, or the average length of time or percentage of time they spend using it during the sampled sessions.

Focus on features and functions used with a low frequency or used only for short periods of time. Try to interpret why these features are underused. You may have to follow up with users and interview them to determine whether these features are simply not useful or not needed often, or whether they are underused due to usability problems.

Focus on features and functions used infrequently or for short periods of time and try to interpret why these features are underused

5. **Draw/document conclusions.** Focus on features and functions that you have determined are underused due to usability issues. Generate suggestions about how to rectify these problems.

See Chapter 17 in the References at the end of the book for a number of published usage studies.

AUTOMATED APPROACHES

Experiments with other techniques for User Feedback have also been reported in the literature. Several papers over the years (see, e.g., Tullis 1986) have reported on attempts to automate general user interface guidelines. One such automated tool is described in Malinowski and Nakakoji (1995). They point out that typically once a software application is implemented, user interface designers are out of the loop, and users are left to communicate their issues to developers. Malinowski and Nakakoji built a tool to extend user-designer communications during and after development and installation of an application. They embedded two knowledge databases in both a development environment and in the final application—one was a knowledge base of *general user interface design guidelines*, the other a knowledge base of *application-specific knowledge.* When designers were designing the interface with the development tool, the knowledge base might interrupt to point out a violation of a user interface design guideline (e.g., menu items should be ordered consistently across different invocations of the menu), or it might point out an aspect of application detail that should impact design (e.g., two actions with different names were actually considered to be analogous by users). Later, during usage, users were given the capability to tailor or adapt the interface to their preferences and needs. When they did so, they might similarly be interrupted to point out that in their tailoring of the interface they were violating some basic user interface design principle that was applied to generate the default interface design. At the time of such an interruption, users could review the general design advice and either take it or choose to ignore it. If they chose to ignore it, they were asked to provide a rationale for why meeting the general design guideline would not support their needs. This information about a design change and the rationale for it from users was then automatically communicated back to designers, who could incorporate this feedback into a general update of the application.

The automation of this feedback loop is attractive, as is the ability to collect usage data and user feedback remotely without any special effort. Such a tool cannot be very general, however, as it depends at least in part on application-specific knowledge, which will be unique for most products. This seems a rather "high-fidelity" approach to the User Feedback task, and it may be more expensive to implement, yet no more effective than some of the "low-fidelity" techniques described above.

S H O R T C U T S

Questionnaires, although they can obtain feedback from a large number of users, are nevertheless a fairly expensive effort. Usability tests and usage studies won't provide feedback from as many users and are still fairly labor intensive. The best techniques to adapt to get user feedback in a "quick and dirty" fashion are thus interviews and focus groups. They require a fair amount of effort per user, but you can abbreviate them by minimizing the number of users you involve. This of course calls into question how representative the feedback is, but nevertheless, it is an acceptable compromise when resources are tight.

The best techniques to adapt to get "quick and dirty" user feedback are interviews and focus groups

WEB NOTES

User feedback can be solicited directly from a Web site or application. This can be done by providing a link on the site that takes users to a structured feedback page, or by offering direct email from the site and asking users to provide free-form feedback. You can even have survey questions pop up as they are "triggered" by specific usage events (see, e.g., Hartson et al. 1996). An advantage of this is that it collects feedback while the user's experience is fresh in his or her mind.

You might need to give users an incentive to take the time to provide feedback, especially if you provide a structured form and it is at all lengthy. Possible incentives include entry in a raffle or discounts on products or services.

The User Feedback techniques that lend themselves most easily to Web sites and applications include questionnaires and usage studies. Other techniques are more difficult to employ since they require the identification and recruitment of users to meet in person with project team members, which may not be difficult on *intranet* sites, but may be next to impossible on *Internet* sites.

SAMPLE WORK PRODUCTS AND TEMPLATES

One sample is provided here: a Sample User Feedback Questionnaire.

SAMPLE USER FEEDBACK QUESTIONNAIRE

This sample is an adapted and abbreviated version of a report I prepared for a client some years ago describing the results of a User Feedback questionnaire. My client was an office automation vendor, and the product was their first release of a word processor. This word processor predated graphical user interfaces, but it was a direct manipulation (as opposed to command language driven) word processor, although it employed a primarily keyboard- and menu-driven interface. My client also designed and developed the workstation and keyboard on which the word processing application ran.

This version of the original report includes parts of the actual questionnaire, summaries of some of the actual data collected via the questionnaire, and some of the analysis and interpretation of the data. The word processor is referred to as "Venus, Release 1.0"—not its real name.

User Satisfaction Questionnaire
Venus, Release 1.0

Executive Summary

A three-part questionnaire was distributed to internal users of the Venus, Release 1.0, word processing application. Part I collected *demographic* information about the user. Part II asked the user to rate *general application characteristics*, and Part III asked the user to rate *very specific word processing functions.* Of 180 questionnaires distributed, 57 were returned, and analyses were performed on these.

Overall, the following conclusions and recommendations were drawn from the questionnaire data:

1. **Conclusion:** Users rated this application with generally high satisfaction ratings. This is probably partly due to the quality of the application and partly due to the fact that the sample of users who returned questionnaires were relatively inexperienced with and had positive attitudes towards technology. Other groups of users will undoubtedly be more critical.

   Recommendation: Conduct a follow-up study to distribute the same questionnaire to a group of more experienced (with both technology in general and word processors in particular) users to discover their general level of satisfaction and pinpoint the aspects of the interface that could be improved for *them.*

2. **Conclusion:** The general application attributes polled in the General Satisfaction section of the questionnaire were considered very important and rated as adequate to good.

"User Satisfaction Questionnaire," cont. next page

"User Satisfaction Questionnaire," cont.

3. **Conclusion:** General areas for improvement suggested by the ratings assigned and comments given to the General Satisfaction items include

   ◆ Clearer error messages
   ◆ Ability to abort or reverse initiated operations
   ◆ Protection from normal human error
   ◆ Ease of learning with minimal dependence on manuals, training, and human assistance

   Recommendations:

   ◆ Analyze and redesign current error messages to clarify what the problem is, offer advice on how to fix the problem, and follow a consistent syntactic format for ease of reading.
   ◆ Provide one consistent way to cancel in-progress operations such as Print, Global Replace, Sort, Super Move/Copy, Search, and so on.
   ◆ Currently, the Clear key exits your document in *overstrike mode*, but erases all text typed when in *insert mode*. This causes many users to lose inserted text by mistake when they forget they are in insert mode and press Clear to exit their document. The Clear key should not be used for both functions. Probably some other key or the menus should be used to exit documents.
   ◆ A prompt should be provided whenever users ask to delete a document, for confirmation before deleting.
   ◆ Provide an Undo function to make reversal of errors easier.
   ◆ Review and redesign all defaults to reduce errors.
   ◆ Review interface to try and discover other ways to improve intuitiveness, consistency, and ease of learning.

4. **Conclusion:** Ratings assigned to individual functions on the Ease of Use, Ease of Learning and Memory, and Key Locations scales ranged from adequate to excellent. Again, these generally high ratings probably partly reflect application quality and partly reflect the particular characteristics of the user sample, pointed out above.

   Recommendation: Conduct a follow-up study to distribute the same questionnaire to a group of more experienced (with both technology in general and word processors in particular) users to discover their general level of satisfaction and pinpoint the functions whose interface could be improved for *them*.

5. **Conclusion:** Individual functions frequently used but considered difficult to use and learn include

   - ◆ Print
   - ◆ List Directory
   - ◆ Auto Underline
   - ◆ Change Format Line
   - ◆ Move
   - ◆ Change Directory
   - ◆ Create Format Line

   Recommendations:

   - ◆ Redesign the Print fill-in screen to make it easier to understand and use. Group fields, order them more logically, and find clearer labels. Provide better defaults, such as last indicated printer in Printer field. Reduce keystrokes required.
   - ◆ Redesign List Directory function to provide more context.
   - ◆ Provide an easy way to undo underlining that doesn't require deleting the text and retyping it. Provide a better cue to remind users that auto underlining is turned on.
   - ◆ Provide a more appropriate default cursor position in the Change Format Line function.
   - ◆ Find a way to make the range of pages controlled by a given format line clearer.

6. **Conclusion:** Individual functions frequently used but considered to have inconvenient key locations include

   - ◆ Clear
   - ◆ Page Break
   - ◆ Indent
   - ◆ Center
   - ◆ Create Format Line
   - ◆ Change Format Line
   - ◆ Auto Underline
   - ◆ Replace

"User Satisfaction Questionnaire," cont. next page

"User Satisfaction Questionnaire," cont.

Recommendations:

◆ Use the Frequency of Use data to decide which keys to locate on the outer edges of the keyboard. (Put least frequently used keys there.)
◆ Put space around the Execute key so it is not pressed in error. Make it bigger than other keys.
◆ Group keys on a functional basis, provide spacing between groups, and use colors to reinforce groups.

7. **Conclusion:** The commands considered to be most difficult to use and remember tend to be those invoked by a combination of a "qualifier" key (e.g., Shift or Command) and a function key. It is probable that the relatively inconsistent and un-mnemonic way (from a syntactic point of view) in which qualifier keys are related to these functions contributes to their difficulty of use.

Recommendation: Design a consistent syntax for all multiple key functions.

8. **Conclusion:** Casual, infrequent users, managers and engineers, and technically experienced users as a group tend to be less satisfied with the application than frequent users, secretaries, and technically inexperienced users.

Recommendation: Besides all the recommendations already listed above, the needs and sources of dissatisfaction of the former user groups should probably be investigated further to help design future releases to better meet their needs. We will need to find ways to improve the general *ease of learning* of the application for *casual, infrequent users*, increase *ease of use* for *expert users*, and *add functionality* of more relevance and use to *managers and engineers*.

Introduction

One thing we as application designers would like to be able to do is to measure the quality of our products from a usability point of view. Quality is always an illusive thing to measure. In the case of software applications, two general categories of measures come to mind:

◆ *performance measures*, which are quantitative and objective, such as time-for-task, words-per-minute, number of errors, and

◆ *satisfaction measures*, which are subjective.

These two measures of quality tend to correlate with each other, but they are not the same thing and don't always correlate. For instance, some studies have found that while performance levels varied across applications, satisfaction levels did not. Both kinds of measures are important and valid. Probably both are needed to get a true measure of application quality.

There are two broad things we need to know in order to effectively measure user satisfaction and application quality:

◆ First, we need to know what attributes of *users* influence performance and satisfaction—that is, we need a sound and complete theory of user psychology.

◆ Second, we need to know what attributes of *applications* are important to users and affect their performance and satisfaction—that is, we need a taxonomy of significant application attributes.

We need to know the former so that we can be sure that observed variations in satisfaction ratings are due to the application user interfaces being rated, rather than differences in the people who are rating them. And we need to know the latter so we can ask the user the relevant and appropriate questions regarding his or her satisfaction.

Thus, my first cut at a questionnaire to measure user satisfaction with Venus, Release 1.0, has three parts: one is designed to collect pertinent data from the users about themselves. The other two are designed to collect satisfaction data on a number of general application attributes and to assess satisfaction with specific functions of the application.

Methodology

First, I found several papers in the literature that helped me decide upon a preliminary set of questions to ask users about themselves. These papers suggested user attributes that are related to performance on and

"User Satisfaction Questionnaire," cont. next page

"User Satisfaction Questionnaire," cont.

satisfaction with software applications. The questions I came up with fall into three general categories:

◆ Attitude and motivation
◆ Experience and knowledge
◆ Job and task factors

As you will see on the following questionnaire, several questions assess each of these factors.

I found only one paper that provided any guidance in designing questions to measure user satisfaction, but it was a particularly good one. It reported on a research project that made a good start at identifying attributes of software applications users consider to be important components of application quality. That study—a good example of how to develop a questionnaire—was conducted as follows:

1. A survey asked 300 experienced users of a variety of software applications to state application properties they considered to be important components of application quality.
2. A subset of 100 of those named application properties were submitted to 233 experienced users, who were asked to rate their relevance/importance on a scale of 1–7.
3. That data was subjected to a statistical method called *factor analysis*, which is a common and accepted method for developing questionnaires for measuring psychological phenomena, such as personality, attitudes, and intelligence.

   Statistically what this method does is take a collection of items and find the particular arrangement of items in groups that *maximizes* the correlations between items *within* groups, and *minimizes* the correlations between items *across* groups.

   Conceptually what it does is identify groups of questions that may in fact be measuring different facets of the same broad underlying factor. In this particular study, seven general factors were found and named. The researchers suggested that a high-quality application must

   ◆ be self-descriptive,
   ◆ give the user a perception of control,
   ◆ be easy to learn,

- ◆ facilitate the task it is used for,
- ◆ behave consistently and predictably,
- ◆ be flexible,
- ◆ be tolerant of human error.

4. These factors were submitted to tests of reliability and validity, and the first five were accepted under these criteria.
5. Then the sample of subjects was subdivided into various categories, and ratings of factor importance were compared, demonstrating that the relative importance of the five factors differed considerably depending on both user *experience level* and *frequency of use*. For instance, whereas task facilitation was most important and ease of learning least important for *frequent* users, this order was exactly reversed for *infrequent* users.

In designing Part II of my questionnaire, I selected those items from the factors that seemed most relevant to office automation applications, rephrased them for clarity and to formulate them as questions, and added some of my own that I thought were important, for a total of five questions per factor. For each question, I provided two 7-point rating scales: satisfaction and importance. This allowed me not only to assess satisfaction, but also to prioritize items as to their relative importance to users in evaluating application quality.

Part III is designed to collect some subjective data on *particular features* or functions of the application. While Part II could be used to evaluate almost *any* software application, Part III is tailored specifically to word processing. This part of the questionnaire would have to be further expanded to assess Release 2.0, which includes more than just word processing functions.

In Part III, all application functions of Venus, Release 1.0, are listed, including

- ◆ Single key functions (e.g., Tab, Sign-off)
- ◆ Single key functions with prompts (e.g., Insert, Go to Page)
- ◆ Multiple key functions (e.g., Change Format Line, Superscripts)
- ◆ Multiple key functions with prompts (e.g., Super Move, Global Replace)
- ◆ Menu selection functions

"User Satisfaction Questionnaire," cont. next page

"User Satisfaction Questionnaire Executive Summary," cont.

Users were asked to rate each function on four 5-point scales:

◆ Frequency of Use
◆ Ease of Use
◆ Ease of Learning
◆ Location of Keys

This provided some more specific data on the usability of particular functions of the application.

Generally, the kinds of analyses I planned to perform on the data were as follows:

◆ Identification of both particular functions and general application characteristics that users consider to be *very important* and *very unsatisfactory*. Solutions to these problems can be proposed for later releases.
◆ Identification of the average level of importance and satisfaction different user subgroups assign to specific functions and general application characteristics. This can help us understand what different groups of users need in applications, how to identify these needs, and how to provide applications that maximally address these needs. For instance, if we can identify specific functions that seem to be primarily used by one type of user, we can tailor the operation of that function to the needs of that type of user.
◆ Comparison of general satisfaction levels across releases, to determine whether our solutions to problems have been successful or unsuccessful, and where we might have introduced new problems.

I anticipated four general ways in which the data from this questionnaire could be useful:

◆ It could help us identify areas for improvement in a consistent, reliable way that informal feedback cannot.
◆ It could provide us with feedback on the level of improvement attained across releases. Over the long run it should help us learn how to address the needs of particular user groups, and what kinds of solutions do and do not work.

◆ It could provide marketing with some concrete data on user satis-faction with the product.
◆ Finally, as the questionnaire is refined and data is collected across a variety and sufficient number of test users, the data is potentially publishable as a contribution of our understanding of the relation-ship between user and application attributes in contributing to user satisfaction.

The rest of this report describes the results of analyses on the ques-tionnaire data. The reader should keep the following in mind when reading these results. Three general kinds of statements are made in the report:

◆ Data: Numerical results are reported. This is *objective* information.
◆ Interpretations: These are my personal views on what the data seems to be telling us. These are *subjective*, an opinion.
◆ Conclusions and recommendations: These again are my personal, *subjective* views on how identified problems might be addressed.

It would have been awkward and cumbersome to repetitively distin-guish these kinds of statements in the text of this report. But keep in mind that while the data is indisputable, interpretations and recom-mendations are only opinions and, as such, are open to debate and discussion.

Results

Out of approximately 180 questionnaires distributed to in-house users, 57 were returned. Analyses on these 57 questionnaires yielded the results described in this section.

Parts of the actual questionnaire, with summary data filled in, are presented below. Following that are discussions offering interpreta-tions and recommendations relating to the data. Note that in this report the numbered questions in the questionnaire are listed in numerical order, and grouped and given group names. In the actual questionnaire as it was distributed to users, questions were not grouped in named groups, and questions were ordered randomly within parts.

"User Satisfaction Questionnaire," cont. next page

"User Satisfaction Questionnaire," cont.

User Satisfaction Questionnaire—Cover Letter

Attached is a questionnaire designed to survey the opinions and satisfaction level of users of the Venus, Release 1.0, word processing application. Information collected through the questionnaire will be analyzed and used as input into the design of subsequent releases of this product.

As a user of this application, your input and feedback are important and necessary to the continuing improvement of this product line. We would like to thank you in advance for your cooperation, time, effort, and frankness in filling out this questionnaire.

The questionnaire has three parts. Part I asks for information about you, your job, and your experience level with the product. Part II asks you about your general level of satisfaction with the application overall. Part III asks you to assess the usability of specific functions of the application. Each part includes instructions.

The questionnaire looks long. However, every question is multiple choice, and it should take very little time to answer each question. Please feel free to go to the application if you need to refresh your memory about particular aspects you are assessing.

Please answer each question in the order it appears in the questionnaire. Ignore the numbers by the questions in Parts II and III: they are only there to assist in later analyses of your responses.

We ask for your name and mail station for several reasons. First, we would like to share with you the results of this survey. Second, we may want to interview some of you to clarify or expand upon the questionnaire results. Third, we may in the future want to carry out related studies requiring the same or different people to participate. To be sure of either, we must have a record of exactly who took part in this survey. Although we cannot offer anonymity in filling out this questionnaire, we ask you to be candid and frank in your answers and judgment of the application. Only by pinpointing areas of dissatisfaction can we hope to improve future releases of the product.

When you are done, simply tear off the preceding page, highlight or circle the statement in capital letters below, and put your questionnaire back in interoffice mail.

PLEASE RETURN TO: DR. DEBORAH J. MAYHEW, MA31–902

Thank you again for your cooperation.

Part I: User Profile

Purpose: The purpose of this section is to gather information about the person filling out each questionnaire so we can interpret his or her responses on the rest of the questionnaire. We want to be able to identify groups of users—such as experienced and inexperienced—and see if they respond differently as a group to the application. Thus this section includes questions about your job, your experience, and your general feelings about working with computers.

Instructions: The questions in this section are multiple choice. Please check only one option for each question. Choose the option that comes closest to describing the answer you would give to the question.

If you find that none of the options provided for a particular question accurately describes your answer, please check the one that comes closest, and also write a note in the margin giving your own answer to the question. We have tried to provide all possible answers for each question, but we may have missed some possibilities and would like to know if we did, so we can refine the questionnaire.

Please answer all questions as best you can.

Please answer the questions candidly. Some of them are questions concerning your attitudes and feelings about working with computers. Your sincerity in answering these questions is necessary if the questionnaire is to yield valid results.

NAME: _____MAIL STOP: _____

"User Satisfaction Questionnaire," cont. next page

Attitude and Motivation:

1. In general, how do you feel about working with computers?
   45 or 79%   I like working with computers.
   0 or 0%   I do not like working with computers.
   12 or 21%   I have no strong like or dislike of working with computers.

2. How do you feel about the way computers have affected your job?
   48 or 84%   Computers have affected my job in a positive way.
   0 or 0%   Computers have affected my job in a negative way.
   8 or 14%   Computers have not significantly affected my job in either a positive or negative way.

3. Would you say computers have facilitated or complicated your job?
   48 or 84%   Computers have made my job more satisfying/easy/interesting/efficient.
   0 or 0%   Computers have made my job more frustrating/complicated/boring/inefficient.
   8 or 14%   Computers have neither facilitated nor complicated my job to any significant degree.

Experience and Knowledge:

4. Have you participated in any Venus, Release 1.0, training programs?
   9 or 16%   No
   48 or 84%   Yes

5. How long have you been working with the Venus, Release 1.0, word processing application?
   2 or 4%   Less than one month
   21 or 37%   One month or more, but less than six months
   24 or 42%   Six months to one year
   10 or 18%   More than one year

6. Before beginning to use the Venus, Release 1.0, word processor, how much experience did you have working with any other word processing applications?

<u>34 or 60%</u>   None
<u>7 or 12%</u>   Less than six months
<u>2 or 4%</u>   Six months to one year
<u>14 or 25%</u>   More than one year

If any prior experience, on which application(s)?

_____

7. How much experience with and exposure to technical language and methodologies have you had (e.g., math, science, engineering, programming)? Please check the *one* option that best applies.

<u>14 or 25%</u>   None above high school level
<u>10 or 18%</u>   Less than four classes at college level
<u>14 or 25%</u>   Four or more classes at college level
<u>19 or 33%</u>   Graduate training or equivalent work experience

Job and Task Factors:

8. How would you classify your job?

<u>6 or 11%</u>   Managerial
<u>14 or 25%</u>   Engineering (hardware/software)
<u>22 or 39%</u>   Secretarial
<u>3 or 5%</u>   Clerical (e.g., technical typist)
<u>11 or 9%</u>   Other_____

9. How important a task is using the Venus, Release 1.0, word processing application within your job as a whole?

<u>7 or 12%</u>   It helps me in one or more *minor* (i.e., incidental, not necessarily infrequent) tasks in my job (e.g., I am an engineer and I use it to produce occasional memos, status reports, etc.).

<u>45 or 79%</u>   It helps in one or more of the *major* (i.e., important, not necessarily frequent) tasks in my job (e.g., I am a secretary and I do a lot of typing, or I am a technical writer, and I use it to produce documentation).

<u>5 or 9%</u>   It *is* my job (e.g., I am a word processing operator).

"User Satisfaction Questionnaire," cont. next page

"User Satisfaction Questionnaire," cont.

10. On average, how often do you use the Venus, Release 1.0, word pro-
    cessing application?

    <u>13 or 23%</u>   Less than one hour per day
    <u>28 or 49%</u>   One to four hours per day
    <u>16 or 28%</u>   More than four hours per day

Part II: General Application Satisfaction Ratings

Purpose: In this section, we would like to find out how satisfied you are with a number of general characteristics of the application, and how important those characteristics are to you in your use of the application. This will help us to pinpoint general areas of dissatisfaction and to order them in terms of their relative importance to you, the user.

Instructions: There are thirty questions in this section. Each is an incomplete sentence. You should read each one as if it began with the phrase "How well does this application . . . "

Please answer each question by rating it on two 7-point scales: *satisfaction* and *importance*. For each scale, 1 is the low or negative end of the scale, and 7 is the high or positive end of the scale.

Note that satisfaction and importance mean different things. For instance, you may feel that the application does not satisfactorily "provide shortcuts for experienced users," but this may not be particularly important to you because you use the application infrequently for a very specific function and will probably never be truly "experienced."

Answer the questions relatively—that is, if you are more satisfied with one characteristic of the application than another, give it a higher rating on the scale.

To give a general idea of what different numbers on the scales mean, the following may be assumed:

Satisfaction	Importance
1 = Unsatisfactory	1 = Totally unimportant
2 = Very poor	2 = Very unimportant
3 = Poor	3 = Moderately unimportant
4 = Adequate	4 = Important
5 = Good	5 = Moderately important
6 = Very good	6 = Very important
7 = Excellent	7 = Extremely important

Please circle one rating on each of the two scales for every question in this section.

Under each question is a space for comments. We encourage explanatory or other comments on all items, but we are particularly interested in an explanatory comment under questions you have given a low satisfaction rating to ("low" = 3 or less).

"User Satisfaction Questionnaire," cont. next page

"User Satisfaction Questionnaire," cont.

At the end of this section are some blank items. If you feel we have left out any significant characteristics of the application about which you would like to express an opinion, please describe the characteristic in the blank space, and then provide your ratings in the space provided for them.

How well does this application:

Factor 1:
Self-Descriptiveness   Satisfaction   Importance
1. . . . explain what is required in   1 2 3 4⑤6 7   1 2 3 4 5⑥7
   each fill-in field on the screen,
   so that you don't need to reference a manual to decide
   what to enter?
2. . . . prompt you, so that you   1 2 3 4⑤6 7   1 2 3 4 5⑥7
   always know what the applica-
   tion expects you to do next and
   what your options are?
3. . . . help you keep track of   1 2 3 4⑤6 7   1 2 3 4⑤6 7
   where you are in the application
   so you know how to return to
   other menus?
4. . . . lay out prompts and fields   1 2 3 4⑤6 7   1 2 3 4 5⑥7
   on each screen in a clear, easy
   to read and understand format?
5. . . . give error messages that   1 2 3④5 6 7   1 2 3 4 5⑥7
   clearly indicate what you did
   wrong and what to do next?

Factor 2:
User Control   Satisfaction   Importance
6. . . . allow you to cancel com-   1 2 3 4⑤6 7   1 2 3 4 5⑥7
   mands you have initiated but
   don't wish to execute, without
   undesirable side effects?

7. . . . allow you to bypass irrele- 1 2 3 ④5 6 7   1 2 3 4 ⑤6 7
vant steps and get efficiently to
the menu, field, or function
you want?

8. . . . allow you to abort or reverse 1 2 3 ④5 6 7   1 2 3 4 5 ⑥7
operations during execution
without undesirable side effects?

9. . . . allow abbreviated input of 1 2 3 4 ⑤6 7   1 2 3 4 ⑤6 7
commonly used sequences of
commands?

10. . . . provide a command lan- 1 2 3 4 ⑤6 7   1 2 3 4 5 ⑥7
guage that is consistent?

Factor 3:

Ease of Learning	Satisfaction	Importance

11. . . . facilitate learning with a 1 2 3 4 ⑤6 7   1 2 3 4 5 ⑥7
minimal amount of training and
reference to manuals?

12. . . . facilitate learning for users 1 2 3 4 ⑤6 7   1 2 3 4 5 ⑥7
with no prior data processing or
computer experience?

13. . . . facilitate learning for users 1 2 3 4 ⑤6 7   1 2 3 4 ⑤6 7
with no prior word processing
experience?

14. . . . facilitate learning about it 1 2 3 4 ⑤6 7   1 2 3 4 5 ⑥7
and using it with minimal
ongoing human assistance?

15. . . . facilitate remembering how 1 2 3 4 ⑤6 7   1 2 3 4 5 ⑥7
to use it from one session to
another?

Factor 4:

Task Facilitation	Satisfaction	Importance

16. . . . reduce the effort required 1 2 3 4 ⑤6 7   1 2 3 4 5 ⑥7
to perform routine or repetitive
tasks?

"User Satisfaction Questionnaire," cont. next page

"User Satisfaction Questionnaire," cont.

17. . . . protect the user from catastrophic results of normal human error?   1 2 3④5 6 7   1 2 3 4 5⑥7

18. . . . help you to perform your job more efficiently and effectively?   1 2 3 4 5⑥7   1 2 3 4 5⑥7

19. . . . provide all the functions that you require in your routine use of it?   1 2 3 4⑤6 7   1 2 3 4 5⑥7

20. . . . help you to improve the quality of your work?   1 2 3 4 5⑥7   1 2 3 4 5⑥7

Factor 5:

Consistency and Predictability	Satisfaction	Importance
21. . . . behave similarly and predictably in similar situations?	1 2 3 4⑤6 7	1 2 3 4 5⑥7
22. . . . require similar and predictable operations for similar functions?	1 2 3 4⑤6 7	1 2 3 4⑤6 7
23. . . . provide clear feedback on the results of executed operations?	1 2 3 4⑤6 7	1 2 3 4 5⑥7
24. . . . provide consistent response times across usage of the same functions or commands?	1 2 3④5 6 7	1 2 3 4⑤6 7
25. . . . provide equal response times for similar activities?	1 2 3④5 6 7	1 2 3 4⑤6 7

Factor 6:

Flexibility in Task Handling	Satisfaction	Importance
26. . . . provide reduced required input and output according to user training level?	1 2 3 4⑤6 7	1 2 3 4⑤6 7
27. . . . allow the experienced user to define his or her own set of functions?	1 2 3 4⑤6 7	1 2 3 4⑤6 7
28. . . . provide shortcuts for the experienced user to perform tasks?	1 2 3④5 6 7	1 2 3 4 5⑥7

29. . . . provide alternative ways for   1 2 3 4⑤6 7   1 2 3 4⑤6 7
    doing the same thing in differ-
    ent situations?

30. . . . provide application infor-   1 2③4 5 6 7   1 2 3 4⑤6 7
    mation at different levels of
    detail on request?

"User Satisfaction Questionnaire," cont. next page

Part III: Individual Function Satisfaction Ratings

Purpose: The purpose of this section is to collect more detailed information concerning your opinion of the way *specific functions* operate within the Venus, Release 1.0, application. We are interested here in how frequently individual functions are used, how easy they are to use, learn, and remember, and how conveniently the keys necessary to invoke them are located on the keyboard. This input will be helpful to us in focusing on very specific problem areas and on considering keyboard design and command language syntax.

Instructions: We have tried to include for your evaluation every basic function of the application. This includes single key functions (e.g., Tab, Sign-off), single key functions with prompts (e.g., Insert, Go To Page), multiple key functions (e.g., Change Format Line, Superscripts), multiple key functions with prompts (e.g., Super Move, Global Replace), and menu selection functions (e.g., Move to Archive, Start a Queue). We include a total of sixty functions for your evaluation.

For each function, we ask you to rate the function on four scales, using the following as a guideline:

Frequency of Use
0 = Never
1 = Almost never
2 = Seldom
3 = Sometimes
4 = Often
5 = Very often

Ease of Use

1 = Very hard
2 = Hard
3 = Moderate
4 = Easy
5 = Very easy

Ease of Learning
and Memory
1 = Very hard
2 = Hard
3 = Moderate
4 = Easy
5 = Very easy

Location of Keys
1 = Very awkward
2 = Awkward
3 = Adequate
4 = Good
5 = Excellent

Each scale is meant to measure a different aspect of the function. In particular, as there is a "Location of Keys" scale, do not consider key location when rating "Ease of Use." For instance, you might feel that the Center function key is very easy to use (it only requires one keystroke, and you immediately see the effects), but the location of the Center function key makes it very difficult to find on the keyboard. Thus for Center, you would assign very different ratings on the two scales. Similarly, note the distinction between "Ease of Use" and "Ease of Learning and Memory." The former refers to the complexity of executing the function. The latter refers to two characteristics: how easy or difficult it was to learn when you were just starting to use the application, and how easy or difficult it is to remember how to execute from one work session to another.

Please give *one* rating on each scale for *every* function listed. The exception to this is that if you choose 0 on the "Frequency of Use" scale, you need not provide a rating on the other three scales (if you have never used the function, you most likely do not have an opinion about it).

Again, please provide comments if you have them, especially regarding functions to which you have assigned any low ratings.

	Frequency of Use	Ease of Use	Ease of Learning and Memory	Location of Keys
1. Execute	0 1 2 3 4⑤	1 2 3④5	1 2 3 4⑤	1 2 3④5
2. Clear	0 1 2 3 4⑤	1 2 3④5	1 2 3 4⑤	1 2 3④5
3. Cursor keys	0 1 2 3 4⑤	1 2③4 5	1 2 3 4⑤	1 2 3④5
4. Return	0 1 2 3 4⑤	1 2 3④5	1 2 3 4⑤	1 2 3 4⑤
5. Tab	0 1 2 3 4⑤	1 2 3④5	1 2 3 4⑤	1 2 3 4⑤
6. Decimal tab	0 1②3 4 5	1 2③4 5	1 2 3④5	1 2 3④5
7. Indent	0 1 2 3④5	1 2 3④5	1 2 3 4⑤	1 2 3④5
8. Center	0 1 2 3④5	1 2 3④5	1 2 3 4⑤	1 2 3④5
9. Required space	0①2 3 4 5	1 2③4 5	1 2 3④5	1 2 3④5
10. Sign-off	0 1 2 3 4⑤	1 2 3④5	1 2 3 4⑤	1 2 3④5
. . .				
. . .				
60. Stop a Queue	0①2 3 4 5	1 2③4 5	1 2 3④5	1 2 3④5

"User Satisfaction Questionnaire," cont. next page

"User Satisfaction Questionnaire," cont.

Interpretations of the questionnaire data follow.

Part I: User Profile. The data in this section was summarized by computing the simple percentage of users giving each response to each question. In the actual questionnaire above, I have reported both the number of users who selected a given response and then the percentage of the total that number represents. Thus, "45 or 79%" should be read as "45 users, or 79 percent of the total number of users." All users did not answer all questions, so the percentages across answers to a given question do not always add up to 100 percent.

Based on the data, this sample of users can be generally described as follows:

◆ All users were either positive or neutral in their general attitudes towards computers.

◆ Most users had taken a formal training program in the use of the application.

◆ Most users had less than a year's experience on the application, and a little less than half of them had less than six months' experience.

◆ More than half of these users had no prior experience on other word processing applications.

◆ These users were very evenly spread across levels of technical experience and training.

◆ These users represented the full range of user types, including managers, engineers, secretaries, and technical typists.

◆ Among these users, there were as many managers and engineers (together) as there were secretaries.

◆ Enough users described themselves as falling in the "other" job category to suggest additional categories on subsequent versions of the questionnaire. These users included technical writers, personnel staff, administrative staff, support staff, etc.

◆ Most users indicated that they used this application to assist them in the major tasks of their jobs.

◆ About half of these users indicated that they use the application, on average, between one and four hours per day. One quarter said they use it less than this, and one quarter said they use it more.

In summary, as a whole, this sample of Venus, Release 1.0, users may be characterized as *positive in attitude, relatively inexperienced, diverse in their organizational roles*, and *"semicasual" users* (in frequency of use and type of use) of the application.

Part II: General Application Satisfaction Ratings. In the questionnaire, the average (i.e., mean) rating for each question on each scale is indicated by a circle. Actual averages were rounded up or down to the nearest whole number.

Almost every question in Part II received an average *satisfaction* rating between 4 ("adequate") and 5 ("good") on a scale of 1 to 7.

On one hand, this is quite positive. None of the areas polled here were considered to be unsatisfactory.

On the other hand, one might have expected high ratings overall from a group of users who are both relatively unsophisticated and inexperienced with—and generally positive in their attitudes towards—computers. Given their low word processing experience, it is likely most users were comparing Venus, Release 1.0, to a typewriter. And, on a scale of 1 to 7, 4s and 5s certainly indicate room for improvement.

Almost every question in this section received an average *importance* rating of between 5 ("moderately important") and 6 ("very important"). This suggests a couple of things.

First, the questions selected for this section seem to have been good ones, capturing application characteristics considered important by users of the application. This is not too surprising, as the questions were based on previous research that established them as important.

Second, the fact that *importance* ratings are almost uniformly one point above *satisfaction* ratings suggests the general sentiment that the application is not as satisfactory as it could be.

Third, although satisfaction ratings were generally high, it is useful to focus on those areas where users expressed relatively less satisfaction. One way of identifying possible areas for improvement is to identify those questions considered *above* the scale average in *importance*, and *below* the scale average in *satisfaction*. This is an arbitrary, but I think useful, criterion for focusing further attention. Questions in Part II meeting this criterion are listed below, along with users' comments:

How well does this application:
5. . . . give error messages that clearly indicate what you did wrong and what to do next?

"User Satisfaction Questionnaire," cont. next page

"User Satisfaction Questionnaire," cont.

- "almost never"
- "sometimes gives them for no reason!"
- "some of the messages are wrong, some of the messages do not clearly define the problem"
- "what the hell is 'document handling error' or 'system error'?"

8. . . . allow you to abort or reverse operations during execution without undesirable side effects?

- "you can't stop some operations"
- "many functions are unstoppable—this causes terminal hangs and reboots"

11. . . . facilitate learning with a minimal amount of training and reference to manuals?

- "have to consult a manual on nearly all the complex operations"
- "five mornings of classes was not enough time to learn the system without becoming somewhat confused"
- "I try what I think are logical steps to get what I want, and most times I have to go for a manual"
- "this is true mostly for people who have WP experience or can easily catch on to the concept"

14. . . . facilitate learning about it and using it with minimal ongoing human assistance?

- "I can never understand why it refuses a command"
- "secretaries having problems . . . most systems people don't for the most part"
- "you need assistance! Sometimes you'll do everything you can think of to clear up an error or some message that comes up and get nothing but a headache. You have to have human assistance or you'd be up a creek without a paddle"
- "I think that it takes the average new user on the system a *while* to build up confidence"

17. . . . protect the user from catastrophic results of normal human error?

- "forget you are in insert mode after typing two pages of text and hit clear to get out of your document (or so you think). Your 2 pages are gone for good"

- "need an alarm to warn on delete a document"
- "many systems allow the user to recover from the last 5–10 operations such as delete. Venus doesn't"
- "too easy to delete a document on publishing menu. Should default to 1 when deleting"

Part III: Individual Function Satisfaction Ratings. In the questionnaire, the average (i.e., mean) rating for each function on each scale is indicated by a circle. Actual averages were rounded up or down to the nearest whole number.

Ratings on the three usability scales (Ease of Use, Ease of Learning and Memory, and Location of Keys) were generally high, with averages ranging from 3 to 5 on the 5-point scales.

These generally high ratings were again probably in part due to the quality of the application, and in part due to the relative inexperience and positive attitude of the users.

Again, we can probably learn something useful from focusing on those areas that received relatively lower ratings. Using the same criterion as in analyzing data from Part II, we can sort the functions on each scale, and then focus on those functions that received below scale average ratings. We can potentially read a lot into the data when we look at it in this way. Here I present three analyses.

1. I might argue that, given that there will always be design trade-offs and compromises, the most frequently used functions should also be the easiest to use. Based on this argument, we can take the subset of functions that received *above* average *frequency of use* ratings, and then focus on the subset of those that received *below* average *usability* ratings. This subset then represents a good starting point for improvement, and users' comments on these functions can help set some direction for that improvement. Functions singled out in this way, plus some user comments on them, follow.

Ease of Use

◆ Print

- "system should default to operator selected printer queue instead of back to Q01 all the time"
- "too many keys to punch"

"User Satisfaction Questionnaire," cont. next page

◆ List Directory

- "list doesn't tell you where you are. This is very bad"
- "I found the directory does not list everything you have in there. You have to ask it two or three times!"

◆ Auto Underline

- "don't always remember to turn it off"
- "it's aggravating to have to delete words in order to get rid of underline"

◆ Change Format Line

- "I always get messed up!"
- "cursor always starts in column 1 of format line. Inconvenient"

◆ Move

- "takes too long"
- "does not always move when and where you want it to go"

◆ Change Directory

- "cursor should go to directory field"
- "want to do it without returning to publishing"

Ease of Learning and Memory

◆ Create Format Line

- "confused as to what pages get impacted: before, after, headers, footers"
- "too close to the Execute key"

Key Location

◆ Clear

- "too small, too separated"

◆ Page Break

- "too close to Execute key"

◆ Indent

- "too close to Execute key"

◆ Center

   • "this is the second hardest key for me to find"
◆ Create Format Line
◆ Change Format Line
◆ Auto Underline
◆ Replace

It is interesting to note that all the functions identified as *unsatisfactory* from the analysis of *frequency of use* and *key location* are either on the top row or on the far right cluster of keys on the keyboard. From the users' comments, there seem to be two sources of dissatisfaction: difficulty of *reaching* and difficulty of *locating*. Only so many keys can be located conveniently close to the home row. Some simply have to be inconvenient (although decisions on which ones should be in these harder-to-reach locations could be based on the frequency-of-use data). On the other hand, making the more distant keys at least easier to *locate* might help. The top row of keys might be improved by grouping keys on a functional basis and by using colors and spacing to further group keys. This would allow the user to scan the row more efficiently and thus reduce search time.

2. An interesting trend can be observed in the Ease of Use and Ease of Learning and Memory scales. Functions that are invoked by a *single keystroke* and are *well prompted* tend to be rated as more satisfactory than functions requiring *multiple keystrokes* involving a "qualifier" key such as Shift or Command followed by a function key. One possible explanation for this is that the qualifier keys assigned to the latter functions seem arbitrarily assigned and have no mnemonic value. It is hard to remember, for instance, whether global replace is Shift Replace and pagination is Command Page, or global replace is Command Replace and pagination is Shift Page. There is no consistent underlying "syntax" to the command language structure that would help users learn and remember these more complex commands. In general, structure and consistent rules in any kind of language greatly facilitate learning. Computer languages are no exception.

3. The relative frequency of use of the application functions as indicated by this data can be of ongoing use. When designing future

"User Satisfaction Questionnaire," cont. next page

releases, frequency of use information can be used to help make decisions involving design trade-offs. In general, it is probably advisable to make the most frequently used functions both easier to use and easier to execute on the keyboard.

Additional Analyses: The preceding analyses of Parts II and III of the questionnaire summarized data across all 57 users in the sample. Users can also be divided into subcategories based on the user profile questions in Part I and then compared in their responses to the rest of the questionnaire. For instance, we could pose the question: are relative *novices* (e.g., with less than one month's experience on the application) more or less satisfied than relatively *experienced users* (e.g., with more than one year's experience)? Making these kinds of comparisons can help us pinpoint what groups of users are least satisfied with the application, and we can then try to better address the needs of these subgroups of users in later releases.

Since this study was relatively "uncontrolled," before making these comparisons, we need to determine whether any of the user dimensions were "confounded." For instance, if all secretaries in the sample use the application more than four hours a day, while all managers use it less than one hour per day, then we wouldn't be able to conclude whether any differences in satisfaction ratings between secretaries and managers were due to their *job type* or due to their relative *frequency of use*.

To help interpret any interesting differences noted between user groups, I took each subset of users—such as novices—and computed their profile on all other dimensions. I found an overall tendency for user dimensions to be somewhat correlated with one another, making interpretation of any single comparison of user groups difficult. However, some conclusions were possible. In particular, it could be noted that the *least satisfied* users tend to be

◆ more experienced in technology in general, and word processing in particular;
◆ users who have not participated in a formal training program;
◆ casual and infrequent users;
◆ managers and engineers, versus secretaries.

More controlled research would be necessary to untangle and explain the effects of individual user dimensions on satisfaction. On the other hand, probably improving the general ease of use and ease of learning of the application for casual, *infrequent* users, increasing the efficiency of operations for *expert* users, and adding functionality of more relevance and use to *managers and engineers* would increase the satisfaction of these less satisfied users.

Final Notes: Two important issues must be considered when developing any questionnaire: reliability and validity. Both reflect how well a questionnaire measures the phenomenon of interest—in this case user satisfaction with a software application.

Reliability refers to the tendency for similar results to be obtained in successive distributions of the questionnaire to samples of people from the same population. It is a measure of how well the responses from your *sample* represent potential responses from the *total population*. Since this questionnaire has only been distributed once, reliability cannot yet be assessed. The findings presented above should not be interpreted too generally until reliability can be assessed.

Validity refers to the extent to which the questionnaire is really measuring what we think it is measuring. Validity, unlike reliability, cannot be established statistically. It is usually assessed by comparing the results of a questionnaire with the results of some other measure of the phenomenon of interest that we have confidence in. I base my confidence in the validity of this questionnaire on several factors. First, the results make intuitive sense. They were not unexpected or difficult to interpret. Second, they are consistent with informal feedback from users. Third, the trends in the effects of user dimensions on satisfaction were very similar for both Parts II and III of the questionnaire. That is, Parts II and III tend to validate each other. And finally, the importance ratings in Part II were similar to the importance ratings given in the study from which the questions were drawn, which in turn were validated as a part of that study. Together these observations suggest that the questionnaire is in fact measuring user satisfaction with the application, and users interpreted the rating scales in the way intended.

Finally, it should be noted that the questionnaire only measures satisfaction with two aspects of the application: very *general characteristics* (Part II) and very *specific functions* (Part III). What the questionnaire does *not* measure is how well the application helps users to accomplish particular *meaningful tasks,* such as writing memos, writing reports, or producing publications. I believe satisfaction at the *task* level would be a useful thing to study and would add significantly to our understanding of how well the application meets the needs of its users, but it was not addressed in this questionnaire.

IV

Organizational Issues

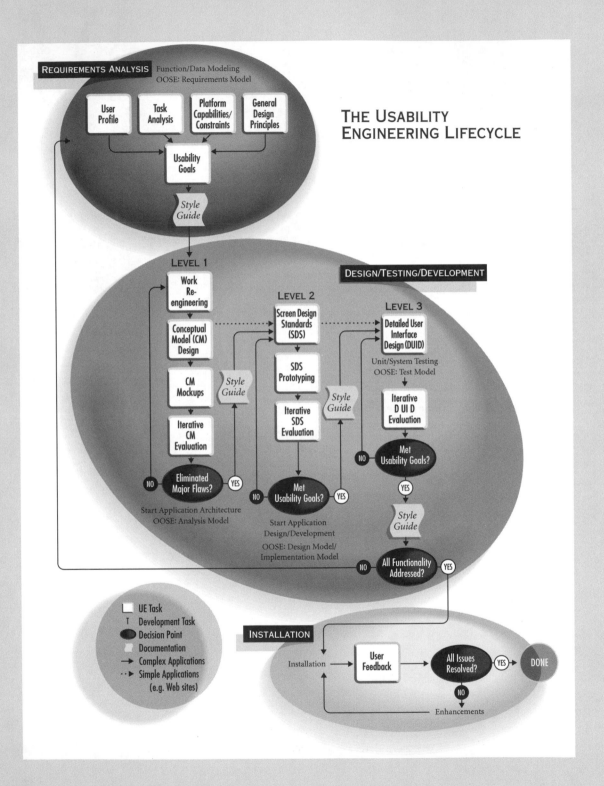

Promoting and Implementing the Lifecycle

INTRODUCTION TO ORGANIZATIONAL ISSUES

Chapters 1 through 17 describe the tasks in the Usability Engineering Lifecycle that should be applied in some tailored way to specific product development projects. In this and the next three chapters, I discuss other related issues that are more managerial in nature and a bit wider in scope than a single development project. These issues include

- Promoting and implementing the Usability Engineering Lifecycle (this chapter)
- Usability project planning (Chapter 19)
- Cost-benefit analysis (Chapter 20)
- Organizational roles and structures (Chapter 21)

An understanding of these four issues helps ensure the success of implementing the Usability Engineering Lifecycle approach within any particular development project and of ultimately institutionalizing it within a development organization and methodology.

Before turning to a discussion of promoting and implementing the Usability Engineering Lifecycle, let's briefly summarize Chapters 1–17. The Usability Engineering Lifecycle consists of three basic phases: Requirements Analyses, Design/Testing/Development, and Installation. Specific Usability Engineering tasks within each of these phases work interdependently with one another and with traditional software engineering tasks, to contribute to the development of products that are tailored to and usable by their intended users. Exactly which *techniques* are

403

applied to accomplish each lifecycle *task* can be adapted to fit the complexity, requirements, and available resources of individual development projects. Much of the lifecycle is applicable not only to the development of traditional software applications but also to the development of Web sites and other interactive products.

This is all very logical—makes perfect sense. But let me pose the question that I know must be on your mind: how can you get your development organization to actually *do* all this stuff?

MANAGING ORGANIZATIONAL CHANGE

If you are introducing Usability Engineering techniques and practices into a development organization for the first time, you have to view yourself as a change agent

Whether you are a usability practitioner or not, if you are pursuing the goal of introducing Usability Engineering techniques and practices into a development organization for the first time, you have to view yourself first and foremost as a *change agent;* not as a usability specialist, engineer, technical writer, product manager, marketer, or whatever else you might be, but as an agent of organizational change. Failing to take this view of your role will most likely result (and indeed often *has* resulted) in a failure to introduce Usability Engineering into the software engineering methodology of a given development organization in a lasting, integrated way. All the technical skills, good intentions, and sound logic in the world will not necessarily cause organizational change. Understanding what motivates organizations and causes them to change is key.

In any organization, there are inherent obstacles to change. They may differ from organization to organization in their exact nature, but they are always there. Anyone who aspires to be a change agent must recognize this basic fact, identify the particular and unique obstacles that exist in the organization, and address them directly and specifically. Failing to do so will usually result in failure to effect the desired results. You must understand the *sources* of resistance in order to overcome them.

Anyone who aspires to be a change agent must identify the unique obstacles that exist in the organization and address them directly

As a change agent, you will have factors, approaches, techniques, tactics, and strategies that can serve as *facilitators* in effecting change. Facilitators can be divided into two types, *motivators* and *success factors.* Sometimes motivators are present outside of the change agent's influence and can simply be taken advantage of. Sometimes the change agent must create or at least draw attention to a potential motivator.

Once an organization recognizes a motivator, an opportunity exists, but your ability to effect change is still dependent on strategic application of pertinent success factors. If the appropriate success factors are not applied, it is entirely possible to fail in effecting change even when a strong motivation is present.

In the following sections, I present typical existing obstacles to the introduction of Usability Engineering techniques into software development organizations. Then I offer specific motivators and success factors for implementing Usability Engineering techniques and practices. Note that information in this chapter is adapted from Mayhew and Bias (1994), which covers the topic of promoting and implementing the Usability Engineering Lifecycle within a development organization in detail.

Once an organization recognizes a motivator, an opportunity exists, but the change agent's ability to effect change still depends on strategic application of pertinent success factors

Obstacles

It is important for anyone attempting to facilitate organizational change to understand the forces at work in the organization to maintain the status quo. In the case of a Usability Engineering pioneer attempting to introduce Usability Engineering techniques and practices into a software development organization, these forces fall into several categories, which are discussed in turn.

◆ Myths, beliefs, and attitudes
◆ Organizational incentives
◆ Organizational practices
◆ Organizational structures

Myths, Beliefs, and Attitudes. The commonly held myths, beliefs, and attitudes of the software development culture regarding usability and Usability Engineering account in part for resistance to change. In my experience, the following myths, beliefs, and attitudes are still often dominant in development organizations, and they must be addressed to create receptivity to Usability Engineering techniques and practices.

◆ **The quality of the user interface doesn't really matter.** Back in the late 1970s and 1980s, it was common to hear managers and developers actually make this statement. And, to a certain extent, it was true. Before usability became an aspect of competitive edge, the user interface really didn't matter—at least to vendors and developers in a bottom-line sense. Now that software usability *is* an aspect of competitive edge (directly or indirectly), it's rare to hear anyone express this belief openly. However, the true measure of what people believe is not what they say, but what they do. And if behavior is the measure, it's clear that this is still a common belief. Even today, how many development organizations actually commit significant time, money, and resources to usability?

♦ **As long as designers are familiar with available user interface principles and guidelines, they will design good user interfaces.** Another common myth or belief among software managers and developers is that as long as there is a usability guru or two around in the organization, his or her expertise and knowledge will somehow find its way into the design of products. Nothing could be farther from the truth. Just like software engineering in general, Usability Engineering in particular is a process that must be managed.

♦ **User interface design tasks don't arise until the detailed design phase of a development project.** Many software engineers still believe that interface design is a simple matter of screen design and therefore does not really arise as an issue until individual screens are designed—usually in the detailed design phase. Thus, they see no reason to introduce new techniques and methods at earlier stages— or later stages—in the overall development methodology.

♦ **Usability is subjective and cannot be measured or engineered.** This is perhaps the myth most responsible for resistance to organizational change. Because developers do not understand that usability is any more than a matter of common sense, aesthetics, and subjective opinion, they cannot see how it lends itself to an engineering approach, and they therefore cannot see how their engineering process should be altered to accommodate it.

♦ **User interface design can be done right the first time, in the design phase.** This myth comes partly from software engineers' belief that usability is subjective and user interface design is a matter of common sense. But it also comes partly from the fact that they are unaware of the techniques from experimental psychology that objectively measure human performance. Thus, they see the process of interface design as a simple one of making decisions based on common sense, rather than as an engineering process requiring the familiar phases of goal setting and iterative testing and redesign.

◆ **User interface design is an implicit part of software design and development, and need not be explicitly planned and budgeted for.** User interface design has, since the first interactive software, been a part of many software development projects. Yet it has rarely—if ever—been made an explicit, formal part of any software development methodology. It has almost always been treated as an implicit part of the design process. People are always hard pressed to see why they should change a way of doing things that seemed to work for such a long time. Every interactive system that has ever been built has had an interface designed, but usually without any explicit planning and budgeting for this to happen. So why should it be necessary to radically alter an accepted and established development methodology? Until developers accept the importance of the goal of improved usability, they will be resistant to the idea of change to their development process, which requires new tasks that must be planned and budgeted for.

Organizational Incentives. In Chapter 20 I offer a technique for performing cost-benefit analyses of usability activities, that is, techniques for establishing the bottom-line value of the Usability Engineering Lifecycle. However, even the most convincing cost-benefit analysis can fall on deaf ears if the right organizational incentives are not in place.

Even the most convincing cost-benefit analysis can fall on deaf ears if the right organizational incentives are not in place

For example, software managers are typically held accountable for staying within planned budgets and schedules and for providing agreed upon functionality. Their incentives—performance reviews, salaries, and promotions—are tied to these deliverables. Software managers are *not* typically held accountable for such things as user productivity (in an internal development organization) or sales (in a vendor company). Other organizations (user groups and sales and marketing staff, respectively) are held accountable for these things, in spite of the fact that the user interface to the software largely determines these outcomes.

The cost-benefit analyses described in this book entail a set of costs and a set of benefits. But they also assume that the costs can be directly compared to the benefits, so that an overall benefit to the organization as a whole can be calculated. However, if development groups and user or marketing groups are organized as separate profit centers with separate

If development groups and user or marketing groups are organized as separate profit centers with separate budgets, why should the manager of one profit center incur costs when the manager of another profit center will realize the benefits?

budgets, as they are in many organizations, it is easy to see how a case for introducing Usability Engineering Lifecycle tasks based on a cost-benefit analysis might fail to attract attention. Such an analysis assigns most of the costs to the development organization and most of the benefits to the user or marketing organization. And why should the manager of one profit center (development) be expected to incur costs, when it is the manager of another profit center (users, marketing) who will realize all the benefits?

The problem here is not one of failing to understand the value of Usability Engineering, but of inappropriate incentives in the organization. Certainly a company as a whole would be inspired to spend money in order to save money, but organizations and individual managers within the company—if they are set up as separate profit centers with unique goals—cannot be expected to focus on companywide goals if they are neither held accountable for them nor rewarded for contributing to them.

Other goals and incentives in development organizations besides (but often related to) budgets and schedules, which may directly conflict with the goal of better user interface design, also present obstacles to introducing better interface design ideas and methodologies. These goals (from Grudin 1991a, b) fall into different categories. *Technical goals* include

◆ Minimizing computer memory and processor use, and maximizing system response time.

◆ Modularizing code, which may discourage smooth integration of functionality.

Cognitive processes and *individual goals* include

◆ The desire to collect and maintain organizational "turf."

◆ The desire to apply new technologies (such as color, voice technology, windowing) simply to keep skills current.

Social, group, and *team goals* include

◆ Need to reward programmer effort (designs that prominently feature novel, difficult-to-implement functions may not present those features in their most usable form).

◆ Desire for cooperation, which often leads to design compromises that reflect good negotiating practices but negatively affect usability.

(Grudin, 1986, gives an example in which developers working on the same application for two different workstations could not agree on whether to place a message line on the first or last line of the screen; they finally compromised by agreeing to always put it on line 25, which was the last line on one workstation, but would cause wrap-around to the first line on the other workstation!)

Marketing and *business goals* include

◆ Desire to maintain installed base by not innovating in ways that might create a retraining overhead for customers.
◆ Desire to avoid copyright violation lawsuits.

All these conflicting incentives and goals can set up resistance to the introduction of Usability Engineering methods and goals.

Organizational Practices. Well-established practices, based in the historical roots of current software development methodologies, present sources of resistance and set up obstacles to change. Some of these practices are described next.

◆ **Limitation of contact between designers/developers and users.** Typically, developers and users are isolated and "protected" from having contact with one another, and customer contact is delegated to groups such as marketers, trainers, and field support. Even marketers are often restricted to contact with "customers" (buyers, user managers) rather than with actual end users. It is generally feared that if developers have continual contact with users they will fail to stick to project plans and schedules, users will be "contaminated" with false expectations, or that highly proprietary secrets of corporate strategy and new product design will be prematurely revealed.
◆ **Traditional emphasis on up-front, thorough design.** Traditionally, different aspects of a product—such as hardware, software, documentation, training, and marketing—have been the responsibility of separate organizational groups under separate management. Often these groups are separated geographically as well as organizationally. The desire to coordinate the efforts of these separately managed and located groups led to development of methodologies that emphasized complete and thorough design up front, frozen before development began, and communicated through formal specification documents.

Iterative design such as that described in the Usability Engineering Lifecycle would require significant organizational and methodological changes in many development organizations.

◆ **Traditional lack of efficient development tools.** Typical development methodologies evolved before the development of efficient prototyping and development tools. The lack of these tools made empirical, iterative design impractical. Even though such tools are now available, taking advantage of them would require radically altering existing methodologies.

◆ **Traditional focus of systems analysis.** One of the sources of poor interface design is a *focus on features and functions*, rather than on overall *user tasks*. Traditional systems analysis and lack of contact with real users encourages this focus.

◆ **Tendency to mimic the manual world.** Poor interface design is sometimes due to a simple-minded tendency to mimic the manual world. This made perfect sense back in the days when noninteractive software applications were designed to automate simple number-crunching functions. However, in today's highly interactive applications, mimicking the manual world often means that those inefficiencies in the manual processes that computers are meant to automate are carried forward into the user interface. In some ways, GUIs contributed to this tendency to mimic the manual world by promoting the idea of metaphors in user interface design. The power of the computer often goes unexploited due to a simple lack of analysis and creative thought on the part of designers.

Organizational Structures. Traditional organizational structures within software development organizations can also inadvertently present obstacles to good Usability Engineering practices.

Sometimes the design of an interface reflects the organization of the product development team assigned to build it

Sometimes the design of an interface reflects the existing organization of the product development team assigned to build it (Grudin 1991a, b). For example, graphics and word processing capabilities that are part of an overall office automation package may be separated into different applications rather than integrated, not so much because of technical implementation constraints, but because different organizational entities were assigned responsibility for these different functions. Database inquiry capabilities of an application and on-line help systems may be implemented as separate, unintegrated functions in a whole application because separate development groups with specialized skills in these areas have traditionally designed and built these functions.

In other cases, something similar happens—project teams are organized in a way that facilitates management of the project and division of labor. Then interfaces reflect this organization. For example, it may be easier to get additional programmers assigned to a project if their role can be mapped to a separate, distinct—rather than a more vague but smoothly integrated—feature or function.

In any case, it is always easier for specialized groups to work relatively independently than to have to coordinate with one another. Thus, ease of management and division of labor in implementation often take precedence over ease of learning and ease of use in interface design.

Ease of management and division of labor in implementation often take precedence over ease of learning and ease of use in interface design

This discussion of obstacles to change—including prevalent myths and beliefs, well-established organizational incentives, practices, and structures—presents an intimidating picture of the forces working against the individual Usability Engineering champion trying to effect organizational change to further the goal of usability. However, it is the very identification and recognition of these forces that will allow the aspiring change agent to plan an effective strategy for effecting change. If you don't understand the enemy, it's hard to plan the battle!

Sooner or later, most development organizations will be motivated to make changes. The aspiring change agent must recognize these motivators as opportunities and take strategic advantage of them. Next I turn to identifying potential motivations for change and, after that, to the factors for successful exploitation of them.

By identifying and recognizing these obstacles, the aspiring change agent can plan an effective strategy for effecting change. If you don't understand the enemy, it's hard to plan the battle!

MOTIVATORS

Even though a natural inertia and resistance to change exist in most organizations, they often do respond to strong incentives to make changes. When I look back on my many years of experience as a consultant being brought into development organizations in their first attempt to use the discipline of Usability Engineering, I can ask myself why each organization chose that particular moment to bring in someone with my expertise. Across my experience, I can identify a variety of motivators. I list these below and provide actual examples from my own experience.

Most commonly, it is some disaster that motivates an organization to change

High-Visibility Disaster. Most commonly, a disaster is the incentive that first motivates an organization. Perhaps a high-profile, very expensive development effort fails dramatically, and users clearly state that they reject a product because it is unusable. Or a product fails in the marketplace, and customers point to its user interface as the reason for their rejection.

One insurance company hired me when a $3 million application development effort failed dramatically. Users were employed by independent agencies and were thus discretionary users of the application. The application was intended to encourage and support the agents in selling this company's products as opposed to competitors' products. But the agents simply refused to use the application, citing among other reasons an unlearnable, unusable interface. Such a dramatic disaster, which so clearly pointed to usability as the main issue, inspired this company to experiment with Usability Engineering.

Sometimes it takes the raw organizational power of an individual to effect change

Powerful Internal Advocate. Sometimes a single individual plays the role of change agent. This individual may be at any management level, from a project leader who decides to hire a usability expert onto his or her project team, to a vice president of research and development who decides to make usability a part of his or her organizational territory. In this case, it is the vision of a single individual that motivates change, and it is that individual's raw organizational power that accomplishes change.

For example, Apple Computer's Steven Jobs was a powerful visionary who simply decided to make usability a key aspect of competitive edge in the personal computer market. He created a company dedicated to usability because that was his personal vision, and thus he had the organizational power to implement his vision.

In my consulting experience, one client organization had a powerful vice president who seized upon Usability Engineering as a way to expand his organizational turf, and he began a new Usability Engineering organization and became its manager. In another client organization, a project manager saw a career opportunity in introducing and implementing the Usability Engineering Lifecycle approach across the whole development organization. She successfully won a mandate and funding from her management to do so.

Perception of Competition and Market Demand. Sometimes, in the case of vendor companies, the marketplace clearly provides the motivation for change. Marketers hear a clear request from customers for improved usability and in turn bring pressure to bear on development organizations. Or a company perceives that they are, or may be, losing market share and attribute this to competitive companies doing a better job of usability.

For vendor companies, the marketplace sometimes provides motivation for change

A division of a vendor of very specialized hardware and software products hired me after reading an article in a users' magazine. The magazine had conducted a survey of the buyers and users of their type of product, asking them what was missing in current products and what they wanted to see in future products. Nearly one third of the users' comments indicated that their main complaint with current products—and their desired features in future products—were related to various aspects of usability. This inspired this division to allocate funds and resources to focus on the user interface of their newest product line.

Desire to Address General Business Goals. In the case of internal development organizations building systems for in-house users, a general motivation to address typical business problems, such as low user productivity, high user training costs, and the desire to grow without increasing costs, may become focused on usability issues.

One of my client companies had a stated business goal of increasing their volume of customer service transactions by 10 percent without increasing customer service staff. It was recognized that better computer support for customer service representatives might contribute to this goal, and so I was hired to help redesign the user interface to a particular customer service application. This in turn led to an additional project to design a *product family* Style Guide (see Chapter 14) to govern the design of future applications.

Need for an Objective Means of Resolving Conflicts. Sometimes the motivation to first bring in a usability expert, often on a consulting basis, arises out of a need for an objective, neutral means for resolving internal conflicts over design issues. Opposing parties agree to resolve a design issue by consulting an outside expert. Or opposing parties agree to resolve a design issue through objective usability testing, but they do not have the necessary skills in-house or can agree only to abide by the findings of an outsider.

One product development team had too many conflicting views on the design of a new product among the highest-ranking members of the project team. They could not resolve their differences and come to any agreement among themselves. The only thing they could agree upon was to hire an external (that is, a politically objective and unbiased) usability expert to come in and assess the alternatives through prototype testing and user surveys. They would then abide by the outsider's conclusions and recommendations. Thus, they brought me in. The combination of my lack of a political agenda, and the objective data produced by my prototype testing and user surveys, allowed everyone to comfortably accept my final conclusions and recommendations. In the process, the development organization was exposed to the special skills and techniques of Usability Engineering and later recruited usability consultants on other projects right from the start.

Education. Finally, sometimes education, in the form of short presentations to management or seminars for developers, can motivate and begin the process of change. Many of my consulting projects have been generated by offering workshops and seminars through conferences and professional organizations. When managers and developers attend such seminars, they begin to realize that not everyone is a user interface design expert, and there really are structured techniques and approaches available for engineering usability into products. They begin to realize there is a lot they don't know and that there are experts out there who do know. What they learn about what they don't know is as important as what they can actually learn in such a short course. The realization that a fairly mature and specialized field of expertise exists can provide the impetus for some change in the way they conduct product development.

Unless a specific motivator is present, trying to influence an organization to integrate Usability Engineering techniques into its development process is usually a thankless task

In my experience, unless a specific motivator such as one of those listed above is present, trying to influence an organization to integrate Usability Engineering techniques into its development process is usually a thankless task. But when one of these motivators is present, an opportunity arises for usability champions, either in-house or outside, to have an impact. Once that is accomplished, another set of factors influences the success or failure of the efforts of individuals in their role as change agents.

SUCCESS FACTORS

A variety of strategies seem to contribute to usability practitioners' success in playing the role of change agents in product development organizations and introducing Usability Engineering techniques for the first time. Below I offer success factors, again with some actual examples from my own experience.

Establish Credibility. Usability specialists hoping to create new roles and new methods in their organizations must move quickly to establish personal credibility as well as credibility for the Usability Engineering discipline. Most likely the engineers and managers you work with, rather than recognizing your special skills, will simply see you as someone with a different set of opinions who has been, for some unclear reason, assigned the job of user interface design. Your co-workers may be resentful that this job has been taken away from them and may be looking for validation of their skepticism. Therefore, it is essential that you choose tasks that clearly demonstrate the special skills you bring to the team.

It is essential that usability practitioners choose tasks that clearly demonstrate the special skills they bring to the team

Conducting clear-cut tasks that require special skills, such as a User Profile, Contextual Task Analysis, or formal usability test, may be better choices for initial projects than, say, simply doing design or participating in design meetings. The former types of tasks clearly demonstrate training, skills, and techniques that are usually not in the average developer's repertoire. Design tasks, on the other hand, demonstrate little more than the fact that the usability specialist has one more opinion to offer on design issues—something there is never a lack of among developers.

It is equally important for the usability specialist to demonstrate knowledge of and appreciation for technical and organizational concerns. Part of establishing credibility is being able to speak the language of your organizational peers. While these skills are not necessarily technically required to be a good User Interface Designer or Usability Engineer, they may be politically and socially crucial to being accepted in a software development organization.

Communicate Effectively. Usability practitioners need to be both articulate in their spoken presentations and effective in their written communications to the developers they are trying to influence—who are, in a sense, their users. Usability practitioners not only need to write developer-friendly user interface design specification documents, but also need to find even more effective ways to communicate design standards than specification documents. For example, an oral presentation, well illustrated, can more effectively communicate design standards than any product Style Guide (see Chapter 14) will, and a prototype embodying design standards will be better yet. Best of all might be embedding design standards in development tools.

Usability practitioners must cast themselves as team members rather than critics

Get "Buy-in". Usability practitioners must work at casting themselves as team members rather than critics. They must work towards creating a process through which they can have an impact, and this involves getting other engineers in the development organization invested in their skills, methods, techniques, knowledge, and design ideas.

When I take on design projects with my consulting clients, I have learned in most cases (although there are exceptions that have been successful) to simply refuse to accept the role of sole or even lead designer. Instead, I cast myself as manager, director, and consultant to an internal design team. I teach Usability Engineering Lifecycle tasks such as User Profiles, Contextual Task Analysis, and product Style Guide Development to the design team, who then carry out these tasks themselves under my direction and with my feedback. I run design meetings but rarely attempt to impose design decisions on the group. Instead I facilitate discussion by focusing on the advantages and disadvantages of design alternatives, and always referring back to the results of Requirements Analysis tasks. I try to introduce a process of "ego-less design," in which the focus is on objective goals, principles, data, and analysis, rather than on conflicting opinions. In the end, I try to leave it to the design team to make every design decision themselves, based on the objective and exhaustive analysis I have facilitated. This way, they have a sense of ownership and investment in the final design decisions, and they champion the cause among others in the internal development organization who need to be convinced.

Be an Engineer, Not an Artist. Software developers are engineers. They are trained to think and work in certain ways, and they relate to and work best with other engineers who think and work in similar ways. They view psychologists and artists as very different kinds of thinkers and workers, and they are often put off by the language and cultural differences of these professions.

To be successful working in an engineering environment, you must think and work like an engineer. This is not difficult to do for usability practitioners whose background is in human factors or psychology. Several characteristics from these disciplines help, including

- Reasoning logically from data and principles, rather than arguing opinion and personal preference or experience
- Applying systematic, structured techniques, rather than vague and ill-defined techniques (e.g., usage studies rather than focus groups— see Chapter 17)
- Focusing on concrete, objective, measurable usability goals (e.g., time and error performance data), rather than on aesthetics or informal, anecdotal feedback from users

The more you can make Usability Engineering techniques seem familiar to the engineer, the more likely they are to be respected and accepted.

To be successful working in an engineering environment, you must think and work like an engineer

Be an Ally, Not an Enemy. It is easy to be viewed as the "usability police." You want instead to cast yourself as an ally to development projects—an invaluable resource that can help them succeed, rather than someone who will reveal their flaws and shortcomings to others. For example, Wixon and Wilson (1997) caution that you should be careful about whom you distribute testing reports to. Remember that usability testing usually reveals problems and flaws in design. Normally, you should not distribute reports outside the project team without the permission of project management. You want the testing process and the reports you generate from it to be viewed as important tools for success rather than as performance evaluations of the project team.

Cast yourself as an ally to development projects—an invaluable resource who can help them succeed—rather than a critic

Produce Well-Defined Work Products. Usability practitioners should certainly participate in design meetings, but not just to throw in one more set of opinions. Use the meetings to identify opportunities for defining and conducting short Requirements Analysis or evaluation tasks aimed at answering questions being raised and debated in these meetings. Highlight these tasks—rather than your "expert design advice"—as your primary role. This way, you cast yourself as an expert with specialized skills who can be used as a resource in making design decisions, rather than as an adversary or competitor for "turf."

On the other hand, even expert advice, when packaged as a distinct work product, can be effective. Sawyer, Flanders, and Wixon (1996), internal usability engineers at Digital Equipment Corporation, describe how they deliver Heuristic Evaluations, or expert reviews of designs (see Chapter 10 for a definition of this technique). First, they write a clear proposal, specifically describing the format of their proposed deliverable and how they will arrive at their conclusions. In this proposal, they also ask for a commitment from their client to respond in writing once the team has identified problems and offered explicit redesign advice. The response documents which recommendations the client will implement and which they will not and why.

Then, in their written deliverable, Sawyer and colleagues clearly identify problems, cite the general design principles upon which their analysis of problems is based, and offer detailed and technically specific solutions. In addition, they rate each identified problem on a relative severity scale, so their client can select those problems to devote resources to that will pay off the most in terms of improved usability.

This Usability Engineering team has found that providing a written, well-structured deliverable, and making a contract with their client that calls for the client to research the feasibility of their recommendations and put in writing which ones they plan to implement, makes the whole process seem more like an engineering process to their clients. This not only enhances their credibility, but inspires their clients to follow through, make use of their suggestions, and live up to their written commitment to make changes.

Usability Engineering tasks of any type should have a clearly defined scope, schedule, and deliverable, so the usability practitioner's contribution is clear, concrete, and readily identifiable

Usability Engineering tasks of any type should have a clearly defined scope, schedule, and deliverable, so the usability practitioner's contribution is clear, concrete, and readily identifiable. Tasks should be as short as possible to accomplish two goals: results must be timely enough to have an impact on a development project, and a clear association must be established between design dilemmas and conflicts and Usability Engineering solutions.

Manage Expectations. One of the easiest mistakes to make as a usability practitioner trying to gain respect and acceptance in a development organization is to feel you must have all the answers. Credibility is seriously damaged when unrealistic expectations are encouraged. For example, it is important to make the limitations—as well as the value—of prototype testing clear. Developers led to believe that prototype testing is the answer to user interface design will inevitably feel disappointed and disillusioned with the field. Usability practitioners must carefully point out that testing

◆ identifies problems but does not solve them,

◆ focuses on ease of learning but not on ease of use (or vice versa),

◆ reflects on performance but not on preference or satisfaction (or vice versa),

◆ reflects only on the part of the product being tested, not on the whole product,

◆ will not necessarily predict sales.

Usability practitioners should also clarify the limits of general design principles and guidelines. Be careful not to give the impression that there is a simple cookbook approach to interface design. Educate developers on the heuristic, "rule-of-thumb" nature of principles and guidelines, and the ultimate necessity of Requirements Analysis and evaluation tasks.

Never be afraid to admit what you don't know, haven't done, and aren't good at. Managers and developers can usually tell—or will eventually discover—that you are bluffing, and this will do great damage to your credibility. People who are confident enough to make disclaimers about their experience and skills enhance their credibility immeasurably. If on one issue you state that you have no idea which design alternative will be best, and on the next express complete confidence in one design alternative over another, people will have much more faith in the latter. They will trust your strong opinions more if you are willing to admit when you don't have a strong opinion.

Never be afraid to admit what you don't know, haven't done, or aren't good at

The value of managing expectations cannot be overstated. If you are up front about the limitations of the field and its knowledge base and techniques, managers and developers are more likely to appreciate what you *can* contribute, rather than conclude that their disappointed expectations reflect on your personal professionalism—or worse yet, on the whole Usability Engineering discipline.

Clarify "Value-Added". At least initially, it can be very helpful to use the techniques outlined in Chapter 20 of this book to cost-justify plans for

It is crucial to begin by applying life-cycle tasks that will quickly and dramatically demonstrate the value of Usability Engineering techniques

Initial usability efforts should be aimed at high-visibility, mission-critical projects, where there will be maximum recognition and appreciation of the results of the lifecycle tasks

Usability Engineering Lifecycle tasks. It is not usually obvious to development engineers and managers what the potential payoff of Usability Engineering techniques might be, at least in the bottom-line sense. They will be reluctant to spend time, money, and resources for some vaguely defined benefit, especially in the heat of tight budgets and schedules. You must make a good business case to clarify the bottom-line value of adding usability tasks to the overall project budget.

It is also crucial to begin by applying Usability Engineering Lifecycle tasks that will quickly and dramatically demonstrate the value of Usability Engineering techniques. For example, it may be wiser to start by proposing a usability testing task, rather than a design task such as the development of a corporate Style Guide (see Chapter 14). The former will take a relatively brief amount of time, and the results are not only objective and concrete, but also usually quite dramatic and convincing. The latter may take a great deal of time, and the payoff will not be immediately obvious. In fact, it may never be obvious if no objective data is gathered to evaluate its impact.

Choosing the right development project to get involved in is also important. If possible, initial usability efforts should be aimed at high-visibility, mission-critical projects where, again, there will be maximum recognition and appreciation of the results of the Usability Engineering Lifecycle tasks. A contribution to a project not many people in the organization are aware of or invested in simply will not have the same impact, no matter how useful a contribution it might be to that project. Related to this, try to choose projects for which management has shown a real commitment to Usability Engineering, so that there is a high probability of visible, measurable impact.

Wixon and Wilson (1997) suggest that a good way to test for commitment is to establish usability goals and get a commitment to them at the very beginning of a project. They point out that resistance to setting and committing to usability goals at this stage should be interpreted as a red flag, indicating a fundamental lack of commitment to Usability Engineering. In such cases, usability practitioners who have any choice in the matter should consider offering their services elsewhere, where they are more likely to have an impact and a successful experience that will help them promote Usability Engineering further in their organization.

To sum up, usability specialists hoping to change the development process of a large organization should initially choose clear-cut Usability Engineering Lifecycle tasks with concrete, objective results and apply

TEST THE WATERS . . . AND KNOW WHEN TO BAIL

I once served as a consultant on a project for a newly formed Usability Engineering organization working on their first project with a development team. There were many early signs that the team was very resistant to input from usability specialists, and the project manager was not at all supportive of the usability specialists when issues of control, authority, and responsibility came up. I strongly advised my client—the Usability Engineering organization's manager—to demand that the project manager clearly define to the project team the scope of authority of usability specialists, and to back them up. I advised her that if the project manager was unwilling to be supportive in this way, she ought to withdraw from the project and find a more receptive project to work with. I thought this was especially important since it was the first project for the new Usability Engineering organization, and a success was crucial to their long-term survival in the organization. Unfortunately, precisely because the Usability Engineering organization was new and the manager was inexperienced, she ignored this advice. In the end, the Usability Engineering organization was eventually "fired" by the project manager under pressure from the project team.

Demanding certain conditions necessary for them to have any chance of success, and simply quitting if these basic conditions were not met would have prevented this highly visible failure—a serious setback for the new organization.

---

them to high-visibility, important development projects, in order for the projects to have the impact of organizational change, not just product change. Also, when trying to "sell" Usability Engineering within a development organization, it is important to understand your audience. Wixon and Wilson (1997) suggest benefits of Usability Engineering that might be emphasized depending on the audience, as follows. To appeal to high-level management, benefits to stress include

◆ Usability data can improve marketing literature, influence early adopters, and convince potential users that training costs will be low.
◆ Usability Engineering can reduce development costs and minimize distribution and support costs.
◆ Usability Engineering can reduce project risk.

Usability specialists hoping to change the development process of a large organization should initially choose clear-cut lifecycle tasks with concrete results and apply them to high-visibility development projects

When trying to sell Usability Engineering within a development organization, it is important to understand your audience

To appeal to a project manager, benefits to stress include

◆ Usability Engineering can reduce time wasted in redesign.
◆ Usability Engineering can reduce overall development time.
◆ Usability Engineering can provide an objective way to identify and prioritize problems so they can be fixed early at minimum cost.

To appeal to a software engineer, benefits to stress include

◆ Usability Engineering is objective and unbiased.
◆ Usability can be measured, just like other engineering attributes.
◆ Usability Engineering provides for creativity in the design process and provides a framework to structure design and allow a team to design quickly.

It can also be very useful for usability practitioners to track the number of problems they identify in testing and the number of those that are actually addressed (either immediately fixed, or at least planned for the next release) across projects, as a concrete measure of their contribution to the development organization (Wixon and Wilson 1997). You will find this invaluable down the line when trying to win (or just maintain) funding and resources from management, and trying to "sell" services to other projects in the development organization.

To get a development organization to climb on the usability bandwagon, there is no substitute for formal, objective usability testing

Test Whenever Possible. At least when initially introducing Usability Engineering skills and techniques into a development organization, data is always better than expert opinion. This is a political truth, not an objective truth. I am talking about methods for effecting change in a development organization, not about objectively optimal methods in an unpolitical, completely accepting environment. In reality, simply soliciting an expert opinion can often be a much more cost-effective technique than formal usability testing. However, in getting a development organization to climb on the usability bandwagon, there is usually no substitute for formal, objective usability testing (see Chapters 10, 13, and 16).

Sawyer and colleagues (1996) suggest that while projects with limited budgets and an openness to "expert opinion" might be served best by Heuristic Evaluations or expert reviews by usability experts (see Chapter 10), on projects with more resources and less receptivity to expert opinion, you are more likely to have an impact by conducting objective usability testing. Data is dramatic, inarguable, and convincing. Use usability testing as a strategic political tool. It works.

PUTTING IT ALL TOGETHER

The usability champion who wishes to succeed in the role of change agent needs first to analyze and identify obstacles to change, and then consider whether the proper motivators are present in the organization. If none is present, the creative and ambitious professional can create one, for example, by educating appropriately powerful managers, making problems visible, or clarifying value added. A usability test on a high-visibility project that clearly demonstrates dramatic usability problems can also be a powerful motivator. Until such a motivating force is present, most efforts, no matter how professional, will fail.

Once the motivator is present, the usability champion must take care to operate strategically and apply the success factors discussed above. It is entirely possible to fail even in a receptive environment. Being a change agent requires political skills as well as technical skills, and using the strategies discussed here in choosing and conducting projects is the key not only to moving a development organization in the direction of Usability Engineering but also to establishing integrated roles for usability practitioners.

Finally, bear in mind that you will not likely be able to take a development organization with little or no prior experience with the Usability Engineering Lifecycle and convince them to try—and then succeed in—implementing the whole Usability Engineering Lifecycle, as described in this book, *overnight*. Instead, you will need to take small, strategic steps in leading the organization to evolve gradually towards integrating a full-blown Usability Engineering Lifecycle into their standard development methodology.

In my experience, what has most often worked best is introducing Usability Engineering Lifecycle tasks one at a time, on one project at a time. Usually, starting (across projects, that is) by introducing tasks and techniques from the end of the lifecycle and then working backwards is most successful. For example, usability testing at design level 3 (Detailed User Interface Design) is a good place to start. On a given project, this is really too late to apply Usability Engineering techniques effectively, but doing it almost always demonstrates the value of Usability Engineering

Data is dramatic, inarguable, and convincing. Use usability testing as a strategic political tool. It works

Change agents require political skills as well as technical skills, and strategically choosing and conducting projects is the key to moving a development organization in the direction of Usability Engineering

Usually, starting by introducing tasks and techniques from the end of the lifecycle is most successful

Begin by focusing your efforts on the projects of one section of the overall development organization—the one that seems most receptive

techniques and wins the support and funding for more Usability Engineering work involving earlier lifecycle tasks on later projects. Then move on to introducing higher-level design and evaluation tasks and, finally, to Requirements Analysis tasks and techniques.

Similarly, start out focusing your efforts on the projects of one particular section of the overall development organization—the one that seems most receptive. Later, when successes have become visible and convincing, you can expand the Usability Engineering resource and introduce the Usability Engineering Lifecycle to other parts of the organization.

Finally, carefully choose high-visibility, high-impact projects to apply Usability Engineering techniques to first; then expand to cover all projects. Change is slow. Be patient. Be strategic.

CASE STUDIES

The lessons I have learned about how to be successful in promoting and implementing the Usability Engineering Lifecycle, I have learned the hard way, as much by my failures as by my successes, over many years and many projects. I have been teaching and otherwise promoting the Usability Engineering Lifecycle approach since 1986, the year I began my consulting practice. Initially, I had no success convincing client organizations to adopt the whole lifecycle and institutionalize it. In fact in the earliest days of my practice, the best I did was to convince client organizations to simply apply one Usability Engineering technique, such as usability testing, on one project. This reflected in part my own limited experience in being a change agent, and in part the level of maturity of the software industry in recognizing the value of Usability Engineering. In many cases, this experience did inspire my client to go on and do additional Usability Engineering on other projects, and sometimes even grow their own in-house Usability Engineering resource. But I never had the opportunity to apply all or even most of the Usability Engineering Lifecycle tasks across a single project.

More recently, I have begun to have this opportunity. I have been able to convince clients to apply some tailored and adapted version of the whole lifecycle to a particular project. This is a trend in the right direction. Here I describe (without divulging any proprietary information) two examples of such projects.

Case Study 1: An Insurance Company

A project manager in an insurance company got funding to hire a Usability Engineering consultant for help with a project building a GUI front end or "shell" to be used by certain users in the company. The shell would allow users to navigate more efficiently and effectively among the many existing mainframe applications they currently used to perform the over 100 daily business tasks their jobs entailed. A meta-goal for this specific design and development project was to allow the development organization to experiment with Usability Engineering techniques on a small, low-risk scale, as the first step toward a long-term goal of creating and institutionalizing a Usability Engineering process integrated within the company's standard and well-established development methodology.

I was brought in at the beginning of the development project, and so the project team had an opportunity to try out all the tasks in the Usability Engineering Lifecycle. My role on the project was part teacher, part project planner, part manager, part mentor, and part reviewer. The in-house project manager ran the project, and she and her staff did most of the actual usability work. I introduced the Usability Engineering Lifecycle tasks and techniques, taught them how to do them, and guided them and provided feedback as they carried them out.

I stayed involved primarily through design level 1 (see the lifecycle chart at the beginning of this chapter). We did an extensive User Profile, sending a questionnaire to 400 of 600 users and receiving back about 300 to analyze. We also did a fairly extensive Contextual Task Analysis involving field observations and interviews, and several rounds of validating reengineered work models. Then we designed and built running prototypes of three alternative Conceptual Model Designs and conducted three iterations of formal usability testing on these prototypes to evolve to a final Conceptual Model Design.

At this point in the project, my involvement phased out, and the team went on to do Detailed User Interface Design and more iterative testing at that level (given the simplicity of their application, they collapsed levels 2 and 3 of design). When their design process was complete, they proceeded into development and then installation at pilot sites.

Throughout the development process, users involved in the process gave us strong positive feedback. They were amazed and delighted to be intimately involved in the design and development of their latest software tool. And, when the final product was rolled out, there were rave reviews from both users and user management. All were delighted at the relative ease of learning and ease of use of this application—its usability was unprecedented in their experience.

The project manager was delighted with her success and decided to submit her project to a national technology contest sponsored by a major technology trade magazine. About twenty corporations submitted projects, and six finalists were selected, including my client. She and her team went to an awards dinner and were thrilled to take first prize. This involved a substantial cash prize to their company and a great deal of publicity. The team was told that what made their project unique and deserving of the first prize was its innovative and clearly effective approach to usability. This project is further described in Kerton (1997) and in Casselman (1997). The project manager has since gone on to work on refining and institutionalizing the Usability Engineering techniques her project introduced across the company's development organization.

Here, one devoted project manager convinced her management and project team to experiment with Usability Engineering

In this case study, the motivation came from one devoted project manager, who managed to convince both her management and her project team—all of whom were initially somewhat skeptical—to experiment with Usability Engineering. She recognized the high level of frustration within her user population with the unusability of most of their existing software tools and used this as leverage to convince management to fund her efforts.

Her project had high visibility and impact because the user group was essential to the company's operations, and her product affected every aspect of their daily jobs. She wisely chose to try out Usability Engineering techniques on a specific project, rather than just focus on designing and building a Usability Engineering process in the abstract. And she took every opportunity to publicize her success, within and outside her company. All these things contributed to the success of the project.

CASE STUDY 2: A METROPOLITAN POLICE DEPARTMENT

This project is still in progress as I write, and it also involves applying the whole Usability Engineering Lifecycle to a single project. It differs from the first case study in that it is hugely complex. The application is intended to support the work of police officers and other personnel in the local police stations of a metropolitan police department. My role on this project also differs from my role on the insurance company project. In that case the project manager and her team had a hands-on involvement with all Usability Engineering Lifecycle tasks, and I played mainly a role of educator and facilitator. On this project, I (and two of my associates) have taken full responsibility for carrying out all Usability Engineering Lifecycle tasks, with some support from the client's project team.

We were allocated the budget and resources to do a very extensive User Profile, distributing and analyzing about 800 questionnaires. This data was thoroughly analyzed and documented. Then we conducted an extensive Contextual Task Analysis, making five different site visits to local police stations, of about three full days each, to do our contextual observations/interviews. The results of this task were also thoroughly documented.

Documentation is another difference between this project and the previous one. In the insurance project, very little documentation was produced. The application was relatively small and simple, its time frame fairly short, and the entire project team jointly carried out all Usability Engineering Lifecycle tasks. For these reasons there was not a great deal of payoff to be realized from the effort of documentation. This project, on the other hand, is complex and long term, and the designers (us) and developers are two separate organizations, geographically dispersed. Thus, thorough documentation plays a much more important role.

We then synthesized and documented explicit Usability Goals (unlike the insurance project, in which we skipped right to Conceptual Model Design). Based on all the Requirements Analysis data gathered and analyzed, my staff took a first pass at Conceptual Model Design and then had a three-day review meeting to get feedback from key project team members from the client organization. Based on their input, we designed a mock-up of the revised Conceptual Model Design and implemented it as a running prototype. Next, we did a first iteration of Conceptual Model Design testing, identified problem areas, did a redesign and modified the prototype, and conducted a second iteration of testing. At this point, we documented the current Conceptual Model Design in a detailed product Style Guide. This is where the project stands at this writing. Next steps are to continue to level 2 and then level 3 design, and then go through the whole process again for several other layers of functionality of this highly complex and functionally rich application.

At the time of this writing, we have validated a very effective Conceptual Model Design. This took only two iterations of design and testing, and I attribute this efficiency to having been allocated the resources for conducting a thorough User Profile and Contextual Task Analysis and for establishing and documenting clear usability goals. In addition, through our User Profile, Contextual Task Analysis, and iterative usability testing activities, we have had much contact with users and generated a lot of positive PR for the project. This population of users was initially extremely technology-phobic and hostile, due directly to very bad past experiences with highly unusable and unreliable software. Just as in the first case study, the user-centered approach to design has had a profound effect on the receptivity of the user population to the coming application. The user-centered nature of the Usability Engineering Lifecycle has the happy side effect of improving the traditionally uneasy and often hostile relationship between development and user organizations.

OTHER PUBLISHED CASE STUDIES

In both case studies described above, a key factor is an individual project manager strongly committed to investing in Usability Engineering and powerful enough to win the resources from management to fund the Usability Engineering effort. The projects differ widely in a number of other ways (e.g., project team size, application complexity, project time frame, and available resources), and as described, I tailored the general Usability Engineering Lifecycle accordingly. For example, I collapsed levels of design, skipped documentation tasks, and tailored my role. Such flexibility is another key to success: you will always need to appropriately adapt the overall lifecycle approach to fit the unique set of requirements and resources of each individual development project.

Another case study of introducing the Usability Engineering Lifecycle approach into a development organization is reported in Miller (1996). She describes the formation of a centralized Usability Engineering organization and the introduction of a Usability Engineering Lifecycle approach into a development organization with an existing software engineering methodology in place. She identifies two "motivators" that created an opportunity for introducing Usability Engineering into her organization:

- An understanding of the history behind current usability problems, for example, heavy decentralization of the development organization had resulted in pervasive inconsistencies across products
- A corporate mandate from a very high organizational level to improve product usability

Then Miller identifies the following "success factors":

- An interdisciplinary team of usability specialists, with a mix of skills, including methodological (i.e., Usability Engineering) and design skills; practical experience in the real world of software development organizations; organizational change management skills; understanding of the corporate culture; and team-building skills.
- Selection of strategic projects (i.e., high visibility, high impact) for initial introduction of Usability Engineering techniques.
- A centralized Usability Engineering staff, who mentored designers on project teams.
- Up-front training of project teams to motivate them and increase project team receptivity to early and sustained Usability Engineering involvement.
- Education in the existing software engineering methodology and explicit tailoring of the Usability Engineering Lifecycle approach to smoothly integrate with it.
- "Do-it-yourself" training in Usability Engineering techniques for developers to best leverage the small Usability Engineering staff.
- Project team participation in all Usability Engineering tasks.
- Adaptation of the lifecycle and Usability Engineering techniques to the unique requirements of projects (e.g., using shortcuts or "quick and dirty" techniques to accommodate aggressive schedules).

This published case study provides a good example of many of the points made in this chapter and elsewhere in this book.

Another case study (Bradley and Johnk 1995) documents the use of a Usability Engineering Lifecycle of tasks very close to what is described in this book, at a division of Hewlett-Packard. The project involved designing a new GUI front end to an existing product with a command language user interface. The project team first analyzed users and tasks and set quantifiable usability goals that were intended as release criteria. They carried out several iterations of design and evaluation, in which they used inspection techniques in earlier iterations, and formal testing of usability goals in the final iteration. They evaluated the success of the Usability Engineering Lifecycle approach by comparing user performance on the original command language–driven product with user performance on the new GUI interface developed with the lifecycle approach. They found dramatic increases in usability realized from the Usability Engineering Lifecycle approach. The authors of the paper documenting this case study cite the following success factors:

- Recruiting a multidisciplinary project team
- Getting a commitment from the team to a Usability Engineering approach
- Maintaining that commitment through periods of doubt and frustration
- Setting aggressive but realistic quantifiable usability goals and using them as minimal acceptance criteria
- Using usability goals to drive design
- Using iterative design with feedback from real users early and often

Two other sources are Moll-Carrillo and colleagues (1995), who document a lifecycle approach including requirements analysis, design, and evaluation tasks, and Rudisill and colleagues (1996), who document a number of case studies.

Directions for Future Work

The process of writing this book, which involved pulling together all the work of my colleagues from the literature and adding to it all I have learned from my own experience to document the framework and details of the Usability Engineering Lifecycle, highlighted for me where the "holes" are in our field at this time. Here, I summarize what I see as the main weak spots in the set of currently available Usability Engineering techniques. They represent opportunities for future contributions to the discipline of Usability Engineering.

- **Requirements Analysis Shortcuts:** Most of the traditional techniques for Requirements Analysis tasks are fairly demanding of time and labor, and currently available shortcuts for these tasks sacrifice reliability and accuracy. We could use more techniques for Requirements Analysis tasks that can be executed quickly without sacrificing adequate accuracy and reliability.

◆ **Work Reengineering:** In general, we lack good formal methods both for the process of generating Reengineered Task Organization Models and Task Flow Models from Contextual Task Analysis data (see Chapters 3 and 7), and for clearly capturing and specifying them in detail.

◆ **Documentation/Specification Tools:** In general, we lack automated and integrated tools for capturing and revising (during iterative cycles) the outputs of all Usability Engineering Lifecycle tasks.

◆ **Integration of the Usability Engineering Lifecycle with the Existing Software Development Lifecycle:** We do not yet have very specific ideas about *exactly* how to most efficiently and smoothly integrate Usability Engineering Lifecycle tasks with standard software development tasks. This is partly due to the many different software development methodologies in use, but it is mostly due to the state of maturity of the Usability Engineering discipline. Work specifically aimed at seamlessly integrating Usability Engineering Lifecycle tasks into existing software development methodologies such as OOSE, so a single process, rather than two parallel processes, is being executed, would be extremely productive. This will require that systems engineering experts and systems development methodology experts work collaboratively with Usability Engineering experts.

◆ **Mainstreaming of the Usability Engineering Lifecycle:** In the several decades since Usability Engineering emerged as a distinct discipline, it still has not become a part of *mainstream* software engineering practice. The presence of Usability Engineering specialists and techniques in software development organizations in industry and government is still the exception rather than the rule. It should be a major goal of the profession for Usability Engineering specialists to become as mainstream as systems analysts, system architects, and programmers, and for their techniques to become as standard as data/object modeling and debugging.

◆ **Education of Software Engineers:** Academia has been slow to pick up on the growing interest in Usability Engineering within the software industry. The profession needs to work on getting courses and tracks in Usability Engineering and user interface design integrated into computer science curricula at both the undergraduate and graduate levels. If all software engineers entering the workforce had at least a basic background in this field and its techniques, the job of trying to institutionalize the Usability Engineering Lifecycle and its tasks and techniques in development organizations and methodologies would be much easier and more likely to succeed.

◆ **Basic Research:** In surveying the published literature for works related to the topics covered in this book, I noted some areas where very little *recent* basic research or even case studies have been reported. The field could use more published research in the following areas:

- User Profiles (Chapter 2)
- Conceptual Model Design (Chapter 8)
- Mock-ups and prototyping (Chapters 9 and 11)
- Detailed User Interface Design specification techniques (Chapter 15)
- User Feedback (Chapter 17)

A Historical Perspective on the Future

The projects described in the Case Studies section are relatively unique in my experience (which dates from the earliest days of the field of software Usability Engineering) in that they represent a willingness to embrace the notion of a whole Usability Engineering Lifecycle as part of an overall software engineering methodology. I wish I could say I have had more projects of this sort, but at least they are my most recent projects, and as such, they suggest an encouraging trend.

I believe it is inevitable that the software engineering discipline will embrace and incorporate the Usability Engineering Lifecycle approach, and it will become widely institutionalized in development organizations, just as software engineering methodologies have become institutionalized in most development organizations.

I started my career in the software industry in the late 1970s. At that time I was a programmer, project manager, and technology management consultant in a consulting firm that did contract software development and technology management consulting. This was a high-powered and prestigious firm founded by several MIT graduates, which offered state-of-the-art consulting on software engineering and strategic technology planning and management. I particularly remember one thing that occurred during the four years I worked for that firm—the introduction of a structured methodology for software development. The firm experimented with this in-house on contract development projects and then turned their methodology into a product that they sold.

Until then, development teams within the firm, like development organizations everywhere at that time, had no structured development methodology. Each project manager and each programmer conducted projects and tasks as they pleased according to their own experience. There was very little specialization. There were project managers, and then there were programmers. Individual programmers played all the roles of systems analysts, architects, programmers, and testers. Part of the structured methodology being introduced involved the specialization of individuals into these separate roles.

I particularly remember the hostility, resentment, and resistance of the firm's development staff to the very idea of a standardized, structured, institutionalized development methodology with specialized roles. After all, they would lose not only their freedom to be creative, but also the responsibilities and "turf" that they had previously held. They feared they would become bored with narrowing job responsibilities and limits on their ability to experiment and innovate.

Today, of course, few people in the industry resist the concept of a structured software development methodology. It has simply become a given. As entry-level software engineering professionals enter the marketplace, they come with an expectation that they will specialize and participate in a structured development lifecycle. It is taken for granted and hardly questioned. This will happen, too, with Usability Engineering. We are simply at the same point in the evolution of the discipline as software engineering was twenty years ago. We need to be patient, and we have a lot of work to do, but I have no doubt that we will eventually get to the point where software engineering as a discipline and practice is today: methodologies vary and evolve and are tailored by each organization to its needs, but the *concept* of a structured methodology is universally accepted and has become institutionalized in the industry. With time and effort, I have no doubt that the Usability Engineering Lifecycle approach will become universally accepted and institutionalized within the software engineering industry and will begin to evolve along with it.

Today few people resist the concept of a structured software development methodology. This will happen, too, with Usability Engineering. The lifecycle approach will eventually become accepted and institutionalized within the software engineering industry

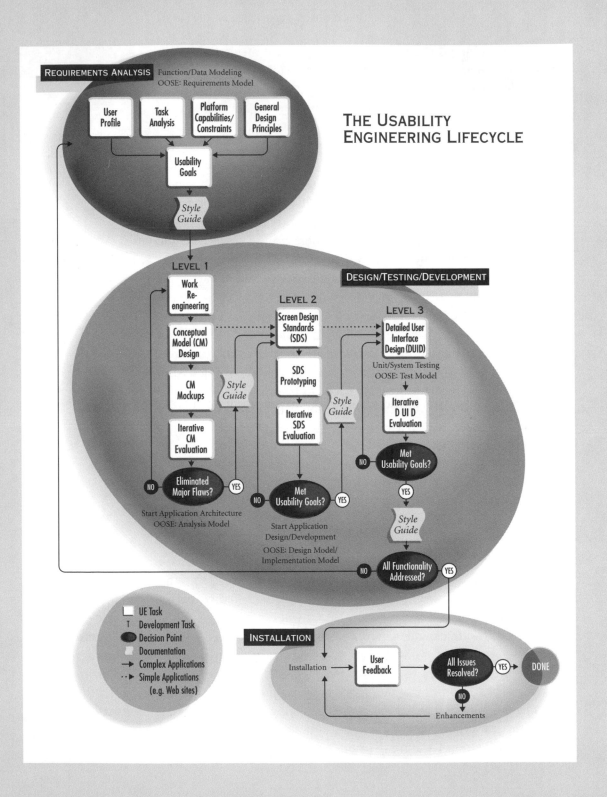

THE USABILITY ENGINEERING LIFECYCLE

REQUIREMENTS ANALYSIS   Function/Data Modeling
OOSE: Requirements Model

User Profile
Task Analysis
Platform Capabilities/ Constraints
General Design Principles

Usability Goals

Style Guide

LEVEL 1

DESIGN/TESTING/DEVELOPMENT

Work Re-engineering

Conceptual Model (CM) Design

CM Mockups

Iterative CM Evaluation

Style Guide

NO   Eliminated Major Flaws?   YES

Start Application Architecture
OOSE: Analysis Model

LEVEL 2

Screen Design Standards (SDS)

SDS Prototyping

Iterative SDS Evaluation

Style Guide

NO   Met Usability Goals?   YES

Start Application Design/Development

OOSE: Design Model/ Implementation Model

LEVEL 3

Detailed User Interface Design (DUID)

Unit/System Testing
OOSE: Test Model

Iterative D UI D Evaluation

NO   Met Usability Goals?   YES

Style Guide

NO   All Functionality Addressed?   YES

UE Task
T Development Task
Decision Point
Documentation
→ Complex Applications
··▸ Simple Applications
   (e.g. Web sites)

INSTALLATION

Installation → User Feedback → All Issues Resolved?   YES → DONE

NO

Enhancements

Usability Project Planning

PURPOSE

There are at least four good reasons to develop and document specific Usability Project Plans for product development projects:

◆ Project planning is a standard management technique on most product development projects.

◆ Planning allows you to more effectively manage your own work efforts.

◆ Getting the Usability Project Plan included in the overall project plan increases the likelihood that it will actually be executed.

◆ Through effective planning and management of usability efforts on individual projects, you take a first step towards institutionalizing the Usability Engineering Lifecycle within the overall development organization and methodology.

Project planning is a standard management technique on most product development projects. These days, most software development organizations have adopted a structured methodology for software engineering. Some methodologies are commercially available, and development organizations buy them, adapt them, and institutionalize them. Other organizations develop their own in-house methodologies. Some methodologies are very structured, and organizations may require complete compliance with the methodology. Other methodologies are more informal and flexible, and organizations may use these methodologies as loose guidelines rather than strictly enforced procedures. In any case, most of these development methodologies specify phases, tasks within phases, and steps or procedures for carrying out tasks, as well as examples and templates, just like the Usability Engineering Lifecycle described in this book.

In addition, most development organizations develop project plans at the beginning of the project, taking the methodology as a starting point to define phases, tasks, and steps. Then assign staff, hours, and dates to those phases, tasks, and steps. Many organizations even use automated project planning tools to create and update their plans.

Project plans are an important managerial tool, allowing project managers to conduct cost-benefit analyses, present projects for funding approval, track project progress, and generally manage the project to successful completion. Managers also use past experiences in creating and tracking project plans to become better estimators, planners, and managers on future projects. With careful planning, record keeping, and "postmortem" analyses on the detailed records of past projects, you learn to accurately estimate required resources and accurately justify and plan for new projects.

Consulting and contracting organizations who sell their services on a fixed-price or time-and-materials basis quickly learn the importance of accurate estimating and planning

Consulting and contracting organizations who sell their services on a fixed-price or even time-and-materials basis quickly learn the importance of accurate estimating and planning. If they misestimate or mismanage a fixed-price contract, they lose money. If they misestimate or mismanage time-and-materials projects too often, they develop a poor reputation and lose business opportunities.

Good managers within well-run internal development organizations also understand the value of planning and tracking. In most cases, bottom-line success depends on good estimation and planning skills combined with cost-benefit analyses and tight management against detailed project plans. If usability practitioners conduct Usability Project Planning for Usability Engineering Lifecycle tasks, they will simply fit into the management processes in product development organizations more easily and naturally.

Planning allows you to more effectively manage your own work efforts. Usability practitioners, whether they are outside or in-house consultants, need to consider themselves project managers of sorts. They must learn to accurately estimate the level of effort required for the different Usability Engineering Lifecycle tasks, to develop overall Usability Engineering project plans based on cost-benefit analyses, and to manage Usability Engineering efforts against their plans.

The best way to do this is to simply start doing it. If you have never been required to plan and track your Usability Engineering efforts before, simply take a stab at planning and estimating your efforts on your next project, task, or even step. You can use or adapt the sample task and step Level of Effort estimates in Chapters 2–17 as a first pass. Then, actually track (to the nearest hour) your efforts against these plans. When you complete tasks or steps, you will be able to compare your actual effort with your estimated effort. You will learn from this, and you will be a little more accurate in estimating the next task or step. Eventually, with experience, you will become an accurate estimator, planner, and manager.

I have been an independent consultant since 1986. When I began, I really had no idea how to estimate and lay out a project plan for my clients, because as an in-house employee in my previous jobs, I had never been asked to plan, estimate, or even track my time. At this point, however, I am a very accurate estimator and rarely exceed (or come in under) my initial estimates. I prepare detailed, step-by-step project plans for my clients, and on longer projects, I submit regular status reports tracking my progress against my initial plan. In-house usability practitioners would do well to follow this example, whether they are required to or not, simply to become better managers of their own efforts and to be able to make better cost-benefit cases (see Chapter 20) to their management.

Getting the Usability Project Plan included in the overall project plan increases the likelihood that it will actually be executed. In my experience, even planned usability efforts are rarely explicitly included in the overall project plan. There may be usability practitioners on the project team, but their role and efforts are largely unplanned, or only vaguely specified. What usually happens in this case is that while plenty of lip service is paid to the importance of usability efforts initially, as push comes to shove and the project gets behind schedule and budget, time and money for usability efforts are the first things to go.

For this reason, usability practitioners should explicitly plan their efforts and make sure their tasks, with specific resources, budgets, and time frames, are integrated into the overall project plan. Only if they are planned for up front—with specific budgets and time frames allocated, documented, and committed to along with the rest of the project plan—are they likely to be carried out.

Through effective planning and management of usability efforts on individual projects, you take a first step towards institutionalizing the

Usability practitioners should make sure their tasks, resources, budgets, and time frames are integrated into the project plan

Usability Engineering Lifecycle within the overall development organization and methodology. Ultimately, our goal as usability practitioners is to get Usability Engineering Lifecycle tasks institutionalized as part of the overall development methodology. All too often, I have seen usability efforts start in one part of a development organization, and enjoy popularity and funding for some period of time, only to be completely discarded some time later. Part of the reason for this is that the Usability Engineering Lifecycle tasks are only applied in certain organizations and on certain projects, and are never formally integrated into the established, documented, and enforced overall product development methodology.

I believe getting the Usability Engineering Lifecycle tasks written into the documented product development methodology—and taught through general training classes introducing new employees to the overall development methodology—should be an important agenda for in-house usability specialists interested in keeping their jobs over the long term. This is not necessarily an easy or quick thing to accomplish, but it should be a long-term, strategic goal that always drives any choices you are allowed to make about how to spend your time as a usability practitioner.

Description

Learning to estimate accurately is not necessarily easy and requires a fair amount of experience, but drawing up a Usability Project Plan is not in itself very difficult. It is a matter of deciding which lifecycle tasks to include and which techniques to apply for each task, and then calculating the resources required for each of those tasks and techniques. In turn, calculating the resources required for a given technique is a fairly simple matter of breaking down the technique into its steps, estimating the time, skill set, and other resources for each step, and calculating a total. It is wise to do a cost-benefit analysis (see Chapter 20) on any Usability Project Plan before submitting it to project management for inclusion in the overall project plan. This allows you to make a convincing argument in support of the budget your plan calls for.

Once you calculate all task times and obtain budget approval, you can integrate the Usability Project Plan into the overall project plan. You must synchronize Usability Engineering Lifecycle tasks with other traditional development tasks to accommodate interdependencies (see Scheduling and Integration with Other Tasks in Chapters 2–17). Then you can assign start and end dates to them. Finally, identify and assign tasks to available staff.

Scheduling and Integration with Other Tasks

Ideally, the Usability Project Plan should be drawn up at the same time that the overall project plan is being put together, so it can be integrated with it and can influence it where necessary. When usability practitioners are lucky enough to be involved at the inception of a project, they have the best chance of implementing the whole Usability Engineering Lifecycle, as described in Chapters 1–17.

When usability practitioners are invited to participate in projects already in progress, which is often the case for outside consultants, they have less chance of including all lifecycle tasks and of influencing overall schedules and budgets. In all likelihood, you will have to live with pre-existing schedules, platforms, and system architectures, use only shortcut techniques for early lifecycle tasks, and minimally impact budgets. However, in my experience, it is almost always possible to create a Usability Project Plan that will make a significant contribution to a project, even when you come in relatively late. Nevertheless, when you do this, it is always important to emphasize to project management the importance and desirability of getting usability experts involved—and a Usability Project Plan in place—earlier on in future projects.

Ideally, the Usability Project Plan should be put together concurrently with the overall project plan so they can be integrated and can influence each other where necessary

It is almost always possible to create a Usability Project Plan that will make a significant contribution to a project, even when you come in relatively late

Roles and Resources

During Usability Project Planning, the usability roles might participate as follows:

Task leader: The Usability Engineer should take the lead role in this task.

Other resources: The User Interface Designer should participate as an assistant in planning, especially on those tasks for which he or she will be responsible (see Chapter 21). Project management, project team members, and others should participate and at least sign off on the plan, to be sure there is commitment from all project stakeholders.

SAMPLE TECHNIQUE— A STEP-BY-STEP PROCEDURE

Creating a Usability Project Plan involves six steps.

❶ **Decide which Usability Engineering Lifecycle tasks to include.** This will depend on many things, such as:

♦ What stage the overall project is currently in (e.g., just beginning, the prototyping stage)
♦ Budget and schedule constraints
♦ Complexity of the product (e.g., simple Web page vs. very complex traditional application)
♦ Politics (some tasks may have a better chance of acceptance than others, given management's past experience, if any, with usability techniques)

Ideally, you would hope to be able to conduct all the tasks discussed in Chapters 2–17.

❷ **Decide which techniques to employ for each Usability Engineering Lifecycle task.** This will depend on most of the same factors named in step 1. Ideally, you would like to be able to carry out each task with the most rigorous available technique, but you will not always (or perhaps even often) have this luxury. Usually, even at least a "quick and dirty" technique for each and every task is better than skipping tasks altogether. For example, if you cannot obtain the resources to do a comprehensive User Profile (see Chapter 2) and Contextual Task Analysis (see Chapter 3), at least try to conduct shortcut versions of both these tasks. You could, for example, interview user management and ask them to characterize the whole user population as best they can, using a User Profile Questionnaire (see Chapter 2 for an example). You could also conduct just a few contextual observations/interviews (see Chapter 3) and take extensive notes rather than document your findings formally.

❸ **Estimate resources for each task/technique.** Referring back to the appropriate chapter for help, break down each task/technique you have chosen to use in your plan into its steps. Try your best to estimate the number of hours and the type of skill set required for each step. It helps to create a general planning form for tasks/techniques such as Figure 19.1.

Figure 19.1 Usability Task Plan Form

Usability Task Plan

Task Number: _____ Start Date: _____
Task Name: _____ End Date: _____
Responsible Staff: _____

Steps   Hours

1. _____   _____
2. _____   _____
3. _____   _____
4. _____   _____
5. _____   _____
6. _____   _____
7. _____   _____
8. _____   _____

TOTAL   _____

Other Required Resources: _____
_____
_____

Then, for each task/technique, you fill in a blank form (see Figure 19.2).

Figure 19.2 Usability Task Plan Form with Input

Usability Task Plan

Task Number: _____14_____   Start Date: _Jan 2, 1999_
Task Name: _____Usability Test_____   End Date: _Feb 2, 1999_
Responsible Staff: _____D. Mayhew_____

Steps   Hours

1. _Design/Develop Test Materials_   _32_
2. _Assemble Test Environment_   _8_
3. _Run Pilot Test_   _8_
4. _Revise Test Materials_   _8_
5. _Run Test/Collect Data_   _32_
6. _Analyze Data/Draw Conclusions_   _16_
7. _Document/Present Results_   _40_
8. _____

TOTAL   _144_

Other Required Resources: _Usability Lab time, video tapes, 4 users for_
2 hours each, 1 lab assistant for 40 hours

Initially, you would leave the Start Date, End Date, and Responsible Staff fields blank and just compute the number of hours of usability staff required. In later steps described below, you will fill in these other fields.

As an aid for planning each task, you can use the Sample Technique—A Step-by-Step Procedure sections in each chapter of this book to remind you of all the steps required for each task/technique that you need to estimate. Don't forget to allocate resources for *all* steps, for example, preparing documentation and presentations, having reviews and getting feedback, and so on. You can also refer to the Level of Effort sections of Chapters 2–17 to help you with initial estimates.

❹ **If appropriate, submit the Usability Plan to a cost-benefit analysis.** This will be appropriate if you have to "sell" management on the plan to get your funding. How to conduct a cost-benefit analysis is described in Chapter 20.

❺ **Obtain approval for the Usability Project Plan.** Present the Usability Project Plan and cost-benefit analysis (if appropriate) to project management for approval. Make modifications as necessary to obtain final approval.

❻ **Integrate the Usability Project Plan into the overall project plan.** Synchronize the Usability Engineering Lifecycle tasks with all other development tasks to accommodate interdependencies (see the Scheduling and Integration with Other Tasks sections of Chapters 2–17). Assign specific staff members to each task, and establish start and end dates for each task. In the end, Usability Engineering Lifecycle tasks should appear in the overall project plan just like any other tasks. For example, an excerpt from a (simplified) project planning chart might look something like Figure 19.3.

Figure 19.3 Project Planning Chart

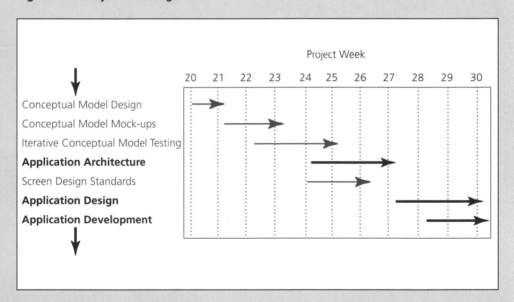

In Figure 19.3, the lighter text and arrows denote Usability Engineering tasks, while the thicker text and arrows denote traditional development tasks.

WEB NOTES

Web designers should also plan the Usability Engineering Lifecycle tasks into their overall project plan. Generally, the Usability Engineering Lifecycle can be contracted for simple Web sites and applications, as discussed in Chapter 1 and also in the Web Notes sections of Chapters 2–17. In addition, generally more "quick and dirty" techniques may be employed for Requirements Analysis tasks. Remember though, in the case of relatively simple Web sites and applications, the plan itself may specify less effort and resources as compared to traditional applications, but the planning process is just as important for all the same reasons.

SAMPLE WORK PRODUCTS AND TEMPLATES

One sample is offered here: Sample Usability Project Plan.

SAMPLE PROJECT PLAN

The following is a slightly adapted excerpt from a Usability Project Plan that I wrote as part of a proposal for a client. It represents a plan for level 1 (Conceptual Model Design) of the Design/Testing/Development phase of a project, on which I had already completed the Requirements Analysis phase.

Usability Project Plan

Deliverable	Tasks	Hours
1: First Draft CM Design Mock-ups —Paper Mock-ups	1: Phase One Review —My staff will spend some time reviewing all our Requirements Analysis phase work products, and any additional up-to-date project documentation you can provide.	16
	2: Trip: Overview of Reengineering —Your team will present to us the XYZ project reengineering of the work process, so that we can base our UI design ideas on your planned architecture and information flow.	54
	3: Design Brainstorming —My staff will work closely together to generate our initial Conceptual Model Design ideas.	45
	4: First Draft CM Design Mock-ups —My staff will work to document our initial Conceptual Model Design ideas in a paper-and-pencil format we can use to communicate them to you in the meeting planned for the next step.	30
2: Second Draft CM Design Prototype —VB UI Design Prototype —Testing Materials	1: Trip: Design Brainstorming with XYZ Project Team —We will present our design ideas to your team and spend two days discussing them with you, getting your input, and refining it according to your feedback.	38
	2: Prototype Second Draft CM Design (VB) —My staff will build a very simple Visual Basic prototype of our current Conceptual Model Design ideas to use as the basis of our first usability test with real users.	92

"Usability Project Plan," cont. next page

"Usability Project Plan," cont.

Deliverable	Tasks	Hours
	3: Develop Testing Materials —My staff will develop all the required supporting materials to run the usability test.	28
3: First Iteration CM Design Testing —Revised UI Design Prototype —Revised Testing Materials	1: Trip: Run First Iteration Testing with Users —I will direct you in recruiting and scheduling between eight and twelve users to participate in our test. My staff will bring the prototype down on a laptop and conduct the testing in the user work environment.	54
	2: Redesign Meeting —My staff will spend two days analyzing the results of the testing and generating redesign ideas.	45
	3: Rebuild Prototype —My staff will revise our Visual Basic prototype to reflect our redesign ideas.	40
	4: Redesign Testing Materials —My staff will update the testing materials as necessary to reflect the revised design.	90
4: Second Iteration CM Design Testing —Conceptual Model Standards Document —Phase Two Level 2 Work Plan	1: Trip: Run Second Iteration Testing with Users —My staff will repeat the testing with a new set of eight to twelve users and the revised prototype.	54

Deliverable	Tasks	Hours
	2: Document Conceptual Model Design —My staff will redesign based on our test results and then document our final design ideas as a high-level design standards document.	60
	3: Phase Three Work Plan —I will prepare a proposal for Phase Two Design Level 2 (Screen Design Standards) and also prepare step-by-step guides for the tasks in that phase.	38

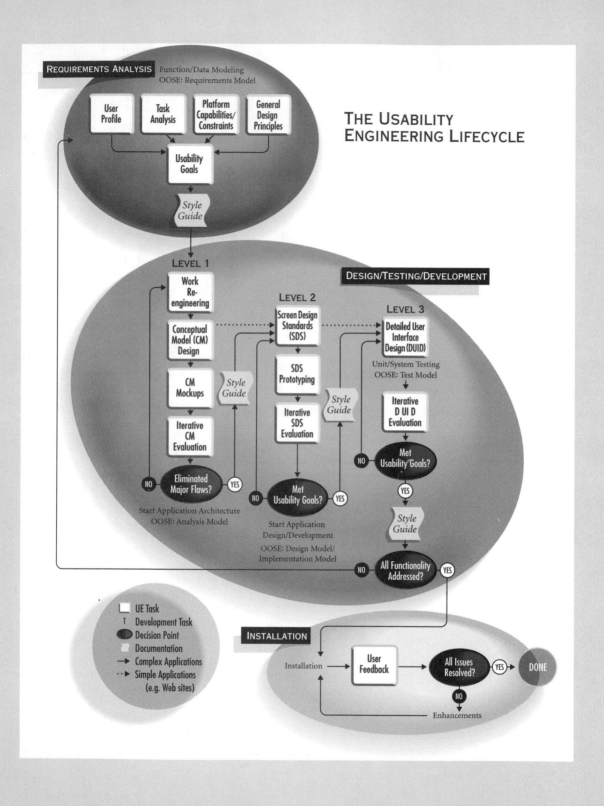

THE USABILITY
ENGINEERING LIFECYCLE

20

Cost-Justification

PURPOSE

This chapter presents a framework for cost-justifying Usability Engineering efforts by describing how to go about calculating the costs and estimating the benefits of the Usability Engineering Lifecycle tasks described in Chapters 2–17. This topic is covered extensively in *Cost-Justifying Usability* (Bias and Mayhew 1994). In particular, Chapter 2 in that book elaborates on the simple framework offered in this chapter. Other chapters in that book offer further discussion and case studies. If you are interested in learning more about how, when, and why to cost-justify Usability Engineering efforts, I refer you to that book for more detail than can be provided here.

There are two possible purposes for conducting a cost-benefit analysis of a Usability Project Plan:

◆ To sell Usability Engineering in general
◆ To plan for a particular project

Very general cost-benefit analyses of hypothetical Usability Engineering efforts can be prepared as a strategy to win general support for trying out Usability Engineering techniques in an organization. When an organization has no experience with Usability Engineering, cost-benefit analyses can help win resources to experiment with it for the first time. In more mature organizations, cost-benefit analyses can be used to plan the Usability Engineering effort for a particular project.

To help settle on a final Usability Project Plan for a specific development project, you could start out by calculating the costs of the most

In organizations new to Usability Engineering, cost-benefit analyses can help win resources to experiment with it. In more mature organizations, cost-benefit analyses can help plan the Usability Engineering effort for a particular project

449

aggressive Usability Engineering program that you might like to implement, including rigorous techniques for all lifecycle tasks. Then you could calculate a conservative estimate of benefits. If benefits still outweigh costs dramatically, as they usually will when crucial parameters are favorable, you could easily make a good argument for even the most aggressive Usability Project Plan. Because only the most conservative claims concerning potential benefits have been made, you can easily defend them. In fact, you can go back and redo the benefits estimates using more aggressive yet still realistic assumptions, and show that in all likelihood an even more dramatic overall benefit will be realized, even from a significant investment in usability.

Use cost-justification to develop a sensible Usability Project Plan that is likely to pay off as predicted

If, however, benefits and costs in the initial analysis seem to match fairly closely, you will want to scale back your initial, aggressive Usability Project Plan, maybe even to just a bare-bones plan. Perhaps you should plan to use shortcuts on the User Profile task, by interviewing user management, and the Contextual Task Analysis, by doing just a few rounds of contextual observations/interviews. Then do just one round of iterations of usability testing on a complete design (i.e., all three levels), to catch major flaws and be sure you have achieved the predicted benefits. You are still likely to realize the very conservative assumptions made concerning benefits, and thus you could predict with confidence a healthy return on investment from a more minimal approach to Usability Engineering. This is probably wiser in the long run than making overly optimistic claims concerning potential benefits, spending a lot to achieve them, and then perhaps *not* achieving them and losing credibility. This is one way to use a cost-benefit analysis, to develop a sensible Usability Project Plan that is likely to pay off as predicted.

When an organization is first experimenting with Usability Engineering techniques and is still skeptical about their value, it is wise to make cost-benefit arguments based on very conservative estimates of benefits, and then to show after the fact that much larger benefits were in fact realized. Once an organization has several positive experiences investing in Usability Engineering, it will be more receptive not only to proposals for more aggressive Usability Engineering programs, but also to more optimistic benefits estimates in the corresponding cost-benefit analyses. See Bias and Mayhew (1994, ch. 2) for more concrete examples of how to use cost-benefit analyses to tailor Usability Project Plans.

DESCRIPTION

To cost-justify a Usability Project Plan, you simply adapt a generic and widely used cost-benefit analysis technique. Having laid out a detailed Usability Project Plan (see Chapter 19), it is a fairly straightforward matter to calculate the costs of the plan. Then you need to calculate the benefits. This is a little trickier, and it's where the adaptation of the generic analysis comes into play (see step 5 in Sample Technique—A Step-by-Step Procedure later in the chapter). After that, you simply compare costs to benefits to find out whether, and to what extent, the benefits outweigh the costs. If benefits do outweigh costs to a satisfactory extent, you have cost-justified the planned effort.

Here's the cost-justification described more specifically. The Usability Project Plan specifies techniques to employ for each Usability Engineering Lifecycle task, breaks the techniques down into steps, and specifies the personnel hours and equipment costs for each step. The cost of each task is then calculated by multiplying the total number of hours for each type of personnel by their hourly wage and adding in any equipment and other costs. Then the costs from all tasks are summed to arrive at a total cost for the plan. Next, overall benefits are predicted by selecting relevant benefit categories, calculating expected benefits by plugging project-specific parameters into benefit formulas, and summing benefits across categories and across the expected product lifetime.

Potential benefit categories depend primarily on whether the development organization is in-house, developing products for use by in-house users, or a vendor organization (or contractor), selling products (or services) on the open market. Sample benefit categories potentially relevant to in-house development organizations (and contractors) include

- Decreased late design changes
- Decreased user training
- Increased user productivity
- Decreased user errors
- Decreased need for user support

Sample benefit categories potentially relevant to vendor development organizations include

Once you've laid out a detailed Usability Project Plan, it is a fairly straightforward matter to calculate the costs of the plan, calculate the benefits, and compare costs to benefits

◆ Decreased late design changes
◆ Increased sales and market penetration
◆ Decreased need for customer training
◆ Decreased need for customer support

In a cost-benefit analysis, focus attention on the potential benefits that are of most interest to the audience for the analysis

Note that while the primary benefit relevant to the in-house development organization might be increased user productivity, this is not usually of direct concern to a vendor company or contractor (even though it should be). The vendor company is more concerned with selling more products and decreasing product support costs. Thus, in a cost-benefit analysis, focus attention on the potential benefits that are of most interest to the audience for the analysis.

Also note that these benefits are only a sample of what might be relevant in these two types of organizations. Other benefits might be included as appropriate, given the business goals of the organization and the primary concerns of the audience, and they could be calculated in a similar way (see step 5 in Sample Technique—A Step-by-Step Procedure).

Your final step is to compare overall benefits to overall costs to see whether, and to what extent, the overall Usability Project Plan is justified. In Sample Technique—A Step-by-Step Procedure, and also in Sample Work Products and Templates, the basic technique for carrying out a cost-benefit analysis of a usability effort is summarized through examples.

Scheduling and Integration with Other Tasks

Ideally, the Usability Project Plan should be drawn up at the same time that the overall project plan is being put together, so it can be integrated with it and can influence it where necessary. Thus, the cost-benefit analysis technique is ideally applied at the very beginning of a project.

When usability practitioners are invited to participate in projects already in progress, which is often the case for outside consultants, they have less chance of including all Usability Engineering Lifecycle tasks and of influencing overall schedules and budgets. They are more likely to have to live with preexisting schedules, platforms, and system architectures, to use shortcut techniques for Requirements Analysis tasks, and to minimally impact budgets. Nevertheless, it is almost always possible to create a Usability Project Plan that will make a significant contribution to a project. And you can use the cost-benefit analysis technique to prepare and support even those Usability Project Plans that involve only parts of the overall Usability Engineering Lifecycle and shortcut techniques for tasks within it.

Roles and Resources

In cost-justification of the Usability Project Plan, the usability roles might participate as follows:

Task leader: The Usability Engineer should take the lead role in this task.

Other resources: All project stakeholders (including users) should be the audience for the cost-benefit analysis of the Usability Project Plan. It is used to gain their commitment to the final plan.

Sample Technique— A Step-by-Step Procedure

Let's consider a hypothetical Usability Project Plan for a software development project and then see how to conduct a cost-benefit analysis of that plan for that project. First, I present the final results of such an analysis. Then, in the steps below, I show how they were derived.

Imagine an in-house development organization is planning to develop an application for use by an in-house user organization. (See the Sample Work Products and Templates section for a sample cost-benefit analysis for a vendor organization.) The project is of moderate complexity and cost and will result in an application that will be used by 250 users. Once developed and installed, the application is expected to be in production for approximately five years.

Table 20.1 shows the overall calculation of the cost of the Usability Project Plan proposed by the project Usability Engineer (see Chapters 1 and 21 for definitions of all Usability Engineering roles). The first column identifies the overall project phase. The middle column identifies which Usability Engineering Lifecycle tasks are planned in each phase, and the numbers in parentheses after some of these tasks indicate the number of planned iterations of that task. The third column summarizes the expected cost of *all* iterations of each task. A grand total for the cost of the whole plan is given at the bottom of the chart.

In this hypothetical plan, the project Usability Engineer has calculated the expected benefits of carrying out this Usability Project Plan in the first year of application installation as shown in Table 20.2, and the predicted benefits over the expected product lifetime are summarized in Table 20.3.

Comparing these benefits and costs, the project Usability Engineer argues that in the first year alone, a net benefit of $88,284 is expected:

Benefits = $175,104

Costs = $87,660

Net Benefit = $87,444

**Table 20.1
Estimated cost of the sample plan**

Phase	UI Task	Cost
Requirements Analysis	User Profiles	$ 7,000
	Contextual Task Analysis	$11,170
	Usability Goal Setting	$ 7,100
	Platform Capabilities/Constraints	$ 2,100
Design/Testing/Development	Work Reengineering	$ 3,530
	Conceptual Model Design	$ 7,140
	Conceptual Model Mock-ups	$ 2,800
	Iterative Conceptual Model Evaluation (2)	$ 9,960
	Screen Design Standards	$ 6,300
	Screen Standards Prototype	$ 5,320
	Iterative Screen Standards Evaluation (2)	$ 9,960
	Detailed UI Design	$ 5,320
	Iterative Detailed UI Design Evaluation (2)	$ 9,960
Installation		
Total		$87,660

Table 20.2
Expected benefits of the sample plan—first year

Benefit	
Increased productivity	$ 23,958
Decreased errors	$ 71,846
Decreased training	$ 62,500
Decreased late design changes	$ 16,800
Total	$175,104

Table 20.3
Expected benefits of the sample plan—lifetime

Benefit	
Increased productivity $23,958 per year × 5 years =	$119,790
Decreased errors $71,846 per year × 5 years =	$359,230
Decreased training $62,500 in first year =	$ 62,500
Decreased late design changes $16,800 in first year =	$ 16,800
Total	$558,320

Over the expected five-year lifetime of the product, a net benefit of $471,500 is predicted:

> Benefits = $558,320
>
> Costs = $87,660
>
> **Net Benefit = $470,660**

The project Usability Engineer expects her plan to be approved based on this cost-justification.

Here are the steps the project Usability Engineer used to arrive at the final results.

❶ **Start with the Usability Project Plan.** Chapter 19 discussed how to prepare such a plan. If it has not already been done, it is the first step in conducting a cost-benefit analysis. The Usability Project Plan identifies which Usability Engineering Lifecycle tasks and techniques will be employed and breaks them down into required staff and hours. Costs can then be computed for these tasks in the next two steps.

❷ **Establish analysis parameters.** Many of the calculations for both planned costs and estimated benefits are based on project-specific parameters. These should be established and documented before proceeding with the analysis. Sample parameters are given below for our hypothetical project.

- Product for in-house use (vs. commercial product)
- End users number 250 (vs., for example, 50 users, or 10,000 users)
- User, customer support, usability, and developer staff all work 230 days per year
- Users' fully loaded hourly wage = $25
- Customer support's fully loaded hourly wage = $25
- Usability and developer staff's fully loaded hourly wage = $35
- Usability lab or sufficient resources in place
- Changes made early in development cost 1/4 of changes made after installation (see Mantei and Teorey 1988)
- Typical system lifetime = 5 years (vs., for example, 2 years or 20 years)

It should be emphasized that when using the general cost-benefit analysis technique illustrated here, these particular parameter values should not be assumed. The particular parameter values of your project and organization should be substituted for those above. They will almost certainly be different from the parameters used in this example.

You should note in general that certain parameters in a cost-benefit analysis have a major impact on the magnitude of potential benefits. For example, when considering productivity—of primary interest to the in-house development organization—the crucial parameters are the number of users and the volume of transactions and, to some extent, the users' fully loaded hourly wage. When you have a large number of users and/or a high volume of transactions, even very small performance advantages (and low hourly wages) in an optimized interface add up quickly to significant overall benefits. On the other hand, when you have a small number of potential users and/or a low volume of transactions, benefits may not add up to much, even when the potential per-transaction performance advantage seems significant and the users' hourly wage is higher.

For example, consider the following two scenarios. First, imagine a case with 5,000 users and 120 transactions per day per user. Even a half second advantage in this case adds up:

5,000 users × 120 transactions × 230 days × 1/2 second = 19,167 hours

If the users' hourly rate is $15, the savings are

19,167 hours × $15 = $287,505

This is a pretty dramatic benefit for a tiny improvement on a per-transaction basis!

On the other hand, if there were only 25 users, and they were infrequent users, with only 12 transactions per day; even if a per-transaction benefit of 1 minute could be realized, the overall benefit would only be

25 users × 12 transactions × 230 days × 1 minute = 1,150 hours

At $15 per hour, the overall productivity benefit is only

1,150 hours × $15 = $17,250

Thus, in the case of productivity benefits, costs associated with optimizing the user interface are more likely to pay off when there are more users and more transactions.

In the case of the *sales* benefit for a vendor, the crucial parameter is usually *profit margin*. If the profit margin per product is low, a very large number of additional sales would have to be achieved due to usability alone for the usability costs to pay off. On the other hand, if the profit margin per product is high, only a small number of increased sales due to usability would be necessary to pay for the usability program. Thus, these crucial parameters are going to directly determine how much can be invested in usability and still pay off. (See Bias and Mayhew 1994, ch. 2, for more discussion of analysis parameters.)

❸ **Calculate the cost of each Usability Engineering Lifecycle task in the Usability Project Plan.** In the Usability Project Plan, the number of hours required by each necessary type of staff were estimated for each step of each task/technique in the plan. You now simply add up the total number of hours of each type of staff required for each task, and multiply it by the fully loaded hourly wage of that type of staff. Additional costs, such as equipment and supplies, are also estimated. From these subtotals, a total cost for each task is computed. If multiple iterations of a task are planned, simply multiply the task cost per iteration by the planned number of iterations. This is how the total costs for individual tasks were calculated in Table 20.1.

Fully loaded hourly wages are calculated by adding together the cost of salary, benefits, office space, equipment, and other facilities for a type of personnel, and dividing this by the number of hours worked each year. If outside consultants or contractors are used, their simple hourly rate plus travel expenses would apply.

Remember that both the hourly wage figures and the predicted hours per task used to generate the sample analysis here are just examples. You would have to use the actual fully loaded hourly rates of personnel in your own organization (or the rates of consultants being hired), and the expected time of your own Usability Engineers to complete each task based on their experience and the techniques they plan to use, in order to carry out your own analysis. For example, the cost for the User Profile task in the sample was calculated as shown in Table 20.4.

Similar derivations for all the other tasks in the cost summary chart can be found in the Sample Work Products and Templates section later in the chapter.

❹ **Select relevant benefit categories.** Since this is an in-house development organization, you would choose benefit categories to include in your analysis that are of most interest to this type of organization. In this hypothetical case, the Usability Engineer decided to include the following benefits:

- Decreased late design changes
- Decreased user training
- Increased user productivity
- Decreased user errors

She selected these because she knows they will be most relevant to her audience, the project management.

❺ **Estimate benefits.** Next the Usability Engineer estimated the magnitude of each benefit that would be realized if the Usability Project Plan (with its associated costs) were implemented, compared to if it were not. Thus, for example, she estimated how much more productive users would be on the application if it were engineered for usability compared to if it were not.

Table 20.4
Sample calculations of User Profile task

Usability Staff Time		User Time	
Step	Hrs	Step	Hrs
Needs finding	24	Needs finding	24
Draft questionnaire	12		
Management feedback	2	Management feedback	2
Revise questionnaire	6		
Pilot questionnaire	8	Pilot questionnaire	8
Revise questionnaire	6		
Select user sample	4		
Distribute questionnaire	6	Respond to questionnaire	50
Data analysis	24		
Data interpretation/ presentation	24		
Document user profiles	24		
Total	140	Total	84
	× $35 = $4,900	+	× $25 = $2,100
			= $7,000

To estimate each benefit, choose a unit of measurement for the benefit, such as time per screen or per task in the case of productivity, or number of major errors per year in the case of errors. Then—and this is the tricky part—make an assumption concerning the magnitude of the benefit for each unit of measurement; for example, a one-second savings per screen or a reduction of four errors per year. (Tips on how to make this key assumption are discussed below.) Finally, multiply the estimated benefit per unit of measurement by the number of units. Benefits can be expressed in units of time and then converted to dollars, given the value of time.

Imagine our hypothetical project is developing a typical data entry application. Based on her in-house experience, the Usability Engineer assumed there would be two to four primary screens on this system representing the main entry screens where users would spend most of their time, and that users on the average would process about sixty of these screens per day. Recall (see step 2 above) that these users work 230 days a year, at a fully loaded hourly wage of $25. The Usability Engineer made the assumption that if her Usability Project Plan were implemented during development, the result would be screens that would allow users to process them 1 second faster than screens that were developed without the benefit of Usability Engineering techniques. Assuming a benefit of 1 second per screen, 60 screens per day, 230 days per user, and 250 users, she thus calculated the total productivity benefit in a year as follows:

> **Increased Productivity:**
> 60 transactions per day
> Time per transaction decreased by 1 second
> 250 users $\times$ 230 days $\times$ 60 transactions $\times$ 1/3600 hours $\times$ $25 =
> **$23,958 in first year**

Note that if the application is in production over several years, as most are, this benefit is realized *each year*. It is not a one-time benefit, even though the costs of achieving the benefit are one-time costs incurred only in the first year during development.

Calculations of all other estimated benefits in this hypothetical example are given in the Sample Work Products and Templates section.

The basic assumption of a cost-benefit analysis of a Usability Project Plan is that the improved user interfaces that are achieved through Usability Engineering techniques will result in such tangible, measurable benefits as those calculated in this hypothetical example (e.g., 1 second per transaction; 10 hours per course; 1 1/2 errors per day @ 2 minutes each; early design changes cost 1/4 of late changes).

The audience for the analysis is asked to accept these assumptions of certain estimated, quantified benefits as reasonable and likely minimum benefits, rather than as precise, proven, guaranteed benefits. Proof simply does not exist, for each specific application and its users, that an optimal user interface will provide some specific, reliable performance advantage over some unspecified but suboptimal user interface that would result if the Usability Project Plan didn't exist.

How can you generate—and convince your audience to accept—the inherent assumptions in the benefits you claim in a given cost-benefit analysis? First, point out that any cost-benefit analysis for any purpose must make certain assumptions that are really only predictions of the likely outcome of investments of various sorts. The whole point of a cost-benefit analysis is to try to evaluate in advance, in a situation in which there is some element of uncertainty, the likelihood that an investment will pay off. The trick is in basing the predictions of uncertainties on a firm foundation of known facts. In the case of a cost-benefit analysis of Usability Engineering, there are several foundations upon which to build realistic predictions of benefits.

First, there is ample research published that shows measurable and significant performance advantages of specific user interface design alternatives (as compared to other alternatives) under certain circumstances. Just a few examples of design alternatives for which performance data exists include

- Use of color
- Choice of input devices
- Use of windowing
- Use of direct manipulation
- Screen design
- Menu structure

The research does not provide simple generic answers to design questions. However, what the research does provide are general ideas of the magnitude of performance differences that can occur between optimal and suboptimal interface design alternatives. The basic benefit assumptions made in any cost-benefit analysis can thus be generated and defended by referring to the wide body of published research data that exists. From these studies, you can extrapolate some reasonable predictions about the order of magnitude of differences you might expect to see in user interfaces optimized through Usability Engineering techniques (see Bias and Mayhew 1994, ch. 2, for a review and analysis of some of the literature for the purpose of defending benefit assumptions).

Besides consulting and citing relevant research literature, there are other ways to arrive at and defend your benefit assumptions. Actual case histories of the benefits achieved as a result of applying Usability Engineering techniques are very useful in helping to defend the benefit assumptions of a particular cost-benefit analysis. A few published case histories exist (e.g., Karat 1989; Bias and Mayhew 1994). Wixon and Wilson (1997) and Whiteside, Bennet, and Holtzblatt (1988) report that across their experience with many projects over many years, they find an average overall performance improvement of about 30 percent when at least 70 percent to 80 percent of the problems they identify during testing are addressed by designers.

But even anecdotes are useful. For example, colleagues working at a vendor company once told me they had compared customer support calls on a product for which they had recently developed and introduced a new, usability-engineered release. Calls to customer support after the new release decreased by 30 percent. This savings greatly outweighed the cost of the Usability Engineering effort. For another, even more dramatic anecdote, see Nielsen (1993, 84).

Finally, experienced Usability Engineers can draw upon their own general experience evaluating and testing software user interfaces as well as their specific experience with a particular development organization. Familiarity with typical interface designs from a particular development organization allows the Usability Engineer to decide how much improvement to expect from applying Usability Engineering techniques in that organization. If the designers are generally untrained and inexperienced in interface design and typically design poor interfaces, the Usability Engineer would feel comfortable and justified defending more aggressive benefit claims. On the other hand, if the Usability Engineer knows the development organization to be quite experienced and effective in interface design, then more conservative estimates of benefits would be appropriate, on the assumption that Usability Engineering techniques will result in fine-tuning of the interface, but not radical improvements. The Usability Engineer can also assess typical interfaces from a given development organization against well-known and accepted design principles, usability test results, and research literature, to help defend the assumptions made when estimating benefits.

In general, it is usually wise to make very conservative benefit assumptions. This is because any cost-benefit analysis has an intended audience who must be convinced that benefits outweigh costs. Conservative assumptions are less likely to be challenged by the relevant audience, thus increasing the likelihood of acceptance of the analysis conclusions. In addition, conservative benefit assumptions help to manage expectations. It is always better to achieve a greater benefit than predicted than to achieve less benefit, even if the lower benefit still outweighs the costs. Having underestimated benefits will make future cost-benefit analyses more credible and more readily accepted.

When each relevant benefit has been calculated on a per-year basis, it is time to add up all benefit category estimates for a benefit total. The benefit total can be based on the first year alone and/or on the expected product lifetime.

6. **Compare costs to benefits.** Recall that in our hypothetical project, the Usability Engineer did this, and according to her figures at the beginning of this section, in the

first year alone, a net benefit of $88,284 is expected. And over the expected five-year lifetime of the product, a net benefit of $471,500 is predicted. Her initial Usability Project Plan appears to be well justified. It was a fairly aggressive plan, in that it included all lifecycle tasks and rigorous techniques for each task. Given the very clear net benefit, she would be wise to stick with this aggressive plan and submit it to project management for approval.

If the net benefit had been marginal, or in fact there had been a net cost, she would be well advised to go back and rethink her plan. She might scale back on the rigorousness of techniques for certain tasks or even eliminate some tasks (for example, collapse the design process from three to two or even one design level) in order to reduce the costs.

WEB NOTES

Web designers should also plan Usability Engineering Lifecycle tasks into their overall project plans and use the cost-benefit analysis technique to justify their proposed plans. Generally, the Usability Engineering Lifecycle can be contracted for simple Web sites and applications, as discussed in Chapter 1 and also in the Web Notes sections of Chapters 2–17. In addition, more "quick and dirty" techniques may be employed for Requirements Analysis tasks such as the User Profile and Contextual Task Analysis (see Chapters 2 and 3). And, design levels 2 and 3 might be collapsed into a single process of iterative design and evaluation. Thus, calculated costs will likely be less than for traditional product development projects.

Benefit categories might also be a bit different for Web developers. Most Web sites and applications are not really productivity tools; neither are they commercial products. They are built to serve many different purposes, such as to advertise, to sell products or services, to educate, and to reduce the cost of disseminating information. You will need to formulate new benefit categories to correspond to the main motivations for providing Web sites and applications. For example, if the purpose of a Web site is to advertise and sell products or services, the measure of its success might be number of visitors, number of pages visited by visitors, and, more directly, the number of sales that originate directly from the Web site. Thus, one benefit category might be increased sales through a usability-engineered Web site as compared to one designed and built without the benefit of Usability Engineering techniques.

Sample Work Products and Templates

The following sample work products for cost-justification are offered here:

- Sample Cost-Benefit Analysis—In-House Development
- Sample Cost-Benefit Analysis—Vendor

Sample Cost-Benefit Analysis— In-House Development

Below is the full cost-benefit analysis for the hypothetical project summarized in the Sample Technique—A Step-by-Step Procedure section of this chapter. See Bias and Mayhew (1994, ch. 2) for more details and discussion with a similar example.

Cost-Benefit Analysis—In-House Development

Analysis Parameters

- Product for in-house use (vs. commercial product)
- End users number 250 (vs., for example, 50 users, or 10,000 users)
- User, customer support, usability, and developer staff work 230 days per year
- Users' fully loaded hourly wage = $25
- Customer support's fully loaded wage = $25
- Usability and developer staff's fully loaded hourly wage = $35
- Usability lab or sufficient resources in place

◆ Changes made early in development cost 1/4 of changes made after installation (see Mantei and Teorey 1988)
◆ Typical system lifetime = 5 years (vs., for example, 2 years or 20 years)

Project Plan

Phase	UI Task
Requirements Analysis	User Profiles
	Contextual Task Analysis
	Usability Goal Setting
	Platform Capabilities/Constraints
Design/Testing/Development	Work Reengineering
	Conceptual Model Design
	Conceptual Model Mock-ups
	Iterative Conceptual Model Evaluation (2)
	Screen Design Standards
	Screen Standards Prototype
	Iterative Screen Standards Evaluation (2)
	Detailed UI Design
	Iterative Detailed UI Design Evaluation (2)
Installation	

"Cost-Benefit Analysis—In-House Development," cont. next page

"Cost-Benefit Analysis—In-House Development," cont.

Cost Calculations

User Profiles

Usability Staff Time		User Time	
Step	**Hrs**	**Step**	**Hrs**
Needs finding	24	Needs finding	24
Draft questionnaire	12		
Management feedback	2	Management feedback	2
Revise questionnaire	6		
Pilot questionnaire	8	Pilot questionnaire	8
Revise questionnaire	6		
Select user sample	4		
Distribute questionnaire	6	Respond to questionnaire	50
Data analysis	24		
Data interpretation/ presentation	24		
Document user profiles	24		
Total	**140**	**Total**	**84**

$\times$ \$35 = \$4,900   + $\times$ \$25 = \$2,100

= \$7,000

Contextual Task Analysis

Usability Staff Time (two staff sharing all tasks)

Step	Hrs
Review requirements spec	24
Interview project team	16
Interview user reps	16
Identify key Actors/Use Cases	8
In-context observations	80
Work Environment Analysis	24
Task Scenarios	16
Task Analysis Document	24
Low-level tasks	16
First pass task model	8
Obtain user task model	32
Document Task Model	8
Total	272

$\times$ \$35 = \$9,520

User Time

Step	Hrs
Interview user reps	8
In-context observations	40
Obtain user task model	18
Total	66

+ $\times$ \$25 = \$1,650
= \$11,170

Usability Goal Setting

Usability Staff Time

Step	Hrs
Refer to User Profile	6
Refer to Contextual Task Analysis	6
Research business goals	12
Draft qualitative goals	12
Formulate quantitative goals	6
Prioritize usability goals	6
Document prioritized goals	24
User/management review	8
Establish benchmark data	90
Total	170

$\times$ \$35 = \$5,950

User/Management Time

Step	Hrs
Research business goals	6
User/management review	16
Establish benchmark data	24
Total	46

+ $\times$ \$25 = \$1,150
= \$7,100

"Cost-Benefit Analysis—In-House Development," cont. next page

"Cost-Benefit Analysis—In-House Development," cont.

Platform Capabilities/Constraints

Usability Staff Time

Step	Hrs
Identify HW/SW platform(s)	4
Review platform documentation	12
Interview technical staff	6
Document platform constraints and capabilities	16
Validate Platform Constraints and Capabilities	6
Total	44

$\times$ \$35 = \$1,540

Developer Time

Step	Hrs
Identify HW/SW platform(s)	4
Interview technical staff	6
Validate Platform Constraints and Capabilities	6
Total	16

+ $\times$ \$35 = \$560
= \$2,100

Work Reengineering

Usability Staff Time
(two staff sharing all tasks)

Step	Hrs
Reengineer work models	48
Validate work models	24
Document work models	16
Total	88

$\times$ \$35 = \$3,080

User Time

Step	Hrs
Validate work models	18
Total	18

+ $\times$ \$25 = \$450
= \$3,530

Conceptual Model Design

**Usability Staff Time
(three staff working as a team in meetings)**

Step	Hrs
Design products/processes	48
Design rules for windows	36
Identify major displays	36
Define navigational pathways	36
Document design	48
Total	204

$\times$ $35 = $7,140

Conceptual Model Mock-ups

**Usability Staff Time
(two staff, one a prototyper)**

Step	Hrs
Select functionality	8
Sketch out design(s)	24
Prototype designs	48
Total	80

$\times$ $35 = $2,800

"Cost-Benefit Analysis—In-House Development," cont. next page

"Cost-Benefit Analysis—In-House Development," cont.

Iterative Conceptual Model Evaluation

First Iteration:

Usability Staff Time	
Step	Hrs
Design/develop test materials	32
Design/assemble test environment	8
Run pilot test	8
Revise test tasks/materials	8
Run test/collect data	32
Summarize/interpret data, draw conclusions	16
Document/present results	40
Total	144
	× $35 = $5,040

User Time	
Step	Hrs
Design/develop test materials	8
Run pilot test	6
Run test/collect data	16
Total	30
+	× $25 = $750
	= $5,790

All Other Iterations:

Usability Staff Time	
Step	Hrs
Design/develop test materials	6
Design/assemble test environment	
Run pilot test	4
Revise test tasks/materials	4
Run test/collect data	32
Summarize/interpret data, draw conclusions	16
Document/present results	40
Total	102
	× $35 = $3,570

User Time	
Step	Hrs
Design/develop test materials	4
Run pilot test	4
Run test/collect data	16
Total	24
+	× $25 = $600
	= $4,170

Screen Design Standards

Step	Hrs
Draft control standards	12
Draft product/process window standards	32
Draft dialog box standards	32
Draft message box standards	8
Draft input device interaction standards	16
Draft feedback standards	24
Document all draft standards	56
Total	180

$\times$ \$35 = \$6,300

Screen Design Standards Prototyping

Step	Hrs
Select subset of functionality	8
Prepare paper-and-pencil spec	64
Build prototype	80
Total	152

$\times$ \$35 = \$5,320

"Cost-Benefit Analysis—In-House Development," cont. next page

"Cost-Benefit Analysis—In-House Development," cont.

Iterative Screen Design Standards Evaluation

First Iteration:

Usability Staff Time	
Step	Hrs
Design/develop test materials	32
Design/assemble test environment	8
Run pilot test	8
Revise test tasks/materials	8
Run test/collect data	32
Summarize/interpret data, draw conclusions	16
Document/present results	40
Total	144
	× $35 = $5,040

User Time	
Step	Hrs
Design/develop test materials	8
Run pilot test	6
Run test/collect data	16
Total	30
+	× $25 = $750
	= $5,790

All Other Iterations:

Usability Staff Time	
Step	Hrs
Design/develop test materials	6
Run pilot test	4
Revise test tasks/materials	4
Run test/collect data	32
Summarize/interpret data, draw conclusions	16
Document/present results	40
Total	102
	× $35 = $3,570

User Time	
Step	Hrs
Design/develop test materials	4
Run pilot test	4
Run test/collect data	16
Total	24
+	× $25 = $600
	= $4,170

Detailed User Interface Design

Step	Hrs
Complete identification of pathways	40
Complete design of menu bar and/or all action widgets	40
Complete design of content of all windows, dialog/message boxes	80
Complete design of input device interactions	80
Total	240

$\times$ \$35 = \$8,400

Iterative Detailed UI Design Evaluation

First Iteration:

Usability Staff Time

Step	Hrs
Design/develop test materials	32
Design/assemble test environment	8
Run pilot test	8
Revise test tasks/materials	8
Run test/collect data	32
Summarize/interpret data, draw conclusions	16
Document/present results	40
Total	144

$\times$ \$35 = \$5,040

User Time

Step	Hrs
Design/develop test materials	8
Run pilot test	6
Run test/collect data	16
Total	30

+ $\times$ \$25 = \$750

= \$5,790

"Cost-Benefit Analysis—In-House Development," cont. next page

Iterative Detailed UI Design Evaluation cont.

All Other Iterations:

Usability Staff Time			User Time	
Step	Hrs		Step	Hrs
Design/develop test materials	6		Design/develop test materials	4
Run pilot test	4		Run pilot test	4
Revise test tasks/materials	4			
Run test/collect data	32		Run test/collect data	16
Summarize/interpret data, draw conclusions	16			
Document/present results	40			
Total	102		Total	24

$$\times \$35 = \$3,570$$

$$+ \quad \times \$25 = \$600$$

$$= \$4,170$$

Cost Summary

Phase	UI Task	Cost
Requirements Analysis	User Profiles	$ 7,000
	Contextual Task Analysis	$11,170
	Usability Goal Setting	$ 7,100
	Platform Capabilities/Constraints	$ 2,100
Design/Testing/Development	Work Reengineering	$ 3,530
	Conceptual Model Design	$ 7,140
	Conceptual Model Mock-ups	$ 2,800
	Iterative Conceptual Model Evaluation (2)	$ 9,960
	Screen Design Standards	$ 6,300
	Screen Standards Prototype	$ 5,320
	Iterative Screen Standards Evaluation (2)	$ 9,960
	Detailed UI Design	$ 5,320
	Iterative Detailed UI Design Evaluation (2)	$ 9,960
Installation		
Total		$87,660

Benefit Calculations

Increased Productivity

60 transactions per day
Time per transaction decreased by 1 second
250 users $\times$ 230 days $\times$ 60 transactions $\times$ 1/3600 hour $\times$ $25
 = **$23,958 per year**

Decreased Errors

1.5 errors per user per day
2 minutes in recovery time per error
250 users $\times$ 1.5 errors $\times$ 230 days $\times$ $0.833/error
 = **$71,846 per year**

Decreased Training

Typical one-week training course reduced by 25% or 10 hours
250 users $\times$ 10 hours $\times$ $25 = **$62,500 in first year**

Decreased Late Design Changes

20 changes made early
1 day per change
Early change cost = 20 $\times$ 8 hours $\times$ $35 = $5,600
Late change cost = 4 $\times$ $5,600 = $22,400
Difference = **$16,800 in first year**

"Cost-Benefit Analysis—In-House Development," cont. next page

"Cost-Benefit Analysis—In-House Development," cont.

Benefit Summary

First Year:

Benefit	
Increased productivity	$ 23,958
Decreased errors	$ 71,846
Decreased training	$ 62,500
Decreased late design changes	$ 16,800
Total	$175,104

Product Lifetime:

Benefit	
Increased productivity $23,958 per year × 5 years =	$119,790
Decreased errors $71,846 per year × 5 years =	$359,230
Decreased training $62,500 in first year =	$ 62,500
Decreased late design changes $16,800 in first year =	$ 16,800
Total	$558,320

Conclusion

Comparing these benefits and costs, in the first year alone, a net benefit of $87,444 is expected:

Benefits = $175,104
Costs = $87,660
Net Benefit = $87,444

And over the expected five-year lifetime of the product, a net benefit of $470,660 is predicted:

Benefits = $558,320
Costs = $87,660
Net Benefit = $470,660

Sample Cost-Benefit Analysis—Vendor

Below is a sample cost-benefit analysis for a hypothetical project within a vendor development organization. The *cost* calculations are identical to those in the sample analysis for an in-house development organization given in the previous sample. The *benefits and conclusions* are calculated differently and are shown here. See Bias and Mayhew (1994, ch. 2) for more details and discussion with a similar example.

Cost-Benefit Analysis—Vendor

Analysis Parameters

- Commercial product (vs. product for in-house use)
- Customers number 6,600
- Usability and developer staff's fully loaded hourly wage = $35
- Customer support's fully loaded wage = $25
- Typical expected sales = 6,000 units
- Profit margin per unit = $75
- Typical length of customer support calls = 5 minutes
- Expected product lifetime = 2 years

"Cost-Benefit Analysis—Vendor," cont. next page

"Cost-Benefit Analysis—Vendor," cont.

Project Plan

Phase	UI Task
Requirements Analysis	User Profiles
	Contextual Task Analysis
	Usability Goal Setting
	Platform Capabilities/Constraints
Design/Testing/Development	Work Reengineering
	Conceptual Model Design
	Conceptual Model Mock-ups
	Iterative Conceptual Model Evaluation (2)
	Screen Design Standards
	Screen Standards Prototype
	Iterative Screen Standards Evaluation (2)
	Detailed UI Design
	Iterative Detailed UI Design Evaluation (2)
Installation	

Cost Calculations

The same project plan as in the previous example for an in-house development organization is used. Refer to that example for all cost calculations. Summary costs are reproduced below.

Phase	UI Task	Cost
Requirements Analysis	User Profiles	$ 7,000
	Contextual Task Analysis	$11,170
	Usability Goal Setting	$ 7,100
	Platform Capabilities/Constraints	$ 2,100
Design/Testing/Development	Work Reengineering	$ 3,530
	Conceptual Model Design	$ 7,140
	Conceptual Model Mock-ups	$ 2,800
	Iterative Conceptual Model Evaluation (2)	$ 9,960
	Screen Design Standards	$ 6,300
	Screen Standards Prototype	$ 5,320
	Iterative Screen Standards Evaluation (2)	$ 9,960
	Detailed UI Design	$ 5,320
	Iterative Detailed UI Design Evaluation (2)	$ 9,960
Installation		
Total		$87,660

"Cost-Benefit Analysis—Vendor," cont. next page

"Cost-Benefit Analysis—Vendor," cont.

Benefit Calculations

Increased Sales

10% increase in sales (10% of 6,000 = 600)
Profit margin per unit = $100
$100 × 600
   = **$60,000**

Decreased Customer Support

6,600 customers
Reduce calls by 2 per year per customer or 13,200 calls
10 minutes per call
1/6 hour × 13,200 calls × $25/hour
   = **$55,500 per year**

Benefit Summary

First Year:

Benefit	
Increased sales	$ 60,000
Decreased customer support	$ 55,000
Total	$115,000

Product Lifetime:

Benefit	
Increased sales $60,000 in first year=	$ 60,000
Decreased customer support $55,000 per year × 2 years =	$110,000
Total	$170,000

Conclusion

Comparing these benefits and costs, the project Usability Engineer argues that in the first year alone, a net benefit of $27,340 is expected:

Benefits = $115,000
Costs = $87,660
Net Benefit = $27,340

And over the expected five-year lifetime of the product, a net benefit of $82,340 is predicted:

Benefits = $170,000
Costs = $87,660
Net Benefit = $82,340

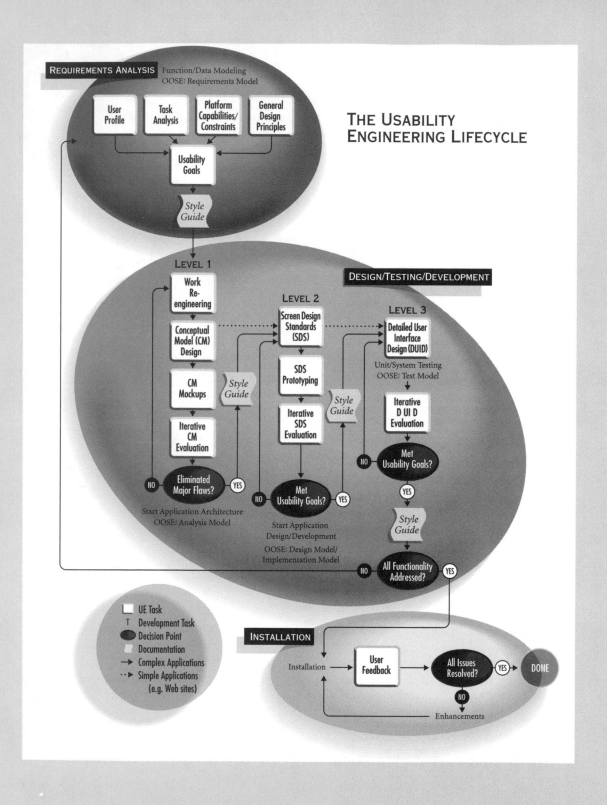

THE USABILITY
ENGINEERING LIFECYCLE

21

Organizational Roles and Structures

INTRODUCTION

In this chapter I offer one way to define some organizational roles relevant to Usability Engineering, assign these roles to appropriate people, and organize them into the overall reporting structure of a development organization. What I describe here is not the only way to do this, but it is one common way that has been successful in my experience. A role is a set of specified responsibilities. Bear in mind in the following discussion that roles are abstract and as such do not necessarily correspond one-to-one to individual people. That is, one person can take on more than one role within a given project and also across projects. And more than one person can share a role, within and/or across projects.

At least four major roles with responsibility for different aspects of the Usability Engineering Lifecycle in a product development organization can be distinguished:

◆ Usability Engineer
◆ User Interface Designer
◆ User Interface Developer
◆ User

The responsibilities that define these roles can be described in terms of which Usability Engineering Lifecycle tasks the role has *lead, or primary,* responsibility for (other roles may participate in these tasks but do not bear primary responsibility for them).

A role is a set of specified responsibilities. Roles are abstract and do not necessarily correspond one-to-one to individual people. One person can take on more than one role within and across projects, and more than one person can share a role within and across projects

The Usability Engineer role takes responsibility for Requirements Analysis and usability evaluation tasks

Very briefly, the Usability Engineer role takes responsibility for Requirements Analysis and usability evaluation tasks. A person playing this role should have acquired the skills necessary for these tasks through a combination of an advanced degree program in a related field and on-the-job experience. Specifically, Usability Engineering Lifecycle tasks that are the primary responsibility of this role include

◆ User Profiles
◆ Contextual Task Analysis
◆ Usability Goal Setting
◆ Iterative Conceptual Model Evaluation
◆ Iterative Screen Design Standards Evaluation
◆ Iterative Detailed User Interface Design Evaluation
◆ User Feedback

The User Interface Designer role primarily performs design tasks

The User Interface Designer role primarily performs design tasks and requires a skill set relevant to that responsibility. This role is not responsible for implementation of the user interface, only for design. The role does not necessarily require any academic degrees related to usability, and the person playing this role might have acquired the necessary skills primarily through on-the-job experience and on-the-job training. Specifically, Usability Engineering Lifecycle tasks that are the primary responsibility of this role include

◆ General Design Principles
◆ Platform Capabilities and Constraints
◆ Work Reengineering
◆ Conceptual Model Design
◆ Conceptual Model Mock-ups (design and implementation of paper mock-ups, although not necessarily of live prototypes)
◆ Screen Design Standards
◆ Screen Design Standards Prototyping (design but not necessarily implementation)
◆ Product Style Guide Development
◆ Detailed User Interface Design

The User Interface Developer role is primarily responsible for the implementation of the user interface

The User Interface Developer role is primarily responsible for the *implementation* of the user interface, not for its design. The only Usability Engineering Lifecycle tasks this role takes responsibility for are

- Conceptual Model Mock-ups (if they are implemented as live prototypes)
- Screen Design Standards Prototyping (implementation but not design)

The main responsibilities of this role are tasks from the overall development methodology, including

- Prototype development
- User interface architecture design
- User interface development

Finally, another important role relevant to implementing the Usability Engineering Lifecycle is that of the user. The User role does not bear primary responsibility for any Usability Engineering Lifecycle tasks, but it is important to note those tasks in which *participation* of users is crucial. These include

- User Profiles
- Contextual Task Analysis
- Usability Goal Setting
- Iterative Conceptual Model Evaluation
- Iterative Screen Design Standards Evaluation
- Iterative Detailed User Interface Design Evaluation
- User Feedback

The User role does not bear primary responsibility for any lifecycle tasks, but note those tasks in which user participation is crucial

Many authors and practitioners believe passionately in participatory analysis and participatory design, in which users play primary, active roles (rather than serve as more passive sources of information and feedback) in Requirements Analysis and design tasks. I believe in these practices in theory, and imagine they have a great deal of potential, but I have not had the opportunity to experiment with them much in practice because of the constraints my clients have placed on my consulting projects. Many an in-house Usability Engineer has suffered the frustration of blocked access to users, and this problem is usually even more difficult to overcome for an outside consultant. Involving users in analysis and design as something more than subjects of study (e.g., in Contextual Task Analyses) and test users (e.g., in usability testing) requires a much bigger commitment from the development and user organizations, and this commitment is not always easy to obtain for an outsider. This is why

Many authors and practitioners believe passionately in participatory analysis and participatory design, in which users play primary, active roles in Requirements Analysis and design tasks

the lifecycle as described in Chapters 1–17 has mentioned but not emphasized the participatory analysis and design techniques. If you are interested in learning about the potentially more active roles of users during Requirements Analysis and design tasks, I refer you to Muller and Kuhn (1993), Karat and Dayton (1995), Bloomer, Croft, and Wright (1996), and Chin, Rosson, and Carroll (1997). These papers also have references of their own that will point you to most of the key literature on participatory analysis and design.

A number of authors (see, e.g., Karat and Dayton 1995) also point to the utility of recruiting active involvement of all other project stakeholders in most if not all Usability Engineering Lifecycle tasks. Other stakeholders might include user management, marketers, documentation specialists, trainers, and product support specialists. All such stakeholders can provide invaluable perspectives and input into the tasks of the Usability Engineering Lifecycle, and you should try to recruit their participation as much as possible. In this discussion of roles, I primarily focus on which roles should lead and bear primary responsibility for which lifecycle tasks. This does not preclude all manner of other roles participating in all tasks.

How roles are assigned and organized can have a profound impact on the overall success of the lifecycle in developing usable products

The roles as defined above are abstract—independent of the individuals to whom the roles are assigned—and are defined simply as a set of responsibilities. How you might assign these roles to project staff and how you might organize staff playing these roles within the overall development organization are the main topics of this chapter. As it turns out, how roles are assigned and organized can have a profound impact on the overall success of the Usability Engineering Lifecycle in supporting the development of usable products.

ASSIGNING ORGANIZATIONAL ROLES

In assigning roles to specific staff members on a specific development project, you will want to consider two main issues:

- What qualifications should be required for each role?
- Should more than one role be assigned to a single staff member?

What Qualifications Should Be Required for Each Role?

In theory almost anyone could be trained in the skill sets required for each role. However, it is most efficient either to hire people who already have the requisite skills for a role or to recruit in-house staff who have skills close to the required skills for a role and support them with mentoring and on-the-job training. One way or another, to carry out the Usability Engineering Lifecycle tasks that define each role, staff would need more or less the equivalent of the following qualifications and ongoing on-the-job training (see also Karat and Dayton 1995). A sample of a more detailed job description for a Usability Engineering manager is offered in the Sample Work Products and Templates section later in the chapter.

For a **Usability Engineer,** minimum requirements might include

- Ph.D. or M.A. in Cognitive Science or Human Factors
- Three to five years' experience as a Usability Engineer in the relevant industry
- Experience managing usability projects and staff
- Training, experience, and skill in most if not all Usability Engineering Lifecycle tasks
- User interface design experience and skill
- Strong interpersonal and negotiating skills

On-the-job training could include

- Short courses on advanced topics in Usability Engineering
- Annual attendance at ACM SIGCHI and other related conferences

For the **User Interface Designer,** minimum requirements might include

- Three to five years' experience working in the relevant industry
- Experience and recognized talent as a User Interface Designer
- Motivation and interest in usability and user interface design
- Strong interpersonal and negotiating skills

On-the-job training could include

- Short courses on user interface design and cognitive science
- Annual attendance at ACM SIGCHI and other related conferences
- Mentoring by Usability Engineers

For the **User Interface Developer,** minimum requirements might include

◆ Three to five years' experience working in the relevant industry
◆ System architecture skills and experience
◆ Experience building user interface software
◆ Experience with relevant technology platforms and tools
◆ Motivation and interest in usability and user interface design
◆ Strong interpersonal and negotiating skills

On-the-job training could include

◆ Short courses on system architecture, technology platforms, and tools
◆ Annual attendance at conferences on user interface technology
◆ Mentoring by Usability Engineers

One qualification common to all three roles is "strong interpersonal and negotiating skills." Successful implementation of the Usability Engineering Lifecycle requires a multidisciplinary team of people with very different backgrounds and skill sets. These team members must work together cooperatively towards the common goal of usability. Constructive teamwork is required for success, and so team-oriented skills are required in all team members.

SHOULD MORE THAN ONE ROLE BE ASSIGNED TO A SINGLE STAFF MEMBER?

Traditionally on product development projects, particularly in the software industry, the three usability roles are spread across various development staff who do not necessarily have the requisite skills

Traditionally on product development projects, particularly in the software industry, the three roles we are discussing here are spread across various development staff who do not necessarily have the requisite skills. The tasks for which Usability Engineers should be responsible (i.e., Requirements Analysis and usability evaluation tasks) are not carried out at all. Both user interface design and user interface development are carried out by many different developers with no particular background or even interest in usability, depending on what subset of product code they are assigned responsibility for. The result of such role assignment and organization is almost always poorly designed user interfaces and unusable products. Unfortunately, many software development projects still operate this way.

The first important point to bear in mind is that anyone assigned one of the usability roles, as defined here, should at least have the requisite skills and background to play that role. The next issue, though, is whether it is necessary to have one individual for each separate role, or whether more than one of these roles can successfully be assigned to a single staff member. This will depend in part on the size and complexity of the product and project. On very small projects in very small development organizations, it will probably not be practical to have individual team members play each of the three roles. For example, the roles of User Interface Designer and User Interface Developer may be combined in a single staff member, who is in fact also the architect and implementor of the rest of the product, not just the user interface. In theory, this can work, as long as the developer has the background and skill set defined for a User Interface Designer. But this is unusual, and a better bet for small development organizations and small projects is to hire outside Usability Engineering expertise on a consulting basis as needed.

On very small projects in very small development organizations, it may be impractical to have individual team members play each of the three roles—it might be better to hire outside Usability Engineering experts on a consulting basis

On larger projects in large development organizations—and even on small projects within large development organizations—it makes a great deal of sense to have individual staff members assigned to each of the three usability roles. There are several arguments in favor of this approach.

◆ **The roles require different skill sets.** As you can see in the qualifications for each role, they require very different sets of background, experience, and skills. It is fairly unusual today to find one individual with strong skills in more than one of these roles. Someone who is a strong User Interface Designer may have no background relevant to performing Contextual Task Analyses or usability testing. Someone skilled with architecture, platform, and development tools may know little about effective user interface design. At this point in the evolution of the Usability Engineering and software engineering disciplines, it is unrealistic to expect a single person to develop and maintain a high level of skill in all these areas. For each role, you want someone who specializes in the skills required to play that role successfully, not someone who simply dabbles in those skills.

Each role requires different sets of background, experience, and skills; it is fairly unusual to find one individual with strong skills in more than one of these roles

◆ **The roles represent conflicting agendas.** The overriding agenda of a Usability Engineer is to serve the requirements of the users. User Interface Developers, like other developers, are usually motivated by technical constraints, budgets, and schedules. These agendas usually come in direct conflict with one another. In many cases successfully serving the needs of users may take more technology, time, and money than would be needed if their requirements were assigned a lower priority. It is unrealistic to expect a single person playing multiple roles to balance these conflicting agendas. Usually, people will take on one role with more passion than another and will thus have a biased agenda. Separating the roles across individual staff members means that each agenda is equally represented, and they must negotiate with one another and find practical compromises (but see the discussion in "Setting Up Organizational Structures" later in the chapter). This, again, is why "strong interpersonal and negotiating skills" is a prerequisite for all roles.

◆ **The roles require different perspectives**. This is related to the two previous points but slightly different. Each role requires a very different way of looking at a problem. The Usability Engineer role requires the perspective of human learning and performance. The User Interface Developer role requires the perspective of technology. The User Interface Designer role requires the perspective of a design discipline—of design elements and how they can work together. Again, it is unusual (although not unheard of) for one individual to have all perspectives, let alone to be able to juggle them and apply them all in a balanced, unbiased manner.

◆ **Each role represents a full-time job**. On any but the smallest projects in the smallest development organizations, any one of the usability roles easily represents a full-time job. On very large projects, all three roles may be kept busy full time on just one project. On smaller projects in large organizations, a small centralized staff of each type of role can easily be kept busy full time by working on multiple projects simultaneously. Given that an individual can be productively kept busy playing a single role, and given all the other arguments above, it is much more effective and efficient to have individuals specialize in a single usability role so that they can develop and practice the skill set required in that role in an optimal way.

There will always be exceptions to these arguments. For example, I consider myself skilled in both the Usability Engineer and the User Interface Designer roles. And I have worked with some developers who have

A PERSPECTIVE ON MULTIPLE ROLES

I remember hearing a speaker at a conference describe himself as holding two Ph.D.'s, one in Software Engineering and one in Human Factors (i.e., Usability Engineering). He then went on to say that when he worked on development projects, he sometimes took on a developer role and sometimes a Usability Engineer role, and he noticed that in spite of his dual backgrounds, when officially playing either role, he found it extremely difficult to maintain the perspective and agenda of the other. The point is that even if you happen to have strong skills relating to more than one role, it is simply hard to play multiple roles simultaneously, given the different perspectives required, the different (and often conflicting) agendas involved, and the time demands of each role. Thus, project managers would be wise to consider separating these several roles across people and filling the roles with people who have the requisite skill sets to play each role.

very strong user interface design skills. But I do not consider myself qualified to play the User Interface Developer role, and I have also worked with very skilled Usability Engineers who simply cannot design. It is not impossible, but it is unusual, for a single person to have a high degree of skill in more than one usability role.

SETTING UP ORGANIZATIONAL STRUCTURES

The next issue to consider is how the different usability roles can best be positioned in the reporting structure of the development organization. First, let's look at the possible reporting relationship between the User Interface Designer and the User Interface Developer. Figure 21.1 illustrates three possible reporting relationships for these two roles, assuming they both report directly within a specific project team. You can probably guess which reporting relationship I consider to be appropriate. The first two are inappropriate because when one role reports to the other, then by definition, the perspective and agenda of that role become subordinate.

Figure 21.1 Three possible reporting relationships

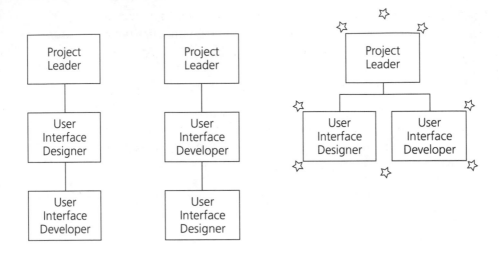

In any design decisions, usability issues should carry equal weight compared to all other issues, such as budgets, schedules, ease of implementation, response time, and maintainability. They are not more important, but neither are they less important. Trade-offs between all these conflicting agendas should be carefully made without bias, to optimize the product. Casting the designer and the developer as peers in the reporting structure with a common manager encourages each to fully represent the agenda their role assigns them and to negotiate on equal terms with other important agendas to find optimal compromises.

Reporting structures do not guarantee that people will work effectively together. Nor are they always necessary for people to work together effectively. Peers can butt heads and work counterproductively and also a person in a managerial role can treat a subordinate more like a peer and encourage group decision making. But you cannot count on people in managerial positions to act objectively upon the advice of their subordinates, and it is safer to choose a reporting structure that maximally supports the end result you hope for. In this case, you want usability issues and other development issues to be given equal consideration and weight, and optimal trade-offs and compromises to be forged. Casting the designers and developers of the user interface as peers simply gives you the best chance of achieving this goal, without relying completely on the

Casting the designer and the developer as peers with a common manager encourages both to fully represent their role and to negotiate with other important agendas to find compromises

personalities and objectivity of the particular people placed in the usability roles.

Now, where does the role of Usability Engineer fit in? Again, assuming that a given person will play this role and not other roles, one possible organizational structure (which I have seen work well in several organizations) is shown in Figure 21.2.

Here you see the User Interface Designer and the User Interface Developer cast as peers reporting to a common manager within a project team, as just discussed. Note that the role of Usability Engineer has a "dotted line relationship" to the User Interface Designer. The idea here is that the Usability Engineer is a floating or centralized resource reporting primarily outside any given project team. He or she is assigned to work with projects on an as-needed basis, with the main contact in the project team through the User Interface Designer.

There are well-documented reasons why it works well to have all Usability Engineers in a company or organization reporting to a centralized Usability Engineering department (see, e.g., Bias and Alford 1989). Similarly, there are reports of successes in decentralizing Usability Engineers and having them report directly to projects or development groups

Figure 21.2 Sample organizational structure for usability roles

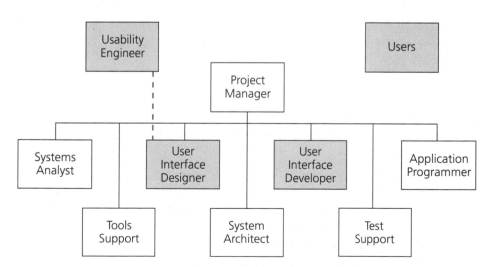

(see, e.g., Bias and Smith-Kerker 1986.) Just as one interface style does not succeed for all types of users, one organizational structure for Usability Engineers does not succeed in all corporate organizations and cultures. But in any organization, either model for positioning the Usability Engineering resource—centralized or decentralized—has its pitfalls.

In the case of the centralized Usability Engineering organization, the biggest hurdle to overcome is the potential for an "us versus them" attitude, which can inhibit the natural integration of Usability Engineering into the development process. This potential is increased when Usability Engineers cast themselves—or are cast as—the authors and enforcers of user interface standards that User Interface Designers and Developers must then follow. When Usability Engineers are presented instead as valuable resources to designers and developers all during the design process, available to help them accomplish common goals, then the potential for this drawback of centralization is decreased. One other drawback, as Wixon and Wilson (1997) point out, is that centralized Usability Engineers often are called in too late and have no continuous contact with projects, minimizing their potential impact.

Decentralized Usability Engineers, who report directly to development project teams and are full-time team members, are regarded less often as outsiders and obstacles, but they face a different set of pitfalls. First, if the Usability Engineer has been too intimately involved with the design and development of a product, he or she may be less objective. He or she might begin negotiations for a more usable interface from a compromised position, simply because of the intimate awareness of the constraints of the development environment, or by falling victim to "group think."

Also, when Usability Engineers report directly to a development manager rather than a Usability Engineering manager, it is likely that the development manager will fail to understand how to adequately evaluate the Usability Engineer's contribution. Similarly, there may be little support to help the Usability Engineer maintain and develop his or her expertise if the manager doesn't understand the field, and it can be professionally lonely to work in an organization without any professional peers. Too many highly trained and expert Usability Engineers have gradually been converted to developers because they did not have the support of a Usability Engineer as their manager and a group of Usability Engineers as their peers.

Miller (1996) gives a good example of the importance of a centralized organization to support Usability Engineers who are assigned to work on particular projects. In her organization, Usability Engineers working with project teams reported back regularly to the centralized group to brainstorm solutions to problems and obtain moral support. In addition, centralized Usability Engineers trained and mentored project team members to carry out Usability Engineering tasks, to better leverage the small centralized Usability Engineering staff across many project teams.

There are approaches to both centralization and decentralization of the Usability Engineering role that can work. In the case of *centralization*, a combination of effective education about and marketing of the resource, and Usability Engineers who have good interpersonal and team-building skills, can overcome the potential of being viewed as outsiders. In *decentralization*, efforts can be made to develop less formal organizational relationships with other Usability Engineers within and outside the company, both for professional support and to help avoid falling victim to "group think." All organizational structures have their potential drawbacks, but the drawbacks can be overcome with proper attention and effort. The key is to choose an organizational positioning for the Usability Engineer role that is compatible with the overall corporate culture in which it must operate. Then address any inherent potential drawbacks constructively before they become serious inhibitors to success.

One advantage of the organization proposed in Figure 21.2 is that it combines the advantages of both centralization and decentralization and minimizes the disadvantages of each. In this organization, the Usability Engineer is part of a *centralized* organization, but the User Interface Designer is *decentralized* in the project team. The User Interface Designer thus has the advantage of continuity and intimacy with the project, but has as a mentor and resource the centralized Usability Engineer, who has a broader perspective and more in-depth Usability Engineering skills. The Usability Engineer acts as a "technology transfer agent" to project teams that have their own internal designers (Wixon and Wilson 1997).

In my experience, and also as reported in Karat and Dayton (1995), it can be very effective to have a small organization of highly trained and specialized Usability Engineers. They can provide basic education in Usability Engineering techniques to other members of the development organization, including User Interface Designers (but also users, marketers, product support staff, trainers, writers, and any other product

In the case of centralization, a combination of effective education about and marketing of the resource, and Usability Engineers who have good interpersonal and team-building skills, can overcome the negative potential of being viewed as outsiders

In decentralization, efforts can be made to develop less formal organizational relationships with other Usability Engineers within and outside the company for professional support and to avoid falling victim to "group think"

stakeholders). Then, Usability Engineers lead, mentor, and apprentice these team members as they learn to put into practice the Usability Engineering skills that were presented to them in formal training classes or workshops. In this approach, everyone on the project team is a participant and becomes invested in the usability engineering of their product. In the words of Karat and Dayton (1995): "Nearly everyone in software development and marketing organizations should practice Usability Engineering to some extent, but the degree and type of activity will vary dramatically with the person's particular role and the system under development."

Taking this approach maximally leverages the usually scarce Usability Engineer role. It also maximizes the long-term success of introducing Usability Engineering into development organizations by integrating it tightly into the overall development activity, rather than casting it as specialized activities performed by specialized personnel. Again, to quote Karat and Dayton (1995): ". . . usability engineering is not a field separate from the base engineering activity, but is a special perspective on that activity."

The training provided by the centralized Usability Engineering staff is most successful when set in the context of a particular project at the kickoff and attended by the whole project team

My experience has shown that the training provided by the centralized Usability Engineering staff is most successful when set in the context of a particular project at project kickoff and attended by the whole project team. With one of my clients, I started the project by providing basic training in Usability Engineering and GUI design for the whole project team. I then directed and mentored them as they applied these new skills to their immediate project. For other clients, I have provided a general training course integrated with consulting. That is, within a three- or four-day training course attended by a whole project team, we would stop about twice a day and try to apply the principles being taught to the team's ongoing project. This approach has proven successful in my experience and could productively be adopted by in-house Usability Engineers. Karat and Dayton (1995) point to some of the specific advantages of this approach of combining formal education with project-based consulting and mentoring:

> Thus the workshop participants' learning environment is a good approximation of the software development environment in which they must apply

their skills after the workshop. They do not return to their job only to be frustrated in explaining the methods to people who were not at the workshop, because most of the members of their real team were in the workshop with them. They do not wonder how to apply the lessons from the workshop to their real projects (or wonder *whether* the lessons can be applied), because the lessons were made with their real project instead of an artificial example. Perhaps most importantly, students and managers can justify the time spent in the workshop partly as getting consulting help on their project, rather as time in class away from their project.

WEB NOTES

On very small project teams, common on Web development projects, it may not be practical to have separate, full-time in-house staff play the different Usability Engineering roles. In these circumstances, two options are available. First, if the project is small but the development organization is large, it will usually make sense to have a centralized Usability Engineering group in-house, and this group can delegate expertise as needed to small projects such as Web development projects.

If the project is small and the development organization is also small, it may not be cost effective to maintain all the different types of Usability Engineering expertise in-house. In this case, since Usability Engineering expertise is just as important to Web design and development as to traditional development, a good alternative is to hire outside expertise on a consulting basis as needed.

In addition, graphic designers have a particularly important role to play in Web design projects. While Web sites must be usable, they must also accomplish other goals not particularly important in traditional software development, such as corporate branding, marketplace differentiation, and image. Thus on Web projects, graphic designers might play the role of User Interface Designers, while Usability Engineers focus on Requirements Analysis tasks, Work Reengineering, and specifying the types of rules necessary in Conceptual Model Design and Screen Design Standards. The actual design of these rules can then be left up to the graphic designers. See related comments in the Web Notes in Chapter 12.

Graphic designers have a particularly important role to play in Web design projects

SAMPLE WORK PRODUCTS AND TEMPLATES

The following samples are offered here:

◆ Sample Proposal for a Usability Engineering Organization
◆ Sample Job Description—User Engineering Manager

SAMPLE PROPOSAL FOR A USABILITY ENGINEERING ORGANIZATION

If you want to obtain support and funding to establish an in-house, centralized Usability Engineering organization, you will need to develop and present to the appropriate level of management a detailed proposal, complete with a plan for the activities of the group, a yearly budget, and job descriptions for the staff you want to recruit. Below I offer an abbreviated and otherwise slightly modified version of just such a plan I once prepared for the development organization in a vendor company. Following that is one of four job descriptions that went along with this proposal.

At the time I wrote this proposal, I had just spent about a year conducting various projects for the Company, introducing Usability Engineering techniques to a particular development organization within it and demonstrating their value. The Company was then ready to consider building an organization of in-house Usability Engineering expertise, and solicited the following proposal.

Note that this proposal was tailored to the needs of a particular organization, given its then current maturity with regard to the application of Usability Engineering, and the state of the Usability Engineering discipline at the time in its history that this plan was prepared. As such, it does not necessarily represent an ideal plan for any other organization at any other point in its own or the discipline's history. As always, you will need to tailor a plan for your organization, taking into account its current receptivity to and readiness for Usability Engineering, as well as the state of the Usability Engineering discipline at the time.

Proposal for an Internal Usability Engineering Department

Executive Summary

On August 11, I met with Mr. Development Organization Manager, Ms. Developer, Mr. User Interface Designer, Ms. Architect, and Mr. Product Line A Manager to discuss developing an in-house Usability Engineering organization within the Company. As a result of that meeting, I drafted a proposal outlining the need for Usability Engineering personnel and describing a plan for filling that need. This proposal was circulated to the meeting participants, and I received significant feedback and input from them and revised the proposal accordingly. This document presents that revised proposal, which I believe now represents a consensus on what the Company needs.

The bottom line of this proposal is that in the immediate future the Company could make good use of a total of four in-house Usability Engineers working within the Development Organization, organized in a centralized Usability Engineering Department.

The rest of this proposal describes the rationale justifying the proposed new positions, the specific activities to which these positions should be immediately applied, both an immediate and long-term organizational plan for making most effective use of these positions, and a more detailed description of the type of people the Company should try to attract into these positions. In addition, I include a budget estimate for the proposed Usability Engineering Department, a sample six-month work plan for assigning personnel to the proposed projects, and four job descriptions.

Background

In the Company's products, the user interface is one of the crucial components meriting special attention. There are of course others, such as functionality, cost, technical performance, and required development effort, and there are always trade-offs to be made among these. But we all understand that the user interface is becoming of increasing importance in the marketplace, and the Company's products must be competitive in this aspect as well as others.

"Proposal for an Internal Usability Engineering Department," cont. next page

"Proposal for an Internal Usability Engineering Department," cont.

I see three general categories of activities to which Usability Engineering expertise should be applied in the Development Organization to help improve the quality of your products. I define these categories along the two dimensions of time frame (immediate vs. future) and relative priority (high vs. moderate). Immediate needs are defined totally within Product Line A. Future needs include those in other Product Line organizations within the Development Organization as well.

Below I describe these three categories of activities and needs as proposed projects, including specific tasks where appropriate. Then I propose a near-term and a long-term organizational plan designed to meet these needs and describe the type of personnel required to address these needs. The work plan near the end of this document roughly estimates the person weeks needed to complete all the projects as described, and it presents one possible way to delegate these projects to the proposed staff.

Activities

(These are summarized here in very abbreviated form compared to my original document.)

A. Immediate Needs—High Priority

1. **Lead role in analysis and design on development projects:** In my view, the primary immediate-term role for Usability Engineers in the Company is not as academic consultants or abstract researchers, but as active members of the development teams taking a lead role in user interface design. The kind of person you want is not only someone with a Usability Engineering background and perspective, but also someone who has systems development and software user interface design experience and can play the role of lead designer on a design team, as appropriate to specific projects.

   There are a number of development projects ongoing or planned within the next several months within Product Line A that either are or will be at the stage of user interface design and to which Usability Engineers could immediately and across the next several months be assigned. These include

- ◆ Calendar
- ◆ Calculator
- ◆ Electronic mail
- ◆ Spelling dictionary
- ◆ Graphics package
- ◆ Help facility

It should be clear that one Usability Engineer cannot possibly play a significant role on all these projects, especially since many of them are being developed in the same short time frame. The Company does not currently have the Usability Engineering resources to cover all these projects.

2. **Product X, Release 3.0:** The new release is scheduled for next year and has not yet been started. It represents the first opportunity for the Company to plug Usability Engineering techniques into a development project at the right stage and with the right level and type of involvement.

3. **Performance measurement:** Usability Engineers should also interface with the Product Test and Documentation groups within Product Line A. Usability criteria should eventually be a formal part of general release criteria. Usability Engineers could provide a resource to Product Test in developing ease-of-learning and ease-of-use criteria and measurement tools, and Product Test could provide a resource to Usability Engineering as a vehicle for obtaining feedback on the usability of the Company's products. In order to improve the effectiveness of the design process, the Company is in need of better tools and methods for assessing the success of current products and for evaluating product design.

B. Immediate Needs—Moderate Priority

Besides actively participating in the development and testing activities within Product Line A, a number of other activities would make valuable contributions to the quality of the Company's products. I believe the Company should apply Usability Engineering resources to these projects to the extent possible.

"Proposal for an Internal Usability Engineering Department," cont. next page

"Proposal for an Internal Usability Engineering Department," cont.

4. **Library research/market segment analysis:** One way Usability Engineers can provide help to planners and designers is to carry out literature searches as input to product planning and design. Since the Company's strategy is to build on and improve currently available technologies and products (rather than be cutting-edge innovators of totally new technologies/products), an important part of your business is keeping up with the research and development efforts of your competitors and developments in the field in general. This is true in the area of user interface design as well as in other areas. There is much available literature to guide you, but someone needs to locate it, digest it, and make it available in summary form to Planning and Development management. In the area of user interface design, Usability Engineers could provide this service.

   Additionally, for the purpose of planning for future products, it would be useful to perform some field research of the Company's target market segments. Such studies would include a thorough assessment of a business segment, a typical organizational structure, and typical jobs and tasks, for the purpose of identifying opportunities for new products to support organizational goals in a sociotechnical environment. Usability Engineers could provide the methodologies for and carry out such studies.

5. **User feedback questionnaires:** In a previous project for the Company, I conducted assessments of user satisfaction with existing products through user satisfaction questionnaires. I completed a questionnaire study on one product and started similar studies on two other products. These need to be completed, and they could be completed by your own internal Usability Engineering staff once you have them on board.

6. **Competitive analyses:** Usability Engineers could interface with the Competitive Analysis group. Competitive products are a source of alternative design approaches. They also offer a vehicle for applied research in usability issues. A usability assessment of competitive products would also be useful to marketing.

7. **Product X, Release 2.0, analysis:** In a previous project for the Company, I initiated a usability analysis of the user interface to Release 2.0 of Product X and prepared a report on one subset of functionality of that product. The intent was mostly to sensitize designers and developers to usability issues, using Release 2.0 as a concrete exam-

ple, rather than to recommend changes to the product, which of course was already in the marketplace. However, this kind of analysis can be useful when the Company begins planning new related products. The analysis should be completed for other aspects of Release 2.0 functionality, and internal Usability Engineers could carry on this project once on board.

8. **Documentation:** Just as important as the usability of the product user interface is the usability of training, on-line tutorials, user guides, and reference materials. Usability Engineers can make significant contributions here.

9. **Market support:** Marketing has been getting requests from prospective customers for information on the ergonomic qualities of the Company's hardware products. Usability Engineers could compile some ergonomic guidelines from the literature and measure and compare our hardware products against them. Marketing would then be able to provide this information to customers.

10. **Corporate Style Guide:** In a previous project for the Company, I prepared a draft *corporate* User Interface Style Guide for Product Line A. A general corporate Style Guide, and also specific Style Guides for other Product Line organizations, should be developed. Internal Usability Engineers in a centralized organization could carry out these projects.

11. **Informal consulting:** In addition to concentrated involvement on specific development projects, I have experienced a demand throughout the Company for spontaneous informal consulting on usability issues. I have often received calls soliciting my opinion or input on some problem developers perceive to have usability implications. I have received such calls from planning, documentation, and testing groups from different Product Line groups, as well as from marketing. Internal Usability Engineers will undoubtedly also receive such calls, and they need to be able to respond to them.

12. **Committee participation:** There are other interfaces for Usability Engineers outside Product Line A that I have been involved with and that I think internal Usability Engineers should continue to be involved in. Examples include various Development Organization-wide committees on such things as voice technology and international products.

"Proposal for an Internal Usability Engineering Department," cont. next page

"Proposal for an Internal Usability Engineering Department," cont.

C. Future Needs

The preceding activities represent things I believe Product Line A should staff in order to address in the near term. There should also be a longer-term vision of the role of Usability Engineering in the Company as a whole. Following are suggestions for future roles for Usability Engineers.

13. **Future products:** Usability Engineering can be a resource to the Strategic Planning group within Product Line A to help specify the objectives and requirements for the user interfaces to identified potential future products. Then, engineers can stay involved as these proposed products enter development.
14. **Other product lines:** Ultimately, Usability Engineering services should be expanded and made available to all Product Lines within the Development Organization.

Organizational Plan

I have identified a fairly extensive list of potential activities above and proposed that a total of three to four Usability Engineers would be necessary to address them all. You will note that these activities span a number of different organizational groups. Because of this, because of the sporadic nature of involvement in any one organization, and because some of the activities do not relate only to one organization, I recommend that the proposed four Usability Engineers be organized in a single centralized department. Because many of the near-term activities involve Product Line A, I suggest that the Usability Engineering Department initially reside within that organization, as illustrated in Figure A.

A Usability Engineering Department Manager role should be created. This position is responsible for recruiting the proposed additional personnel, delegating activities to them, and managing their participation in those activities. This position also provides a central point for receiving and responding to requests from the various organizations for Usability Engineering resources. This managerial role should only take a quarter to half of the position's time, leaving the rest for direct participation in some activities.

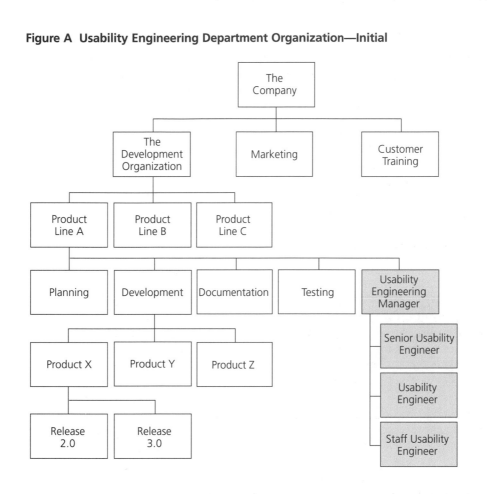

Figure A Usability Engineering Department Organization—Initial

As Usability Engineering participation expands to involve other product lines within the Development Organization, and other organizations within the Company, it should move as considered appropriate—intact as a single group—up to a staff position, reporting to the Director of the Development Organization, as shown in Figure B.

I think this organizational plan accomplishes several things. First, a single department managed by a Usability Engineering manager is the optimal way to effectively utilize the resources. If, instead, you hire several

"Proposal for an Internal Usability Engineering Department," cont. next page

"Proposal for an Internal Usability Engineering Department," cont.

Figure B Usability Engineering Department Organization—Expanded

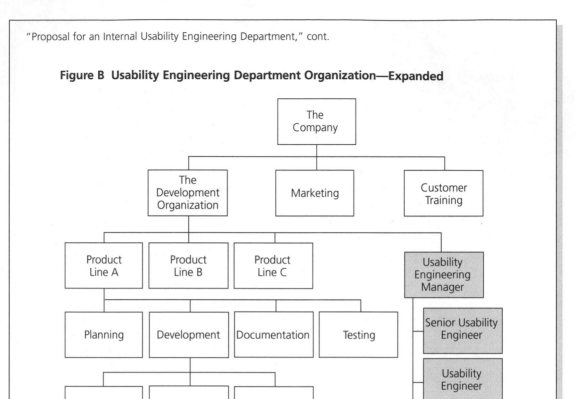

people and have them each report directly and independently to existing product managers, you invite several problems: (1) a person is idle between activities for a single product project to which he or she reports; (2) consistency and coordination of Usability Engineering input into different products is not assured; and (3) many things never get done because nobody with the big picture of what needs to be done is managing the resources.

The success of Usability Engineering in having an impact on your products will also depend to a significant extent upon positioning the centralized resource appropriately in the overall organization of the Company. Placing individuals as outside consultants inside the product development projects, where they have no decision-making responsibility and are not directly endorsed by anyone with decision-making responsibility, simply does not work in my experience. I also think that, like any other job, in order to attract good people into these positions, you need to offer an interesting job and a convincing career path. The job will be viewed as more interesting if it consists of assignments to a wide variety of projects in different organizations. Providing the beginnings of a managerial structure and a plan for the function to expand and move up in the overall organization over time defines a clear career path within the Company's "dual ladder" career path policy for technical specialists. Individual contributors reporting to product development project managers not of their profession, on the other hand, are in what looks like a dead-end job with little opportunity for growth and advancement. Thus, I think that this organizational proposal effectively addresses both the needs of the Company and of the individuals you hope to attract into the positions.

Staffing

The qualifications needed to conduct the activities described here and in the job descriptions attached include a combination of training/education/skills in the following areas:

◆ cognitive science
◆ software development
◆ user interface design
◆ office automation
◆ human physiology/hardware ergonomics
◆ applied experimental/test design
◆ quantitative data analysis techniques
◆ design of training aids and methods
◆ organization/job/task analysis

In addition, you should look for people with experience working in business organizations (vs. only academic experience), good communication

"Proposal for an Internal Usability Engineering Department," cont. next page

skills, the ability to be relatively self-directing, and the ability and willingness to work effectively as part of a team.

Realistically, it will be hard enough to find anyone with just the combination of experience in cognitive science and software development. Thus, you probably will have to be flexible in defining your requirements. It is probably not too important if required skills have been developed through academic training or on-the-job experience. In my mind, several combinations of type and level of experience would be acceptable. For example, people with a combination of advanced degrees in cognitive science and experience in software design and development would be most desirable in all four positions. Alternatively for the non-managerial positions, and more likely available, would be a more junior-level person with, say, a B.A. or M.A. in cognitive science and significant software experience, not necessarily in your business application areas, or a B.A. or M.A. in computer science with significant training in cognitive science. Within the organizational structure I have proposed, this sort of person could quickly become effective under the direction of a senior Usability Engineer playing a managerial and mentoring role. In general, you should be willing to interview people across this spectrum of backgrounds and experience levels and assess their ability to contribute on an individual basis.

In addition to the proposed Usability Engineering staff, you should consider hiring (from outside or within) specialists who can provide technical support to the Usability Engineers. Their duties would include such things as building automated usability testing tools and implementing prototypes.

Following are a sample six-month work plan outlining the delegation of the identified activities to the proposed personnel, an estimated budget for the proposed Usability Engineering Department in its first year, and four job descriptions corresponding to the proposed positions. All these should be regarded as tentative proposals, subject to the kinds of candidates you are actually able to find and to further clarification and development of the Usability Engineering plans and needs of the Company.

Sample Six-Month Work Plan

(Unit is person weeks of time)

Activity	Staff (by job level)			
	13	12	9	7
1. Interface design	4	10	4	3
2. Product X, Release 3.0	1	4		
3. Performance measurement	2		8	
4. Library research/ market segment studies	8	8	4	3
5. Questionnaire	2			8
6. Competitive analysis	1		4	5
7. Release 2.0 analysis	1			4
8. Documentation	1		4	
9. Marketing support	1		1	
10. Style Guide	2	2	2	3
11. Informal consulting	2	2		
12. Committee participation	1			
13. Recruiting	1			
Total weeks per position	27	26	27	26

Estimated Usability Engineering Budget—First Year

Salaries	$285,000
Travel (professional conferences)	6,000
Journal subscriptions	1,000
Books and library services	1,000
Total	$293,000

"Proposal for an Internal Usability Engineering Department," cont. next page

SAMPLE JOB DESCRIPTION— USABILITY ENGINEERING MANAGER

Below is the job description of the level 13 Usability Engineer identified in the organizational plan above. This Usability Engineer manages the Usability Engineering Department.

Job Description—Usability Engineering Manager

Position Purpose

This position manages, directs, and coordinates the activities of the Usability Engineering Department within Product Line A of the Development Organization of the Company. It works with the manager of Product Line A to determine the activities within Product Line A in which Usability Engineering should participate and delegates these activities to the Usability Engineers reporting to this position. In addition, the position takes part in these activities as an individual contributor. The general responsibility of the Usability Engineering Department is to take an active role in the design and development of the Development Organization's products, to ensure the quality of the user interface of those products, and to conduct research and development efforts aimed at improving products and planning for future products from the point of view of usability concerns.

Nature and Scope

This position initially will report to the manager of Product Line A, but it also interacts directly with all managers and many professionals within the Development Organization. The position has three Usability Engineers reporting to it: a Senior Usability Engineer (level 12), a Usability Engineer (level 9), and a Staff Usability Engineer (level 7).

The primary responsibility of this position is to manage the efforts of the Usability Engineering Department in contributing to the improvement of the Development Organization's products by designing or assisting in the design of the user interfaces for those products. By managing and participating in these activities, the incumbent ensures that products are

- Easy to learn to use
- Easy to use
- Easy to remember how to use

- Efficient for highly skilled users to use
- Psychologically satisfying to use

The following job responsibilities are included in this position.

1. **Design consulting:** Because the Usability Engineering Department is a new organization, the incumbent must analyze the current design procedures and develop, propose, and initiate the mechanisms or processes by which usability considerations will be incorporated into product design. The incumbent will both manage subordinates' efforts and participate directly in the following activities:

   - Appraise the quality of the user interfaces of current products
   - Provide recommendations during the specification of new products
   - Audit those products through the testing phase to ensure usability criteria have been met
   - Develop performance measures for assessing the impact of design features on user productivity and satisfaction
   - Provide design consulting through the development of documents outlining usability standards and guidelines for user interface design
   - Help design and participate in studies of target market segments to identify potential new products and specify usability objectives for those products
   - Provide consulting on the design of user training programs and user documentation

2. **Education:** Part of the incumbent's job will be to educate and update other Usability Engineers in the department, as well as managers and developers across the Development Organization, in the state of the art in the field of Usability Engineering. This would include both general education in cognitive science and specific information related to very particular design issues. The incumbent will develop and conduct educational activities to accomplish this goal, such as contracting outside speakers to give seminars, identifying external seminars for subordinates to attend, and distributing relevant literature.

3. **Library Research:** Often the incumbent and his or her subordinates will not be able to resolve design issues or choose between design

"Job Description—Usability Engineering Manager," cont. next page alternatives based on their own experience and knowledge. In this case it is the responsibility of the incumbent to coordinate a consultation of the available literature on the issue at hand. In general, part of the incumbent's job is to keep abreast of current research and articles in this area, review and analyze that data, and propose ways to apply it to products.

4. **Basic Research:** Sometimes design issues will arise that have not been addressed by published research. When the design issues are of enough significance to merit the effort, it is the responsibility of the incumbent to plan, design, develop, and conduct or direct research activities to resolve these issues. The research activities may range from resolving specific interface design issues to planning, research, and development for new products.

Other job activities that support the incumbent's basic responsibilities might include

♦ Contributing to the Usability Engineering profession and to the Company's image through the publication of research findings in relevant journals and trade magazines
♦ Participating in the activities of professional societies, such as attending and presenting at society meetings

A major challenge in this job is to coordinate and integrate the consideration of usability issues in systems design with the often conflicting issues of technical constraints, budgets, and schedules. This requires that the incumbent not only have expertise in relevant areas of Usability Engineering, but also have substantial understanding of the systems engineering process, the technology itself, and the business goals and organizational procedures of the Development Organization.

Since the Usability Engineering Department will be a new organization, an additional challenge is to integrate the Usability Engineering function effectively into the Development Organization. This requires creativity in organization and job design and the ability to implement and manage organizational change.

A further challenge to this job is the necessity to work effectively both independently with minimal supervision and interactively as a team member, with a wide variety of people. As the Usability Engineering Department manager, the incumbent holds a unique job and brings unique expertise to the Company. In this sense, the incumbent has no peers and performs the job somewhat under his or her own direction. Thus, the incumbent must be able to direct his or her own activities, manage his or her time well, and be innovative and creative in devising methods for accomplishing the goals of the Usability Engineering Department.

On the other hand, close interaction is required between this position and the different roles within the Development Organization, training personnel, marketing groups, internal user groups, and customer users. Good interpersonal skills and an understanding of the jobs within these other groups are required if the goals of the Usability Engineering Department are to be effectively fulfilled.

Because the formation of the Usability Engineering Department has yet to be accomplished, the incumbent must build an organization. This includes recruiting the appropriate personnel, facilitating their interaction with a wide variety of groups within the Development Organization, and providing them with motivation and incentives in the form of a satisfying job and career path.

The incumbent will represent the Usability Engineering Department on any committees across the Company that require input from or participation by the Usability Engineering Department.

One challenge of this position is the variety of roles it involves and the range of skills it demands. The incumbent must have experience and skills in cognitive science, systems design, data analysis, educational methodologies, organizational design, job analysis, communications, and management.

The responsibilities of those positions reporting to this position include carrying out the activities described herein, delegated to them by the incumbent.

The manager of the Usability Engineering Department must manage the organization within the administrative policies and procedures of the Company and within the constraints of approved plans.

The effectiveness of the position is measured by the total success of the Usability Engineering Department in making a significant contribution to the quality of near-term and future products of the Development Organization.

Qualifications

The basic qualifications required to fill this position include

◆ Ph.D. in Cognitive Science
◆ Advanced skills in all Usability Engineering tasks

"Job Description—Usability Engineering Manager," cont. next page

"Job Description—Usability Engineering Manager," cont.

◆ Significant experience in software development organizations
◆ Managerial experience and skill

Additional desirable experience includes

◆ Experience designing office automation products
◆ Experience using competitive office automation products
◆ Prior job experience as a Usability Engineering Manager
◆ Good communication skills
◆ Ability to work with others in a team
◆ Ability to work independently with minimal supervision

Principal Accountabilities

The principal accountabilities of the incumbent include participating in and managing the efforts of the other Usability Engineers in the group in the following activities:

1. Review and assess current office automation products for quality of user interface and usability to provide benchmarks for future products.
2. Contribute to the marketability of new office automation products by assisting in the design of effective user interfaces and ensuring the usability of these products.
3. Audit the design of new products through test phase and at user and customer sites to ensure usability criteria have been met.
4. Contribute to the effectiveness of both training programs and user documentation by providing insights from learning theory and educational psychology.
5. Provide state-of-the-art consulting in user interface design by keeping abreast of current research and articles in the areas of cognitive science and Usability Engineering.
6. Plan, design, develop, and conduct research activities directed at resolving specific design issues from a usability perspective.
7. Plan, design, develop, and conduct research activities directed at the development of future products.
8. Contribute to the Company's image through publications and participation in professional societies.

References

PREFACE

Beyer, H., and K. Holtzblatt. 1998. *Contextual Design: Defining Customer-Centered Systems.* San Francisco: Morgan Kaufmann.

Bias, R. G., and D. J. Mayhew. 1994. *Cost-Justifying Usability.* Chestnut Hill, Mass.: Academic Press.

Dumas, J. S., and J. C. Redish. 1993. *A Practical Guide to Usability Testing.* Norwood, N.J.: Ablex Publishing.

Hackos, J. T., and J. C. Redish. 1998. *User and Task Analysis for Interface Design.* New York: John Wiley & Sons.

Mayhew, D. J. 1992. *Principles and Guidelines in Software User Interface Design.* Englewood Cliffs, N.J.: Prentice Hall.

Nielsen, J. 1993. *Usability Engineering.* Chestnut Hill, Mass.: Academic Press.

Nielsen, J., and R. L. Mack. 1994. *Usability Inspection Methods.* New York: John Wiley & Sons.

Wixon, D. R., and J. Ramey, eds. 1996. *Field Methods Casebook for Software Design.* New York: John Wiley & Sons.

CHAPTER 1

Beyer, H., and K. Holtzblatt. 1998. *Contextual Design: Defining Customer-Centered Systems.* San Francisco: Morgan Kaufmann.

Brown, D. S., and S. Motte. 1998. Device Design Methodology for Trauma Applications. *CHI '98 Proceedings* (April): 590–3.

Button, G., and P. Dourish. 1996. Technomethodology: Paradoxes and Possibilities. *CHI '96 Proceedings:* 19–26.

Chin, G., Jr., M. B. Rosson, and J. Carroll. 1997. Participatory Analysis: Shared Development of Requirements from Scenarios. *CHI '97 Proceedings:* 162–9.

Coble, J. M., J. S. Maffitt, M. J. Orland, and M. G. Kahn. 1996. Using Contextual Inquiry to Discover Physicians' True Needs. In *Field Methods Casebook for Software Design*, edited by D. R. Wixon and J. Ramey. New York: John Wiley & Sons.

Dray, S. M., and D. Mrazek. 1996. A Day in the Life of a Family: An International Ethnographic Study. In *Field Methods Casebook for Software Design*, edited by D. R. Wixon and J. Ramey. New York: John Wiley & Sons.

Dumas, J. S., and J. C. Redish. 1993. *A Practical Guide to Usability Testing*. Norwood, N.J.: Ablex Publishing.

Gould, J. D., and C. Lewis. 1985. Designing for Usability: Key Principles and What Designers Think. *Communications of the ACM* 28, no. 3 (March): 360–411.

Hackos, J. T., and J. C. Redish. 1998. *User and Task Analysis for Interface Design*. New York: John Wiley & Sons.

Holtzblatt, K., and H. Beyer. 1996. Contextual Design: Principles and Practice. In *Field Methods Casebook for Software Design*, edited by D. R. Wixon and J. Ramey. New York: John Wiley & Sons.

Jacobson, I., M. Christerson, P. Jonsson, and G. Overgaard. 1992. *Object-Oriented Software Engineering: A Use Case Driven Approach*. Reading, Mass.: ACM Press/Addison-Wesley.

Juhl, D. 1996. Using Field-Oriented Design Techniques to Develop Consumer Software Products. In *Field Methods Casebook for Software Design*, edited by D. R. Wixon and J. Ramey. New York: John Wiley & Sons.

Karat, J., and T. Dayton. 1995. Practical Education for Improving Software Usability. *CHI '95 Proceedings* (May): 162–9.

Mantei, M. M., and T. J. Teorey. 1988. Cost/Benefit Analysis for Incorporating Human Factors in the Software Lifecycle. *Communications of the ACM* 31, no. 4 (April): 428–39.

Mayhew, D. J. 1992. *Principles and Guidelines in Software User Interface Design*. Englewood Cliffs, N.J.: Prentice Hall.

Nielsen, J. 1992. The Usability Engineering Lifecycle. *Computer* (March): 12–22.

Nielsen, J., and R. L. Mack. 1994. *Usability Inspection Methods*. New York: John Wiley & Sons.

Page, S. R. 1996. User-Centered Design in a Commercial Software Company. In *Field Methods Casebook for Software Design*, edited by D. R. Wixon and J. Ramey. New York: John Wiley & Sons.

Rosson, M. B., and J. M. Carroll. 1995. Integrating Task and Software Development for Object-Oriented Applications. *CHI '95 Proceedings* (May): 377–84.

Rowley, D. E. 1996. Organizational Considerations in Field-Oriented Product Development: Experiences of a Cross-Functional Team. In *Field Methods Casebook for Software Design*, edited by D. R. Wixon and J. Ramey. New York: John Wiley & Sons.

Shneiderman, B. 1992. *Designing the User Interface: Strategies for Effective Human-Computer Interaction*. 2d ed. Reading, Mass.: Addison-Wesley.

Wixon, D. R., and J. Ramey, eds. 1996. *Field Methods Casebook for Software Design.* New York: John Wiley & Sons.

Wixon, D., and C. Wilson. 1997. The Usability Engineering Framework for Product Design and Evaluation. In *Handbook of Human-Computer Interaction.* 2d ed. Edited by M. Helander, T. K. Landauer, and P. Prabhu. Englewood Cliffs, N.J.: Elsevier Science.

Chapter 2

Comstock, E. M., and W. M. Duane. 1996. Embed User Values in System Architecture: The Declaration of System Usability. *CHI '96 Proceedings:* 420–7.

Mayhew, D. J. 1992. *Principles and Guidelines in Software User Interface Design.* Englewood Cliffs, N.J.: Prentice Hall.

Potosnak, K. 1984. Choice of Interface Mode by Empirical Groupings of Computer Users. *Proceedings, Interact '84 2* (September): 262–7.

———. 1986. Classifying Users: A Hard Look at Some Controversial Issues. *CHI '86 Proceedings* (April): 84–8.

Chapter 3

Bauersfield, K., and S. Halgren. 1996. "You've Got Three Days!" Case Studies in Field Techniques for the Time-Challenged. In *Field Methods Casebook for Software Design,* edited by D. R. Wixon and J. Ramey. New York: John Wiley & Sons.

Beyer, H., and K. Holtzblatt. 1996. Contextual Techniques Starter Kit. *Interactions* 3, no. 6 (December): 44–50.

———. 1998. *Contextual Design: Defining Customer-Centered Systems.* San Francisco: Morgan Kaufmann.

Brown, D. S. 1996. The Challenges of User-Based Design in a Medical Equipment Market. In *Field Methods Casebook for Software Design,* edited by D. R. Wixon and J. Ramey. New York: John Wiley & Sons.

Butler, M. B., and M. Tahir. 1996. Bringing the Users' Work to Us: Usability Roundtables at Lotus Development. In *Field Methods Casebook for Software Design,* edited by D. R. Wixon and J. Ramey. New York: John Wiley & Sons.

Button, G., and P. Dourish. 1996. Technomethodology: Paradoxes and Possibilities. *CHI '96 Proceedings:* 19–26.

Chin, G., Jr., M. B. Rosson, and J. Carroll. 1997. Participatory Analysis: Shared Development of Requirements from Scenarios. *CHI '97 Proceedings:* 162–9.

Coble, J. M., J. Karat, and M. G. Kahn. 1997. Maintaining a Focus on User Requirements throughout the Development of Clinical Workstation Software. *CHI '97 Proceedings:* 170–7.

Coble, J. M., J. S. Maffitt, M. J. Orland, and M. G. Kahn. 1996. Using Contextual Inquiry to Discover Physicians' True Needs. In *Field Methods Casebook for Software Design*, edited by D. R. Wixon and J. Ramey. New York: John Wiley & Sons.

Comstock, E. M., and W. M. Duane. 1996. Embed User Values in System Architecture: The Declaration of System Usability. *CHI '96 Proceedings:* 420–7.

Dray, S. M., and D. Mrazek. 1996. A Day in the Life of a Family: An International Ethnographic Study. In *Field Methods Casebook for Software Design*, edited by D. R. Wixon and J. Ramey. New York: John Wiley & Sons.

Ford, J. M., and L. Wood. 1996. An Overview of Ethnography and System Design. In *Field Methods Casebook for Software Design*, edited by D. R. Wixon and J. Ramey. New York: John Wiley & Sons.

Hackos, J. T., and J. C. Redish. 1998. *User and Task Analysis for Interface Design.* New York: John Wiley & Sons.

Harper, R., and A. Sellen. 1995. Collaborative Tools and the Practicalities of Professional Work at the International Monetary Fund. *CHI '95 Proceedings* (May): 122–9.

Holtzblatt, K., and H. Beyer. 1996. Contextual Design: Principles and Practice. In *Field Methods Casebook for Software Design*, edited by D. R. Wixon and J. Ramey. New York: John Wiley & Sons.

Jacobson, I., M. Christerson, P. Jonsson, and G. Overgaard. 1992. *Object-Oriented Software Engineering: A Use Case Driven Approach.* Reading, Mass.: ACM Press/Addison-Wesley.

Juhl, D. 1996. Using Field-Oriented Design Techniques to Develop Consumer Software Products. In *Field Methods Casebook for Software Design*, edited by D. R. Wixon and J. Ramey. New York: John Wiley & Sons.

Lewis, S., M. Mateas, S. Palmiter, and G. Lynch. 1996. Ethnographic Data for Product Development: A Collaborative Process. *Interactions* 3, no. 6 (December): 52–69.

Lokuge, I., S. A. Gilbert, and W. Richards. 1996. Structuring Information with Mental Models: A Tour of Boston. *CHI '96 Proceedings*: 413–9.

Mackay, W. 1995. Ethics, Lies and Videotape . . . . *CHI '95 Proceedings* (May): 138–45.

Malinowski, U., and K. Nakakoji. 1995. Using Computational Critics to Facilitate Long-Term Collaboration in User Interface Design. *CHI '95 Proceedings* (May): 385–92.

Muller, M. J., and R. Carr. 1996. Using the CARD and PICTIVE Participatory Design Methods for Collaborative Analysis. In *Field Methods Casebook for Software Design*, edited by D. R. Wixon and J. Ramey. New York: John Wiley & Sons.

Page, S. R. 1996. User-Centered Design in a Commercial Software Company. In *Field Methods Casebook for Software Design*, edited by D. R. Wixon and J. Ramey. New York: John Wiley & Sons.

Ramey, J., A. H. Rowberg, and C. Robinson. 1996. Adaptation of an Ethnographic Method for Investigation of the Task Domain in Diagnostic Radiology. In *Field Methods Casebook for Software Design*, edited by D. R. Wixon and J. Ramey. New York: John Wiley & Sons.

Rosson, M. B., and J. M. Carroll. 1995. Integrating Task and Software Development for Object-Oriented Applications. *CHI '95 Proceedings* (May): 377–84.

Rowley, D. E. 1996. Organizational Considerations in Field-Oriented Product Development: Experiences of a Cross-Functional Team. In *Field Methods Casebook for Software Design*, edited by D. R. Wixon and J. Ramey. New York: John Wiley & Sons.

Wilson, S., M. Bekker, P. Johnson, and H. Johnson. 1997. Helping and Hindering User Involvement—A Tale of Everyday Design. *CHI '97 Proceedings*: 179–85.

Wixon, D. R., C. M. Pietras, P. K. Huntwork, and D. W. Mussey. 1996. Changing the Rules: A Pragmatic Approach to Product Development. In *Field Methods Casebook for Software Design*, edited by D. R. Wixon and J. Ramey. New York: John Wiley & Sons.

Wood, L. 1996. The Ethnographic Interview in User-Centered Work/Task Analysis. In *Field Methods Casebook for Software Design*, edited by D. R. Wixon and J. Ramey. New York: John Wiley & Sons.

CHAPTER 4

Bennett, J. 1984. Managing to Meet Usability Requirements: Establishing and Meeting Software Development Goals. In *Visual Display Terminals: Usability Issues and Health Concerns*, edited by J. Bennett, D. Case, J. Sandelin, and M. Smith. Englewood Cliffs, N.J.: Prentice Hall.

Bias, R. G., and D. J. Mayhew. 1994. *Cost-Justifying Usability.* Chestnut Hill, Mass.: Academic Press.

Butler, K. A. 1985. Connecting Theory and Practice: A Case Study of Achieving Usability Goals. *CHI '85 Proceedings* (April): 85–8.

Comstock, E. M., and W. M. Duane. 1996. Embed User Values in System Architecture: The Declaration of System Usability. *CHI '96 Proceedings*: 420–7.

Hix, D., and H. R. Hartson. 1993. *Developing User Interfaces.* New York: John Wiley & Sons.

Whiteside, J., J. Bennett, and K. Holtzblatt. 1988. Usability Engineering: Our Experience and Evolution. In *Handbook of Human-Computer Interaction*, edited by M. Helander. Amsterdam: North-Holland.

Wixon, D., and C. Wilson. 1997. The Usability Engineering Framework for Product Design and Evaluation. In *Handbook of Human-Computer Interaction*. 2d ed. Edited by M. Helander, T. K. Landauer, and P. Prabhu. Englewood Cliffs, N.J.: Elsevier Science.

CHAPTER 5

Forsythe, C., E. Grose, and J. Ratner. 1998. *Human Factors and Web Development.* Mahwah, N.J.: Lawrence Erlbaum.

CHAPTER 6

Baecker, R. M., J. Grudin, W. A. S. Buxton, and S. Greenberg, eds. 1995. *Readings in Human-Computer Interaction: Toward the Year 2000.* 2d ed. San Francisco: Morgan Kaufmann.

Brown, C. M. 1988. *Human-Computer Interface Design Guidelines.* Norwood, N.J.: Ablex Publishing.

Dumas, J. S. 1988. *Designing User Interfaces for Software.* Englewood Cliffs, N.J.: Prentice Hall.

Fowler, S. L., and V. R. Stanwick. 1995. *The GUI Style Guide.* Chestnut Hill, Mass.: Academic Press.

Galitz, W. O. 1996. *The Essential Guide to User Interface Design: An Introduction to GUI Design Principles and Techniques.* New York: John Wiley & Sons.

Hix, D., and H. R. Hartson. 1993. *Developing User Interfaces.* New York: John Wiley & Sons.

Horton, W. 1994. *The Icon Book.* New York: John Wiley & Sons.

Malinowski, U., and K. Nakakoji. 1995. Using Computational Critics to Facilitate Long-Term Collaboration in User Interface Design. *CHI '95 Proceedings* (May): 385–92.

Mayhew, D. J. 1992. *Principles and Guidelines in Software User Interface Design.* Englewood Cliffs, N.J.: Prentice Hall.

Mosier, J., and S. Smith. 1985. Application of Guidelines for Designing User Interface Software. *Proceedings, Human Factors Society 29th Annual Meeting* (September): 946–52.

Nichols, S., and F. E. Ritter. 1995. A Theoretically Motivated Tool for Automatically Generating Command Aliases. *CHI '95 Proceedings* (May): 393–400.

Nielsen, J. 1990. *Designing User Interfaces for International Use.* Englewood Cliffs, N.J.: Elsevier Science.

Norman, D. A. 1989. *The Design of Everyday Things.* New York: Doubleday.

Shneiderman, B. 1992. *Designing the User Interface: Strategies for Effective Human-Computer Interaction.* 2d ed. Reading, Mass.: Addison-Wesley.

Tetzlaff, L., and D. R. Schwartz. 1991. The Use of Guidelines in Interface Design. *CHI '91 Proceedings* (April): 329–34.

Tufte, E. R. 1990. *Envisioning Information.* Cheshire, Conn.: Graphics Press.

———. 1997. *Visual Explanations.* Cheshire, Conn.: Graphics Press.

CHAPTER 7

Beyer, H., and K. Holtzblatt. 1998. *Contextual Design: Defining Customer-Centered Systems*. San Francisco: Morgan Kaufmann.

Button, G., and P. Dourish. 1996. Technomethodology: Paradoxes and Possibilities. *CHI '96 Proceedings*: 19–26.

Hackos, J. T., and J. C. Redish. 1998. *User and Task Analysis for Interface Design*. New York: John Wiley & Sons.

Holtzblatt, K., and H. Beyer. 1996. Contextual Design: Principles and Practice. In *Field Methods Casebook for Software Design*, edited by D. R. Wixon and J. Ramey. New York: John Wiley & Sons.

Jacobson, I., M. Christerson, P. Jonsson, and G. Overgaard. 1992. *Object-Oriented Software Engineering: A Use Case Driven Approach*. Reading, Mass.: ACM Press/Addison-Wesley.

Ramey, J., A. H. Rowberg, and C. Robinson. 1996. Adaptation of an Ethnographic Method for Investigation of the Task Domain in Diagnostic Radiology. In *Field Methods Casebook for Software Design*, edited by D. R. Wixon and J. Ramey. New York: John Wiley & Sons.

Rosson, M. B., and J. M. Carroll. 1995. Integrating Task and Software Development for Object-Oriented Applications. *CHI '95 Proceedings* (May): 377–84.

Wood, L. 1996. The Ethnographic Interview in User-Centered Work/Task Analysis. In *Field Methods Casebook for Software Design*, edited by D. R. Wixon and J. Ramey. New York: John Wiley & Sons.

CHAPTER 8

Bloomer, S., R. Croft, and L. Wright. 1997. Collaborative Design Workshops: A Case Study. *Interactions* 4, no. 1 (Jan.–Feb.): 31–9.

Carroll, J. M., and J. R. Olson, eds. 1987. *Mental Models in Human Computer Interaction*. Washington, D.C.: National Academy Press.

Chin, G., Jr., M. B. Rosson, and J. Carroll. 1997. Participatory Analysis: Shared Development of Requirements from Scenarios. *CHI '97 Proceedings*: 162–9.

Furnas, G. W. 1991. New Graphical Reasoning Models for Understanding Graphical Interfaces. *CHI '91 Proceedings*: 71–8.

Gardiner, M. M., and B. Christie. 1987. *Applying Cognitive Psychology to User-Interface Design*. Chichester, UK: John Wiley & Sons.

Halasz, F., and T. P. Moran. 1982. Analogy Considered Harmful. *Proceedings, Human Factors in Computer Systems* (March): 383–6.

Hanisch, K. A., A. F. Framer, C. L. Hulin, and R. Schumacher. 1988. Novice-Expert Differences in the Cognitive Representation of System Features: Mental Models and Verbalizable Knowledge. *Proceedings, Human Factors Society 32d Annual Meeting:* 219–23.

Jacobson, I. M., M. Christerson, P. Jonsson, and G. Overgaard. 1992. *Object-Oriented Software Engineering: A Use Case Driven Approach.* Reading, Mass.: ACM Press/Addison-Wesley.

MacLean, A., V. Bellotti, R. Young, and T. Moran. 1991. Reaching through Analogy: A Design Rationale Perspective on Roles of Analogy. *CHI '91 Proceedings:* 167–72.

Malinowski, U., and K. Nakakoji. 1995. Using Computational Critics to Facilitate Long-Term Collaboration in User Interface Design. *CHI '95 Proceedings* (May): 385–92.

Mander, R., G. Salomon, and Y. Y. Wong. 1992. A Pile Metaphor for Supporting Casual Organization of Information. *CHI '92 Proceedings:* 627–34.

Manktelow, K., and J. Jones. 1987. Principles from the Psychology of Thinking and Mental Models. In *Applying Cognitive Psychology to User-Interface Design*, edited by M. M. Gardiner and B. Christie. New York: John Wiley & Sons.

Mayhew, D. J. 1992. *Principles and Guidelines in Software User Interface Design.* Englewood Cliffs, N.J.: Prentice Hall.

McDonald, J. E., S. W. Dearholt, K. R. Paap, and R. W. Schvaneveldt. 1986. A Formal Interface Design Methodology Based on User Knowledge. *CHI '86 Proceedings* (April): 285–90.

Nilsen, E., H. Jong, J. S. Olson, K. Biolsi, H. Rueter, and S. Mutter. 1993. The Growth of Software Skill: A Longitudinal Look at Learning and Performance. *CHI '93 Proceedings:* 149–56.

Norman, D. A. 1987. Some Observations on Mental Models. In *Readings in Human-Computer Interaction,* edited by R. M. Baecker and W. A. S. Buxton. San Francisco: Morgan Kaufmann.

Rieman, J., C. Lewis, R. M. Young, and P. G. Polson. 1994. "Why Is a Raven Like a Writing Desk?" Lessons in Interface Consistency and Analogical Reasoning from Two Cognitive Architectures. *CHI '94 Proceedings* (April): 438–44.

Rosson, M. B., and J. M. Carroll. 1995. Integrating Task and Software Development for Object-Oriented Applications. *CHI '95 Proceedings* (May): 377–84.

Rouse, W. B., and N. M. Morris. 1986. On Looking into the Black Box: Prospects and Limits in the Search for Mental Models. *Psychological Bulletin* 100, no. 3: 349–63.

Rubinstein, R., and H. Hersh. 1984. *The Human Factor: Designing Computer Systems for People.* Maynard, Mass.: Digital Press.

Smith, R. B. 1987. Experiences with the Alternative Reality Kit: An Example of the Tension between Literalism and Magic. *CHI '87 Proceedings* (May): 61–8.

Snyder, K. M., A. J. Happ, L. Malcus, K. R. Paap, and J. R. Lewis. 1985. Using Cognitive Models to Create Menus. *Proceedings, Human Factors Society 29th Annual Meeting:* 655–8.

Sumner, T. 1995. The High-Tech Toolbelt: A Study of Designers in the Workplace. *CHI '95 Proceedings* (May): 178–85.

Tognazzini, B. 1993. Principles, Techniques and Ethics of Stage Magic and Their Application to Human Interface Design. *CHI '93 Proceedings:* 355–62.

Young, R. M., and A. MacLean. 1988. Choosing between Methods: Analyzing the User's Decision Space in Terms of Schemas and Linear Models. *CHI '88 Proceedings* (May): 139–44.

CHAPTER 9

Bloomer, S., R. Croft, and L. Wright. 1997. Collaborative Design Workshops: A Case Study. *Interactions* 4, no. 1 (Jan–Feb.): 31–9.

Virzi, R. A., J. L. Sokolov, and D. Karis. 1996. Usability Problem Identification Using Both Low- and High-Fidelity Prototypes. *CHI '96 Proceedings:* 236–43.

Wixon, D., and C. Wilson. 1997. The Usability Engineering Framework for Product Design and Evaluation. In *Handbook of Human-Computer Interaction.* 2d ed. Edited by M. Helander, T. K. Landauer, and P. Prabhu. Englewood Cliffs, N.J.: Elsevier Science.

CHAPTER 10

Bailey, G. 1993. Iterative Methodology and Designer Training in Human-Computer Interface Design. *CHI '93 Proceedings* (April): 198–205.

Bellotti, V., S. B. Shum, A. MacLean, and N. Hammond. 1995. Multidisciplinary Modelling in HCI Design . . . In Theory and in Practice. *CHI '95 Proceedings* (May): 146–53.

Byme, M. D., S. D. Wood, P. Sukaviriya, J. D. Foley, and D. Kieras. 1994. Automating Interface Evaluation. *CHI '94 Proceedings* (April): 232–7.

Comstock, E. M. 1983. Customer Installability of Computer Systems. *Proceedings, Human Factors and Ergonomics Society 27th Annual Meeting* (Norfolk, Va.): 501–4.

Dumas, J. S., and J. C. Redish. 1993. *A Practical Guide to Usability Testing.* Norwood, N.J.: Ablex Publishing.

Ehrlich, K., and J. Rohn. 1994. Cost-Justification of Usability Engineering: A Vendor's Perspective. In *Cost-Justifying Usability,* edited by R. G. Bias and D. J. Mayhew. Chestnut Hill, Mass.: Academic Press.

Hartson, H. R., J. C. Castillo, J. Kelso, and W. C. Neale. 1996. Remote Evaluation: The Network as an Extension of the Usability Laboratory. *CHI '96 Proceedings:* 228–35.

Jeffries, R., J. R. Miller, C. Wharton, and K. Uyeda. 1991. User Interface Evaluation in the Real World: A Comparison of Four Techniques. *CHI '91 Proceedings* (April): 119–24.

John, B. E., and H. Packer. 1995. Learning and Using the Cognitive Walkthrough Method: A Case Study Approach. *CHI '95 Proceedings* (May): 429–36.

Karat, C., R. Campbell, and T. Fiegel. 1992. Comparison of Empirical Testing and Walkthrough Methods in User Interface Evaluation. *CHI '92 Proceedings* (May): 397–404.

Kieras, D. E., S. D. Wood, and D. E. Meyer. 1995. Predictive Engineering Models Using the EPIC Architecture for a High-Performance Task. *CHI '95 Proceedings.* (May): 11–8.

Knox, S. T., W. A. Bailey, and E. F. Lynch. 1989. Directed Dialogue Protocols: Verbal Data for User Interface Design. *CHI '89 Proceedings* (April): 283–8.

Koenemann-Belliveau, J., J. M. Carroll, M. B. Rosson, and M. K. Singley. 1994. Comparative Usability Evaluation: Critical Incidents and Critical Threads. *CHI '94 Proceedings* (April): 245–52.

Mackay, W. 1995. Ethics, Lies and Videotape . . . . *CHI '95 Proceedings* (May): 138–45.

Meister, D. 1986. *Human Factors Testing and Evaluation.* Englewood Cliffs, N.J.: Elsevier Science.

Nielsen, J. 1992. Finding Usability Problems through Heuristic Evaluation. *CHI '92 Proceedings* (May): 373–80.

———. 1993a. *Usability Engineering.* Chestnut Hill, Mass.: Academic Press.

———. 1993b. Estimating the Relative Usability of Two Interfaces: Heuristic, Formal and Empirical Methods Compared. *CHI '93 Proceedings* (April): 214–21.

———. 1994. Enhancing the Explanatory Power of Usability Heuristics. *CHI '94 Proceedings* (April): 152–8.

Nielsen, J., and T. Landauer. 1993. A Mathematical Model of the Finding of Usability Problems. *CHI '93 Proceedings* (April): 206–13.

Nielsen, J., and R. L. Mack. 1994. *Usability Inspection Methods.* New York: John Wiley & Sons.

Nielsen, J., and R. Molich. 1990. Heuristic Evaluation of User Interfaces. *CHI '90 Proceedings* (April): 249–56.

Norman, D. 1982. Steps toward a Cognitive Engineering: Design Rules Based on Analysis of Human Error. *Proceedings, Human Factors in Computer Systems* (March): 378–82.

Rowley, D. E. 1994. Usability Testing in the Field: Bringing the Laboratory to the User. *CHI '94 Proceedings* (April): 252–7.

Sawyer, P., A. Flanders, and D. Wixon. 1996. Making a Difference—The Impact of Inspections. *CHI '96 Proceedings:* 376–82.

Wixon, D., and C. Wilson. 1997. The Usability Engineering Framework for Product Design and Evaluation. In *Handbook of Human-Computer Interaction.* 2d ed. Edited by M. Helander, T. K. Landauer, and P. Prabhu. Englewood Cliffs, N.J.: Elsevier Science.

CHAPTER 11

Bloomer, S., R. Croft, and L. Wright. 1997. Collaborative Design Workshops: A Case Study. *Interactions* 4, no. 1 (Jan.–Feb.): 31–9.

Chin, G., Jr., M. B. Rosson, and J. Carroll. 1997. Participatory Analysis: Shared Development of Requirements from Scenarios. *CHI '97 Proceedings:* 162–9.

Gale, S. 1996. A Collaborative Approach to Developing Style Guides. *CHI '96 Proceedings:* 362–7.

Malinowski, U., and K. Nakakoji. 1995. Using Computational Critics to Facilitate Long-Term Collaboration in User Interface Design. *CHI '95 Proceedings* (May): 385–92.

Mayhew, D. J. 1992. *Principles and Guidelines in Software User Interface Design.* Englewood Cliffs, N.J.: Prentice Hall.

Miller, A. 1996. Integrating Human Factors in Customer Support Systems Development Using a Multi-Level Organizational Approach. *CHI '96 Proceedings:* 368–75.

Sumner, T. 1995. The High-Tech Toolbelt: A Study of Designers in the Workplace. *CHI '95 Proceedings* (May): 178–85.

CHAPTER 12

Bowers, J., and J. Pycock. 1994. Talking through Design: Requirements and Resistance in Cooperative Prototyping. *CHI '94 Proceedings* (April): 299–305.

Catani, M. B., and D. W. Biers. 1998. Usability Evaluation and Prototype Fidelity: Users and Usability Professionals. *Proceedings, Human Factors and Ergonomics Society 42d Annual Meeting:* 1331–6.

Miller-Jacobs, H. H., J. M. Spool, and B. Verplank. 1992. In Search of the Ideal Prototype. *CHI '92 Proceedings* (May): 577–80.

Uceta, F. A., M. A. Dixon, and M. L. Resnick. 1998. Adding Interactivity to Paper Prototypes. *Proceedings, Human Factors and Ergonomics Society 42d Annual Meeting:* 506–11.

Virzi, R. A., J. L. Sokolov, and D. Karis. 1996. Usability Problem Identification Using Both Low- and High-Fidelity Prototypes. *CHI '96 Proceedings:* 236–43.

CHAPTER 13

See the references for Chapter 10.

CHAPTER 14

Brown, J., T. C. G. Graham, and T. Wright. 1998. The *Vista* Environment for the Coevolutionary Design of User Interfaces. *CHI '98 Proceedings* (April): 376–83.

Gale, S. 1996. A Collaborative Approach to Developing Style Guides. *CHI '96 Proceedings:* 362–7.

Karsenty, L. 1996. An Empirical Evaluation of Design Rationale Documents. *CHI '96 Proceedings:* 150–6.

McCormick, K., and T. Bleser. 1985. Developing a User Interface Styleguide. *Proceedings National Computer Graphics Association.*

Miller, A. 1996. Integrating Human Factors in Customer Support Systems Development Using a Multi-Level Organizational Approach. *CHI '96 Proceedings:* 368–75.

Shneiderman, B. 1998. Codex, Memex, Genex: The Pursuit of Transformational Technologies. *CHI '98 Summary* (April): 98–9.

Thovtrup, H., and J. Nielsen, 1991. Assessing the Usability of a User Interface Standard. *CHI '91 Proceedings* (April): 335–42.

CHAPTER 15

Brown, C. M. 1988. *Human-Computer Interface Design Guidelines.* Norwood, N.J.: Ablex Publishing.

Galitz, W. O. 1996. *The Essential Guide to User Interface Design: An Introduction to GUI Design Principles and Techniques.* New York: John Wiley & Sons.

Helander, M., T. K. Landauer, and P. Prabhu, eds. 1997. *Handbook of Human-Computer Interaction.* 2d ed. Englewood Cliffs, N.J.: Elsevier Science.

Herbsleb, J. D. 1993. Preserving Knowledge in Design Projects: What Designers Need to Know. *CHI '93 Proceedings* (April): 7–14.

Mayhew, D. J. 1992. *Principles and Guidelines in Software User Interface Design.* Englewood Cliffs, N.J.: Prentice Hall.

Nielsen, J., ed. 1989. *Coordinating User Interfaces for Consistency.* Chestnut Hill, Mass.: Academic Press.

Norman, D. A. 1989. *The Design of Everyday Things.* New York: Doubleday.

Shneiderman, B. 1992. *Designing the User Interface: Strategies for Effective Human-Computer Interaction.* 2d ed. Reading, Mass.: Addison-Wesley.

CHAPTER 16

See the references for Chapter 10.

CHAPTER 17

Malinowski, U., and K. Nakakoji. 1995. Using Computational Critics to Facilitate Long-Term Collaboration in User Interface Design. *CHI '95 Proceedings* (May): 385–92.

QUESTIONNAIRES

Chin, J. P., V. A. Diehl, and K. L. Norman. 1988. Development of an Instrument Measuring User Satisfaction of the Human-Computer Interface. *CHI '88 Proceedings* (May): 213–8.

Coleman, W. D., and R. C. Williges. 1985. Collecting Detailed User Evaluations of Software Interfaces. *Proceedings, Human Factors Society 29th Annual Meeting* (September): 241–4.

Hartson, H. R., J. C. Castillo, J. Kelso, and W. C. Neale. 1996. Remote Evaluation: The Network as an Extension of the Usability Laboratory. *CHI '96 Proceedings:* 228–35.

INTERVIEWS

Malone, T. W. 1983. How Do People Organize Their Desks? Implications for the Design of Office Information Systems. *ACM Transactions on Office Systems 1:* 99–112.

Nielsen, J., R. L. Mack, K. H. Bergendorff, and N. L. Grischkowsky. 1986. Integrated Software Usage in the Professional Work Environment: Evidence from Questionnaires and Interviews. *CHI '86 Proceedings* (April): 162–7.

USAGE STUDIES

Aucella, A., and S. F. Ehrlich. 1986. Voice Messaging: Enhancing the User Interface Based on Field Performance. *CHI '86 Proceedings* (April): 156–61.

Gaylin, K. B. 1986. How Are Windows Used? Some Notes on Creating an Empirically Based Windowing Benchmark System. *CHI '86 Proceedings* (April): 96–100.

Good, M. 1985. The Use of Logging Data in the Design of a New Text Editor. *CHI '85 Proceedings* (April): 93–106.

Hanson, S. J., R. Kraut, and J. M. Farber. 1984. Interface Design and Multivariate Analysis of UNIX Command Use. *ACM Transactions on Office Information Systems:* 42–57.

Page, S. R., T. J. Johnsgard, U. Albert, and C. D. Allen. 1996. User Customization of a Word Processor. *CHI '96 Proceedings:* 340–6.

Tullis, T. S. 1986. A System for Evaluating Screen Formats. *Proceedings, Human Factors Society 30th Annual Meeting* (October): 1216–20.

Wixon, D., and M. Bramhall. 1985. How Operating Systems Are Used: A Comparison of VMS and UNIX. *Proceedings, Human Factors Society 29th Annual Meeting* (September): 245–9.

CHAPTER 18

Bradley, R. F., and L. D. Johnk. 1995. Replacing a Networking Interface "From Hell." *CHI '95 Proceedings:* 538–45.

Casselman, G. 1997. ITX Awards: London Life Bridges Systems with CoPilot. *ComputerWorld Canada* (21 November).

Grudin, J. 1986. Designing in the Dark: Logics That Compete with the User. *CHI '86 Proceedings:* 281–4.

———. 1991a. Systematic Sources of Suboptimal Interface Design in Large Product Development Organizations. *Human-Computer Interaction* 6: 147–96.

———. 1991b. Interactive Systems: Bridging the Gap between Developers and Users. *Computer* (April): 59–69.

Kerton, B. 1997. Introducing Usability at London Life Insurance Company: A Process Perspective. *CHI '97 Proceedings.*

Mayhew, D. J., and R. G. Bias. 1994. Organizational Inhibitors and Facilitators. In *Cost-Justifying Usability,* edited by R. G. Bias and D. J. Mayhew. Chestnut Hill, Mass.: Academic Press.

Miller, A. 1996. Integrating Human Factors in Customer Support Systems Development Using a Multi-Level Organizational Approach. *CHI '96 Proceedings:* 368–75.

Moll-Carrillo, J. J., G. Salomon, M. Marsh, J. F. Suri, and P. Spreenburg. 1995. Articulating a Metaphor through User-Centered Design. *CHI '95 Proceedings:* 566–72.

Rudisill, M., C. Lewis, P. B. Polson, and T. D. McKay. 1996. *Human-Computer Interface Design: Success Stories, Emerging Methods and Real-World Context.* San Francisco: Morgan Kaufmann.

Sawyer, P., A. Flanders, and D. Wixon. 1996. Making a Difference—The Impact of Inspections. *CHI '96 Proceedings:* 376–82.

Wiklund, M. E., ed. 1994. *Usability in Practice.* Chestnut Hill, Mass.: Academic Press.

Wixon, D., and C. Wilson. 1997. The Usability Engineering Framework for Product Design and Evaluation. In *Handbook of Human-Computer Interaction.* 2d ed. Edited by M. Helander, T. K. Landauer, and P. Prabhu. Englewood Cliffs, N.J.: Elsevier Science.

CHAPTER 19

I am not aware of any references specifically on Usability Project Planning. This would be a good area for future work.

CHAPTER 20

Bailey, W. A., S. T. Knox, and E. F. Lynch. 1988. Effects of Interface Design upon User Productivity. *CHI '88 Proceedings* (May): 207–12.

Bias, R. G., and D. J. Mayhew. 1994. *Cost-Justifying Usability.* Chestnut Hill, Mass.: Academic Press.

Karat, C. 1989. Iterative Usability Testing of a Security Application. *Proceedings, Human Factors Society 33d Annual Meeting:* 273–7.

Mantei, M. M., 1986. Techniques for Incorporating Human Factors in the Software Lifecycle. *Proceedings of STA-III Conference: Structured Techniques in the Eighties: Practice and Prospect*, Chicago (June).

Mantei, M. M., and T. J. Teorey. 1988. Cost/Benefit Analysis for Incorporating Human Factors in the Software Lifecycle. *Communications of the ACM 31*, no. 4 (April): 428–39.

Nielsen, J. 1993. *Usability Engineering.* Chestnut Hill, Mass.: Academic Press.

Whiteside, J., J. Bennett, and K. Holtzblatt. 1988. Usability Engineering: Our Experience and Evolution. In *Handbook of Human-Computer Interaction.* edited by M. Helander. Amsterdam: North-Holland.

Wixon, D., and C. Wilson. 1997. The Usability Engineering Framework for Product Design and Evaluation. In *Handbook of Human-Computer Interaction*, 2d ed. Edited by M. Helander, T. K. Landauer, and P. Prabhu. Englewood Cliffs, N.J.: Elsevier Science.

CHAPTER 21

Bias, R. G., and J. A. Alford. 1989. Factoring Human Factoring, in IBM. *Proceedings of the IEEE International Conference on Systems, Man and Cybernetics:* 1296–1300.

Bias, R. G., and P. L. Smith-Kerker. 1986. The Mainstreamed Human Factors Psychologist in the Development of the IBM RT PC. *Proceedings of the IEEE International Conference on Systems, Man and Cybernetics:* 153–8.

Bloomer, S., R. Croft, and L. Wright. 1997. Collaborative Design Workshops: A Case Study. *Interactions 4*, no. 1 (Jan.–Feb.): 31–9.

Chin, G., Jr., M. B. Rosson, and J. Carroll. 1997. Participatory Analysis: Shared Development of Requirements from Scenarios. *CHI '97 Proceedings:* 162–9.

Karat, J., and T. Dayton. 1995. Practical Education for Improving Software Usability. *CIII '95 Proceedings* (May): 162–9.

Mayhew, D. J., and R. G. Bias. 1994. Organizational Inhibitors and Facilitators. In *Cost-Justifying Usability*, edited by R. G. Bias and D. J. Mayhew. Chestnut Hill, Mass.: Academic Press.

Miller, A. 1996. Integrating Human Factors in Customer Support Systems Development Using a Multi-Level Organizational Approach. *CHI '96 Proceedings:* 368–75.

Muller, M. J., and S. Kuhn. 1993. Participatory Design. *Communications of the ACM 36*, no. 4: 24–8.

Wiklund, M. E., ed. 1994. *Usability in Practice.* Chestnut Hill, Mass.: Academic Press.

Wixon, D., and C. Wilson. 1997. The Usability Engineering Framework for Product Design and Evaluation. In *Handbook of Human-Computer Interaction.* 2d ed. Edited by M. Helander, T. K. Landauer, and P. Prabhu. Englewood Cliffs, N.J.: Elsevier Science.

Index